Archival Anxiety

and the Vocational Calling

Archival Anxiety

and the Vocational Calling

By Richard J. Cox

Litwin Books, LLC
Duluth, Minnesota

Copyright Richard J. Cox, 2010

Published in 2011 by Litwin Books
PO Box 3320
Duluth, MN 55803
http://litwinbooks.com

This book is printed on acid-free paper that meets all present ANSI standards for archival preservation.

Library of Congress Cataloging-in-Publication Data

Cox, Richard J.
 Archival anxiety and the vocational calling / by Richard J. Cox.
     p. cm.
 Includes bibliographical references and index.
 ISBN 978-1-936117-49-9 (alk. paper)
 1. Archives—Social aspects. 2. Archives—Study and teaching (Higher) 3. Archives—Moral and ethical aspects. 4. Archivists—Training of. 5. Archivists—Professional ethics. I. Title.
 CD971.C68 2011
 027—dc22
                                                    2010044942

Table of Contents

	Introduction	vii
1.	The Archival Calling	1
2.	Public Memory Meets Archival Memory: The Interpretation of Williamsburg's Secretary's Office	37
3.	Public and Private History in Colonial Williamsburg: A Memoir of a Half-Century and a View to a Calling	55
4.	Empty Temples: Challenges for Modern Government Archives and Records Management	67
5.	Secrecy, Archives, and the Archivist	87
6.	The National Archives Reclassification Scandal	103
7.	Archival Ethics: The Truth of the Matter	129
8.	The Archives & Archivists Listserv Controversy	147
9.	The Anthony Clark Case, SAA, and Professional Ethics	183
10.	Revisiting the Archival Finding Aid	205
11.	Teaching Unpleasant Things	227
12.	Arguing About Appraisal in the Age of Forgetfulness	243
	Conclusion	259
	Endnotes	272
	Works Cited	315
	Index	345
	About the Author	356

Introduction

As I have gotten older and more experienced, my worries about the archival profession and its mission have increased. That is what this book is about. The initial part of the book consists of three essays exploring the notion of archival calling, including a lesson about a lost opportunity for advocating the critical importance of the archival mission and a very personal reflection on my own calling into the archival field. The second part of the book concerns one of the pre-eminent challenges of our time, government secrecy, and how, if left unchallenged, it can undermine the societal role of the archival profession. The third part of the book considers what I see as one of the most important issues facing archivists, indeed, all information professionals, the possession of a practical ethical perspective. The fourth and final part of the book concerns the matter of teaching the next generation of archivists in the midst of all the change, debates, and controversies about archives and archivists. My sense, as reflected in these various essays, is that a substantial portion of the archival profession is also anxious about a variety of issues. Whether I am exaggerating *how* anxious is a matter for debate.

In the first chapter, "The Calling," I wrestle with a topic that many professionals, including archivists and records managers, seem to neglect. Any conversation with a records professional about how he or she entered the field will inevitably have lots of references to personal interests and fortitudinous circumstances, but rarely will there be any commentary about pursuing such a career because they responded to a calling. This may have to do with the swiftly changing society we live in, one where vocational callings and meanings are drowned out and where the predictions of the ends of experts and disciplines make one reluctant to use such seemingly old-fashioned language. We worry that if we use the notion of a calling, we will be designated as a religious nut or just too old-fashioned (although we soon learn that we have to believe in something). It is true we have to slow down, even stop, and listen closely to hear such a calling, but I argue that is necessary because our mission in administering and protecting records is about far more than just holding a job. It may be that society's misunderstanding of archives and other forms of records and information management work is as much the result of us promoting it as little more than just clerical duties and skills. We need to bring passion to our workplaces and make more obvious the pathways into a profession that is committed to a societal good. Understanding that the popular perceptions of archivists and record managers often weaken the idea of a calling is a good first step. Being a professional is more than being paid to do something; it is, among other things, committing to a lifelong pursuit of enhancing one's knowledge, whether through formal education, self-directed reading, continuing education opportunities, or a mentoring relationship. However, given the modern university's embracing of the corporate model, with a focus more on credentials than learning, a commitment to a calling is even more critical. We need to extend this notion of a calling to encompass both reading the professional literature and contributing to it by our own research and writing. While holding a job may be about skills and attitudes, responding to a calling is about possessing knowledge (both applied and theoretical), a knowledge that is important to draw on as we face numerous reports on the abuses and mismanagement of records critical for all sectors of our society and our lives.

The second chapter, describing the history, preservation, and interpretation (or lack of it) of the Secretary's Office in Williamsburg, Virginia suggests why responding to an archival calling might be difficult. Built in 1748, subsequently acquired by Colonial Williamsburg in the mid-twentieth century, the Secretary's Office is one of the oldest public records offices in North America. Strategically located in one of the most prominent and visited historic sites in the United States, the structure has been seen and visited by millions, although its purpose as a public records office has been hidden. Despite the reliance of Colonial Williamsburg on the rich archival sources of early Virginia to reconstruct the history of this colonial government center, it has not devoted much attention to interpreting the building as a public records facility (the building has been used as an exhibition area, public program venue, administrative offices, gift shop, and ticket office). With the exception of a couple of popular articles and some sporadic references in the archival professional and scholarly historical literature, the old public records building has been largely forgotten as a testament of early America's resolve to preserve its governmental records. Yet, it could be refurbished to present the importance and nature of archival work in our society, in a way that sends a message that might call the next generation of archivists. Given the manner in which the architects of the American Republic, such as Thomas

Jefferson, viewed the preservation of their records and that of the new democratic governments, this seems like a fitting use of the building.

The third chapter rounds out my discussion of the notion of calling by offering a very personal account of more than fifty years connecting with Williamsburg, Virginia and the nurturing of my interest in history. Some have been surprised about my intense interest in the past, assuming that some of my criticism about the relationship between historians and archivists or the assumptions by some archivists that archives exist solely for the use of such scholars means that I do not possess such an interest. I hope this essay clarifies that I understand that archives are critical for historians and historical research, even though I long ago expanded my sense of the value of archives to concerns such as accountability and evidence that place archives squarely in the midst of public policy and other matters. Here I testify how such personal interests can become a deeper sense of calling.

The fourth chapter concerns the problem of growing secrecy in the use of Presidential and other government records. Several recent, and compelling, books about modern government records raise a variety of issues about the nature and purpose of the administration of such information sources. The books critique the presidential library system, government secrecy, and the nature of recordkeeping even in a totalitarian, repressive regime — each posing in its own way critical issues for government archivists. Government secrecy is a compelling issue for records professionals, raising leadership issues, how we view the role of records in applications such as the accountability of public officials to citizens, the ownership and control of public records, the sometimes difficult challenges of balancing secrecy against real needs for providing security, and how issues such as secrecy throw greater light on the need for good recordkeeping. We can wonder if archivists and records managers who seek to ignore the implications of such activities as blacking out records don't figuratively black out themselves as relevant in government work. What we begin to see here is the collision between governments' efforts to be more secretive and the ethical values of archivists pushing for greater access.

The next chapter, also concerning government secrecy, examines five recent books on this topic by political scientists, a journalist, a lawyer, and an archivist. This essay summarizes how archivists have compiled an interesting, but generally uneven, set of opinions about how they should contend with such secrecy. These books suggest that while secrecy is not new or limited to government, it has become ingrained in every aspect of our society. Instead of the information age we may be living in the surveillance or security age. Archivists, whether they are aware of it or not, are being asked to work within classified parameters. Yet, a plausible argument can be made that archivists, as advocates for access, must always be working for the opening of records. What this means is open to negotiation and debate, but it is unlikely that any strong case can be made for archivists to be part of secret regimes, at least in democratic societies. It is another reason why some archivists feel anxious.

Chapter six is a final look at the problems and challenges of government secrecy, concerning secret agreements the National Archives made to reclassify previously declassified government records. While most archivists decry the increasing secrecy of our Federal Government as antithetical to the archival mission, archivists also have learned that their leading national program was part of this problem. This chapter provides a blow-by-blow account of the unfolding of the news about the reclassification effort, the debate surrounding it, and the implications of this scandal for both the National Archives and the American archival community. Most of the story is reconstructed by using the Archives and Archivists listserv, a forum ultimately threatened with oblivion by a recommendation of dumping its online archives by the archival community itself. As I mention in this chapter, we can look at this in a very positive way: A researcher stumbled upon the re-classification program, secret agreements were revealed, the media cast a spotlight on the case, a national professional association spoke out about the situation, the Archivist of the United States pledged that the National Archives would operate transparently and more responsibly in the future, and proposals for reforming the classification of government records were introduced. We almost can detect a process of checks and balances in what occurred.

Starting with chapter seven is my section on ethics as part of both professional knowledge and practice. This chapter considers what has become known as "Raisingate" within the American archival community, demonstrating how easy it is to become the focus of ethics discussions if you are the one to raise the issue (not unlike what occurs with whistleblowing). This essay explores the question of whether records professionals are as aware of the ethical dimensions of their work as they should be. Archival ethics, as such matters go, is a relatively recent issue for this professional community. In this case, exploring the debate about the use of a labor poster on the cover of the *American Archivist* and the reactions of business archivists to it, we find a disturbing example of the problems of how we view ethics. For example, before this debate, there was little evidence of ethics as a topic in the business archives literature.

The next chapter in this section deals with a brief, but intense, controversy concerning The Society of American Archivists' sudden, unanticipated announcement in 2007 that it intended to destroy the online archives of the Archives and Archivists listserv. In this essay I consider the history and nature of listservs, their use by archivists, and why archivists ought to be concerned with learning how to manage these as document-producing entities. The archives threatened with destruction provided many insights into the archival community, how it saw itself, appraisal issues, electronic records management concerns, and professional leadership. When considering this case, it emerges as not merely a disagreement about appraisal or a lack of ease with digital documentation but just as much about professional vision, mission, and leadership; the debate was a means for remembering that in carrying out appraisal or seeking to maintain digital information and evidence many other factors intrude.

The final chapter in this section brings together a set of blog and listserv postings concerning the story of Anthony Clark's efforts to gain access to the records of the Office of Presidential Libraries at the National Archives. I have presented here the original messages, with some introductory and reflective commentary, in order to document this debate. This will enable readers to determine for themselves just how important this debate was and whether SAA leadership or myself over-reacted or, more likely, that this captured something of the manifold unresolved aspects of professional ethics and leadership in the archives community. This case represents one that may only be worked out in the long-term, as the next generation of archivists takes over both SAA and the National Archives or, perhaps just as likely, a new archival discipline with different perspectives, commitments, and vision takes over, or side-steps, both the older professional associations and the largest archival agency. In my opinion, the case, along with the others in this section, demonstrates that archivists often create their own anxiety (we are just as often the victims of our own actions as well as because of contending with complicated issues generated by outside societal, political, legal, and technological forces).

The final section of the book concerns issues of teaching and cases that also suggest contentious or controversial changes facing the archival community. Chapter 10 provides a skeptical view of one of the most cherished of archival products, the finding aid. How could the simple finding aid be controversial? For one thing, it has been, despite its aim at providing a nexus between researchers and archivists, a remarkably inward-looking artifact, part of a process of archivists talking to themselves. In this essay, I explore three ways archival finding aids might be examined from outside our own professional community. Ultimately, they might be evaluated like museum exhibitions have been by historians, anthropologists, and other scholars, as artifacts defining their particular view of the world. Or, archival finding aids can be studied by those who are experts on design, considering the message they intend to convey to society. And, finally, archival finding aids might be one other means by which archivists are, or could be, held accountable to society.

The next chapter considers the teaching of advocacy in graduate archival education, a challenge, I argue, because it can bring up many unpleasant things (unpleasant, especially, for students just beginning to prepare for their careers). As graduate archival education programs have grown in scope, the variety of courses offered has changed to include some that prepare students to grapple with challenging and sometimes controversial aspects of the profession. This essay offers insights gained from teaching a course on archival advocacy, one that expanded over more than a decade from a focus on access to public outreach, and, then, to ethical issues. This shift in focus created particular problems in engaging students who come to the graduate program with basic presuppositions about archival work that do not often mesh with the reality of this professional community; challenges also arise because of the kinds of training students expect from professional schools within the university. The essay places this course in the context of the modern university and the changing archival community and considers the challenges and potential successes of engaging graduate students within a professional school. In this essay I also suggest how difficult challenging students to re-think their assumptions can be in professional schools in the modern corporate university.

The last major chapter wrestles with a favorite subject of mine, a favorite because it is both complex and so critical to the archival mission and the role of archivists in society. We used to think of archives as possessing bedrock stability, but now we understand, sometimes begrudgingly, that archives and the appraisal function are constantly changing. Society's views about records are shifting, and we are all learning that history is much messier than we ever assumed. A lot of attention is now devoted to the notion of public memory and a feel-good heritage industry, and this transformation suggests how easy it is for archivists to get into trouble for just doing their jobs. Postmodernism, truth, evidence, privacy, security, intellectual property, the empowering of citizens to assume archival tasks, ethical quandaries, and a host of other issues are reminding us that working to protect the materials that enable us to remember the past is not a form of pain relief. And the ultimate issue is how archivists formulate new stories to engage the public in supporting their mission. How can they do this if so much time is spent debating such issues rather than resolving them?

The making of this book involved years of teaching, researching, and writing, with some of the chapters having appeared in earlier forms or as presentations at professional conferences. Chapter One originally appeared as a three-part essay: "Hearing the Call," *Records & Information Management Report* 23 (January 2007): 1-13; "Heeding the Call," *Records & Information Management Report* 23 (February 2007): 1-13; and "Sustaining the Call," *Records & Information Management Report* 23 (April 2007): 1-14. Chapter Two was published originally as "Public Memory Meets Archival Memory: The Interpretation of Williamsburg's Secretary's Office," *American Archivist* 68 (Fall/Winter 2005): 279-296. Chapter Four was published as "Empty Temples: Challenges for Modern Government Archives and Records Management," *Records & Information Management Report* 22 (October 2006): 1-13. Chapter five was published as "Secrecy, Archives, and the Archivist: A Review Essay (Sort Of)," *American Archivist* 72 (Spring/Summer 2009): 213-230. Chapter six was originally published as "The National Archives Reclassification Scandal," *Records & Information Management Report* 22 (November 2006): 1-13. Chapter seven originally appeared as "Archival Ethics: The Truth of the Matter," *Journal of the American Society for Information Science and Technology* 59, no. 7 (2008): 1128-1133. Chapter eight originally appeared as a two part essay, "Listservs and Difficult Appraisal Decisions: The Archives and Archivists List Great Debate," *Records & Information Management Report* 23 (September 2007): 1-14 and "Listservs and Difficult Appraisal Decisions: The Archives and Archivists List Great Debate (Part Two)," *Records & Information Management Report* 23 (October 2007): 1-14. Chapter ten was first published as "Revisiting the Archival Finding Aid," *Journal of Archival Organization* 5, no. 4 (2007): 5-32. Chapter eleven was originally published as "Unpleasant Things: Teaching Advocacy in Archival Education Programs," *InterActions: UCLA Journal of Education and Information Studies*. Vol. 5, Issue 1, Article 8 (2009), available at http://repositories.cdlib.org/gseis/interactions/vol5/iss1/art8. Chapter three has not been published and the final chapter was presented as the keynote address at the New England Archivists meeting in Boston in November 2009.

Even though these essays have appeared in many other venues through the last half-dozen years, I believe that assembling them into one volume provides a glimpse into why archivists have so many reasons to be anxious about the state of their profession and its mission (beyond the normal concerns about issues such as information technology). I believe that the challenges archivists face are the result of a growing recognition of the importance of records in our society and its organizations, although these challenges are pushing archivists to think well beyond the cultural mission so many archivists have chosen to emphasize. Some readers of this volume might conclude that the anxiety is really all mine, and, if that is the case, I accept this is a result of being one seeking to challenge students in my classroom contemplating becoming archivists or archival faculty. I believe the topics I explore here are essential to assisting these students to prepare for their careers, since the days of archivists sitting quietly in their stacks and waiting for the occasional researcher to appear are long gone (if they ever really existed). Archival anxiety may be the result of this community being shaken out of its complacency.

In these contemplations I have been assisted by conversations and debates with an array of archivists and other colleagues, including Elizabeth Adkins, Jeannette Bastian, David Bearman, Karen Benedict, Frank Boles, Bernadette Callery, Toni Carbo, Paul Conway, Terry Cook, Barbara Craig, Elena Danielson, Bruce Dearstyne, Wendy Duff, Phillip Eppard, Timothy Ericson, John Fleckner, James Fogerty, Elsie Finch, Anne Gilliland, David Gracy, Karen Gracy, Mark Greene, Larry Hackman, Verne Harris, Margaret Hedstrom, Randall Jimerson, H. G. Jones, Joan Krizack, Cal Lee, Sue McKemmish, Heather MacNeil, Jennifer Marshall, Bruce Montgomery, Sue Myburgh, Richard Pearce-Moses, J. Michael Pemberton, Mary Jo Pugh, Helen Samuels, DongHee Sinn, Helen Tibbo, David Wallace, Tywanna Whorley, Thomas Wilsted, and Elizabeth Yakel. I am sure I have missed some individuals, but I am also sure that they are happy not to be mentioned. I also have benefitted from a group of recent doctoral students, each of whom in their own fashion have pushed me to clarify or even to change my views, including Allen Benson, Joel Blanco, Janet Ceja, Brian Cumer, Hea Lim Rhee, Robert Riter, Heather Soyka, and others.

As I put the finishing touches on this book, I do wonder if this is my last one aimed at the archival community. In a brief concluding reflection, I offer some final advice to the archival community in charting its future. By this I do not mean that this is my last book about archives (indeed, I am presently finishing two others), but these other books are not aimed at the archival profession (although, perhaps, some members of this community may read these and subsequent books and articles of mine in the future). I have reached my fourth decade working in the archival trenches, and while my commitment to this profession does not waver, I believe I have said what I needed to say to this audience. However, there is much to be said to those outside of this community about the value and power of archives.

There is also much more to be said to graduate students, at both the masters and doctoral levels, in our archives programs. Teaching is a form of both scholarship and publishing, and I think it is time for our graduate archives programs to break away from notions of traditional values and practices. And I think this is beginning to happen. Much of what is in this book falls into the ethical, policy, and accountability aspects of archival work, and this is the third in a set of books on such topics I have been involved in over the past decade. Tackling such topics is not easy. Schooling, even at the graduate level, has been threatened to become only technical and competencies-based. Mark Rose, considering the general state of education, notes, "It is entirely reasonable that a society will turn to its basic institutions to solve pressing needs. My concern ... is that the economic motive and the attendant machinery of standardized testing has overwhelmed all the other reasons we historically have sent our children to school. Hand in glove, this motive and machinery narrow our sense of what school can do. We hear much talk about achievement, the achievement gap, about equity, about increasing effort and expectations, but it is primarily technical and organizational talk, thin on the ethical, social, and imaginative dimensions of human experience."[1] David A. Hackema, in an essay about the role of ethics in professional schools, shines light more closely on my own educational home: "Rather than encourage students to reflect on the qualities that constitute a virtuous character, professional school ethics courses tend to focus on how many months an engineer or lawyer must wait after resigning from a firm or partnership before going to work for a competitor or a government regulation agency."[2] I am committed to offering more than technical-vocational training, where the practical overwhelms important and messier matters such as ethical issues of practice, and for this reason I offer this volume. And I am reasonably sure the reader will hear more from me on this and related topics in the future (especially since most of the present book emerged as reactions to events and controversies within the archival profession rather than as part of some sustained research agenda).

Richard J. Cox
Pittsburgh, Pennsylvania
September 2010

Chapter One

The Archival Calling

Introduction

We live in a restless age. Not only does change seem constant, but the concept of change is longed for and lauded, driven by our information technologies, rapid global communication, and fast and efficient delivery of consumer goods. As we evolved from moving under our own power to the use of domesticated animals to a succession of machine-driven vehicles, our sense of the world and our neighbors expanded, even if our ability to understand this universe has not always kept pace.

Archivists and records managers, as information professionals, might be expected to hold ambivalent feelings about our society and its unrelenting passion for speed and the next technological gadget. Records professionals expect to harness some of the benefits associated with the use of these technologies, while fearing that these same technologies also threaten to transform records work and displace them. Even more traditionally focused librarians are reading books guiding them to expand their own work parameters and counseling them that they will make substantial changes during their working lives.[1] While the predictions of the end of the utility of archivists or records managers have subsided, there still remains angst about the need for records professionals to grasp fully the information technologies or risk their obsolescence or relegation to lower level staff positions. One of the continuing claims by those who herald technologies supporting the use and maintenance of cyberspace is that the control by experts over knowledge will be broken and access to and application of such knowledge will be possible by many operating outside of the disciplinary guilds. This is particularly grim since the work of archivists and records managers has more often than not been seen to be little more than commonsense or, at its worst, an impediment to organizations' competitiveness. Filling out forms, filing documents, storing records, and retrieving them when needed — whether done with paper and file cabinets or virtually — often seems needlessly cumbersome in the nearly mythological belief in digital speed and deliberative communication and decision making.

The incessant fast pace of life in our post-modern era creates a kind of static that makes it difficult for people to hear what they need to hear. News, facts, events, sounds, and experiences flow over and around us in ways working against us being able to absorb and understand them. Instead of reflecting on information to build knowledge, we seem to be intent on chasing and grabbing more information than we can really use. We seem less content to participate in communal environments where we exchange and debate ideas, and more intent on sitting at our computers and surfing the World Wide Web. We seem less inclined to work for an education, and much more interested in having education delivered to us in digestible nuggets more like snacks than nourishment. Silence and reflection appear to be part of a dying art, replaced by multi-tasking and frenetic activity. Even conversation has been challenged, especially as we have been buried under "conversation avoidance devices" such as iPods, computers, video games, and e-mail while listening to radio and television talk shows that promote anything but civil discourse.[2] Under such circumstances it can be difficult to hear or respond to advice and influences essential to us as both working professionals and human beings. How much is done becomes more important than how well it is done. Longer-term missions are buried under short-term gains and activities.

In the midst of all this, some of us feel compelled to work as archivists or records managers. Those who work with records are often chastised for being absorbed with rather pedestrian concerns in our Information Age. Nevertheless, archivists and records managers serve a particularly important role in society, a role that is probably increasing in importance as we continue to move into the digital era and we face new challenges in preserving our documentary heritage, especially as new needs for organizing what seems like the chaos generated by this new age.[3]

Calling: Religious and Secular

The problem of living today is that the pace of life, and its many distractions, weakens our ability to hear or respond to a vocational call. The notion of being called to a profession is an ancient idea, and it is one that many have forgotten or think old-fashioned, especially as calling brings religious imagery of burning bushes, voices from above, and dramatic conversions — notions usually not associated with work in the twenty-first century, unless we are discussing religious faith *and* vocation.[4] There are valuable lessons here - such as the reminder of the larger purposes of human work and the self-fulfilling aspects of vocation that we often have seemed to have forgotten or pushed aside in the quest for money, fame, and security — but this is not the topic here.

There are ways to consider a vocational calling without the religious fervor, while including something about personal conviction and purposefulness. William Sullivan, in one of the best explications of the nature of work and professionalism, suggests that what distinguishes a sense of professionalism from any other concept of work is its sense of "calling," the notion that "professions contribute to the wider civic order." Professions draw their meaning from how they contribute to the "good society and the good life." In terms bordering on the theological, Sullivan argues that the "professions are important because they stand for, and in part actualize, the spirit of vocation. Professionalism promises to link performance of specific tasks with this larger civic spirit. By enabling workers to connect their activities and careers to the service of public ends, professionalism suggests how to organize the complex modern division of labor to ensure that specific functions are performed well and with a sense of responsibility for the good of the whole."[5] Such an assessment suggests that we not only pay heed to our employing organizations but to the societal needs and concerns that may be affected, positively or negatively, by our deeds. For archivists and records managers this means keeping our eyes on the global importance of records, as well as striving to have clear and relevant professional missions, strong and practical ethics codes, and well-developed senses of personal morality. And these activities are not always as easy as they seem.

Such attitudes and aspirations are not always universally understood or even known. Many students are in the classroom because they don't know what else to do, they are looking to gain a credential in order to get a job, or because they are seeking to change, for the second or third time (or even more), careers. We can go one step farther. Many gainfully employed records professionals are on the job by accidental circumstances, because they do not know what else to do with themselves, because it is the best position they can secure for the moment, or because they are there temporarily as they contemplate their next career. The idea of calling has little to offer to them; it is a purely idealistic notion, far removed from their own realities or needs. The lack of calling undermines the records professions because it weakens higher concepts of the significance of records and recordkeeping systems for society. It explains why so few pay attention to the role of records and their systems for purposes such as evidence, transparency, accountability, and cultural memory. Without a true sense of calling, it is easy for archivists and records managers to assume clerical roles they fear to be associated with or to function in a way legitimizing such a perspective by their employers and society at large.

Such attitudes are not unique to the records professions. In assessing the plight of keeping mature workers (where certainly a large portion of the records professions reside), several observers about the nature of the workplace note a "growing gap between employees' effort and satisfaction. Mid-career workers tend to be loyal and hard-working employees. The majority would contribute extra effort to help the organization succeed, yet only 43 percent say they are passionate about their jobs, and only 33 percent feel energized by their work. We also sense midcareer workers finding fault not only with employers, but with themselves — failure to live up to ambitious youthful expectations, to make a difference in their lives and career."[6] This suggests that such challenges influence how employers define work and professional positions.

Perhaps the greatest problem today, however, is the vastly different ways we approach work. There are many individuals, trapped in poverty and cut off from educational opportunities, who rarely reflect on a profession, striving to maintain shelter, feed themselves and their families, and pay the basic bills. Others, such as trailing spouses or individuals with family responsibilities such as ailing parents, often do the best they can, securing a job to meet basic needs with little thought of a career. Even those who once contemplated their professional lives, aided by solid educational preparation and resources to stay current in any field, now change careers three, four, five, and more times in their working years. Why do they go through so many occupations? One reason may be the restlessness of our high-tech society, where attention spans seem short and expectations for success and riches are intense. One is always searching for a break, never satisfied or happy. Perhaps the constant bombardment of information brings with it suggestions of better opportunities and greatest happiness in an occupation other than the one a person is working in. It is hard to hear a calling when so much other noise is present.

Constant occupational change may be the result of other factors. Is there such a thing as a real vocational calling once we strip away its supernatural or religious aspects? Given that parents and others start applying pressure earlier and earlier to our youth to decide what they want to do, it may be that a vocational calling has been replaced by market and economic forces unprecedented in their ferocity and pressure. The World Wide Web, blogs, wikis, instant messaging, email, and the never ceasing stream of facts, figures, advice, falsehoods, exaggerations, and rumors coming our way only adds to the confusion muddling our lives and our sense of livelihoods.

Whatever one might think about such pressures on individuals as they determine precisely what they want to do vocationally, it is certainly the case that employers must pay more attention to what is happening to their workforces. With the retiring baby boomers, longer life expectations, and declining birth rates, companies, organizations, and governments "will have too few young workforce entrants to replace the *labor, skills, and talent* of boomer retirees."[7] There are too few new professionals coming into the workforce.[8] And my impression is that the records professions will not be immune from such trends. Developing a message attracting new and young professionals to become archivists and records managers not only will be essential, but it will be a task that is competitive; that is, other professions also will be seeking to attract new workers to their fields as well.

Regardless of the challenges one might encounter in hearing a call, I remain convinced of three things. First, the notion of a calling to a vocation is not an antiquated idea. Without the sense of the commitment that is a calling, a professional position can be an empty vessel or one too porous to hold anyone's attention for very long. Second, it is especially difficult to hear a genuine call in our present information era. With the immense calls for equality offered via the relatively free access to lots of information on the Web, the notion of a deeper calling or even the relevancy of a profession has been challenged. Younger workers function in a manner very different from older ones; they are more tribal, more connected with peers, more independent, more networked, less formal, and less structured — all of these characteristics building within them the thirst for more "engaging" jobs, greater opportunities to "learn and grow" on the job, and more demands to have "attentive management."[9] And, third, information professionals, like archivists and records managers, need to re-evaluate the importance and meaning of such calls. What is a calling for a records professional, and what is their concept of mission in organizations and society?

We must be sensitive to how the notion of calling and vocation has changed over time from merely holding a position to mastering knowledge.[10] It may be that records professionals are in such a situation today, with a focus on professionalism as merely holding a job. We need to reflect more seriously on how individuals approach the field, and mulling over the notion of a calling into the records profession is one means of doing this.

The Importance of a Calling

Why is the idea of a calling to a profession so important? It is essential because the notion of a calling affirms the importance of any discipline. There are many workers complaining today about their jobs, many justifiably because of mismanagement, manipulation, unfair labor practices, loss of pensions, and other such problems. However, there are also many whining because they really don't understand their vocation, because they are in it for the wrong reasons or because they have simply burned out.[11]

There is ample evidence of such problems in the records professions. Archivists, on their listservs and in conference hotel bars, often lament their lower salaries, the lack of public recognition, and the misunderstanding by their employers of what it is that they do. Records managers, in the same venues, often pine for greater recognition as information workers and worry about how their association with records suggests that they are merely clerks or bureaucratic clogs. Such complaints and laments mirror what is happening in other professions, attributable to changing demographics, new workplace pressures, and vacillating notions of how information technologies impact and redefine the duties of those in the information disciplines. Such problems really suggest, however, a lack of understanding about the importance of records in society.

What is the essence of a calling for someone to join the records professions? In the past, individuals have become archivists or records managers in a variety of ways. For many years, individuals seeking to become archivists did so because of an interest in history or concern about the management of cultural resources. When they thought about joining archival ranks, they usually thought of working in museums, historical societies, historic sites, or academic special collections. Many individuals are attracted to the archives field not because they have a clear notion of what it is (given the confused way the media report on archives and archivists, how could they?), but because there is some connection (sometimes a vague one) between an interest in the past and old stuff. Ultimately, of course, these individuals, if they enter the field, discover that archival work is not about playing with old stuff, but that managing and preserving archives involves constantly ruminating about the mission of the work, advocating for it, and wrestling with new and complex digital information systems.

Why have individuals become records managers? Many have become records administrators by stepping up from clerical positions or other administrative positions within organizations. There are two points to be made about this. First, their emphasis has usually been on the managerial aspects of records, often derived from interests and backgrounds in electronic information systems. Second, some have found their way into records management by following a process within an organization. They start out in a lower position, involving some aspect of responsibility for records and information systems and then are offered higher paying administrative positions based on experience and success. Many never came to the organization to be a records professional. While some eventually connect to the larger profession and its various organizations and conferences, a good number know what they know about records management based on experience and self-directed reading.

We face a weakening of opportunity to respond to a true vocational calling for records work. Despite a central core concept of a life cycle for records, one that must include both the administration of current records and the identification and caring for records with archival (or continuing) value, the very different career paths and sets of interests for those attracted to become archivists and records managers produce a muddled sense of mission. We have had interesting calls for other missions, focusing on information or knowledge, but these lead us away from the central responsibility to work with records. Records may be increasingly in digital form, but the characteristics of what makes something a record do not fundamentally change. While some might exclaim that downplaying records is good for a variety of reasons, it is difficult to see what else has emerged that provides a coherent or substantial focus for a professional mission or calling. Information seems too soft, as does knowledge — although many disagree with this assessment. Records continue to be a focus in governments, corporations, universities, and other organizations.

Without a strong sense of a calling, individuals who join the ranks of records professionals may not stay there. The era when individuals worked for one organization or company all their careers has long since ended. With corporations jettisoning pensions, benefit packages being trimmed, and longer hours the norm, the idea of loyalty to an organization seems old-fashioned. Without some sense of purpose or commitment, workers' lives lose some of their purpose or meaning. Archivists and records managers require a strong connection to what it is that they are doing (their disciplines), no matter what their feelings may be regarding their employers. Given some of the illegal or immoral acts some organizations engage in concerning the maintenance of their records and information systems, records professionals had better possess a greater sense of meaning; they may be asked to indulge in activities counter to their acceptable responsibilities, and without a sense of calling how will they be able to sort out their options when this occurs? Indeed, Dychtwald and his colleagues suggest that this is the difference between satisfaction and engagement: "Satisfaction is about sufficiency — enough pay, benefits, flexibility to work and live, and no major problems or unfair treatment to sour one's attitude toward the employer." While I am sure many records professionals might argue that satisfaction is an ideal enough goal to achieve, it is not enough to hold someone in a particular position or even a career; a focus on satisfaction produces the perspective of someone constantly looking for the next opportunity (in effect, causing them never to be satisfied). We need something more than satisfaction: "Engagement is about passion and commitment — the willingness to expend one's discretionary effort on the employer's success."[12] To be engaged requires something greater than being focused on the employer's needs and concerns, such as a greater mission in society and contributing to a larger public good.

Positioning Oneself to Hear the Call

In order to hear anything, one needs to be in a position to hear. We can't isolate ourselves by not following the news, reading narrowly or hardly at all, or not mixing with professionals and others who are experts and good potential advisors. Records professionals, like any group, need to be aware of what is happening around them, if, for no other reason than that records seem to be on the front pages of major newspapers every day, the topic of crusading journalists and social commentators writing for news weeklies and public opinion outlets, and featured in a growing number of blogs. If archivists and records managers lack the societal, political, economic, and technological understanding of records and recordkeeping systems — an understanding requiring them to stay current with breaking developments — it is difficult to comprehend how they could administer effectively their records and recordkeeping systems.[13]

We need to develop means of staying current with the relevant professional literature and other sources, recognizing that the knowledge supporting records work is not static, but one that is being enhanced, revised, and strengthened. Even with the professional literature, however, we must be concerned with the clarity of its message. Within archival circles there has been a deepening of both theory and basic research in its journals, and a growing number of monographs discoursing on issues relevant to archival work. Records managers have tended to stick with basic practice issues, with little interest in testing the assumptions of their work. With both, however, there have been only modest efforts to reach beyond their own practitioners to the public, employers, or policymakers. When I am ruminating about the idea of a call, I am not interested in a jargon-laden language but one that connects to the greater good of our society and its citizens. We have enough examples of professions that have lost their way in their own academic debates because they have lost sight of their mission and audience.[14] It is probably the case that very few who might read our professional literature are going to walk away with a full understanding of the importance of records or our professional mission. Even when other disciplines study the nature of records, it is extremely rare that they utilize the literature of archivists or records managers, and archivists and records managers rarely cross-disciplinary borders in their own reading or research.

What some archivists and records managers have wished for is one or two powerful books, aimed at a general audience, easily, powerfully, and convincingly conveying the right message about what records professionals do and why records are important. We generally lack these, although there are indicators that there may be changes on the horizon. The book about Nelson Mandela's time in prison conveys a powerful message about the role of documents with lavish illustrations, and it may capture a broader reading audience's interest in why and how records ought to be maintained. If I found reading the volume to be a compelling and moving tale, I ought not to be surprised someday to be talking with a new student or a new archivist or records manager and discover that they joined our ranks because of having read it.[15] And, given the importance of records to society, archivists and records managers ought to be surprised that there are not multiple examples of such books — along with movies, television shows, radio programs, short stories, and Web sites — extolling the virtues of records and recordkeeping systems. And, indeed, they may be there save for the fact that we misuse them or react to them in a hypercritical mode. Records professionals need to be more creative and open about such matters.

We also make ourselves responsive to hearing a call by our relationships to others. Every year I note that there are new students who have discovered the records professions because they have had a university or college job that ultimately led to working in an archives or records management unit. A chance conversation may have sent them down a path where they begin to discover that there are careers where they can work with records. Others have somehow gotten to know someone working in the field, and they have become informed about the records professions, its mission, and its employment opportunities. This type of informal, early mentoring is very important. If a picture is worth a thousand words, then knowing a working archivist or records manager is worth far more. Although the limitations in the breadth of knowledge and experience of any archivist or records manager will impact just how important such mentoring may be, it is nevertheless clear that there is high potential of this being influential in enabling a calling to be heard or, at least, a greater depth of knowledge gained from talking to or watching a working professional.

The immense range of ways that individuals discover the archives and records management fields suggest both hope and the need for more calculated reflection on the part of the records professions. Students discuss being influenced by family members, inspired by visits to museums or historic sites, motivated by experiences working in libraries and archives as students or volunteers, led by their personal collecting, engaged by their own diaries or blogging, captivated by doing research in archives, intrigued by examining their own family papers, interested by media coverage of events concerning archives or records and recordkeeping, advised by a professor, and possessing a passionate love for history or intense joy in reading and books or even an innate love in order. We can be hopeful because individuals seem to find their way to our disciplines in virtually any way possible, but we need to consider approaches that do not pin recruitment into the records professions on a completely serendipitous process (or, worse, lack of process).

The challenge with positioning oneself to be able to hear a true calling is daunting. Lots of channels send information in our direction, often in muddled or inaccurate forms. More to the point, how records systems and records professionals are described often adds to confusion rather than providing any clarification. Archivists are described as librarians. Records are poorly described or merely seen as problems for organizational efficiency. Records managers are often more invisible than archivists. Records managers desire to be seen as information or knowledge workers, sending mixed or confusing signals about their mission and responsibilities. Archivists lean as much towards museum curators or historians than towards information professionals, creating their own obstacles for clear messages about their practice and mission.

Even if the message is not always clear enough to capture the attention of most people, the conflicting messages and differing perspectives can enable us to consider the tensions in our own lives in a useful fashion. Parker Palmer, a sociologist and motivational speaker, has written about vocational calling in a manner suggesting that all this noise can be good;

Palmer emphasizes that "If we are to live our lives fully and well, we must learn to embrace the opposites, to live in a creative tension between our limits and our potentials."[16] Both records managers and archivists have done relatively poorly in reaching out to a broader public, even if we consider that our professional associations and employing organizations have been a lot more active in the past decade than ever before. If we want to attract people to work in the records community then we need to be very clear about what this work represents. Given the growing predictions about future shortages in many professional arenas, records professionals need to do this better, especially since organizational leaders and policymakers have been mesmerized by the promises of information technologies to believe that records problems and issues have been resolved. To the contrary, the power for the individual to manage effectively their own documentation using personal computers, laptops, and hand-held computing devices only makes the need all the greater for archivists and records managers to explain what it is they do.

Rethinking the Call

There are many ways to think about what constitutes a calling to be an archivist or records manager, but the best place to start may be with the essence of what records constitute. Writer Wendy Lesser provides this interesting tidbit about an interview with a filmmaker: "Madmen always have files, or at any rate madmen of a certain sort, the ones who seek to organize experience by chronicling and alphabetizing every idea that floats through their minds, every act of real or supposed injustice committed against them, every seed of potential enormous wealth."[17] The connection of recorded documentation with every human activity, from the most benevolent to the most evil, has been affirmed over and over again in the past half-century. Media coverage of a war criminal quickly moves to discussing the evidence, and truth commissions around the world have generated millions of documents as sort of alternative archives. So, why is it so difficult to have a meaningful conversation with anyone about what archivists and records managers do? Why are these professionals, despite their employment in every kind of organization around the globe, among the least well known of all professional groups? Or, even, is it more proper for records professionals to be invisible, in order to convey that they are objective custodians rather than activist shapers of the documentary universe?

Archivists and records managers have been content to let society develop any view of them, often where the notion of records, archives, and recordkeeping systems are mangled beyond any reasonable utility. General perceptions about archives as old stuff for genealogists and historians, and records management as a function to clean out the old stuff predominate, and, it might be added, weaken any idea of a real calling. These perceptions are more like housekeeping functions, or the dreaded clerical tasks so many want to avoid, rather than anything that grabs one's attention. And that is a serious problem. It is not dark basements and dank attics that archivists and records managers want to be associated with; records professionals need to be seen at meetings, in the main hallways of the organization, and with the groups working on the primary products of any organization (whether corporate or non-profit). Otherwise, records will be perceived as the documentary detritus of an organization, stuff to be cleaned up and shuffled off after the important work is done.

When we are ruminating about the essence of a calling, we are doing something far more profound than assembling encyclopedia entries, dictionary definitions, or professional glossaries. And we are engaged in something that is very different than just reflecting on the nature of a profession, although one goes with the other. Sometimes, as we read the many postings on professional listservs complaining about poor salaries, inadequate recognition, and improper image, we hope to read a message affirming what archivists and records managers contribute to their organizations and society. However, this omission may be reflective of other aspects of twenty-first century culture where personal agendas and objectives seem to cloud anything that may be bigger or more important.

There is a bigger picture needed for thinking about the calling to the records professions. When I went into class on the morning of September 11, 2006 — the fifth anniversary of the terrorist attacks on the World Trade Center and the Pentagon — it was a class coincidentally focused on the "power of records." I commenced class with a brief statement to mark the anniversary and to start my lecture on this topic, mentioning among other things, that "This is a particularly poignant day for archivists, records managers, and others associated with the records and information professions. Over the past half decade we have witnessed not just war and threats of war, but we have seen the erosion of civil liberties, the weakening of access to information and evidence, and the risk to government transparency and accountability normally associated with democratic regimes." I also mentioned that we have the "extraordinary opportunity for records professionals to expound more clearly and profoundly the importance of records in our society. However, in order for this to happen, archivists must have the right mission and the most powerful message.

Records document all activities, keep governments and organizations accountable, enable the maintenance of our civil liberties, and sustain societal memory. It is only if we can maintain such attributes, and others deeply embedded in our democratic governance, that there will be meaning for 9/11 in our anniversary events." As I explained to my class, this statement was not intended to suggest any particular political perspective but only to remind them that contemporary events both challenge our professional mission and provide a new context for understanding it. We ought to reevaluate constantly whether our call is relevant. Some might argue that if there is not a clearly articulated public good associated with any occupation, then such work ought not to be deemed a profession. Considering someone to be a professional just because they are paid to work is a very short-sighted notion of the concept of a profession. There must be something to *profess*![18]

If we adopt a historical perspective, even for a moment, the relationship of a call to society becomes clearer. The earliest emphasis of archivists was on gathering the documentary record, not unlike what museums and other cultural organizations had been doing for generations. Increasingly, archivists' focus shifted to the organizational management of institutional and government archives and records programs, from which the concept of records management emerged. As digital information technologies had an increasing array of implications for archives and records work, the work of records professionals became more concentrated on technical issues, extending beyond preservation and access issues. There were deliberate shifts from collecting to managing records and then to considering the nature of the record, the forming of both records systems and our documentary heritage, and the practical uses of records for accountability and evidence.

Both the nature of a calling was changing and, the significance of a calling was becoming more prominent. Suggesting a different calling from where individuals express a love of history or for old things (for archivists) or where there is an innate sense of efficiency and organization (for records managers) is simply not good enough. It is certainly not good enough when teaching about archives and records management in the graduate or undergraduate classroom. None of this is intended to suggest that someone with an interest in history or old stuff won't eventually adopt a broader sense of an archival or records management mission (I offer myself as testimony to this). What is important to reconsider, however, is how we attract people directly into the records professions because they have such an understanding.

There is some danger in possessing a strong sense of vocational calling. Neurologist Alice W. Flaherty, in an analysis of various physiological and psychological aspects blocking writing, offers this aside on the notion of vocation: "So a sense of vocation doesn't guarantee happiness at work. Nor does it guarantee being good at the job. Perhaps it merely gives its possessor a subtle feeling of megalomania, a sense of being in some manner chosen for a higher goal. ... When your work is part of who you are, and you feel you are working badly, you become foul to yourself."[19] Another way of looking at this is to understand that holding a strong sense of personal mission, especially one with ideas of the accountability function of records, also can place archivists and records managers in very different roles within their organizations and society, roles requiring them sometimes to speak out or even to place their jobs and careers in jeopardy.

We also are in a time of transition in the records professions. Most archivists and records managers have tended to believe that the source of this change is due to the transforming nature of the always-new digital systems and digital recordkeeping approaches. However, the main issue is that these systems throw into the light the importance of records for a much broader cluster of values than what archivists and records managers have generally assumed to be the case. Traditional notions of archival work for history or cultural memory and records management for efficiency and economy are not going to disappear. Other values and agendas are slowly emerging. Dorothy Sayers, in her book about Christian doctrine many years ago, made an interesting comment about belief: "What we in fact believe is not necessarily the theory we most desire or admire. It is the thing that, consciously or unconsciously, we take for granted and act on."[20] We are now moving from theoretical notions of the importance of records to understanding these as a critical part of the records professional's toolkit. Some of this is becoming more evident in how individuals heed the call to become an archivist or records manager.

Heeding the Call

How does one heed the call to become an archivist or records manager? What may be most important in entering is the first employer. Mihaly Csikszentmihalyi reminds us "that finding a job should never be just a matter of finding a source of income. The organization you work for will shape your entire identity. It will either enable you to grow or stunt you; it will either energize you or drain you; it will strengthen your values or make you cynical."[21] It is surprising to listen to individuals desiring to be an archivist or records manager who have little sense of the variety of jobs within these professions, the differences between archivists and records managers, or the great variety of organizations where records professionals ply their trade.

People looking for work are not always searching just for a means of financial support, but they are looking for personal fulfillment and identity, especially as we realize more than ever that jobs are subject to economic shifts, corporate changes, emerging sources of cheaper labor, and other fluctuations in our society.[22] As Russell Muirhead suggests, the revamped notion of a calling or vocation remains critically important in our present culture, making "labor a duty instead of a curse. The calling established work's necessity apart from our material necessity. But taking work to be a calling also requires that individuals see themselves related to their jobs in a way that is not accidental or arbitrary. Callings, in short, involve a fit between individuals and their work that not only links individual aptitudes with specific occupations but also connects work, however ordinary, with the highest purposes individuals can serve."[23] Some surmise that the nature of a vocation has changed because the greater use of information technology has transformed both how we prepare to work and what we might actually do as an occupation. If we adopt a more holistic historical perspective we find that "change brings complexity, and a suitable metaphor for social change will be multidimensional and disorienting — as disorienting a model as the real thing would be to have lived through."[24] The ability to respond effectively to a real calling is to start a career in a place where one can be exposed to the full spectrum of ideas about and the practices of records work, as well as be mentored by an able, experienced archivist or records manager. Most professionals spend the majority of their waking hours focused on their work, for whatever reason, and this alone necessitates that they re-evaluate just what professional work means — to them, their families, their employers, and society itself.

Anyone must possess an openness to learn and to develop a broad perspective about his or her vocation. Religious commentator George Weigel observes this about the religious nature of European life: "A thoroughly secularized world is a world without windows, doors, or skylights: a claustrophobic, ultimately suffocating world."[25] Weigel is, of course, making commentary on the role of religion in society, but it is not that much of a stretch to see that any closed, inflexible view of the world limits one's ability to grow or change as they should. Once inside the records professions we need to be open to being influenced about what it means to be an archivist or a records manager. And this is not always as easy as it might seem, and it can take years. Howard Gardner, the prolific

Harvard cognitive scientist, argues that it takes a decade to master a discipline,[26] and my own experience suggests this as well. Developing an understanding of a sense of a professional mission is dependent on a number of variables, including education, early professional experiences, and contacts with other archivists and records managers.

First Institution

Just a few decades ago, most individuals entering into some aspect of records work came to it via apprenticeship, gaining practical experience. Fledgling archivists often took a formal field experience course where the student learned about a variety of basic archival functions (usually reference and arrangement and description). Those entering into records management often came to it from a variety of positions within an organization, such as secretarial work or, increasingly, entry-level information management activities, and were mentored by an experienced records manager. The curriculum was more training than education and, no matter how one might think about such programs, this was somewhat like a medieval guild system. Those who experienced this sort of entry into the records professions are usually honest in reporting that most of this gateway was an accidental rather than a planned or deliberate process. The experience was good, but often the orientation to professional knowledge was marginal (and knowledge supporting records work is derived from application, the codifying of practice, and, to some extent, theoretical speculation and research across the spectrum of records work, systems, and administration).

My own experience working with graduate students preparing for records careers suggests that those students with some range of experience as a paraprofessional, technician, or undergraduate archives work study are best prepared for this next stage of educational preparation. They have sorted out personal connections with the range of work done by archivists or records managers, and they have real experiences to compare with the more theoretical preparation they will receive in the classroom. Practical experience drives the creation of a curiosity for learning more about what archivists and records managers do in a well-rounded, comprehensive exposure to the functions carried out by archivists and records managers — precisely the orientation that can be provided by a full-fledged graduate program. Even the best mentors or internship programs have limitations in their knowledge and experience, but these limitations can be overcome when someone becomes a student and is immersed in the field's theoretical and research literature.

No matter how large or small the first archives or records management program employing someone may be, most individuals working as an archivist or records manager will run headlong into the various pressure points generated by organizational and professional missions. This may have to do with the seemingly relentless change wrought by new information technologies, and our attitudes and reactions to these technologies' implications. The notion of market-driven organizations now cuts across every variety of institution — government, cultural, corporate, and citizen action group — generating a constant need for change that can be confusing and demoralizing.[27] Archival programs in cultural institutions are not immune from this, and, if that is the case, certainly records and information management programs in profit-minded entities are being pressured by such elements. The student who has been in the real world of the records professions can relate to it with a deeper understanding, more critical perspective, and a stronger sense of its implications; at the least, their own personal experience will generate good questions by which to evaluate what I am saying. The vocational calling can be better heard or confirmed by some degree of real experience.

The decision about what institution to enter to gain one's first professional experience is always a challenge, and one probably should seek advice from a veteran records professional. Americans have come to expect some particular promises in their vocational choices, as Robert Reich notes with his assessment that one of these is that "everyone should have an opportunity fully to develop his or her talents and abilities through publicly supported education."[28] Could records professionals hope for any better than this? We continue to hope that such promises remain in place, especially the last one, but the continual restlessness of people for personal meaning in their positions, one that transforms a job to a profession or a profession to a societal mission, often makes such a quest an elusive one. The addition of the concept of a calling gives distinct meaning to a job, and the search for that calling, normally in the early years of one's working life, is essential. The concept of a calling is not a fiction but a necessity.

Education as an Entry Point

Some working records professionals criticize what is offered as formal educational preparation, a topic I explore in the last section of this book, but which I want to discuss here in the context of professional calling. Often such complaints mirror more about the insecurities and personal angst harbored by archivists and records managers who have been working in the field without the benefit of such education, although there is valuable tension between working professionals and academics to keep a focus on professional concerns and practical issues. Even though archivists and records managers seem to operate according to very different educational guidelines, the former having a focus on graduate education and the latter on undergraduate preparation, formal education provides an excellent path for one responding to a call to become a records professional. Bruce Dearstyne writes, as one example, "One of the defining traits of a profession is that it has articulated, recognized educational standards and provisions for regulating or guiding entry into the field," although there is always a need for "new approaches" due to changes such as represented by technology.[29] Educational programs need to be evaluated for how well they equip students to enter the workforce and for how long the skills they possess remain relevant in their early professional positions.

Formal education provides an opportunity to become both immersed in the accumulated knowledge guiding the work of archivists and records managers as well as oriented to the debates and controversies affecting this knowledge. Professional knowledge is constantly expanding, due to the changing technologies of records and information systems, shifting laws and public policies affecting the administration of records, development and testing of new best practices, and new research about records and recordkeeping systems, their management, and their preservation and use. This knowledge, while it encompasses both skills and attitudes, is much more than either or both of these professional attributes. A solid educational foundation provides a usable foundation for the long-term. Mihaly Csikszentmihalyi, discussing the problems associated with corporate and government leaders who want quick fixes and short-term gains at the expense of all else, argues that "we need *hundred-year managers* at the helm of corporations," not individuals who think in terms of one-minute managers.[30] The analogy is particularly relevant since archivists and records managers are the ones responsible for the long-term administration of records and other information sources.

If educational programs provide little more than a basic orientation to practice, there is little opportunity for students to gain a full appreciation of professional mission or to evaluate any sense of a calling to work as an archivist or records manager. Students need to be challenged by their instructors, and this necessitates both a perspective offered by the instructor about the field as well as a challenge to the status quo. Some years ago, Benjamin Barber, assessing the nature of teaching, offered this observation: "With good teaching, as with good art, someone is always offended: the point is precisely to provoke, offend, and spur to critical thinking."[31] We must come into the classroom fully prepared to present divergent perspectives about what archivists and records managers do, offering critiques of and challenges to how they normally approach their work. The point is, there is room for improvement and the necessity for new methodologies, and in the consideration of these discourses will come the opportunity for students to reconsider why they think they want to be an archivist or records manager. I view my mission as getting the students to think of their role as being change agents in the field, not for the sake of just making changes but because records professionals face new and always emerging challenges to their work (and this includes the opportunity for the students to reconsider the nature of a vocational calling).

We can look at this in another way. Sociologist Richard Sennett has aptly noted that the "shelf life of many skills is short; in technology and the sciences, as in advanced forms of manufacturing, workers now need to retrain on average every eight to twelve years."[32] Sennett reminds us that this presents an "idealized new self: an individual constantly learning new skills, changing his or her 'knowledge basis.'"[33] While we must constantly evaluate the merits of this situation, especially according to moral and ethical aspects, on a practical level, as instructors of the next generation of working professionals, we must be both providing new information and methodologies as well as the framework for individuals to evaluate their new circumstances in terms of vocational commitment. Sennett cautions that the "more one understands how to do something well, the more one cares about it. Institutions based on short-term transactions and constantly shifting tasks, however, do not breed that depth."[34] He observes that the quality of institutional life has declined, especially as they "inspire only weak loyalty, they diminish participation and mediation of commands, they breed low levels of informal trust and high levels of anxiety about uselessness."[35] The one thing that professionals such as archivists and records managers possess is that they can connect to a larger professional mission, one extending their focus far beyond their own institutional homes.

Students' changing work and career expectations present new challenges, as Derek Bok suggests when he writes, "They want work that is interesting, well paid, respected, and worthwhile. They want to serve in an ethical environment where they do not feel pressured to do things they consider wrong and can count on being judged fairly in matters of pay and promotion. They want a career that fits their aptitudes and talents yet challenges them in ways that help them develop further."[36] We can create a nurturing environment to start students on the right path, but the road they will be on always will be changing, complicated by new educational approaches such as online education offering new means of auditing our success and holding us accountable.[37] Records professionals might use this to open a dialogue with schools providing an entry point into their fields, arguing for new and improved methods of educational delivery. At the least, archivists and records managers might conduct the same exercise in their own employing organizations, searching for a means of a professional audit and reconsidering the implications for measuring their own performance. Such self-scrutiny aids us in better discerning the nature of a professional call.

Reading

Whether one has the benefit of a formal professional education or not, the new archivist or records manager needs to stay current with the field. This has become both more promising and more challenging. A few decades ago archivists and records managers had only a few journals, a small set of basic practice manuals, and some theoretical works to assist them. One could gain a command of the professional literature with a modest weekly regimen of reading, assuming that they had access to the basic journals, manuals, and other writings; it was not particularly difficult to build, quickly and inexpensively, a working professional library, but now the professional literature has expanded both in depth and breadth.

Today, the professional literature is much more complex. Partly due to new graduate education opportunities and the greater challenges of administering records systems that are both analog and digital, there has been tremendous growth in the professional literature. Put more simply, archivists and records managers have more journals, a greater number of basic practice manuals, and a growing number of research studies in journals and monographs. Adding to the greater complexity of the literature, scholars and professionals from other fields are turning their attention to the nature of records and recordkeeping systems and the importance of the archival and records management functions to society and its institutions. Historians, anthropologists, sociologists, political scientists, cultural and literary studies specialists, ethnographers, linguists, and others are writing about aspects of the documentary process in society and its organizations — and these scholarly discourses add new insights to the knowledge about archives and records. Reading across the disciplines ought to make archivists and records managers understand that their concerns and interests are not so unique as they may think, as well as to provide new insights into the formation of the documentary heritage.

The complexity of this new knowledge beckons archivists and records managers to read across their disciplinary boundary. A scientist-theologian provides an interesting perspective on the nature of interdisciplinary endeavors, suggesting that in our complicated world, "The moral is certainly not that we should all return to the comfort and safety of our professional home grounds. Interdisciplinary work is both essential (for, in the end, knowledge is one) and risky (for we must all venture to speak on topics of which we are not wholly the master). We must attempt a bit of intellectual daring and, above all, we have to be prepared to listen and learn from each other, showing mutual tolerance and acceptance in doing so."[38] Such an assessment adds to the importance of professional reading. While many archivists and records managers claim they have little time for reading, or much of anything beyond meeting daily responsibilities, we must understand that this weakens us. Reading is not just a source of practical advice; it is a window into new possibilities, pushing us to rethink what we are doing. It is one means by which we affirm our call, keeping us open to the possibility of taking our archives and records management mission and message into other venues in ways that strengthen it.

The knowledge supporting records work is made up of theory, methodology, and practice, and professional reading can be directed to support each of these components. Most records professionals gravitate to reading about practice, and since an immense portion of the professional literature is composed of nuts and bolts manuals or practical case studies, it is not difficult to figure why this would be the case. Clearly, it is not hard to understand that archivists and records managers often read to find out if others have confronted and solved problems similar to their own. This certainly dominates the discourse on professional listservs and explains why many Web sites are designed in the manner they are. Of course, the fact that archivists and records managers, after a half-century of separate professional identity, are still struggling to find a common ground for their work is indicative of more serious problems needing to be addressed.[39] However, the new opportunities we have with blogs, wikis, e-journals, and Web sites ought to be re-invigorating what and how we read, as well as how we construct new knowledge (keeping our minds open and active and receptive to new ideas and opportunities).

Mentoring

Forming working relationships with experienced records professionals is important for developing a sense of calling. It is likely that mentoring has been the *most* important means for assisting many to appreciate the nature of archival and records management work, especially as other means, such as formal education, are recent developments.[40] Mentoring also may be important because, as some from within the field argue, records professionals are "not much given to introspection."[41]

Some infer that the various certification programs in the archives and records management fields are an extension of mentoring. Archivists gravitate to their certification to complement educational programs, and records managers, where there is no strong tradition of university-based education, see certification as one of the very few ways of demonstrating competency.[42] Whether certification leads to a stronger mentoring and learning process is questionable or untested, but it is reasonable to assume that credentialing probably helps individuals ramp up their knowledge and improve on their range of work experience. If used in the right way, certification can be a process not merely to earn a credential for practice but one intended to assist individuals to evaluate their careers and to prepare them for new professional opportunities.

Professional associations have established formal mentoring programs. The Society of American Archivists has one "designed to facilitate communication and to cultivate career development between archival generations."[43] While ARMA does not offer such a program, a visit to its web site reveals many services supporting career development in order to "meet the challenges of the increasingly complex records and information management field."[44] Reading such statements makes one realize that professional associations represent a kind of collective mentor, providing advice and guidance from publications, standards, and policy statements to conferences and workshops.

Mentoring may be a path to resolving the highly differentiated records and information professions, where archivists, records managers, information professionals, knowledge managers, and others build unnecessary boundaries and confuse employers and society about the nature of records and information management work. Sue Myburgh suggests that the differences are dissolving because of the changes in information and communications technologies.[45] This is not the first observation about this transformation, but personally I think it is more hopeful than realistic. We need a mentoring program enabling archivists, records managers, and other records and information management professionals to gain a variety of experiences outside of their own institutions so that their perspectives, knowledge, and skills are broadened. Exchange programs where organizations trade employees for a limited time could do much to assist the employing organizations, as well as to begin to help individual professionals begin to talk across professional boundaries. More concerted efforts by professional associations to bring in people from outside their associations who could stretch ideas and perspectives (some limited efforts have been made) also could do a lot to help nurture stronger professional development. The information technologies, theoretically pushing individuals to embrace professional convergence, at least should remind us of such possibilities and the reasons for our own professional choices.

Continuing Education, Conferences, and Informal Networking

If there is any one area of the records professions that has become extremely well developed, it is continuing education, including conferences. Both the SAA and ARMA have excellent continuing education programs, offering workshops from the basic to the advanced level and experimenting with offering courses online. Every regional archival association offers workshops on every topic imaginable and often at bargain basement prices and in convenient locations. The local ARMA chapters also offer interesting programs, usually on a monthly basis, including more extensive workshops. Many universities with graduate programs in the field host workshops, as do many state government archives and records management programs. It is not an exaggeration to say that nearly everyone in North America is a short drive from some continuing education offer.

Continuing education functions best if an individual has a good educational foundation, with grounding in the theories, methodologies, and practices supporting archives and records management. No one gains a comprehensive orientation to all of the elements in the administration of records and information systems in any education program. The programs are too short in time, the field is too complex, and the change is too rapid. They need to gain experience, be mentored, and learn more about what they don't know. It is when someone is able to identify needed additional skills that continuing education opportunities become important. Continuing education is best when it fills gaps in the knowledge of archivists and records managers, building from graduate programs that should provide a foundation for lifelong learning. Not only can everything not be learned in a formal educational experience, neither can everything be mastered via on-the-job experience. The possibility of continuing education workshops and institutes is that individuals can push themselves to learn and prepare for new positions and career options. Workshops and other continuing education programs can be an important source of mentoring.

People go to professional conferences for many different reasons. Some go to gather information about the latest developments in standards, methodologies, and practice. Others go to hear the latest gossip, professional and personal. These two purposes suggest why conference attending is critical to developing both a strong sense of professional identity and helping us re-evaluate where we are in our own career (or where we want to be). Conference attendance builds a sense of professional community. You get to see larger groups of other professionals who are basically doing the same work as you, and you can also learn from others about the challenges they face and the solutions developed to resolve these challenges. Talking with other archivists and records managers is an opportunity to learn about what has drawn them into this field and the range of responsibilities constituting records work.

While sitting through conference presentations is an important mechanism for enhancing professional knowledge, it is the networking with other professionals that is usually the part of any conference that has the most lasting influence and value. Building relationships over time, often started by making acquaintances at conferences, can lead to trusted mentoring relationships and sources of advice. We face challenges, of course, in sustaining conference going and continuing education as sources for personal networking, since so much is now virtual. There are legitimate questions about whether such interaction is as useful as face-to-face interaction, at least for developing closer working relationships that can assist professionals to re-evaluate career goals and aspirations. Fortunately, other aspects of the new digital world support the development of other kinds of useful networking, and some of these may far exceed what we had in place before.

Not too many years ago, we would write a letter and wait weeks for a reply. Or, we would play telephone tag for days trying to locate someone in his or her office or elsewhere. Planning and carrying out a meeting or event had a leisurely pace that we might be nostalgic about now in a world of hyper speed. Yet, the amazing development of new and portable information technologies has provided remarkable opportunities for networking that can be of great assistance to us in our day-to day work. While we all need to occasionally shut off these electronic devices and have some quiet reflective time, when we move to such a mode we are far better informed about what we might be contemplating. Electronic mail has considerably improved our ability to stay in touch with each other, transforming our ability to network (especially internationally). Over two decades I observed a colleague building international partnerships by logging thousands of air miles and many nights of hotel stays. It was exhausting to watch. Today, we can accomplish the same ends without ever leaving home.

We can add cell phones and their increased capability for text messaging, instant messaging, and a host of other approaches that while not always the most socially respectable or polite ways of keeping connected can be very helpful for quick help and advice. Sometimes we might wonder whether those in the airport, loaded down with various electronic devices, might really have a moment to reflect about anything they might be working on, but hopefully each of us can learn how to harness their power in positive ways for our own careers and productivity.

There are new forms of electronic information systems revolutionizing how we build mentoring and advising networks or, as we might better refer to them, communities. Web logs or "blogs" might be the most important of these. As one commentator on blogs suggests, "Weblogs or digital diaries are perhaps primarily about synchronizing one's experience with others, about testing one's evaluations against the outside world. Blogging, besides being an act of self-disclosure, is also a ritual of exchange: bloggers expect to be signaled and perhaps to be responded to. If not, why would they publish their musings on the Internet instead of letting them sit in their personal files?"[46] Now we can develop blogs on a topic of interest to us, go public, and seek commentary, discourse, and debate on the topic. While the value of such blogs can vary tremendously, their potential for building professional communities is unlimited, and they can be of great service in assisting us to understand how well we are following our professional calling.

Professional Education and Calling

The notion of responding to a call has been tied historically to the development of graduate and professional education. Derek Bok, former president of Harvard University, declares, "education is important for its own sake," suggesting that it is accepted as both part of a greater public good and individual calling.[47] In recent years the university has taken on a business-like persona whereby students are customers, revenue is the primary objective, and cost-effectiveness is as critical as any other educational or societal objective. The so-called corporate university has also prompted some re-evaluation of the historic purposes of the university.[48]

Such matters are important for those teaching in professional schools since often we are seen by both external and internal observers as supporting little more than a system of credentialing individuals to ply a trade.⁴⁹ This is why the concept of a calling, societal mission, and public good are critical features for what and how we function, if for no other reason than to offer a better explanation for the existence and functions of professional schools.

More moderate and balanced perspectives have been expressed about the nature of the modern university. English professor Eric Gould reflects that the emergence of the modern American university occurred in a capitalist society, and that the more recent problems enunciated as part of the corporate university are really nothing new.⁵⁰ While such views may be reassuring for those who have been assailed as transforming the university into a business and little more, these perspectives do not lessen our needs, as members of a distinct profession, to work continuously to ensure that the mission of the profession is well connected to the purpose of higher education, and the latter's purpose has often been seen as supporting the generating and archiving of human knowledge, grappling with society's ills and other needs, and instilling the capacity for individuals to develop into well-rounded citizens and human beings.

Whatever perspective one might have, the point is, professional schools ought to be able to thrive in any concept of the university, since such schools ought to be able to present both a public good and generate revenue by attracting students wishing to enter a particular profession. Professional schools suggest that they can appeal to the most basic desire for credentialing, by offering degrees with highly marketable skills and sometimes supported by accreditation processes affirming the degree, while also having much clearer and more specific aims for a public good. Although one of the hallmarks of the rise of the modern university in the past century has been the creation of professional schools and the development of disciplines, the professional schools have often had a tenuous, stormy relationship with the university.⁵¹

Back in 1990, the President of the Society of American Archivists, John A. Fleckner, delivered his penultimate address in the form of three letters to a recent college graduate and volunteer archives intern. In the first letter to Mary Jane, Fleckner describes how, as he worked on his dissertation in history and made a living by doing odd jobs, he discovered a graduate program in archival studies. This program offered him the opportunity to take classes and to work with archival records through an internship. Fleckner relates that he "loved the combination of handicraft and analytical work" and the "intense, intimate contact with the 'stuff' of history."⁵² Fleckner, in his second letter, describes how he truly became an archivist after an "extended apprenticeship," where he was mentored and learned from experienced colleagues "their craft and their wisdom."[53] However, it is in his third letter that Fleckner makes some points most relevant to the topic of this chapter, reflecting that how by becoming an archivist he has joined a professional community, even while acknowledging that the notion of a profession was being debated: "But the notion of a 'profession' also harkens back to a more old-fashioned idea: the idea that as 'professionals' we have something to 'profess,' something more than devotion to the latest techniques. And further, that in this act of 'professing' we tie our own self-interest to the well-being of the larger society so that our 'profession' is not merely that of a self-interested clique, but, instead, a legitimate claim on behalf of the greater public interest."[54] And, finally, Fleckner, with this larger public mission in mind, suggests that this connects archivists to a "wider community of professions, institutions, and individuals" who share that mission, or, at least, some part of it.[55] Calling and education go hand in hand.

There has been considerable consternation about graduate education in the records professions because it suggests, among other things, that there is a hierarchy of possession of knowledge. Some experienced archivists and records managers are anxious because they were not able to acquire a formal educational introduction, and, because of this, they feel that they may be at a disadvantage. This is not unique to our field. Writing a couple of decades ago, Jacques Barzun observed such a problem in our society. "Elite means *elect*, a Puritan idea: few are chosen. It is also a democratic idea. We continually elect representatives, not just for making laws, but for innumerable purposes in the private sector — those endless committees and slates of officers. ... So it turns out that the country is a mass of elites; hardly anybody is left out; privilege is the rule." So, then, Barzun mulled over, why are so many upset about the prospect of elitism? He concludes that this occurs because we worry that an "elite member will make us feel inferior with respect to a talent we think we have."[56] Archivists have been particularly sensitive to issues about elitism, often adopting statements and standards allowing everyone in to the practice, with mixed results (giving many an opportunity to work in the field but also weakening professional standards or the development of stronger educational venues).

Whether there is angst or not about the education of records professionals is beside the point, with interesting and compelling arguments about the strengthening of archival and records management education. Berenika Webster predicts that records management is shifting from a profession to a scholarly discipline, recognized both by a growing body of theoretical literature and emerging research projects and activities.[57] With the hindsight of a decade, her assessment was more optimistic than it deserved to be. Bruce Dearstyne, surveying both changes in the information professions and the responses of various kinds of professional schools, suggests that education "can help us to cope with change, position ourselves for success in fast-changing institutions, and, at the same time, help change and advance the entire information management profession."[58] However, can there be educational programs broad and deep enough for transforming students into the masters of everything? What everyone will agree with is Dearstyne's assertion, posited in a related essay, that records and information management professionals have possessed, at best, an "ambiguous approach to education," embracing an "educational diversity" suggesting no commitment to clear standards for preparing individuals to enter into the field.[59] We need to do better than this, because it is at the heart of what it means to be called to be a professional.

Records professionals need more education than training, so that they can function in increasingly complex organizations using ever more complicated records technologies. They need an education that enables them to develop critical thinking skills, provides the best perspective into the social, economic, political, and administrative aspects of any recordkeeping system, and assists them to understand the historical, organizational, and cultural aspects of records. Training usually targets immediate needs, resolves specific problems, and develops practical solutions to recordkeeping and information system needs. Both long-term, big picture education and short-term, problem-oriented training are needed, but education is always the greater need. In one classic analysis of teaching, the authors describe what is at the heart of teaching in a way that should resonate with archivists and records managers: "Information is to knowledge what sound is to music, the unorganized material out of which the structured result is composed. We do not ask teachers to convey information; we seek information from newspapers, the stock market ticker tape, or price tags on items in a store. Instead, we ask teachers to transmit knowledge, that which is organized and formally known about a subject — facts, findings, explanations, hypotheses, and theories accepted for their proven accuracy, significance, beauty, utility, or power."[60] Such education can only be supported if we support the development of rigorous graduate programs, encourage individuals in our field to answer their own calling to be academics, and support them in the theoretical and analytical work of research. Comprehensive graduate programs are necessary if they are to help anyone respond to their calling to a vocation.

Educators in the field must have a sense of what prospective employers want, of course, and this necessitates them to be sensitive to the knowledge, skills, and attitudes the employers seek in their applicants. It is why academics sometimes face a barrage of questions about the nature of their graduate programs when providing a reference. We discuss how we know the candidate, the individual's interpersonal skills, their oral and written communication skills, and whether they can meet deadlines, work independently, and work under stress or with a certain degree of ambiguity. At some point I am asked to read the job ad, or provided a summary, and asked to speak about the individual's abilities to perform such tasks. This is the point where some interesting discussion occurs about the nature of graduate professional education, about just what I might be teaching these students.

The Society of American Archivists' graduate guidelines suggest a focus on "core archival knowledge," "knowledge from other relevant disciplines," "critical thinking and decision-making skills for records and papers as part of the larger cultural heritage," research methodologies, and a "sense of their professional and social responsibilities and the knowledge of the ethical and legal dimensions of their work." The Society's guidelines provide very strong indicators that education must assist students to reflect on a serious commitment to a profession.[61] What worries me about such professional guidelines is that they do not convey a real passion for the profession, not stressing why it is that anyone would want to go through the trouble and expense of such an education. Jacques Barzun once mused that college students bring many expectations to the classroom, acknowledging that they "want education for their souls, training for life, organized social and artistic activities, psychiatric help, and career planning and placement."[62] While we might think that such objectives are unrealistic, it is nevertheless the case that in order to attract, equip, and retain individuals in a profession such as ours that we must provide *both* a foundation in the knowledge of the field and a reason for why anyone would want to be such a professional.

Some years ago, a graduate of a leading archival education program wrestled with the question of the relationship between theory and practice in his education, concluding that the focus on basic principles and concepts helped provide an "initiation into archival culture," suggesting that working archivists who had not had the benefit of such an education had simply gained their initiation in another way, such as through "reading, conferences, collegial discussion, and work experience."[63] What we must reconsider, however, is the relevance of a formal education, a process more serious than an apprenticeship, for preparing an individual who is serious about responding to their calling. What one can learn in an apprenticeship is limited both to the quality of the institution and that of the archivist or records manager providing the mentoring. Surely as individuals who "profess" to represent a profession, we can do better than merely suggesting that in order to become an archivist or a records manager go work in an archives or records management program and learn by practicing.

Teaching is more than just imparting information, it is mastering and conveying knowledge. [64] It is often tempting for busy working professionals like archivists and records managers to focus their attention on applying new information about basic practices, in whatever manner that this can be accomplished, but this is not what a formal educational gateway into a profession is intended to provide. Educators in the field are expected to be individuals who have mastered a knowledge and are staying current with and adding to that knowledge; that is, they are assistants for helping individuals learn about and discern more about the nature of the calling they are responding to in the early stage of what will become a professional career.

A faculty member has the responsibility to stay current with knowledge regarding the nature of records and recordkeeping systems. This means reading broadly and deeply across disciplines, examining records over time, considering the current issues affecting records systems and their use, and tracking predictions about trends (especially in regards to information technologies) that might affect records and their administration. This requires faculty to have a critical eye. While working archivists and records managers might possess a predilection for basic manuals, faculty teaching the next generation employ these manuals in a very different fashion. We use manuals as a means to get our students immersed in basic principles and practices, but we also utilize these manuals as a way of critiquing basic aspects of archives and records management work. The purpose of the critique is not intended to be nitpicky for its own sake, but it is meant to enable students to understand that basic knowledge is constantly changing as political structures, legal systems, and information technologies continue to evolve. While there has been internal debate about the question of the mutability of archival theory, most faculty assume that their task is to highlight those aspects of this knowledge that seem constant and to suggest where there may be, or should be, changes. It is why a faculty member labors so intensely on looking for new publications, evaluating these publications, and constantly changing course reading lists. It is also why research is at the heart of their work — not as a means to divert their thoughts away from their students and their teaching but as a means to teaching these students what they need to know in order to be competent records professionals.

Faculties play a unique role in assisting individuals to hear a professional calling by their commitment to basic and applied research. Research is what sets off faculty from the typical working records professional, and it can be a source of tension between those in the field and those in the classroom. The working archivist or records manager may see a faculty member reporting about research or requiring that students read and undertake research as being irrelevant to what a records professional does on a day-to-day basis. Practitioners want the focus to be on practical matters, issues relevant to their daily responsibilities, where theory is trumped by projects and deadlines, but where ascertaining the parameters of the practical knowledge desired can be difficult. The needs of working professionals vary greatly, but it is because of such varying needs and perspectives that research studies and theoretical approaches are needed, providing a broader perspective pulling together a variety of working records professionals and bringing order to conflicting opinions and a miscellany of assumptions. And this is why it is so critical for us to introduce students to such issues at the beginning of their careers; we need to make them confident of their ability both to read and conduct research, as well as enabling them to be able to appreciate why there is practical value in reading the professional and scholarly literature about archival and records management issues.

Caught up in this traditional tension between practice and everything with the slightest twinge of being theoretical is the role and nature of research in a profession. A lack of relevant research weakens the notion records professionals also perform a vital public good function for society. Legal trends, public policy changes, intellectual property changes, accounting and other regulatory best practices, advances in information technologies, and a host of other matters all fall within required knowledge for the working professional. And it is the responsibility of educators to orient students to such matters, if for no other reason than helping them to discern that the call to be a records professional involves dealing with some complex and testy social, political, economic, technological, and ethical issues. Moreover, staying current with such concerns require a commitment to staying current not just with our own professional literature but also with an array of publications from other disciplines.

We find many presuppositions about research that are inaccurate or exaggerated. Research about records, recordkeeping systems, the use of records, professionals and their standards, and the programs administering records is vital for success, both institutional and individual. Research studies can add to one's professional knowledge, assist institutional programs to develop new and better approaches, and test every assumption about professional practice in a way that strengthens that practice. Research studies are neither luxury nor fluff; they are essential to every working archivist or records manager. In an era of increasing accountability and performance measures, it is important to be able to answer with specifics not generalities or guesses. For archivists and records managers to appreciate the importance of the research literature they must be introduced to it early in their preparation for a career and understand that part of their own professional calling is to possess a commitment not only to using the literature but to contributing to it.

There are many different research methodologies and experiences available, and the range can be intimidating, including both quantitative and qualitative approaches ranging across many different disciplines. What all this implies is, of course, a commitment to a career-long reading regimen, and the classroom is the forum where the importance of such reading is introduced. While teachers are often worn out by the perpetual complaints by students that the reading requirements are too heavy, faculty must strive to demonstrate the value and necessity of sticking with a reading program after graduating. A records professional who is not systematically reading is a professional who is apt to not be current with the knowledge of their own field.

Like so many parts of our lives, dealing with research studies is an activity that needs to be learned, from developing research questions to using particular research methodologies to analyzing data and drawing conclusions. The analytical part of a research study is very important, primarily because it is where the researcher weighs data, generates findings, and seeks to place his or her research into a larger body of research and professional or disciplinary knowledge. In the classroom, and through prepared assignments where they must critically evaluate the professional literature, students are able to learn how to analyze the research literature and separate it from other dimensions of the literature, such as opinions and theoretical explorations, as well as learning how to avoid common mistakes in conducting research (such as failing to explain why they have selected a particular source, making broad assumptions without searching the existing professional and scholarly literature to support such a view, and citing authors without any identification of their background or perspective or, most importantly, the authority they possess or do not possess to be referred to in a paper).

The purpose of professional education on the graduate level is not about indoctrinating students in basic skills and attitudes. This education is far more complicated than this, seeking to ground students into the values of the field and to equip them to question and critically assess these professional values. Professional education is a means to enable students to learn more about their own sense of a calling or, perhaps, to question about whether they have such a calling at all.

Teaching Values

Writer Eric Lott, reflecting on the changing status of the liberal intellectual in the university, had this very straightforward, if not particularly simple, assertion to make about the mission of the university in society: "Debate, not censure, is the university's hallmark."[65] Such perspectives are difficult for those in professional schools in the university, seeking to balance their roles as scholars and academics with their connections and responsibilities to a field of practice. Faculty members teaching about archives and records management issues and applications grapple with the need to present practical and technical solutions as well as dancing about with theoretical principles, intellectual excursions into professional knowledge, and research. However, anyone knowing anything about archives and records management realizes how difficult it is to segregate basic practice from larger philosophical, legal, and societal concerns, testing anyone's resolve about what led them to seek to become a part of this field in the first place.

We can visualize the difficulty of understanding fully the relationship of teaching with such broader values. For example, a sizable portion of the records community works in government settings, and records professionals should understand that they possess extra responsibilities when they function in a democratic government. In an analysis about how our political leaders are evaluated in a democracy, Paul Woodruff writes, "Even in their specialties, experts are known to go wrong. And when they have their own interests at stake, as is too often the case, they are especially likely to go wrong. Plato, to his credit, tried to fend off this criticism by keeping the expert deciders from having property — in order that they would have no special interests. But if we have learned anything from history we have learned that this is a dream. Leaders always have their own interests, and so they cannot be left immune from scrutiny. And there is no one but us — the ordinary citizens — who can carry out this scrutiny in the last analysis. (If we appoint professional scrutinizers, we must still scrutinize them.) Our best hope, no matter how much expert knowledge is available, lies in our ability — the ability of ordinary people — to judge the advice and performance of experts."[66] This suggests a high level of accountability, and this adds an extraordinary responsibility to archivists and records managers who need to ensure that the records of government and its elected and appointed officials are open. Too often, we hear and read stories of lapses in this responsibility, but the fact that we even know about such problems and can question how government keeps itself accountable to its people is an indication that the process is working. It is also why those of us teaching future records professionals need to stress that the reasons that they will be administering such records goes beyond good clerical and technical means to ensure economy and efficiency.

Even records professionals who work in cultural organizations have responsibilities transcending good management and preservation practices. The world is becoming a far more complicated place, with complex laws and ethical issues confronting us no matter what direction we turn. Oliver Leaman notes that archaeologists have to be working harder to comply with a sense of "good behavior in collecting," and he believes that the "ideal position is where the artifact is not far removed from its original environment, but is left there after having been excavated and placed within both its original natural context, in so far as this is possible, and together with other related objects that form its cultural context."[67] Such values have affected all professionals working with cultural remains, artifacts, and documentary materials, and it is imperative that students be introduced to such concerns as soon as possible in their educational programs. Old notions of merely gathering documentary resources must be tempered with a stronger sensibility to issues about who owns the physical materials and the intellectual property represented in those materials, issues that are not as simple as they once seemed to be. Two archaeologists note how their colleagues have begun to rethink ethical issues: "As stakeholders, professional archaeologists should play an active role in the discussion of these issues, but they should be decided in an arena which recognizes a wide variety of competing stakeholders, among them, indigenous groups, proprietary owners, developers, educators and other communities with an interest in the past. In such a context, archaeologists should act as participants in discussion and debate, not as professionals who decide the issues."[68] Students, as novice professionals, must gain both a basic foundation in the knowledge of their field and the application of that knowledge in a way enabling them to deal with such new roles as negotiators for the preservation of the documentary heritage. Nuance, complexity, and sensitivity are all attributes of a new professional culture students need to be situated in. Some should even be responding to a call specifically to address such contentious issues.

What we can term such an orientation to teaching is really nothing more than trying to assist students, who sometimes bring into the classroom some uninformed or naïve assumptions about the kinds of potential careers represented by archivists and records managers, to sort through the age-old challenge of seeing the forest for the trees (a topic I focus on later in this book). We are seeking to help students get a sense of the big picture of the societal and professional mandate for records professionals while grounding them in some particular skills and attitudes necessary for starting in an entry-level position in the field. Some of this we achieve by having students read the basic manuals or texts of practices, the classic writings of theory and principles, and the seminal explorations into the history of records and recordkeeping systems as well as the evolution of the discipline. We also have them read a wide array of newspapers, news magazines, and other news sources, now easily achieved with the online presence of these and other news and opinion sources.

Conclusion: Whose Calling — Students' or the Faculty?

Faculty in professional schools are accustomed to being asked about just what their intentions are in teaching students, that is, how they perceive the kinds of positions graduates from their programs are prepared to assume. There are a number of things implied by such questions, from insecurity by the questioner about their own educational preparation to sincere concerns about the nature of professional education. It is a good question to ask, and it is a good question for any faculty member to reflect on regularly.

When I first joined the faculty of a professional school, my ambition was to prepare students for entry-level positions as archivists and records managers, and this remains a major component of my educational agenda. However, given my strong sense that there is a calling associated with the work of the records professionals, that archivists and records managers carry out important mandates in their institutions and in society overall, and that records and information systems are often involved in both critical and controversial activities, I also believe that faculty have a responsibility to view their students in ways that are more profoundly complicated than just being potential applicants for entry-level positions.

I am convinced that our role is to educate students to be both leaders and agents for change in the field, more than just equipping them with basic skills, attitudes, and knowledge. Some think that my focus on trying to identify particular students as potential leaders implies either that there are no leaders in the records community or that I have a sinister objective in developing individuals to carry out my personal professional agenda. Individuals sometimes see my focus on the notion of change agents as being an indictment of the field. Instead, my educational emphasis is meant to imply that my hope is to assist students to develop into well-rounded professionals with the tools needed for ultimately assuming leadership roles, especially since a large portion of the graduating students enters into positions with managerial responsibilities. My emphasis on being change-agents is only intended to suggest that students need to be ready to enter into a complicated and fast-changing world where they will face new and complex challenges.

Some think that those teaching in professional schools ought to be exclusively linked to the field's interests and practical concerns. Yet, it is a historic function of university faculty, whether in professional schools or other areas of higher education, to define the knowledge of their field, to study the success and issues of their disciplines, and to be involved in other activities suggesting that they will be constantly questioning professional missions, mandates, and performance. Faculty members also are called to perform such activities, and these activities are the norm not the exception for their positions. We are here to keep students off-balance, to get them to question their own sense of calling, and to develop inquiring and energetic professional agendas equipping them for careers not just jobs. Newman, Coururier, and Scurry argue that "One reason the American workplace has remained the most productive in the world is the widespread — and widely used — opportunity for a worker to attend or return to higher education, certificate programs, or corporate universities over his or her career."[69] In order for this to happen, professional education must be a dynamic, provocative, and useful force.

And this education must support preparing individuals to be able to understand enough about the importance of their discipline to enable them to stick with it. For records professionals, our societal mission is too important for us to think that an individual slipping in and out of it is an acceptable situation. How do we enable them to sustain a sense of a professional calling and commitment? The notion of a calling is essential to how we view ourselves, conduct our business, and deal with the kinds of challenges described in the following chapters.

Chapter Two

Public Memory meets Archival Memory: The Interpretation of Williamsburg's Secretary's Office[1]

Figure 1. — Public Records Office of Colonial Williamsburg

Introduction

One of the most famous streets in America is the Duke of Gloucester Street in Williamsburg, Virginia. Stretching a mile, with the College of William and Mary at one end and the Capitol building, seat of government for the Virginia colony, at the other, this street has witnessed more scenes of historical importance and hosted more tourists than any other street in the nation. President Franklin Delano Roosevelt, dedicating the restored street on October 20, 1934, declared it to be the "most historic avenue in all America."[2] On either side of the length of the elegantly tree-lined thoroughfare are quaint merchant shops and beautiful colonial homes, now pristinely managed as part of America's earliest and best-known historic site.

As one leisurely walks down this street towards the stately Capitol building, there is a compact one story brick structure just off to the left of the government seat that barely catches your eye. Described by Marcus Whiffen in his architectural history of the town as a "handsome little building,"[3] with its distinctive Flemish bond brickwork and rubbed brick doorway, the building is the Secretary's Office, for a long-time referred to as the Public Records Office by Colonial Williamsburg historians and interpreters [Figure 1, preceding page].[4] The structure was built in 1747-48, just after the Capitol building burned to the ground, and it is the only original colonial central government building that is extant. How many archivists and other records professionals know that the antecedents of their profession are well represented on a street that has been traversed by millions of tourists through the years?

This essay considers three lessons for archivists in their quest for greater public understanding and support, drawing on how this old public records structure has been interpreted. First, the essay suggests that the story of the Secretary's Office is not well-known by archivists and those interested in the history of efforts to preserve our documentary heritage. Second, the essay recounts the story of the failure by America's premier and pioneering historic site to interpret fully the legacy of the public records office. This failure is not the result of neglect or conspiratorial activities, but it simply suggests the typical challenges in explaining the archival mission to the public. Third, and finally, the essay indicates that the lack of interpretation represents a lost opportunity to promote public understanding of what records represent, why archives are important, and the work of archivists. In this final area, it undermines the sense of a calling to archival work, described in the first chapter.

Both archival and public memory have been weakened even as the two and a half century Secretary's Office holds a place as one of the best preserved original structures in Colonial Williamsburg. Constructed at a cost of a little over 367 pounds, the 56 by 24 feet building was completed by December 1748. The construction was designed to resist damage by fire, the main threat to records and books, by having no basement or attic, floors of paved stones, plastered walls and window jambs, and as little exposed wood as was possible. The structure also included four fireplaces, generally thought to have been there to keep out the infamous Tidewater humidity, a threat almost as insidious as fire. Consisting of three rooms, a large center room supposedly used by the Secretary and his clerks for copying and referencing records, and two outer rooms, each probably used for records storage, the public records office is one of the smallest buildings on the Duke of Gloucester Street, with only some of the craftsmen and other shops being smaller.

After Virginia's capitol was moved to Richmond in 1781, the Secretary's Office was used as an office for the Court of Admiralty then the Chancery Court, then the home of the headmaster of a private grammar school (the school was briefly located in the old Capitol building), and then was acquired as a private residence. By 1855, the Secretary's Office was privately owned, and altered with the addition of a frame structure on its West side. Colonial Williamsburg acquired the building in 1937 and restored its exterior in 1939-40, as it was doing with many of the other buildings in the area. The last owner of the house, Mrs. David Rowland Jones, lived there until her death in 1964, at which point the remainder of its restoration was completed.

Countless tourists to Colonial Williamsburg have passed by the Secretary's Office. From nearly the moment the idea developed for transforming the sleepy early twentieth century village of Williamsburg back to its former glory as the eighteenth century capitol of Virginia, tourists flocked there to see what was going on. The idea for the town's restoration having generated in the mind of Rev. W.A.R. Goodwin, Rector of Bruton Parish in Williamsburg in the early 1920s, his enlistment of the financial support of John D. Rockefeller, Jr. in 1926 provided the foundation for the creation of the outdoor history museum. By 1932, the first building, Raleigh Tavern, was open to the public, and by the end of that decade it was already well established as a vacation and educational venue.

For many Americans, family history can nearly be charted by visits there, and I am no exception. I went there as a young child in 1957, and the visit sparked my interest in history. I can vividly recall return visits in the 1960s, I went there on my honeymoon in 1975, and I have been a regular visitor there for conferences, golf (there are championship courses throughout the area), and research. While as a child I have only a vague recollection of the Secretary's Office, but I remember it distinctly from the 1970s after I had commenced my archival career.

Despite the significance of the Secretary's Office as a landmark in the history of American archives, records management, and public recordkeeping, it has been generally ignored in the scholarship on these topics. As one example, one of the earliest surveys of the history of efforts to preserve Southern archives made no mention of the building, more than a decade after the creation of Colonial Williamsburg as an outdoor history museum.[5] As another example, Ernst Posner's important analysis of American government archives makes only a passing reference to the 1747 legislation that led to the construction of the building.[6] Other than a few popular articles on the building and sparse references in official guidebooks to the town, the building has been largely ignored by those conducting research on the history of American archives and public recordkeeping.

There is some delicious irony in this. The Colonial Williamsburg endeavor has long been considered the critical benchmark for the modern historic preservation movement, partly because of its scrupulous attention to historical documentation; yet, Williamsburg provides little interpretation of the old public records office or about the nature, preservation, and use of the archival records. Charles Hosmer, in his detailed history of the American historic preservation movement, describes how Williamsburg became the model for others to emulate, as well as a clearinghouse of information: "The work was a success by every standard: It was scholarly, it attracted a great many visitors, and it proved that large amounts of money could be put into preservation projects."[7] Sitting, virtually silent, among all this effort was the public records office, the place where many of the records that would ultimately support the town's restoration had been originally preserved.

Interpretation

The building now known as the Secretary's Office was interpreted almost from the beginning of the creation of Colonial Williamsburg. The 1935 official guide to the restored town provided a brief 89 word description, indicating the time of construction and a modest reference to the building's purpose, its subsequent history, and its then present status as a private residence.[8] Thirty years later, the guidebook's successor had expanded the coverage to about 150 words, adding just a little more detail about the building (more about the structure, that is, than what was going on in it).[9] Visitors who visited the restoration and assiduously read the guidebook would learn that there was a public records facility, that it was built to protect the records after the Capitol building burned, and that it had had a checkered history after the capitol was moved to Richmond, mostly as a private residence.

Besides such brief descriptions, the staff of Colonial Williamsburg put considerable energy into researching the records building (as they did with all of the structures and sites in the town). In 1938, a report indicated that when townspeople and historians met to recommend a name for the structure that they settled on the Public Records Office (rather than others such as Clerk's Office or Chancery Office) because the former name reflected the intent of the 1747 legislative act and because it was believed to be the first such building in America for such a purpose. As this report indicated, the "building has a prestige which only such an explicit name could convey."[10] About this time an archaeological report of the building's site was completed as well, identifying the existence of two privies about forty feet away from the building (suggesting that archives and records centers have always had a preoccupation with restrooms). The same report also did an extensive analysis of the various initials and names carved into the soft brick around the doorway by people ranging from the 1760s until the 1830s, providing the interesting idea that the building itself had become a kind of record as well.[11] [See figure 2, next page.]

Research about the building continued. In 1945 Colonial Williamsburg completed a thorough architectural analysis of the building, providing as much information about the building's various uses as could be done. The report's author, A. Lawrence Kocher, noted various changes to the structure, such as the covering of the stone floors with wood, but more interesting is the conclusion about how little documentation there actually was for the building. Kocher remarked that it was not known how the records would have been stored, and that more research was needed about this aspect of the structure's history.[12] Ironically, from this point on, the substantial research seems mostly to have stopped.

Figure 2. — Carvings around the doorway of the Public Records Office.

By the 1970s the Secretary's Office, now without any residents and open for use and interpretation by Colonial Williamsburg, was being used for changing public exhibitions. A fitting one, perhaps, was its use for an exhibition in 1976 marking the Bicentennial of the American Revolution and the fiftieth anniversary of the Williamsburg restoration.[13] Curiously, given its original construction and purpose, during this year the building suffered from a "humidity problem,"[14] a problem quickly corrected. Soon the building was being regularly used for changing exhibitions, often as part of the popular Williamsburg Antiques Forum, usually displaying portraits, furniture, and drawings.[15] Some of the exhibitions were quite appropriate to the building's original use, as when in 1979 a group of measured architectural drawings documenting thirteen of the Williamsburg buildings, including one done of the Secretary's Office, was put on display.[16] The Secretary's Office also was used for a variety of other interpretive and administrative purposes. It was used at least once for a Christmas tree decoration workshop, during the extremely popular holiday season in the restored capitol.[17]

The increasing diversity of uses for the Secretary's Office was not met without some internal discussion among various Colonial Williamsburg staff. In 1974, archivist Mary R. M. Goodwin, reacting to suggestions about how to utilize the building, indicated that if it were to be used for exhibitions of portraits and documents, it would be best "if it were properly interpreted." She saw only tenuous connection between portraits and records, but she was happy if the building's uses were merely explained that this was due to it being a convenient place for such purposes. However, why not furnish it as the "Secretary's Office," and Goodwin attached a 1699 letter from Virginia Governor Nicholson describing how rooms and boxes for records were used in the original Capitol building.[18] The attachment suggested that while there may not be documentation specifically about the interior uses of the Secretary's Office, there was documentation concerning how records were maintained during the colonial era. This idea had been germinating for some time. Lester J. Cappon, who had been responsible and then adviser for the administration of Colonial Williamsburg's own records, documents a meeting with Ed Alexander and Marge Kocher at the CW archives to discuss the appraisal of its records, noting, "What is needed most is more space for preservation of records of long-time value. The Public Record Office near the Capitol may be a possibility. It has been restored, with a slate floor, and the humidity could be controlled."[19] That Cappon had lived for years a few hundred yards away from the structure must have helped him to see the possibilities.

What was goading some Colonial Williamsburg insiders was the lack of interpretation of the building as a records office. In early 1976 there was discussion about the building needing "more definition from the outside," seeking brief wording indicating that this structure was the "first archival building in America and its superb condition for an original building."[20] Some of this discussion may have been prompted by the publication of the first major, if popular, essay on the public records office, written by Virginia's State Archivist and published in the popular history and tourism serial, *Virginia Cavalcade*.[21] About this time, some more obvious rationales were being made for the multifarious uses of the records office for exhibitions and other public programs. In an interview in early 1979, James R. Short, Colonial Williamsburg's Vice President for Preservation and Research, explained that an exhibition of measured drawings of Westover, William Byrd's magnificent home on the James River, made sense because, "That's an appropriate place because these drawings are public records."[22]

In the early 1980s, a new possibility for the Secretary's Office opened up. In 1982, Colonial Williamsburg received a $90,000 grant from the Pew Freedom Trust Fund to assist the Foundation to develop a new educational program focused on the "traditions of American citizenship." Five buildings in the historic district — the Capitol, the 1770 Courthouse, the Public Gaol, a law office, and the Secretary's Office — were to be included. As the press release announced, the grant would support research on "these structures as the setting for a carefully integrated interpretation of the emergence of American citizenship during the colonial period."[23]

Six years later the research for this project was still underway, with projections of the first phase being ready by 1989. By then it had been renamed the "Legal Traditions Program," with the intention of informing Colonial Williamsburg visitors "how ordinary people learned to conduct the public affairs of their community under the rule of law." In the press release about the project, a mention was made about the "arduous task" in researching the 1770 Courthouse, attributed to the "burning of Richmond in 1865 destroying many local court records which ironically had been sent to the capitol for safe-keeping. Fifty years later, in 1911, a fire destroyed all but the exterior walls of the Courthouse itself."[24] There were, of course, some parallels to the history of the Secretary's Office, but the key element here is to note how the focus had shifted to the Courthouse with no mention of the Secretary's Office, despite an understanding of how the loss of public records had made research for this educational effort more difficult.

Perhaps as a result of the study for this public programming, Colonial Williamsburg's popular magazine, distributed to its contributors and members, featured about this time an essay on the Secretary's Office. Written by one of the restoration's historians, the essay described how colonial Virginians had managed their records, various calamities befell these public records, and the circumstances of the 1747 Capitol fire and subsequent construction of the records building. Howard Gill stated, "The designer's primary objective was to design a building especially for the preservation of records," declaring it, then, to be the "first archival structure in English America and possibly in the Western Hemisphere." Gill again indicated that there was little evidence about how the rooms were used or the interior furnishings or even how the records were stored, obviously drawing on previous research done in the late 1930s and early 1940s.[25] Colonial Williamsburg's popular book, *Williamsburg Before and After*, also featured, nearly at the same time, a couple of pages on the records building, providing a bit more detail than its official guidebooks and, befitting its coffee-table market, included photographs of the structure when it was a private residence and after its restoration to its original appearance.[26]

The ultimate decision about the interpretation and use of the Secretary's Office came in 1988. Cary Carson, then Director of Research, considered a request from the Colonial Williamsburg Educational Administrators Group to use the building as a modern exhibition gallery, considering, as well, whether the restoration for this purpose would meet the needs of describing everyday work of the Secretary's Office. Carson, meeting with historians Carl Lounsbury and John Hemphill, reported, "It is their opinion that too little is known except about the use of the Public Records Office to make a strong case for its restoration as an exhibition building." It is unclear who worked in the building, and there is no evidence of how the records were stored. Carson continued: "The only thing that can be said for certain is that provincial court officials were eager to move their records out of the jailer's lodging into a newly built, fireproof record office." Approval was given for the "adaptive reuse" as an exhibition site.[27] It seems that no new research about the building had been done, as well as any additional investigation about eighteenth century recordkeeping practices.

By the next decade, the Secretary's Office was being used for short public discussions, administrative offices, and a bookstore and gift shop. In the 1990s, the Secretary's Office was used for an hour-long discussion on eighteenth-century marriage.[28] It was during this time that the citizenship project was finally completed and unveiled. The Secretary's Office was used as a "visitor service center" where individuals and groups could secure "program information and tickets." [See Figure 3.] The main room of the Secretary's Office was used to orient visitors to the story of the American Revolution from 1763 to 1781, along with an exhibition on pirates and a bookshop. [See Figure 4.] Mostly the building was to be used as a "venue for historian talks — an opportunity for visitors to take an in-depth look at a particular historical topic."[29] When I last visited in May 2005, the center room was set up for lectures, the room on the right was a bookstore and gift shop (as well as a place to buy tickets for entrance into the Colonial Williamsburg buildings), and the room on the left was closed with a sign indicating that it was being used for "Administrative Offices."[30]

There is another clue about the interpretation of the Secretary's Office found in the current official guidebook to the restoration, originally published in 1998. In the guide, there is a brief mention made of the building's use for the public records, the current exhibition on pirates (an exhibition that has been dismantled between its publication and the present), and the Secretary's Office part in the "Choosing Revolution" story line. As part of this story line, there is more information made available

Figure 3. — Current use of the Secretary's Office.

Figure 4. — Current use of the Secretary's Office main room.

about the care of public records. There is a description about how before the Secretary's Office was built, that the most important public records, both bound volumes and loose papers, were originally stored in an office next to the General Courtroom in the Capitol building.

Then the detail of recordkeeping in the modern guidebook seems to play on every stereotype imaginable: "There, the chief clerk and his deputy oversaw a vast domain of records in the form of bound volumes and of endless files of loose papers tied up in red tape that had been used by bureaucrats to secure legal and official documents since the seventeenth century. Here, generations of clerk-apprentices scribbled away, learning their trade." The description then describes the 1747 fire, the discussion about passing a legislative act to endorse the construction of a public records facility, the nature of the construction of the building, and how the Secretary functioned.[31] Is it possible, then, that the Colonial Williamsburg historians, interpreters, and administrators simply wished to ignore interpretation of the old public records office because records were boring to them or too boring for the public visiting the restoration? The references connecting records, red tape, and bureaucratic inertia seem too obvious, cute or smug for the well-known historic site. At the least, the long known fact that Thomas Jefferson, first while a law student at the College of William and Mary, became interested in the condition of Virginia's early records and copied them as a means to preserve them, confiding that he "passed much time [from 1762 to 1775] in going through the public records in Virginia, then in the Secretary's office," opens up the possibilities of interpreting the more important goal of preserving historical records so vital to Williamsburg's restoration.[32]

Opportunities Lost

The archives and records management professions have not paid much attention to this rather unique structure and evidence of society's interest in administering records in Williamsburg. There have been instances where it appeared this might change. Morgan P. Robinson, head of the archives division of the Virginia State Library, wrote to Colonial Williamsburg's archivist, Helen Bullock, in 1938, asking for assistance in making a case for changing the name of the archives division there to Public Records Office by drawing on the documentation related to the Colonial Records Building. Robinson believed that the term "public records" was a more understandable term for most people.[33] The name change never occurred.

Nearly forty years later, Louis Manarin, holding the same position as Robinson, wrote about the Secretary's Office: "It would be both educational and informative if the building would be opened with exhibits depicting record-keeping methods of the eighteenth century. Such a presentation would pay tribute to the farsightedness of those early Virginians who first conceived 'a building for the preservation of the public records' and thus provided an example for the future."[34] This may have been the best statement, one raising the most basic questions, made regarding the Secretary's Office.

Others, from time to time, expressed an interest in the records structure. Morris Radoff, Maryland's State Archivist, inquired about the building in 1950, and was told that there was little detailed documentation about the original erection of the building in 1747-1748, but the "fact that the building was standing in a fair state of preservation when its restoration was undertaken, more than makes up for this."[35] In 1954, John Melville Jennings, Director of the Virginia Historical Society, also inquired about the uses of the building, and he received a lengthy five page letter describing Colonial era public records care, mostly summarizing earlier research.[36] Yet, in general, with the exception of Manarin's popular essay, the archives and records management community has expressed little interest in the Secretary's Office, and there has been no stream of requests to anyone at Colonial Williamsburg seeking to have the old public records office better interpreted as a landmark in the development of North American archives and records management.

There are other questions to ask, however, regarding the use and interpretation of the public records office. Given Colonial Williamsburg's reputation for meticulous research about its buildings, artifacts, and other historical collections, one might first simply accept the argument that there is little direct evidence that can be mustered to more fully interpret the building as an early records facility. In a description about the 1980s research on the eighteenth century courts and legal practices program, the one that originally included the Secretary's Office, John Krugler attests to the type of research Colonial Williamsburg does, when its "research department undertook extensive field investigations on courthouses and other public buildings in the southern colonies and England," mostly aimed at gathering data for use in the restoration of the 1770 Courthouse.[37] None of this work seems to have influenced how the public records office was interpreted or to re-open discussion about the interpretation of the structure that seems to have been firmly in place for forty years.

There is another way of questioning this, however, that certainly suggests some deep-seated problems with public understanding of the administration of archives and records. As is true of all historic sites, accurate interpretation and sound, ongoing professional educational programs depend on the existence and use of historical documentation. This has been a hallmark of Colonial Williamsburg's work. As I worked my way through its own archives, it was easy to see the painstaking efforts to gather and evaluate documents regarding the Secretary's Office, supplemented by archaeological and architectural analysis. One of the major transformations of the historic site has been the effort to interpret more fully the Colonial experience, utilizing the best of social history methodologies. In the early 1980s, about the time the Secretary's Office was being reduced as an interpretative possibility, the York County Project started and soon was in full swing, under the able direction of Cary Carson, gathering information from the extant public records about every inhabitant in the Williamsburg region in the eighteenth century era, amassing a major archive of its own data.

In addition to this project, the Colonial Williamsburg Foundation has a major research library for its own purposes, the John D. Rockefeller, Jr. Library, holding "72,000 volumes, 12,500 rare books, 150 manuscript collections comprising 50,000 manuscript pages dating largely from the eighteenth century. There are 50,000 architectural drawings, 6,000 reels of microfilm, 10,000 microfiches, and 500,000 images, most of them photographs."[38] The entire Colonial Williamsburg enterprise has been built about the gathering of archival sources. In 1955, it, along with the Virginia Historical Society, the University of Virginia Library, and the Virginia State Library, began to build a massive documentary archive by identifying and copying Virginia-related records in the libraries and archives of Great Britain, Ireland, and France, resulting in 963 microfilm reels by its conclusion in 1985.[39] So, why could not the old public records office be used as a place to educate the public about the nature of archival and other research needed to support the day-to-day interpretations of the historic site?

There are additional clues in a controversy, emerging in the mid-1990s, about the general interpretive and educational programs going on at Colonial Williamsburg. Two anthropologists, Eric Gable and Richard Handler, conducted research on the interpretive activities of history museums, using Colonial Williamsburg as a case study. As they reported in early findings of their work, "Touring the museum repeatedly, we listened as interpreters routinely told the public that history changes because new documents revealing new facts are found." They described in detail how interpreters were provided packets of artifacts and documents for their use, and, at a later date, each building at Colonial Williamsburg was stocked with a notebook with information on all displayed artifacts for the use of its guides and craftspeople. What made their work so controversial was their conclusion that the methods of training, evaluating, and administering the interpreters revealed a complex hierarchy of control and accountability that went far beyond the general business of educating visitors to the site.[40] What is most interesting here, given the focus on the old public records office, is not the substance of their study, and certainly not the more controversial aspects of their work, but that a considerable part of their investigation has to do with how documentary evidence is used for interpretive activities at history museums.

Cary Carson, the head of research at Colonial Williamsburg, and one of the individuals who paved the way for the anthropologists to do the study, hoping to learn some things that would enhance the educational programs of the historic site, also reveals an interesting perspective on the importance of documentary evidence. Carson bluntly questions much of the anthropologists' work, noting that they are "consistent with a mythology widely held by university academics, untold numbers of the general public, and even some conspiracy theorists employed by museums themselves."[41] Indeed, Carson, an innovative museum administrator and accomplished scholar, effectively debunks many of the points made by Gable and Handler.

It is in Carson's analysis of their commentary on the authority of documents that should most interest archivists and other records professionals. Carson indicates that the two "anthropologists have shed light on current practices at Colonial Williamsburg that need correction and improvement." Carson is careful to note, however, that the "historians and trainers can do a better job of explaining to interpreters that there are pedagogical reasons for the selection of the primary sources used in training sessions." And here is the most critical aspect of Carson's statement: "Documents and artifacts do not speak for themselves. They reveal their meaning through the historians and teachers who select some in preference to others, arrange them in one order rather than another, and interpret them to mean this, not that. Every interpreter needs to understand this creative process, whether or not he or she makes that idea explicit to others."[42] With this latter statement, we nearly have in hand a script for what the Secretary's Office could be used to interpret, both for the training of its own guides and the education of the public (unless, one of course accepts that such matters may be too mundane or uninteresting to exhibit).

Exhibitions, especially for the public, are not easy exercises to be done successfully. Museum specialist Barbara Franco, also contributing to the issue of the *Journal of American History* featuring Carson's exchange with the anthropologists, argues, "Exhibitions must consider the needs and desires of the public as the primary audience, merge education and entertainment, and integrate serious content with effective communication."[43] Thinking along these lines, one can easily imagine why the old public records office remains largely un-interpreted, except for identifying its original function and being described in a bit of a light-hearted fashion in official guidebooks about the red tape and bureaucratic aspects of government recordkeeping.

However, Franco is not done with her assessment about the purpose and nature of museum exhibitions:

> My own experience at the Minnesota Historical Society suggests that reexamination of long-standing assumptions and arguments about historical methodology is also needed to reestablish history as a discipline central to public understanding of how past events relate to the present. The distinction between a scientific and objective process of research and analysis and a suspiciously subjective process of communication is no longer tenable. The public is more than willing to engage difficult subjects and complex meanings in exhibits that do not avoid emotion. . . .[44]

Like Carson's rebuttal, this statement suggests directly trying to educate the public about how historical documentation has played a role in more recent interpretative programs at places like Colonial Williamsburg. Of course, the public already senses that something is up, as returning visitors discover more interpretation about African-Americans, women, lower classes, and everyday life in addition to the political, economic, and upper-class orientation that Colonial Williamsburg once doted on.

There is, yet, another barrier that may have been in the way of interpreting the Secretary's Office over the years. Stuart Hobbs, also examining what history museums and historic sites have done in interpreting the past, discusses the long-ago split between architectural historians and other historians in such venues, noting how they have often focused on buildings rather than archival research. Hobbs believes that "Members of the newly professionalizing museum field felt alienated from academic historians who focused on printed rather than material sources and scholarly rather than popular audiences. History museum professionals found intellectual and institutional allies in architectural and art historians, and curators of decorative arts at art museums."[45]

In looking back over the history of interpretation of the Secretary's Office at Colonial Williamsburg, it is possible to read its treatment as a focus more on its architecture than on its function. As to the problems with the interpretation, exhibition, and public programs related to the building, one must ask whether how much more, or how much less, is known about other structures in the Colonial Williamsburg complex that are more fully and richly interpreted. For example, in the criticism by Gable and Handler, as they focus on one building's interpretation (the Wythe House) and the use of the document packets by the interpreters, the anthropologists note that "all such artifacts, and those in the main house itself, were conjectured in the sense that there are no surviving records of the furnishings of the property."[46] I suspect that there is enough evidence from the many Colonial era public records inspections, with many colonial governments doing such an investigation nearly every generation from the late seventeenth century through the next century, that an engaging and accurate interpretation of the old public records could be done.[47]

Such criticisms must be, however, put into a fuller context, one that archivists and records professionals ought to understand as they have experimented with public programs, educational efforts, and advocacy to deepen understanding about the importance of records. Part of the charm and interest of Colonial Williamsburg for many is its architecture, pleasant streets, recreations of street festivals, dining experiences, and shopping for everything from the most garish sweatshirts long associated with popular tourist sites to the very expensive reproductions of furniture and decorative arts. While visitors come to learn, they also come to be entertained. For many, the Secretary's Office is a pleasant bit of architecture, and one can imagine more than one visitor contemplating how they could transform it into a comfortable suburban tract house. Would visitors go into the building to learn about Colonial recordkeeping, the challenges of preserving such records, and the even greater challenges of utilizing the historical documentation to understand and present the history of Colonial Williamsburg? We don't know, because it has not been tried. However, we can speculate about how this might work.

Conclusion

The year 2007 marked the four hundredth anniversary of the founding of Virginia, as well as my own fiftieth anniversary in first visiting the historic village. And, I hope that when I visit there again, as I am sure I will, that I could tour a functioning and dynamic Secretary's Office. I envision entering into the main, central room and seeing an exhibition about the history of recordkeeping with explanation about how the Colonial Williamsburg restoration has made use of the archival documentation. The history of recordkeeping could extend from the Colonial era, when the building was built, up to the present, considering some of the calamities that have befallen the older records through fire, natural disaster, neglect, and wars. The exhibition even could touch on the challenges posed by modern digital technologies, educating the present generation about the importance of records and why no one should take for granted what happens with their electronic mail messages, Web sites, and digital photographs.

I also hope that the room off to the left of the center room, the one now closed for administrative offices, could be turned into a living exhibition about the production of records. Just as the visitor to Colonial Williamsburg can visit the printing office and see how books and newspapers were printed, bound, and marketed, why could the visitor not see an apprentice scribe copying a record, indexing a record, storing a document in a box, or retrieving a document for a public official? Here the visitor could ask the interpreter about the making and keeping of documents, the quaint spellings, and the learning of the Chancery hand used in the making of official records. Here also the visitor could ask about the nature of older records systems that, today, support both the interpretation of the eighteenth century town and the modern genealogist's quest for their ancestors (something most visitors will probably identify with).

Perhaps, walking back into the far room, the visitor could find a bookstore and gift shop, just as presently there is one. However, this shop would feature both scholarly and popular publications (along with multimedia publications) on the nature of archives and manuscripts, genealogical and historical research, historic preservation, and items related to calligraphy or with some other connection to the creating or maintaining of records. It could be the one place in Colonial Williamsburg focused on the preservation of the documentary and material heritage and the relationship between the two. Given the rich and popular literature on such topics that we can now choose from, the only difficult task would be fitting all the materials into the relatively small confines of the room.

Obviously, I am not an exhibit designer and there may be flaws with my ideas, but I do not think that what I am describing here is too ridiculous or far from the range of activities that this history museum now supports. That the Secretary's Office is a now largely silent witness to generations of archival and records work is not something that archivists and records managers should be happy about. It is also not something that the administrators and scholars of Colonial Williamsburg should be content with, given the possibilities for engaging the public about some important matters related to the American experience and the interpretation of the site. Each year hundreds of thousands of visitors walk about the old public records office, mostly missing any sense of the importance of such an operation to the history of their nation or the Revolutionary legacy. There was probably no generation more concerned with preserving the legacy of their own deeds, than that of men like Thomas Jefferson, many of whose public careers had their start just down the street from where the Secretary's Office was located. It is part of the story of Colonial Williamsburg and the formation of the American experience that is not being told well enough. The Secretary's Office deserves more than a modest sign and a brief entry in a guidebook.

And, who knows, maybe some young person entering such a refurbished Secretary's Office could hear the first faint call to pursue an archival career.

Chapter Three

Public and Private History in Colonial Williamsburg: A Memoir of a Half-Century and A View to a Calling

Introduction

In 1957 Virginia celebrated its three-hundredth and fiftieth anniversary, led by yearlong events and parties at Jamestown and nearby Williamsburg. At age seven, I was there, in the company of a portion of my family — my father, great-uncle, and great-aunt. I remember vividly my few days there in the hot late summer days — the costumed docents, the stately Duke of Gloucester Street, standing in the craft shops watching the manufacture of buckets and wrought-iron brackets, the ruins of the church at Jamestown, the reconstructed glassworks at that first settlement, the Colonial Williamsburg cafeteria we ate at repeatedly, and a host of other activities bringing history alive to my grade-school self. I even remember seeing for the first time *The Story of a Patriot*, a then brand new half-hour film produced for the anniversary when lead actor Jack Lord was truly unknown (as apparently was the reason for his selection, a bet that failed as Lord went on to become a popular television actor within a few short years after filming the historical feature).

What I most remember, however, is that this brief visit birthed an interest in history that I have never lost. From this time forward I read history books, gladly visited with my family historical sites and museums, and watched films (good, bad, and indifferent) about historical themes. And, even more surprising, it started a life-long relationship with Colonial Williamsburg, now more than a half-century in duration (with no signs of slowing down), which I am describing in this brief chapter, one knitting together the notion of a calling described in chapter one and the issues related to the interpretation of the Secretary's Office considered in the second chapter. I have now reached that age, just turning sixty, where what I am writing is as much memoir as it is some form of scholarship. As I begin to move into my final decade of an academic and professional (divided neatly between working as an archivist and teaching others to be archivists) career, it seems appropriate to embark on such self-reflection. It seems even more appropriate to write about my connection to Colonial Williamsburg as this restored historical site itself begins to move towards its own seventy-fifth anniversary. Connecting to such events and places is just one way of marking one's life.

Traveling to historic sites is another especially compelling way of marking off the passage of time. My father loved (and still loves) driving to all varieties of historic sites and scenic byways. After Williamsburg, I remember successive trips to Harper's Ferry, Antietam battlefield, Gettysburg National Park, and a variety of other such destinations (usually old forts, historic houses, parks, and museums). The commencement of the Civil War Centennial reinforced my interest in all things historical, with re-enactments and an abundance of new publications on the history of this war. These trips, coupled with a steady supply of history books and incessant playing of board games with historical themes such as Avalon Hill's 1957 breakthrough *Gettysburg*, nurtured my love of the past; in 1962, confined at home for a week with a mild case of scarlet fever, I was given a stack of Random House's Landmark Series, with titles such as *The Pony Express*, and I devoured these in between required naps (this series is still being published, having started in 1950, the year of my birth, and it is considered one of the pioneering history series for children). It is good to know I was in the vanguard in appreciating such publications, although it is just as comforting to know that my discovery of an interest in history is not unlike what others experienced.[1]

College and Early Professional Years

By the time I went to college, there was little question that history would be my major (even with an advisor who suggested that if I wanted to make a decent living I should consider plumbing — evidence that he had never seen me with a tool in my hand). Although I was not to become an academic historian in any traditional sense, I was to become an academic with a focus on historical matters as part of a group of pioneering professors in archival studies. My childhood fascination with the past and the remembrance of those visits to historic sites was to pay dividends in later years in my work as an archivist, getting a chance to handle some of our country's oldest documents and to see history literally from the ground up through the artifacts created by our forebears and somehow preserved through both accident and dedication by various creators, custodians, and collectors. Working in a school of information studies, a humanist amongst scientists, a historian amongst technocrats, has only served to draw on my early-formed passion for history as a means for explaining myself. While some see only a present problem or challenge, I tend to see it as part of a historical continuum. While others persistently view technology in its future potential, I remind myself (and others) of the many other future prognostications that went nowhere.

Thinking like this is only to remind oneself of what the restorers of Colonial Williamsburg, however jaded our present views of our country may be causing us to regard the patriotic overtones of the endeavor with suspicion if not sarcasm, had in mind when they worked to restore it to its late eighteenth-century appearance. Of course, I did not have such sophisticated thoughts when I was seven, or later as a teenager. This only came later as I began to understand the history of historic preservation, the notion of public memory, the challenges of recreating the past, and the complexities of reading records — both textual and artifactual — as signposts to the past. I am not even sure what it was when I was young that attracted me to history on the Duke of Gloucester Street. Years later, I learned how the restoration appealed to many as a means of connecting to a past, even if it was sanitized and cleaned up and served as a model for the faux restoration of many older homes to appear to belong to the Colonial era. I understood years later that the row homes in which I grew up in Baltimore, built in the years just after the Second World War, were tract homes mirroring the Williamsburg style and even borrowing from their decorators' schemes in colors, woodworking, and fireplace mantels if not in floor plans. I grew up inhabiting a couple of these home types in the 1950s and 1960s, and, after getting married, lived in another one in the late 1970s and early 1980s.

As I got older, I did not lose my enthusiasm for the past. Despite my undergraduate advisor's comments, I did major in American history. And not long after I commenced a career as an archivist, completing a masters in history along the way. As part of my conference attendance, I spent a week in 1981 at the American Association of State and Local History (AASLH) annual meeting (and getting an intensive behind the scenes orientation to Colonial Williamsburg and its research and education programs). Ultimately, I worked for sixteen years as an archivist, before becoming a faculty member teaching future archivists (acquiring a PhD in Library and

Information Science with a focus on archival studies). My increasing interest in the history of archives would bring me back to Williamsburg in new and more interesting ways at a later date. I early perceived the similarities, and some differences of course, in the work of archivists, archaeologists, historic preservationists, historians, and museum curators — seeing enough in common that I at times struggled to understand, in some full or final sense, my own professional identity. Years after the AASLH conference, I would become re-acquainted with a scholar, long after his death, who struggled with his own professional identity, leaving a detailed trail of reflections and ruminations in a set of dense personal papers and volumes of diaries.

In the 1960s I made a couple of trips back to Williamsburg, but it was in the middle of the 1970s that my connection to the restored Virginia colonial capital was renewed in meaningful ways. In January 1975 I was married, and we honeymooned in Williamsburg. My wife-to-be was extremely skeptical about going to a place wrapped in both our country's and my own history, but she determined to do this against her own good judgment (if only for the fact that her desired destination — Nova Scotia — seemed a bit forlorn and cold in the midst of winter); our annual summer vacations in mid-coast Maine seem to have assuaged her disappointment with a northerly trip. What happened next was surprising then, and it remains so to this day — she loved her experience. She had never been there, and she embraced the tours through the buildings, the leisurely walks on the streets, and the excursions into the restored but still bustling mercantile shops with a remarkable enthusiasm. Even through several straight days of chilly rain, scratchy muslin sheets in one of the restored houses, and my own droll lectures on early American history (along with a short-lived effort to introduce her to playing the military board games I had grown up with in my youth — leading to a violent scattering of the board and hundreds of complicated markers across the stately Colonial period room), Lynn fell in love with the place. Today, people mistake her for a CW tour guide as she offers information to people she sees lost or confused on the streets of the restored district. Her constant smile, clear voice, and infectious interest in people would stand her well in such a position — and I daresay, someday, she will do something just like this.

With my wife's vibrant interest, we began slowly to make regular trips to Colonial Williamsburg (with the exception of our time spent in Alabama and upstate New York in the mid-1980s, when the drive was just on the too-long side). After our move to Pittsburgh in the late 1980s, putting us within easy striking distance of the ancient colonial capital, we began to make regular trips, exploring more and more of the region. And, it is amazing how the region has changed. When I first visited a half-century ago, the area around the restored historic district was mostly farm land and undeveloped forest, probably not unlike what the first settlers found as they stepped off of their ships. Between that first visit and the honeymoon, little had changed. In fact, I remember how difficult it was to find a decent place to eat on a late Sunday evening when we arrived in Williamsburg, driving along Richmond Road. Now that same road is a beehive of every franchised and other kind of eatery you can imagine, along with outlet malls, specialty shops, and retirement communities. Indeed, the enterprise that has grown up because of Colonial Williamsburg now seems to divert people and families away from the historic district or, more likely, to assist CW to evolve into a more diversified (and healthy) operation combining historical scholarship and interpretation, education, and vacation spa.

I have no idea how many trips we have made to Williamsburg, both together and individually, in our thirty-five years of marriage, but we can certainly chart our changing interests over this time. For a while, we travelled there because we liked to see the changing interpretation of the site, the influence of new social history research, efforts to integrate the history of African-Americans and indigenous peoples, and the changing thematic interpretations intended to bring back families year after year. My wife's interest in such matters was reinforced when she attended the 1982 Seminar in Historical Administration held at Colonial Williamsburg. We also grew to love the colorful gardens, the wintery smell of burning fireplaces, and the transforming seasonal landscapes silhouetting multi-colored clapboarded and rose and orange-colored brick buildings. Later we visited because we found it a convenient place for a winter break, often encountering very mild weather in both December and January, while also enabling us to enjoy the Christmas season there with throngs of people or a much quieter time in January celebrating our wedding anniversary; we are suckers for the dark green magnolia leaves and sprigs of holly bushes with bright berries framing windows and doorways. Finally, my historical and archival interests converged, and I began to plan a series of research trips to use manuscript and records materials at both the College of William and Mary and at the Colonial Williamsburg Foundation. Why it took so long for this to happen is unclear to me, but I am glad I finally reached this point (as is my wife, who enjoys tagging along and dropping me off for quiet mornings in archives while she can plan her own itineraries without worrying about my interests). Like thousands of other marriages, we can mark our married lives by our visits to Williamsburg, the legacy of any restored historic site that has managed to generate its own venerable history. We can see in the restored and even recreated houses from the 1930s our own pasts, as the reconstructed and restored structures have both now aged to seem authentic to the eighteenth century.

My interest in archival work has always included a curiosity about the history of archives and manuscript collecting. My earliest articles, in the mid-1970s, focused on the acquisition of the Calvert Family papers by the Maryland Historical Society, the evolution of collecting by the Society, and the care of Maryland's colonial records.[2] Later, these formed the foundation of my master's thesis completed at the University of Maryland. And as I worked on this topic, I noted in passing that the first public records office was established in Williamsburg, and, moreover, that it was still standing in the historic district (a fact that I don't recall noting when I was a tot meandering around CW's streets).

Lester Cappon and the Struggle with Professional Identity

My archival connections with Williamsburg soon grew deeper roots as I worked to master the knowledge required for archival work, documentary editing, and historical research. I also had been influenced early in my career by the writings and ideas of Lester J. Cappon, archivist, historian and documentary editor, who had a long career with both Colonial Williamsburg and the Institute of Early American History and Culture at the College of William and Mary. When Cappon died in 1981, I proposed to one of his long-time colleagues that an edition of his seminal writings on archival issues would be a good idea. Nothing came of the idea (although I subsequently learned that William Towner, the Director of the Newberry Library in Chicago and the Cappon colleague I had written to, had planned just such a volume when Cappon finished his work on the *Atlas of Early American History* and sort of retired in his late seventies). Inspired by the signs of more sophisticated historical work on the archival profession and current debates about its societal mission and relationship to history (and encouraged by my wife to find *more* reasons to make trips there), more than two decades later, I went to examine Cappon's personal papers at the College to see what they offered as possibilities for research. By then Cappon had become a largely forgotten figure (at least within the archival community), and a new phase in my relationship to Williamsburg opened.[3] What I did not realize, at the outset, was that reading Cappon's documentary legacy was like opening a window into my life, career, and historical interests.

Over the years I had identified a dozen essays written by Cappon that either were critical to understanding archival professional debate and development in the 1950s through the 1970s or that continued to offer important insights in present archival theory and practice. What were difficult to understand about some of his essays were the reasons he had written them in the first place. One of his early essays defining the nature of manuscripts as archival sources I always have considered a seminal essay, but it just seemed to hang in the space of the professional archival community, providing little understanding of why it was written. In 2003 I made a trip during Spring Break to spend what I anticipated to be a day or two (I packed my golf clubs with the expectation of having plenty of time to get in a round or two when I finished) to find clues and answers in Cappon's personal papers about why he had written what he had. What I discovered was a rich treasure trove of material requiring a couple of extended visits to examine his papers (another visit took me to the University of Virginia to examine materials in its archives related to his nearly two-decade career there as an archivist before his move a hundred miles Southeast to Williamsburg). And in it, I learned that Cappon's essay was part of a projected volume (never finished) on historical manuscripts administration, handed over to the *American Archivist* because that journal was short of material. I played no golf that week — nor have I played a round of golf in any of my other ten or so research trips there to investigate Cappon's life and career in the old Virginia capitol.

With the aid of Cappon's rich papers, I wrote a lengthy essay about his career and his archival musings prefacing a collection of his seminal writings, published by the Society of American Archivists. Interestingly, my work on Cappon began to have a stronger influence on my own career than I ever imagined could happen. If Williamsburg's historical recreation had had an influence on my own fledgling historical interests, my work on one of that town's leading citizens in the mid-twentieth century began to have additional influences on my sense of my own career. Surprisingly, when I made an early presentation about Cappon's career and how he wrestled with his professional identity as a historian, an archivist, or a documentary editor, one of the members of the audience remarked that they had no idea that I was as interested in history as my commentary suggested. I was taken aback, and wondered if I had in fact wandered that far from my own interests and roots. My wandering around in Williamsburg at age seven seemed even more distant than ever before. However, there were many more surprises to come.

When I did my original research in the Cappon Papers, I noted that there were two boxes of diaries restricted for a few more years to August 21, 2006 (the twenty-fifth anniversary of his death). I made a note to go back to examine these diaries, but I doubted there was much in them that I needed for my project in evaluating Cappon's contributions to archival theory and practice. My goal became to write an essay about the historian-archivist as a diarist, a creator (not just user) of archival materials, enabling me to delve into the rich historical and literary scholarship on diaries and journals now steadily appearing. My plans would quickly change after I opened the first volume of Cappon's diary.

Yes, I discovered that Cappon was a self-conscious diarist, offering considerable insights into the nature of such documentation. However, I also discovered that he fully documented his personal life and career in the diary volumes, offering insights into a variety of topics including teaching history and engaging with what we now call public history, the fledgling field of documentary editing, scholarly publishing, and collecting archival materials and rare imprints in Early American and Western history. Cappon's diary, extending from 1954 until a few days before his death in 1981, also is full of references to life in Williamsburg and the activities of Colonial Williamsburg, many quite candid (explaining why he kept the diaries closed for a quarter-of-a-century after his death).

From the moment the diary opens, Cappon is wrestling with his lack of time for research and scholarship, with laments that his employers (the College and Colonial Williamsburg) don't sufficiently value such activity because of interests in popularizing the past. In his many entries about such matters, Cappon seeks to make a distinction between the scholarly activities of the Institute of Early American History and Culture and the popular education functions of Colonial Williamsburg (tensions that have lessened, but not completely disappeared, in subsequent decades with more ambitious research activities sponsored by CW and more clearly reflected in the daily educational events offered to the tourists visiting the restored historical town). As Cappon struggled with his own professional identity, using his diary as a personal sounding board and record of his activities, he also wrestled with the notion of popular history (what would become established as public history a couple of decades later).

Nevertheless, Cappon possessed a self-deprecating sense of humor that always got him through the most troublesome of his personal and professional misgivings. In 1960, he readily agreed to play a role in the CW film about music in eighteenth century Williamsburg, noting, "This morning I had a wig-fitting at the Colonial Williamsburg wig dept. on N.

England St. In the CW movie on Eighteenth-Century in Williamsburg I am to play the role of organist, but will not really play the organ. A recording of Arthur Rhea's playing will be made, but since someone thinks Arthur doesn't 'look eighteenth-century,' — and I do! — I am to be the actor."[4]

Throughout the diary, Cappon provides glimpses into the nature of life in Williamsburg in its early years as a restored historic village. In one 1958 entry, Cappon comments on the need for a good bookstore in the town: "The College book store is a dreary untidy, dingy place offering text books & a few paper backs & stationary supplies. The Cole Shop on Duke of Gloucester St. is tiny, limited in stock and open at hours to suit the proprietor, Mr. Prentice. Colonial Williamsburg sells its own publications at its Craft House & Hotels, but only as an adjunct to other merchandise. Both the College and CW are missing an educational opportunity."[5] Right up to the end of his life, Cappon worried about the future of Williamsburg and its historic status. On July 29, 1981, just less than a month before his death, he wrote the following: "Today, the Cappon family visited the Anheuser Busch Gardens and brewery, 5 miles east of Williamsburg. This 'fun place' was built on land purchased by AB from Colonial Williamsburg, Inc., which had bought the land at a low price years ago for 'protection' of the restored area. Thus CW promoted a *competitor* for a huge profit on the sale of the real estate. One wonders how many tourists go to Busch Gardens first, where they spend most of their money, with little left for educational CW."[6]

While the bookstore dilemma has been rectified with the partnership between the College and Barnes and Noble (I always manage to spend a couple of hundred dollars on books there every visit) and the flourishing of some excellent second-hand and rare bookstores in the area, Busch Gardens has grown into a competitor for the attention of children (and probably a lot of adults as well). Fortunately, our daughter is now 25 and grown beyond such debates and temptations, but we have had many conversations with individuals who have had to negotiate visits to both CW and the amusement park of a brewery in order to persuade their children to leave their digital fantasy worlds on the computer and see something with connections to the real past. For kids, entertainment and education need to be sewn together, and my joyful memories of just sitting and reading a history book — with no television on in the background — must seem antique to many. I always hope that another kid visiting Williamsburg for the first time might be inspired, whether by cynicism of what he or she is seeing portrayed or some more romanticized sense of the value of an interest in the past, to take on history as a career.

Public History, but Whose Public?

What I have been engaged in for most of my career is what has become known as public history, the efforts by academically-trained historians to engage the public outside the classroom, wherever the public might gather and might be captured for a few moments to learn something about the past. One of the reasons that some of my own colleagues failed to realize my own interest in history was that long ago in the early years of my archival career I saw both promise and peril in the blessing of public history by university-based historians. It seemed to me then that this interest in public history was clearly little more than an effort to find alternative employment for graduates of history programs, rather than any agenda to teach the public about the importance of understanding history. For the record, Lester Cappon shared skepticism of what was to be baptized later as public history. Commenting on a talk at the 1955 Antiques Forum sponsored by CW, Cappon critiqued a talk given by a historical society director: "There is all too much leeway in the purveying of art and 'culture' and 'history' to the public for reputations of a kind based upon thin foundations. In the academic world one can't make his way on superficial learning too successfully under the scouting of critical scholars; but in historical societies and museums the opportunities and temptations are greater to emphasize promotion and popular appeal at the expense of sound scholarship. The allurements and pitfalls are many in these fields; it is a pity that their 'public contacts,' which should be cultivated, are often of the shoddy variety, in the name of History."[7] Yet, as Director of the Institute, Cappon sought to publish scholarly books with popular appeal, although how well he succeeded is most likely a mixed legacy (his own editing of the Adams-Jefferson correspondence, in print fifty years after its original publication, is probably his greatest achievement in this regard).[8]

The efforts to do public history remain elusive and difficult today, whatever one thinks of the American society's interest in the past. William Hogeland's recent book criticizes efforts in engaging the public about history by museums, historic sites, newspapers, and public broadcasting. What Hogeland worries about is that in order to do this history is made subject to a "kind of simplification that erases our deepest conflicts." He contends, "Public history should try to help all of us imagine and look closely. Too often it tries to do just the opposite."[9] Some writers about Colonial Williamsburg have made such arguments about it. For me, thinking about CW's history and legacy has enriched my own understanding of the past, how we interpret it, and how we engage the past. Cappon wrestled with just such concerns, but, in my estimation, he ironically missed one opportunity while living and working in Williamsburg.

Cappon spent most of his time in Williamsburg living in the John Prentis House on the Duke of Gloucester Street. Just a few hundred yards away from his residence stood the Secretary's Office, the oldest extant public government building in Virginia, a place where secretaries for courthouses were trained, and where Thomas Jefferson did both legal research and research for his famous *Notes on Virginia*. All of these matters tied into Cappon's long-standing interests in the development of archives, manuscript collecting, and documentary editing. Yet, there is no evidence Cappon ever entertained writing a history of this building and its function or arguing that it should be used for educating the many tourists visiting CW about the important work of archivists, documentary editors, and related fields. His many comments (indeed, complaints) about the quality of scholarship supporting the work of CW never broached this building as one place where Cappon himself could help.

After I finished my initial use of Cappon's personal papers for an introduction to his writings on archival studies and while waiting for his diaries to open, I decided to do some research myself about the old Secretary's Office. I did not start at the beginning, since the Virginia State Archivist Louis Manarin had written an excellent essay about the history of the building (perhaps explaining why Cappon never tackled the topic himself).[10] What I focused on was the subsequent history of the building's interpretation as part of Colonial Williamsburg, writing an essay for the *American Archivist*, that saw the lack of the interpretation of the building as a public record office as an inability of CW to see how such a topic could be intrinsically interesting to the public. In the CW research files, I discovered many explanations — such as lack of sufficient evidence about how the building was used and outfitted — but I wondered if the real reason was not because of a perception that any focus on records creating and managing was not just a little too boring (despite CW's reliance on the existence of such rich archives and the public's gung-ho enthusiasm for genealogy and other activities also requiring archives). I concluded my own essay with the hope that I would eventually see the structure educating the public about how the Colonial Williamsburg restoration has made use of the archival documentation, why records were important then and now, how records were created and maintained — maybe all underwritten by a bookstore and gift shop selling publications and other materials about calligraphy, genealogy, and local history archives. If the nearby printing press shop could function as a popular tourist destination, why couldn't the old Secretary's Office?

Conclusion

And, so, it seems that my fifty-year history with Colonial Williamsburg will continue. I have more research to do on another book on Cappon as public historian. My wife wants to make more trips back to visit the gardens, tour the buildings, and enjoy the quieter, even if imperfect, time of the eighteenth century. We are now looking into a timeshare or even contemplating some sort of partial retirement in this part of Virginia's tidewater. At the least, we will combine all of these on our annual anniversary celebrations and a return to Williamsburg. Arthur Clarke, in his classic science fiction novel, writes, "Fifty years is ample time in which to change a world and its people almost beyond recognition. All that is required for the task are a sound knowledge of social engineering, a clear sight of the intended goal — and power."[11] In my own fifty-year observations, the world does not seem to have changed so much, perhaps because it has been anchored by an abiding interest in the past. I know more, for sure, than when I first visited Williamsburg and I use a very different set of technologies. But, I still read, take notes, and write.

It may be that so little change seems to me to have occurred because of my long-term focus on writing. Writing, even as it involves a shift from pen and paper to keyboard and the digital, is a process that is painstakingly slow and laborious. Kathleen Norris describes it this way: "Even as I discovered my vocation as a writer, I had to struggle to maintain the boring work habits necessary for nourishing it. The syndrome that the ancient monks describe is one that I know well. It is just when the work seems most hopeless, and I am hard pressed to care whether I ever write another word or not, that the most valuable breakthroughs are likely to come."[12] There is a repetition to it that slows time down, as Norris again captures: "Because it impedes my illusory forward movement, having to begin again can feel like failure. It reminds me that work I thought finished must be redone, and I resent being reminded of the transitory nature of all things, including myself: when I dust, I am humbled, because I, too, am dust. As a writer I must begin, again and again, at that most terrifying of places, the blank page. And as a person of faith I am always beginning again with prayer. I can never learn these things, once and for all, and master them. I can only perform them, set them aside, and then start over."[13]

Chapter Four

Empty Temples: Challenges for Modern Government Archives and Records Management

"The past is also the repository of downright failures, monuments to ignorance, excessive optimism, and hubris. If heeded, the past thus provides caveats and lessons for future designs. If shunned, it will still haunt the future, always lurking in the shadows of success." Henry Petroski[1]

Introduction

The origins of modern archives and records management rest with government institutions. In the United States, the modern professional community commenced with the origins of state government archives and culminated with the founding of the National Archives in 1934. From these roots emerged the first codifiers of professional practice, the first professional associations, and the concept of modern records management. This relationship between government and the professional community stems from a variety of factors — size of the documentary universe, the range of administrative and other challenges, and the critical mass of staff. Another factor is the natural leadership positions the staff of government archives assumed at an early point in the history of the archives and records management community.

Today, however, it seems that government is generating multiple problems threatening the traditional mission and mandate of archivists and records managers, and these are not just technical challenges (such as the oft-discussed issues associated with electronic records management) waiting for their solutions to be announced. Other than the occasional observatory article, many records professionals seem unaware of or uninterested in the nature of the problems and challenges emerging from government administration of records and information systems, stemming from critical legal, managerial, and cultural sources. This lack of awareness or interest reflects the unfortunate tendency of many records professionals to focus their attention nearly exclusively on the issues and challenges concerning their own organizations. What archivists and records managers risk losing is the need to reassess their mission and role, not only in government, but in all organizations and society at large.

We can think of many examples of government secrecy as it affects access to records and information systems. In early May 2005, the *London Sunday Times* published the until then secret minutes of a meeting of Prime Minister Blair's on national security and foreign policy held a few years before, revealing how the Bush administration had determined to invade Iraq for reasons having nothing to do with the alleged weapons of mass destruction. As Mark Danner reflects, "we live with the legacy of exaggerations and lies of the secret way to war: in the distortion of the public debate, the corruption of our politics, and the collapse of the one element essential to fighting a long and inconclusive conflict — the trust and support of the people."[2] Governments striving to operate in secret still create paper trails, and documents get leaked. What are the implications for records professionals? Many explanations, such as divine calling,[3] have been offered for why particular government administrations and leaders make the kinds of decisions they do in domestic and foreign policy; but I am more worried about the consequence of their activities as it concerns government secrecy and records/information policy (and the response by records professionals).

Problems with government secrecy are not new. In mid 2005 it was reported that "government secrecy has reached a historic high by several measures, with federal departments classifying documents at the rate of 125 a minute as they create new categories of semi-secrets bearing vague labels like 'sensitive security information.'" The newspaper report describing this trend states that a "record 15.6 million documents were classified last year, nearly double the number in 2001," while the "declassification process, which made millions of historical documents available annually in the 1990s, has slowed to a relative crawl, from a high of 204 million pages in 1997 to just 28 million pages last year." Not only was this costing huge amounts of money, over seven billion dollars, but it was prompting many to acknowledge that something was amiss. Thomas H. Kean, chairman of the Sept. 11 commission and a former Republican governor of New Jersey, commented, "We're better off with openness. The best ally we have in protecting ourselves against terrorism is an informed public."[4]

In late February 2006, as just another example from among many concerning government records problems, an article appeared in the *Washington Post* about President Bush's selection of a site for his presidential library. John Wertman, a former Clinton administration staffer, argues that the current president has worked steadfastly against having his records opened for purposes of historical research or the accountability of government to its citizens. Wertman contrasts the Presidential Records Act of 1978, with its mandated opening of records after 12 years, providing the "final check on indiscretion in office and the final basis for presidential accountability" and Bush's Executive Order 13233, signed on November 1, 2001, allowing "former presidents and their heirs to bar the release of documents for almost any reason." The theme of this op-ed essay was that after a brief flurry of protest and activity about this particular presidential pronouncement that interest has abated, with potentially devastating results. Wertman concludes, "Until the original intent of the law is restored, public access to the records of our former presidents stands in limbo. Congress must act now to correct this injustice or one day the George W. Bush Presidential Library and Museum may be derided as a hiding place for secrets concerning matters that dogged the administration."[5] The silence about this is evident in both society at large and from within the professional records community. If it was largely government that generated the impetus for modern records work, it is still the case that it is government and the various crises and challenges confronting it that often shapes the future of records and information management practice.

At virtually the same time as Wertman wrote his editorial on the matter of access to presidential records, an interesting and disturbing story broke about the efforts of the CIA and other federal agencies to reclassify previously opened records located at the National Archives. In late February 2006, the public learned about a project, one that had started in 1999, leading to closing over 55,000 pages of records, through the efforts of an historian, Matthew Aid, working at the National Security Archive (NSA). As the NSA reported, the reclassification program encompassed "50 year old documents that CIA had impounded at NARA but which have already been published in the State Department's historical series, *Foreign Relations of the United States*, or have been declassified elsewhere. These documents concern such innocuous matters as the State Department's map and foreign periodicals procurement programs on behalf of the U.S. intelligence community or the State Department's open source intelligence research efforts during 1948." The justification for this program was that President Clinton's Executive Order 12958, pushing a more rapid declassification of federal records, had led to the release of records threatening national security.[6]

The National Archives immediately responded to the breaking of this story, seeming surprised about the program. In a press release offered on February 22, 2006, the Archivist of the United States, Allen Weinstein, declared, "Inappropriate declassification can subject our citizens, our democratic institutions, our homeland security, and our interactions with foreign nations to potential harm. Inappropriate classification (and reclassification) needlessly disrupts the free flow of information and can undermine our democratic principles which require that the American people be informed of the activities of their Government. This is not an either/or challenge. Deliberate, continuous effort is required to succeed at both. The American people expect and deserve nothing less and the National Archives is determined to fulfill its role in this process." Weinstein indicated that the Information Security Oversight Office (ISOO), an office within the National Archives, would be auditing the situation and issuing a report "to provide the greatest feasible degree of transparency to this classification activity."[7] The question remains, however, how NARA had missed for half-a-dozen years what was going on in this reclassification effort. As it was later revealed, not only had NARA leadership known about this program, but that it had willingly entered into a secret agreement with a number of intelligence agencies. The larger issue is, as represented by this case and increasing concern about a new Bush library, growing government secrecy threatening the administration of records providing for open access.

Several new and compelling books about modern government records raise a variety of issues about the nature and purpose of the administration of such information sources. The books critique the presidential library system, government secrecy, and the nature of recordkeeping even in a totalitarian, repressive regime. These writings suggest a shift in how archivists and records managers view or should view government records. They offer provocative ideas, some of which may seem to be quite controversial, that archivists and records managers ought to be mulling over and, better yet, experimenting with in their employing organizations.

Presidential Temples

Actually, the *one day* Wertman worries about is here now, or at least it seems that way. What Wertman worries about has been building for some time, and it is only because the then incumbent president was so openly aggressive in his pursuits of secrecy (or at least in his rhetoric about secrecy) that one might worry about this as characterized in this essay. The challenges of preserving and managing presidential records have been recounted in a book about presidential libraries, written by Benjamin Hufbauer. The author, a fine arts professor, suggests that the establishment of these libraries "marks the dramatic increase in presidential authority that has occurred during an era when the United States has become the most powerful nation in the world."[8] They are evidence of American civil religion — honoring saints, sacred places, sacred objects, and pilgrimages: "They are meant to be sacred national places where pilgrimages can be made to see relics and reconstruction of presidential history, all in order to elevate in the national consciousness presidents who, even if figures lesser than Washington or Lincoln, are represented as worthy of patriotic veneration."[9] Thus far, none of this might seem all that problematic, and certainly not related to the historical obstructions narrated by Wertman (and numerous other observers about government secrecy and information policy).

Hufbauer argues, however, that these libraries represent a "new kind of commemoration," promoting the "imperial presidency" and threatening the "nature of our constitutional government and the balance of power among its branches."[10] Towards the end of his book, Hufbauer strives to define how this commemoration works: "Presidential libraries try to create the sense that their subjects, if not immortal, are still relevant, and that visitors can acquire through a tourist experience living memory of the dead. One of the most important goals of a presidential library, using documents, displays, audio, film, educational role-playing, and interactive video, is to transform presidential labor into myth, giving it seemingly transcendent value."[11] How does one administer records and information systems which are part of an effort mostly to celebrate a president and his administration's achievements, no matter how poor or checkered these achievements actually constitute?

Presidential Temples commences with an assessment of the origins of the Franklin Delano Roosevelt Presidential Library, the pioneering precedent for what became a system of libraries run by the National Archives. Then Hufbauer shifts to the making of the Truman and Johnson libraries, suggesting that this book might be a traditional history of these institutions. Then the author makes a dramatic change, examining the First Ladies exhibits at the Smithsonian before considering a study in the efforts to reinvent the Truman Library nearly half a century after its opening. The chapter on the First Ladies seems out of place with the rest of the book, even though it probably resonates more of the author's area of expertise and provides an interesting side story about how the wives of the presidents have been interpreted. For example, he comments that the "obsession with preserving these gowns was laudable, but the vast effort put into these examples of fragile upper-class clothing may also have presented the formation of a larger discussion and display of the role of women in political culture. All of the concern about gowns helped reduce first ladies to their clothes, limiting them, and in a sense women in general, to an extremely circumscribed role, politically."[12] Hufbauer doesn't seem to go to great lengths to tie this back to the tale about the libraries (although it is a very intriguing analysis of changing museum interpretations of a particular topic over the course of a century), and the best one can say about this is that the reader should approach it as an interesting respite from the story of libraries. Finally, the author reflects on the various efforts with the more recent libraries, quickly leading the reader through these institutions from the Johnson library to the planning for George W. Bush's contribution to them. What first seems like a quick summing up is transformed into a poignant tale of failed efforts to give these institutions a new life and purpose, but one will find themselves lingering over Hufbauer's words, especially as his description is reminiscent of a kind of Greek tragedy.

Many of the tales of the creation of these libraries has been told elsewhere, although Hufbauer's book may be the best, even as it is a rare, scholarly treatment of the subject.[13] Rather than recount the story of each of them, it is more useful to consider some of the main themes Hufbauer constructs in *Presidential Temples*, themes with much to offer in our understanding about what is happening to the administration of government records and public access to the evidence and information found in them. It is interesting to see how someone from far outside of the archives and records management community can be so insightful into the issues needing to be addressed by this community.

One persistent theme in this work is that of the role of the archival function in these libraries being designed to promote a kind of civil religion. Hufbauer argues that "informing and validating a presidential library's museum are archives that preserve documents and other presidential possessions as national relics."[14] FDR used the mixed track record of preservation of former presidents' archives as a "compelling rationale" for his library, eventually winning over the tough critics of the academic historians.[15] Given Hufbauer's expertise in fine arts, it is not surprising that he dotes on the ways in which the architecture and interior design of these institutions contributes to this kind of religious or memorial function (but he ought to remind all records professionals that their buildings convey messages about their mission, whether it is a Neo-Classical temple or a functional warehouse, that may help or hinder them in meeting this mission). Hufbauer provides a detailed description of the functions played by Thomas Hart Benton's mural in the Truman library, depicting the opening of the American West, again reflecting his own scholarly interests but also expanding what archivists and records managers normally consider. As Hufbauer explains, the "painting heralds Independence [the site of the library] as a microcosm of American society, one that helps explain how Manifest Destiny formed an integral part of the foundation of twentieth-century America and the twentieth-century American presidency. And the mural prepares viewers for the culmination of American power symbolized by the Oval Office replica."[16] As this quotation suggests, Hufbauer then depicts the process and importance of creating this replica of the president's working office and the role these replicas play in all the libraries, contrasting them to other museum exhibitions and dioramas. As he concludes, the "replica at the Truman Library has been so effective at evocatively commemorating Truman's presidency that Oval Office replicas have subsequently been built at the Kennedy, Johnson, Ford, Carter, Reagan, and Clinton libraries. These presidential dioramas, in their different ways with their different stories, continue the project of using the landscape of public memory to naturalize narratives of white supremacy and presidential power in order to make them appear as objective history rather than constructed myth."[17] Is it any wonder, then, that these aspects of the libraries overwhelm eventually their archival function, subordinating the importance of records for matters like evidence and accountability to little more than museum props in supporting the temple functions of commemoration and celebration?

Another theme developed by Hufbauer is that the archival function, even when providing a critical part of the rationale for presidential libraries, is often far below other functions in terms of importance and popular appeal. In discussing the FDR library, Hufbauer notes, "FDR's desire to convert the research room into a display room for paintings and books shows Roosevelt's understanding of the need to appeal to tourists, even if it meant sacrificing facilities for researchers. Roosevelt understood that most tourists would have little interest in using the archive, even if it was what validated the site and informed the displays."[18] Indeed, library was chosen over the term archive for the name of the FDR institution "because it was thought that it would seem less alien to the public."[19] Much of the attention in the formation of the FDR library was in housing and displaying the wide range of personal collections Roosevelt had assembled. Hufbauer observes that "through the organization of his presidential library into a tourist site and museum, Roosevelt was able to elevate the idiosyncrasy of his collections to the level of national relics."[20] Archives as relics suggests, however, documents to be viewed but not really used and studied, relegating records that should be documenting a president's actions to objects that serve as commemorative devices. In this, all records professionals should wonder and question how this perspective is allowed to continue to predominate other legitimate responsibilities for these institutions.

One of the more important issues evident in this tome is that the presidential libraries, while heralding the preservation and increased access to the archives of these national leaders, really have been created and sustained as a means of controlling access. Hufbauer quotes from FDR's speech at the 1939 laying of the cornerstone, where he places more importance on the documents not associated with his presidential administration, referring to the "spontaneous letters which have come to me ... from men, from women, and from children in every part of the United States, telling me of their conditions and problems and giving me their own opinions." Hufbauer interprets FDR's speech in this way: "Roosevelt did value expressions of popular opinion, but his statement screened his desire to prevent access to many of his own sensitive papers."[21] This has continued to be a source of tension and criticism for these libraries to this day. FDR thought of the library as his own, and so have most of the other presidents who have established them. Those who have argued that these institutions have enhanced access to the presidential records have generally adopted rhetoric rather than produced data supporting their contention. Various episodes of continuing family or individual control suggest that problems with full disclosure of the records exist, with little evidence that access is better in this system than in any other mechanism that could be adopted.

Despite this problem, Hufbauer, examining the architectural style of the Johnson library and the use of the archival sources by Robert Caro for a critical biography of Johnson, believes that the libraries also provide access greater than would be possible under other approaches: "The presidential library ... manifests the dramatic increase in presidential power since the 1930s, but democratic access to most of their holdings has yielded publications, which, like Caro's, illuminate the sordid as well as positive aspects of presidential power and counteract the uncritical heroizing of presidents often found in the libraries' museum exhibits."[22] Or, as more bluntly stated, Johnson's "library, a shrine to Johnson's presidential ego, has ended up providing the material that in some places may even shock his critics."[23] Of course, we could probably create another means of making these records available for scholars, journalists, and others without having to suffer through the less critical, more celebratory, exhibitions. This also begs the question of whether the Caro biography or the library exhibits have had the greater impact on the popular memory of Johnson or the public conception of the office of the presidency. Hufbauer suggests just this, in fact, when he writes, "At presidential libraries, at least initially, the history presented in the museum is bought and paid for by interested parties. Historians certainly have a role, and many books have been written primarily through access to the archives at presidential libraries. However, less than 1 percent of the one-and-a-half-million people who visit presidential libraries each year use these archives. Ninety-nine percent of visitors to presidential libraries are there for the museum displays, which at first present a whitewashed and glamorized portrait of each president."[24] Records professionals need to question when their functions are buried under others, such as museum exhibitions or public relations, because this negatively impacts why records are managed and preserved. Touting the importance of records for accountability and evidence, certainly critically important attributes for government records, is likely to be drowned out in the stress on functions such as memorializing and celebrating.

We can discern such issues concerning the mission of these libraries in other ways as well. This is an especially relevant concern since, in reflecting on the Johnson library, with a structure built on a grand scale seeking to reflect Johnson and his native state, Hufbauer muses, "One of the effects of the presidential library, and especially of the Johnson Library, is to elevate the individual president as well as the office above the average citizen by attempting to inspire awe and reverence."[25] Is this appropriate for a democratic state? And what does it do to the archival records housed in these libraries? There is an immense contradiction in the fact that these libraries are run from the National Archives, seemingly possessing a mandate to preserve the records of the national government for the American people, and just what they often present to the public. "Even though presidential libraries are public institutions that carry the imprint of the National Archives," Hufbauer reflects, "those who pay for the initial displays, which often last for decades, largely control them."[26] Exhibitions at these libraries often ignore any topics which might criticize or throw their subjects in a bad light, no matter how much evidence there is that supports wrongdoings, mistakes, and even illegal activity. Again, just like in the more recent reclassification controversy, one must ask why the National Archives leadership doesn't make a greater fuss about such matters.

Perhaps the problem may be the elevation of the libraries to civic temples, ones not to be challenged or tampered with under any circumstances. Even the restricted access to the archives in these institutions adds to their role and mystery as religious shrines. In discussing the first presidential library, Hufbauer argues, "The Roosevelt Library is meant to store and display every preservable trace of Roosevelt's life and labor for as long as possible. The archived traces of Roosevelt's labor became the sacra of the presidency at the site. Archived traces became sacred presidential remains. The mystified quality of this labor is emphasized by Roosevelt's plan to restrict access to the archive, which was to be seen even more than it was to be used."[27] So, then, can't such problems relating to access or, more broadly, basic missions, be addressed and resolved? Or, does this cause us to deface a holy site? While records may be related to religious impulses historically, it is hard to consider that in a democratic society we should place the records of political leaders on such a plane.

Despite the growing prominence of the libraries as molders of the public memory of the presidential office, these institutions are constantly evolving. As other commentators on the presidential libraries have noted, these institutions follow a distinctive life cycle, moving from the initial stage of fund-raising and formation to a focus as a research center when the records begin to open and finally to a tourist site and educational facility. Hufbauer suggests, as have others, that it is the last phase that is the most challenging: "When eventually the interest of scholars, as with tourists, subsides, it becomes a continuing challenge for presidential libraries to justify their existence."[28] The question that can be raised at this point is whether this exercise should be continued or, instead, lead to serious discussion about ending the system and finding other means to preserve presidential archives and interpret presidential administrations. A new system could add the role of the library staffs as kinds of religious figures: "Each generation of presidential library directors, curators, and archivists — who might be thought of as priests and priestesses within contemporary archival temples — reconstructs the story of their president for every new generation of visitor."[29] Is this something that the American people really want continued, especially given the financial costs associated with the task? At the least, if there is a cycle of these institutions there is always the possibility that they could be replaced with something better, more effective, and an improvement for supporting a more logical vision for archives in a democratically governed society.

Some efforts have been made to grapple with such issues in these libraries, and Hufbauer provides a compelling description of Larry Hackman's efforts, after he assumed the directorship of the Truman Library, to do just that. I worked for Hackman for a few years when he was the New York State Archivist, and the same energy and dedication ascribed to him at the Truman was evident in his other positions. Hackman was determined to transform the exhibitions and other programs into ones forcing individuals to reflect on their topics and their relevance to contemporary events. To achieve this, he had to set out on an ambitious fund-raising campaign, win support from the board, set a new mission and agenda, and rebuild or inspire the staff. As Hufbauer suggests, "from the outset, Hackman had a larger goal than merely remaking the Truman Library; he hoped to provide a model for the reinvention of the entire presidential library system."[30] He had tried to do this in New York state government, making that state archives a model for others, and he had also played this role in his years on the staff of the National Historical Publications and Records Commission. And to a certain extent, he achieved this at the Truman, turning its exhibitions into ones unique to the system in that visitors "emerge with an understanding not just of the positive achievements of Truman, but also of his troubled legacy. No other presidential library tries to give visitors such a deep understanding of the costs accompanying presidential choices."[31] Hufbauer discusses how the National Archives' generally decentralized approach to the presidential libraries allowed the Truman to experiment, provided it raised the funds to underwrite the changes, but he also laments how most of the libraries opt not to make such efforts; instead they are content to create a "Happy Meal version of presidential history."[32] And it is here that one of the tragedies of these institutions becomes obvious to the readers.

In the last chapter of *Presidential Temples*, the author analyzes some of the challenges facing the administrators and staffs of the libraries. Hufbauer mentions the obvious secrecy of the present presidential administration, while noting that "Franklin Roosevelt's ideas about how the archive in a presidential library should function were distressingly similar to those of George W. Bush."[33] With secrecy surrounding their archives, it is no wonder that they resort to mythology and spin doctoring to attract visitors. But the end of the book provides a sobering take on such issues. At a meeting with Larry Hackman, the one individual who comes across as a hero (and with good reason), Hufbauer relates how Hackman reacted to what he was hearing about presidential libraries. According to the author, Hackman leaned over and "almost in a whisper," stated, "I don't like it when people say 'Truman's Library,' or 'Reagan's Library.' It is The Truman Library or The Reagan Library. These institutions are not owned by these individuals or their families." And the author's reaction? The last line of the book reads — "Or at least they should not be."[34] But, as one learns, what is occurring with the presidential libraries is part of a larger problem with government secrecy.

Blacked Out

Years ago, I remember my former doctoral student and now colleague, David Wallace, giving a talk on the challenges posed by the classification of government records and the use of the Freedom of Information Act in opening such closed records. First, he showed the results of various efforts to get a particular record released, revealing how a variety of archivists examining the document had blacked out various parts of it; the efforts of many individuals seeking the document had resulted in a set of puzzle pieces that, with a little work, could almost provide a usable version of it. Second, Wallace displayed a record, released through a legitimate FOIA request, one that had been completely blacked out. What could be seen as a practical joke by the individual evaluating the document might also be seen as a less than humorous commentary on the state of government secrecy and an eroding sense of accountability of government to its citizens.

In a way, the problems with the roles of the presidential libraries may be little more than a symptom of government secrecy, a topic sketched out by Alasdair Roberts in a book on the topic. Roberts places more recent concerns with government secrecy in both a historical and international framework. He describes how by the end of the nineteenth century Western democracies had achieved a certain kind of transparency, while a concern with secrecy still existed. Led by the American Freedom of Information Act in 1996, an "oddity" on the international scene, by the 1990s Roberts believes that it seemed as if the "world was on the cusp of an unprecedented era of openness."[35] All this ended with the terrorist attacks on American soil on September 11, 2001, and some argue, according to Roberts, that a return to secrecy contributed to the events of 9/11. Roberts, with his wide-ranging grasp of international developments in regards to access to government records, considering developments in many countries, the changes after the end of the Cold War, and the efforts to create a more transparent global perspective on human rights, presents a compelling argument about the ramifications of government secrecy.

There is no question about how Roberts views government secrecy. Early in the book, he states, "Respect for the fundamental right to self-determination demands greater openness. Secrecy, by contrast, compels the public to defer to the judgment of a narrow elite."[36] And he is highly critical of trends in the United States and in other countries to reverse gains made in opening up government. In this nation, for example, after commenting on a series of acts starting in the 1970s to make government more visible, Roberts comments on controversies such as the leaking of news about the Abu Ghrarb torture case, Executive Order 13233 restricting access to presidential records, the tightening of declassification, and efforts by the Bush administration to curtail the investigation about the 9/11 terrorist attacks. Roberts points to some basic misunderstandings as the source for the debates about recent government secrecy, noting that the "Bush administration and its sharpest critics had one thing in common: a misapprehension about the reversibility of history. The Bush administration believed that it could roll the clock back to the pre-Watergate years, and so launched an assault on the many rules it believed had undercut the power of the presidency and, more broadly, the governability of the American system. The administration's critics accepted the premise that the clock could be rolled back — not only that, but also that it *had* been rolled back."[37] Reading this ought to cause critics of the presidential library system to rally and call for an end to it. This certainly provides a sense of what we might see, or not see, someday in the George W. Bush Library.

What Roberts has given us is not another screed about the attack on civil liberties or a hysterical defense of the need to institute stronger national security measures. Instead, *Blacked Out* provides a balanced analysis of the factors leading to increased government secrecy, some little more than changes in how information is exchanged and stored or government functions carried out. Roberts contends that we have witnessed a shift from the age of bureaucracy to an era of networks, and that this has brought increased threats to open government. For example, while he finds no evidence that open access laws lead to curtailing recordkeeping in government agencies, Roberts does discern some negative impact by technology on open government. He argues that "technology hashed a countervailing effect, by causing millions of undocumented conversations to be transformed into documents [such as the use of electronic mail rather than the telephone] — all at risk for public disclosure."[38] In other words, there are some legitimate reasons why governments are concerned about security, inappropriate leaks, and how to manage their functions related to critical issues like national security. Roberts also argues that some structural changes in how government operates have generated new problems with the notion of open government. He describes how the shift of much of government to private corporations has compromised the utility of disclosure laws: "As work left government departments — to go to contractors, privatized utilities and nonprofit organizations — the principle of access to government documents began to break down."[39] One wonders when we might see government archives and records management work outsourced and the chilling effects this could have on government openness and accountability.

This is a study with considerable references to and insights in the administration of government records and information. Some of Roberts's most important ideas come from his comparison with what is occurring in Western nations versus that of developing countries. He notes that in countries outside of the United States, often having parliamentary systems and more organized political parties, disclosure systems are developed that are "more highly centralized and politically attuned," resulting in greater resistance to opening records and information systems.[40] It is in this area that Roberts suggests some compelling insights into the issues affecting the administration of records and information systems. For example, he believes that disclosure laws "test the administrative capacities of developing countries." He contends that "even in affluent countries, good recordkeeping is a challenge. Preparing a documentary record of official activities, sorting and filing documents — all of this takes time and staff. As the public services of the advanced democracies have been cut back over the last decade, record keeping — often regarded as one of the ancillary functions of government — has deteriorated in many of these countries."[41] And Roberts correctly attributes some of the problems in assuring open government to the personal or human dimension: "Even in countries with long-established disclosure laws, making a request for information requires knowledge about the bureaucratic routine by which information requests are processed and about the legal provisions that should govern decisions on the release of information."[42] Sometimes, in our intense debates about government secrecy and accountability, Americans forget that other countries have greater, or lesser, problems.

Blacked Out provides an interesting assessment of government secrecy and, along the way, develops a set of principles and practices that can be used to develop an understanding of how to have more open government. In summing up, Roberts suggests that a "decent system of record keeping and a reasonably professional civil service are likely to be two prerequisites for an effective disclosure law. A third will be adequate resources for administering the law."[43] What one might wonder is just how the matter of open access to records as a form of democratic accountability meshes with the largely interpretative role of the presidential libraries. Somewhere in the convergence of these factors may reside the fate of democratic governance, and the future of an archival function in government.

Records in a Prison

It seems, however, that the archival mission and function are resilient (despite the preceding discussion), even in the midst of the most insidious totalitarian regime. It is rare that we find a commentary on the creation of archives (in this case created by Nelson Mandela and the South African government) that is as much about attacking individual and societal memory and identity. Those who have been reflecting on the nature of archives understand how such seemingly contradictory forces can operate because they understand that records are as much about power, force, evil, and good as about what we have generally assumed were little more than dull bureaucratic actions or conventional cultural activities. If presidential libraries celebrate rather than document and governments seek to close information, the recordkeeping created by the imprisonment of Nelson Mandela in his crusade against apartheid is testimony to the importance of even the most mundane documents for affirming human dignity and holding individuals and governments accountable.

Mandela, as the world knows, was incarcerated for twenty-seven years by the apartheid government of South Africa until he was released in 1990. The records related to his imprisonment, life, and political activities were scattered for a number of years after his release, until the Truth and Reconciliation Commission intervened in 1997 and 1998 and started gathering the documents. The Promotion of Access to Information Act of 2000 finally gave Mandela the necessary authority to have access to the government records documenting his crusade within this nation. The book, *A Prisoner in the Garden*, grew from an exhibition mounted at the South African National Archives in 2004 by the Nelson Mandela Center of Memory and Commemoration, but it is far from merely a record itself of an exhibition. The volume, heavily illustrated with photographs of the complex and diverse documentation, is a revealing insight into the nature of why records are often created, even for the most insidious of reasons. It gives an account of the archival documentation related to Mandela, details of the range of records, the wrenching tale of the recovery of two of Mandela's prison notebooks, and many texts of crucial records related to his imprisonment. What sounds, in a description like this, like a standard archival finding aid or exhibition catalog is far more than anything as commonplace or utilitarian, as the Center's mission is promoting the "idea of an archive for social justice."[44] While most presidential libraries promote the image and memory of a particular chief executive, this project focuses more on the individual's purpose or mission in a broader conception of recording and social justice.

As the authors of the text suggest, what is being described in this publication is not a normal archives, as they note that "whereas a conventional archive has a single location and a finite number of documents, the Mandela Archive is an infinite one, located in innumerable places." This is an archives "not confined to documents, but includes sites, landscapes, material objects, performances, photographs, artworks, stories and the memories of individuals."[45] The Mandela Archive stretches from his boyhood home to the police state imprisoning and documenting his every move. Although this is no traditional archival finding aid, *A Prisoner in the Garden* provides a list of archival documentation, from the personal to the official and the ephemeral, attesting to the difficult task of assembling a reasonable documentary record of Mandela's life and work: "Many records have been appropriated, some secreted away from their original holding places, others sold or lost; of these, numbers are slowly returning."[46] Some records are fugitive, some dormant (not found), some, like those related to his presidency, are in established archival repositories.

What is described in the exhibition and its accompanying book is a very different kind of archives project, one where the normal concerns about privacy and access are viewed somewhat differently. The authors admit that they are recounting the efforts towards opening a new archive, but that it is one that must "take into account the legacy of the security establishment and its surveillance program, which intruded into the private worlds of activists like Mandela, subjecting their most intimate emotions and actions to invasive scrutiny." In this sense, this is a project much like that encountered by those opening the records related to Holocaust victims or those spied on by the Stasi in East Germany, or, the kind of efforts to circumvent government secrecy as described by Roberts in so many different parts of the world. The authors admit that some records remain closed off from public access, done in the "knowledge that every such act is not simply a gesture of sensitivity, but also an act of power, albeit a retrieval of power for those once so actively disempowered." And, it is here that the theme of the book emerges, as the very next sentence reads, "No archival act, it seems, is ever innocent of power."[47]

As part of this power, the control of documents is seen as reversing "acts of confinement and to make visible those the system rendered invisible." In other words, we are being asked to re-evaluate how we normally approach archival records, as staid, stable, and neutral artifacts of a past that can be fully recovered and put to rest. Those assembling *A Prisoner in the Garden* argue, "Just as the documents of the prison authorities testify to the effort they put into maintaining a rigidly disciplined and coercive system, so too the documents of the prisoners themselves are testimony to how they challenged that power."[48] And the power associated with the records radiate throughout the beautifully illustrated and designed book. This may be a book about archives that reaches a far larger audience than normally would read anything about seemingly dusty and dry old records. They will be pulled in by Mandela's smiling face on the cover, the intriguing title (a caption from a famous photograph of Mandela working in the prison garden), and then the documents lavishly appearing everywhere as they flip through the book. This book pulls the browser in. Hopefully, they will plow into the text and come away with a more fundamental awareness of what archives are about, although it may be a different one than many archivists might wish them to hold.

One of the most astounding aspects of the book is the closeness in detail it provides for describing how archives flourish, at least in the raw accumulation of documentation, in oppressive governments and societies in stress. Emerging from the book is the clear notion that those in power over Mandela, seeking to limit his influence and to eradicate any evidence of his role in South African society, actually created an amazing documentary record, one greater than would be expected for any individual living and working under normal conditions. In considering the prison authorities, the book's authors suggest that these authorities "carefully recorded, duplicated and filed every piece of paper relating to Mandela. These included results of medical tests, correspondence with family and friends, formal complaints against prison conditions and early negotiations with his captors. The prison files reveal the extent of the web of surveillance that existed in apartheid South Africa, the depth of paranoia around Mandela and, most strikingly, the power that this Robben Island prisoner wielded in spite of his status as an inmate."[49] The South African apartheid government captured "Mandela's every word and every move," producing an "extraordinarily rich record of his years in captivity." What we get, then, is an extremely moving story of Mandela's life, as well as a remarkable testament to what records, and archives, can do for us. As the writers note, "This record affords us a unique insight into the psychological, social and political world of his incarceration — his relationships with the warders, with his fellow prisoners, with his own internal world as with the world outside. It is not just a record of his imprisonment, but also that of the birth of democracy in South Africa."[50]

Nestled within the larger archives story are extremely poignant, human-interest vignettes that indicate something of both the remarkable man that is Mandela and the potential power of even the most seemingly normal documents. The prominent example of this is the recounting of the story of the return of two notebooks by a former guard. *A Prisoner in the Garden* describes the intertwined and complicated lives of the guard and the prisoner, as well as the circuitous history of the notebooks and their reuniting with Mandela at a public event. "The story of the notebooks draws attention to the role of the Center in calling out of the texts of the archives from the many unknown places where they have been lodged over the years."[51] It is the story of the opposite side of government secrecy, suggesting the power of records for opening government and making it more accessible to the people it serves. It is not about building temples, but it reflects an awareness of the good that opening records can do for healing a troubled society.

What emerges from this book is a candid and compelling argument about how a person's archives and their own body are indelibly connected. Mandela wears on his face a kind of record, as well as being highly respectful of the power and significance of archival documentation for societal memory. We read this in the book: "The world was astonished by the difference in appearance between the man who had entered prison and the man who emerged. The archive of the prison experience was inscribed in his person, etched on his body, profoundly shaping his consciousness and embedded in his unconscious. . . ."[52] When you finish the book you also have experienced the prison and the efforts to create, hide, peruse, and preserve the documents of this experience.

Conclusion

What we are dealing with in this chapter are two conflicting matters. First, there is the seismic shift in access to government information and records, moving our society to an unprecedented secret government. Second, there are the ethical and professional values of archivists and records managers, values that have tended to lead them to being advocates for broad, open access to records and the evidence they contain. Obviously, these are on a collision course, or, at least one would think that was the case.

Professional values are being eroded, everywhere, when it comes to matters like ethical standards and open access. Media specialist David Allen concludes that corporations have altered the culture of democracy by changing how we evaluate public life. Corporations, he notes, stress "efficiency, maximizing profits, scientific reasoning, and winning as opposed to understanding." Allen notes that professions and corporations likewise share many values, notably efficiency, expertise, and profitability, leading to where professionalism has become a barrier between the public and both the press and government.[53]

The same problem seems to have occurred in the matter of government archives work. The aforementioned NARA reclassification case (described in greater detail in chapter six) quickly moved the American National Archives from being a window into a besieged archival repository to appearing to be a co-conspirator in an effort to close down previously open government records. The revelations that National Archives leadership had signed a secret memorandum of understanding to deceive purposively the public and researchers seem astounding and something out of an Orwellian nightmare. Additional news that neither the incumbent Archivist of the United States or his predecessor knew anything of the agreement or the reclassification program paints a decidedly more awful picture of the leading American archival program having no one in charge. What is worse is that few archivists or other records professionals spoke out, and many who did seemed to express support for the wrong aspects of the case. What emerged was a picture of archivists as meek civil servants, willing to be ordered to do most anything with the records in their charge. It is why we have presidential libraries, government secrecy, and archival gulags.

Chapter Five

Secrecy, Archives, and the Archivist

Introduction

The issue of government secrecy is not a new concern for archivists. Nearly four decades ago, historian Howard Zinn broached this topic at the height of the controversy about the Vietnam War, cautioning archivists that they could not merely ignore the social and political consequences of their work or how aspects of recordkeeping reflect power and control. Zinn, in his customary frank fashion, made two recommendations for archivists, "that they engage in a campaign to open all government documents to the public" and "that they take the trouble to compile a whole new world of documentary material, about the lives, desires, needs, of ordinary people."[1] That was a long time ago, and a lot has changed. At the time Zinn wrote this assessment, government archivists were more agitated about the replevin of stray government archives in private citizens' or dealers' hands. [2] But even in discussions of replevin, there emerged affirmations of the public's ownership of public records, such as when Julian Boyd concluded his analysis of the efforts by the Federal Government to reclaim the journals of William Clark (of Lewis and Clark explorer fame) discovered in an attic in 1953 by reaffirming the public ownership of government records.[3] The issue of government secrecy is now, it seems, a greater concern than ever, and the role or responsibility of archivists as muddled as ever.

Fast-forward three decades to the Society of American Archivists Presidential Address of Tim Ericson, and we see how the matter of government secrecy has become more critical in American archival issues.[4] Ericson carefully documented the growing secrecy and, then, asked where were the archivists and what were they thinking? Ericson argued strenuously that archivists needed to educate themselves about this issue, pushing the SAA to join with other professional associations and allies (such as the American Civil Liberties Union, National Security Archive, and OMB Watch) to become a more effective watch dog in what the Federal Government was doing with its information and the degree of access it was allowing the public and researchers. Ericson's address, as it turns out, is not the first to make such a call from within the archival community for cooperative advocacy on behalf of truly open and accountable government, but it is unique in that it came at a time when the Federal Government seemed to be becoming more closed and less accountable to its citizenry and researchers.

This essay considers five recent books on aspects of government secrecy in the United States, written by external observers and critics of American government and from within the ranks of archivists. Political scientists Robert M. Pallitto and William G. Weaver have co-authored a research study on presidential secrecy and its legalities and illegalities.[5] Investigative reporter Ted Gup has sounded the alarm to the public about the increasing toll secrecy in government operations is having on the country.[6] Lawyer and public policy expert Alasdair Roberts has written an analysis of the U.S government's response to the 9/11 events, much of it focusing on issues of government accountability and access.[7] And archivist Bruce Montgomery gives us a succinct, powerful analysis of the "Bush-Cheney" administration and the demise of open government in two books with ample commentary on the implications of government secrecy for archival work and archivists' mission.[8] This is just a sampling of the growing number of books being published on the issue of government secrecy with implications for archives and records management, but considered together they include some compelling lessons and warnings for archivists, both in and out of government.

Shifting Interests in Government Archives

Along the way, archivists have heard from a growing number of voices about the persistent challenge of government (and other forms of) secrecy. Athan Theoharis, in the early 1980s, described both the "unparalleled insights into the activities of American dissidents"[9] offered by the FBI investigative case files, and the challenges posed by the FBI's efforts to create and conceal shadow recordkeeping systems, the possible destruction of many of these records, and the cumbersome difficulties posed by FOIA procedures. These problems not only weakened the possibility of certain kinds of historical research but undermined government accountability. Historian Joan Hoff-Wilson warned that professional associations, including those representing archivists, needed to develop codes of professional conduct that go beyond moral platitudes and dealt with legal issues concerning the increasing tendency of government and other records creators to hide their archival resources.[10] Sigmund Diamond described his long career of using the Freedom of Information Act to get access to public records and his checkered success in getting private institutions to open up records, concluding that "archivists, as custodians of the records of our times, have an ethical obligation to support the most possible public access to public records."[11]

Archivists also began to probe the nature of access to government records. Some prepared historical studies providing part of the background for current government records laws.[12] Other archivists, involved in acquiring the personal papers of elected federal officials (sometimes embroiled in scandal or controversy), sought to develop approaches that would enable them to secure the papers, even if risking negative publicity.[13] Elena Danielson, in an essay describing controversial cases about access to personal papers and government records, acknowledges that "Providing fair access to archives may appear to be a fundamentally simple operation, until one examines specific cases."[14]

The growing challenges of administering government records, on all levels of government, began to generate a number of case studies about the difficulties of providing access. From within the National Archives emerged balanced accounts of trying to deal effectively with federal records and information systems that had become complex, partly due to their connection with spying on American citizens, notably the FBI field case files.[15] The issue of how best to manage and preserve presidential papers, as records owned by the government for its citizens, continued to stimulate a number of investigations, including some testy explorations into matters concerning the National Archives and its relationship to the Executive Office.[16] Examinations of the efforts to repatriate official government records or to straighten out the control of archival materials of former colonial powers also provide interesting insights into access issues to these records and our notion of archival principles.[17] The Mississippi State Sovereignty Commission, a state agency existing from 1956 to 1973 and charged with keeping surveillance on individuals suspected of being involved in the civil rights movement, created difficult problems of access versus personal privacy for the state archives.[18] This American state government agency had eerie similarities to the circumstances surrounding the East German Stasi (secret police) files, presenting similar challenges to balancing personal privacy with concerns of state history and accountability.

Eleanor S. Danielson, in considering the latter records, argues that archivists must fight for the preservation and access to such records.[19] And, indeed, a number of other case studies confirmed such challenges, notably in former parts of the USSR.[20]

American archivists also began to document cases where federal agencies sought to interfere with access to papers and other records held in non-government repositories. Harold Miller documents the case where the FBI subpoenaed and got access to the papers of Carl and Anne Braden in a suit the FBI was involved in, even though Anne Braden, one of the donors, objected to such use. Miller lamented the precedent that might discourage potential donors from giving their personal papers and worried that the Society of American Archivists declined to become involved in support of the repository.[21] There were also case studies about the control of and access to federal records, such as the Lawrence Berkeley Laboratory, held at universities.[22] Undoubtedly, we will see more case studies in the future, and, it is a good thing given the complexities of such access matters.

Government secrecy and the manipulation of records by government officials have moved such matters to the forefront of archival concerns. Michael Isikoff recounts, in October 2007, the difficulties Sally Bedell Smith had in researching her book about Hillary Clinton at the William J. Clinton Presidential Library, reporting that very little of the materials held at this library have been opened. Isikoff indicates that *Newsweek* obtained through FOIA documents revealing that "Clinton has given the [National] Archives private instructions to tightly control the disclosure of chunks of his archive.'"[23]

Government secrecy is not a new issue (although it is one that has probably been exaggerated by greater media scrutiny in our digital era). Cornelia Vismann, in her study of the concept of files in Western culture, documents how by the mid-seventeenth century, "language had become a sanctuary for political action. Words are more easily ordered than territories, and they are more obedient than mercenaries."[24] As government grew in scope and produced more records, the need to manage and sometimes control access to these documents also changed. There was, for example, a Prussian edict of 1776 stating that affairs can only be made public from the archives when they have "no adverse effect on state and government."[25] From this point on, we have the classic tension between government officials and the public, namely the transparency of government including records and archives. As Vismann summarizes this classic battle, "The state compiles records, society demands their disclosure."[26] As democratic regimes evolved, such tensions were more evident as public debate about government secrecy became a source for both political intrigue and debates about the nature and purpose of the state in society. Indeed, this was one of the grievances against the king leveled by the American patriots in their Declaration of Independence and institutionalized in their Constitution a decade later.

New Scrutiny on Government Secrecy: Who Is the Most Secret of All?

It is easy to misread the efforts of the current president (George W. Bush when I was originally writing this essay) regarding secrecy and national security as being unique to him, partly because he is so aggressive in arguing for the need for it for waging a war on terror. Robert M. Pallitto and William G. Weaver demonstrate that there is a long history predating what "W," Cheney, Ashcroft, Gonzales, and Rove have been doing in keeping their activities behind closed doors. Pallitto and Weaver, political scientists, firmly document that the Bush administration is the most secret of the presidencies, but they also document that no one in this administration invented the idea. What they show is that after 9/11 opportunities appeared to create a presidency that is "inconsistent with constitutional provisions and the functioning of our democracy."[27] Or, seen from another angle, "The second war with Iraq is arguably the only combat action in United States history justified solely on information unavailable to the public and Congress."[28] Things have gotten so out of hand with presidential secrecy that the authors report that when they sought out policy documents governing the definition and application of the notion of state secrets that they could locate no one who knew of such policies. What such issues mean for archivists working for government agencies or for archivists campaigning for the acquisition and opening of government records and information systems is debatable.

The point of this study is to investigate the judiciary's role in presidential secrecy, concluding that while congressional oversight has been weak, the judiciary has opted to ignore or defer to the president when the president claims the right of secrecy or increased national security. The courts have usually sided with the executive office when it has embarked on new wiretapping adventures, looked the other way when the president has taken steps that are contrary to both "political accountability and legal scrutiny,"[29] not been concerned when the Freedom of Information Act has been skirted, records over-classified, executive orders issued hiding more and more information, and national security — a "notoriously vague term"[30] — invoked repeatedly. Pallito and Weaver conclude that while there are legitimate reasons for reacting to "crisis conditions" involving restrictions on civil liberties, this is very different from a "jurisprudence forged in secret, permanently unavailable to congressional oversight, and for practical purposes not subject even to Supreme Court review." That the latter has occurred, Pallito and Weaver describe as "astounding."[31]

There is a lot in this study relating to the work of archivists and records managers, and this is particularly important since government records professionals and the National Archives have been central to the development of this professional community over the past century. In the book there is a particularly compelling chapter, "The Classified President," reviewing the evolving nature of the classification of records and secrecy challenges. Considered with the legacy of the Iran-Contra email case, E.O. 13233 and its additional restricting of presidential records, the increasing power of the attorney general's office, the ramifications of the Patriot Act, and the extraordinary instances of "signing statements" by the president when enacting new legislation, this book is a depressing read for any archivist committed to open access to records and democratic accountability. There is special reason to be concerned for the archivist's role and mission. The Information Security Oversight Office (ISOO), frequently cited by people in the profession about the recent NARA reclassification scandal as a hopeful sign that the National Archives will be more vigilant about such matters in the future, is also described as being "understaffed and overcommitted" and as having no real authority.[32] Such statements reveal how some others outside of the archival community tend to see this government archives.

It Ain't Just Government

At roughly the same time of Pallito and Weaver's study there also appeared investigative reporter Ted Gup's book, *Nation of Secrets: The Threat to Democracy and the American Way of Life*. Gup commences his book by tracking all the news stories appearing in one day related to secrecy in government, corporations, universities, in the media, and even cultural organizations — building a case for how pervasive secrecy has become in our society. Gup seeks to reveal the causes and consequences of such secrecy in American life, and the result is a most depressing read. While it is easy to just toss the Gup book into the growing stack of books decrying growing secrecy (and the loss of personal privacy), this reporter's book is well researched and focused on topics of interest to records professionals.

Secrecy is portrayed as a toxin, contaminating other aspects of society and counteracting even good laws and policies. As Pallito and Weaver hone in on the judiciary's role in the development of secret government, Gup ranges over other institutions, including the courts. The books complement each other, both with many insights in and comments about records and archives, providing historical perspective and analysis of contemporary events. Both conclude that secrecy in government, or any organization, is not new to American culture, while suggesting that the half-decade since 9/11 has given rise to a secrecy far more extensive and deep-grained than at any other time in our history. Gup notes that in the events since 9/11, the "only thing that has been rationed in this strange undeclared war is information,"[33] with government ringing up huge costs to maintain its clandestine activities (far higher than the financial costs associated with essential archiving tasks and responsibilities).

Gup also examines the increase in the quantities of classified records and information, the weakening of FOIA, the growth of executive authority in the Federal Government, the weakening of judicial review, the president's excessive use of signing statements in the enacting of new laws, wiretapping of private citizens, the establishment of secret prison camps, and the hyperbole about the potential of our enemies possessing weapons of mass destruction. By now, the story is a familiar one. The result of all these kinds of activities is, according to Gup, the marginalization of both citizens and consumers. Secrecy has made the information society the surveillance society or the security age. Gup reinforces his arguments with a series of brief case studies humanizing the impact of secrecy on individuals just like us, demonstrating how secrecy has become a bureaucratic tool for building status, securing power and authority, and protecting government officials. How should archivists work in this surveillance or secrecy era? Can they achieve the kind of balance so many have argued for in the past or must they take clearer sides with those arguing for an open society?

Nation of Secrets has a number of archival twists. Gup considers how in the past there has been the idea that somehow history (the future) would ultimately judge and hold accountable political and other leaders in our time through eventual access to their records, with a caveat that "even history is being purged. Dusty old records are being removed from the U.S. Archives and presidential libraries. Other records are being withheld or simply disappearing. The corrective head of history with its distant day of reckoning is itself now manacled by secrecy."[34] Clearly, archivists and records managers now face new challenges, although one must consider just what the role of these records professionals has been in contributing to this purge.

Gup makes a number of references to archivists and their activities. He considers the NARA reclassification program. Gup examines some of the more irrational instances of government secrecy, often involving the closure of much older records with questionable importance. He travels to the Library of Congress Manuscripts Department and requests a list of everything not allowed to be seen, discovering that there are 104 personal collections with national security restrictions. Gup also recounts how Harvard University has placed lengthy restrictions on its official records, with a number of troubling comments about that institution's secrecy and the role of archivists, making the point that the culture of secrecy is now so pervasive that even those who are on the frontlines of preserving and making accessible historical records seem negatively affected by this culture.[35] Gup makes archivists reflect what their role might be in contributing to secrecy or why he or she ought to re-examine personal perspectives or professional practices.

Maybe It Depends On Your Perspective

The recent books by Roberts and Montgomery provide very different interpretations of what has been going on in the George W. Bush Whitehouse since the events of September 11, 2001. Roberts focuses on a crisis of authority, while Montgomery stresses a deliberate agenda of secrecy and an erosion of accountability. Both books offer food for thought for records professionals, with Montgomery, the archivist, not surprisingly offering more about records and information management issues.

Reading Roberts' *The Collapse of Fortress Bush* requires some understanding of Roberts' notion of government, and how it can or ought to operate openly (and this necessitates the reading of his earlier comparative study of government secrecy). In his earlier book, Roberts tracks the evolving transparency of Western democracies where it seemed that the "world was on the cusp of an unprecedented era of openness" (see chapter four for additional discussion about this book).[36] This new transparency is tied to the remarkable advances in information technology and a new global society, and Roberts sees the Bush administration's efforts to be less open as the result of "executive anxiety about the capacity to govern effectively in this new environment."[37] Advocating transparency, Roberts presents a balanced view of the difficulties involved in governing in an open environment. While reviewing all the efforts by the Bush administration to regain control over government information and records and the media, and other criticism these efforts generated (and comparing this to other nations such as Australia, Canada. and the United Kingdom),

Roberts concludes that keeping good records, maintaining practical information systems, and enabling access to the evidence and information in these systems all constitute a major challenge for modern government. He argues that the United States, even with all of the public hues and cries about increasing government secrecy, has "perhaps the most comprehensive set of transparency rules in the world, a vigorous and free media, and an educated and enfranchised population."[38] In other words, Roberts hedges his bets, seeing needs for government to operate in secret with a varying set of effective counterbalances to excessive secrecy. This may be reassuring for some archivists who probably weary of the criticisms about excessive secrecy in American government and the warnings about their role in such secrecy.

Roberts continues the story in his newer book, focusing on government authority, specifically why the government reacted to 9/11 as it did. Considering the scale of its expenditures on defense, Roberts still contends that the "9/11 crisis was notable for the extent to which it did *not* repeat many earlier excesses — such as treason and sedition trials, denaturalization proceedings, internments, blacklists, and programs to disrupt domestic protest movements."[39] He sees the Bush administration as exercising constraint while wrestling with its military capabilities, reflecting a "peculiar system of governance: in one sense deliberately crippled, to protect political and economic freedoms; in another, overmuscled, as a result of a prolonged contest between superpowers."[40] Roberts is painting a portrait of an American tragedy, arguing that the Bush administration lacked coherent and legitimate policies in nearly every area. Certainly there is nothing we can describe as an archives or records policy.

Although we have read countless screeds about the Bush administration's disregard for truth, openness, and the American citizenry, Roberts depicts an administration twisted in its own rhetoric. The Bush administration "did not plan" and it could not get various federal agencies to work together effectively.[41] He likens the Bush story to a "moral tale about the difficulties of asserting control within contemporary U.S. government."[42] Embedded deep in this moral tale was how records and information were administered. Roberts indicates that one of the factors in the 9/11 crisis was the tendency by the government to overuse the classification of information for blatantly political ends. However, there is another important part of the story involving information technology: "The revolution in information and communications technology has undercut presidential authority as well. Digitization has made it easier to leak information, increased the volume of incriminating information (such as email) that is available for leaking and increased the impact of leaks by allowing the instantaneous dissemination of leaked information."[43] This is another way of depicting the major change in how people and government create, store, and access information, and it begs the question of how this might transform archival agencies in the digital era.

Bruce Montgomery: Government Secrecy from Inside the Profession

Bruce Montgomery is an experienced archivist who has been writing about government recordkeeping and accountability, human rights and ethical issues, and other matters for many years. One of his most notable, earlier writings on presidential records was his 1993 essay on the twenty-year legal battle over the Nixon White House papers and tapes, providing excellent detail about the nuances of that case and the lack of archival leadership in promoting that presidential papers were public property, for him the most critical archival issue in a republic.[44] Such a perspective, about the imperative for open government and flexible access to most archival materials, also comes across in his writings about Amnesty International and those of other human rights groups.[45]

In *Subverting Open Government*, Montgomery brings together a group of essays on Nixon's battles to control his presidential materials, Henry Kissinger's struggles to restrict access to telephone transcripts created while National Security Advisor, challenges to the Presidential Records Act of 1978 (whereby presidential records were declared to be public records), and the strenuous activity by Vice President Dick Cheney to keep the documentation related to his Energy Task Force inaccessible to the media, public, and Congress. All of these cases are examples of challenges to open government, and, as Montgomery writes, "The open records laws, which were designed to act as a bulwark against excessive secrecy, have served the American public enormously well."[46] Given the topics Montgomery has chosen, it is also logical for us to wonder what role archivists should play in defending and implementing such laws.

The core part of Montgomery's first book is Nixon's legal wars to lay claim to the presidential papers he lost after his resignation and the passing of the Presidential Recordings and Materials Preservation Act in 1974. If archivists declare FDR to be a great friend for his establishment of presidential libraries, then they also should think more kindly of Richard M. Nixon with his creation of the most documented presidential administration to that point. Montgomery is careful to state that much of what Nixon, his lawyers, and his heirs argued for in controlling his presidential papers was no different than what tradition had allowed earlier presidents to do. This translates into a tremendous battle about executive privilege, and Montgomery helps the reader navigate through the various court battles, legislative acts, executive orders, and policies. The Presidential Records Act, enacted in 1978, declaring that all presidential papers after 1981 would be public property, was intended to end the problems associated with the administration, preservation, and access to these records.

In the other cases Montgomery examines, the persistent theme is the diminution of control for the public good of the papers of former presidents and their aides. The Kissinger case, also marked by legal wrangling, highlights how appointed officials could operate in secretive fashion and continue to maintain that secrecy by the control of their papers (Kissinger's papers reside in the Library of Congress, wrapped up in restrictions and the personal oversight of Kissinger, although most of the telephone transcripts were released in 2004). Montgomery's assessment of the continuous challenges to the Presidential Records Act — the PROFS case, the Bush-Wilson agreement giving George H. Bush power to review requests for his materials, George W. Bush's Executive Order 13233 giving the incumbent president the authority to stop the opening of his predecessor's records — reveals a depressing legacy of the power of law to manage presidential materials. We get a glimmering of the archival mission, making what Montgomery has to tell us a kind of Shakespearean archival tragedy.

Being an archivist, Montgomery is sensitive to the National Archives's role in these cases. Concerning Nixon and his lawsuits, Montgomery writes that Nixon's efforts to control his papers and legacy meant "he would have to wage an unrelenting guerilla war against the Archives and its employees working to make his presidential tapes and records public."[47] Montgomery chronicles the intense political pressure placed on the National Archives, the public criticism the Archives received for being too timid in its efforts to work with these records, the "complicity of top Archives officials on behalf of Nixon," and the acquiescence of Archives officials to Nixon's demands that "set a troubling precedent" for future work with presidential materials.[48] These and other problems suggest the limitations of the presidential libraries system and the lack of authority and ability of the National Archives to play an effective role in the administration of presidential records.

Montgomery has continued writing about presidential records and government information over the years, and he has pulled these into another powerful essay, *The Bush-Cheney Administration's Assault on Open Government*. Montgomery pulls no punches in his assessment of what has been happening in presidential affairs in the twenty-first century, stating that this "administration has launched the most aggressive campaign in modern times to expand executive authority at the expense of the nation's key open government and accountability laws."[49] He considers, in succession, the Freedom of Information Act, the Presidential Records Act, the work of the General Accountability Office, the Federal Advisory Committee Act, and the Federal Intelligence Surveillance Act. As one might expect with Montgomery's professional experience, he provides considerable attention to issues of recordkeeping and information management.

In nearly every law or policy Montgomery considers, he includes references to the impact or implications for the administration of government and presidential records. He alludes to George W. Bush sending his Texas gubernatorial records to his father's presidential library in order to keep them closed. There are multiple references to Vice President Dick Cheney's efforts to keep the Energy Task Force records secret and Executive Order 13233 restricting the opening of a former president's records without the approval of the incumbent. Executive Order 13292, issued on March 25, 2003, gave Cheney the unprecedented authority to classify intelligence, part of an evolving effort to make the Vice President's office a co-equal partner with that of the presidency, all part of the Bush administration's commitment to curtailing a "decades-long erosion of presidential authority."[50] At times, Montgomery admits the motive in the various Bush administrations might be unclear (is it in the interests of national security, protecting business allies, or expanding the executive office?), but nearly always these efforts led to more secrecy. What expense this has for the archival community is not an issue Montgomery considers here, but given the generally low level roles of the National Archives and archival leadership in dealing with such issues, it is reasonable to guess that this has not been a positive influence for the authority and public image of archives.

Montgomery sees the 1977 Supreme Court ruling about Nixon's claims to his presidential materials as a pivotal case in the battles about presidential privilege and secrecy. He notes, for example, that "it is perhaps one of the great ironies surrounding the troubled history of the [Presidential Records] act that Nixon, whose extreme claims of privilege failed to win back his presidential materials, became the model for later presidential attempts to undercut the law."[51] In other words, thirty years later the battles about presidential records continue, unabated and more muddled than ever. Is this merely a sign of how complicated the work will be for future archivists in our nation? It is in his chapter on the PRA that Montgomery reveals some of the abiding weaknesses of the archival approaches to managing presidential papers. Why the archival community has stood by the presidential library system is complicated, perhaps better explained historically with the system itself.[52]

For Montgomery, Executive Order 13233 seals the fate of presidential libraries, creating a dynastic rule over presidential papers.[53] Even with the archival community and the media speaking out about such decrees, they stay in effect and embolden the next presidential administration. Indeed, in Montgomery's analysis of other key laws regarding information access and secrecy, he recounts efforts to weaken oversight, resist turning over documents when requested, holding secret meetings, engaging in secret wiretapping when it suits the administration's purpose, detaining citizens and others whenever to defend national security, and losing critical e-mails without recrimination. Admittedly, many of these incidents are destined to become court cases extending far beyond the end of the Bush administration, with consequences yet to be seen for our nation or its documentary heritage. However, there is little good expected for the archival community and its mission, especially as many working archivists contend with challenges, from technology issues to intellectual property quagmires, in their own repositories.

One finds considerable overlap between Montgomery's two volumes (he is working on another book on Cheney and the vice-presidency), but the second book is the extended conclusion to his first one. I always thought that his 2006 book needed a conclusion for one coherent argument about the failure of the Presidential Records Act. I believe that conclusion is found in his second book, and both ought to be read together.

It's Hard to Hide

Archivists would never suggest that contending with the challenges of managing public records and archives in a society where government is growing more secretive is an easy task or a responsibility they relish. What makes it particularly difficult is that the media is keen to focus on this problem and many investigative reporters and public scholars find this a salable topic. There are some benefits, however, as the opportunity for greater public exposure to the work of archivists and other records professionals improves. Kate Doyle's story about the Guatemalan National Police Files in *Harper's* is one of those rare media occasions.[54] Doyle, a member of the National Security Archives (NSA) staff, recounts the subsequent events of the discovery in May 2005 in Guatemala City of the Guatemalan National Police archives, documenting the police's role in the 36-year civil war ending in 1996. Doyle's essay is a stark reminder of the social and political importance of government records.

Doyle makes very clear the importance of such records to society, for both "human-rights investigators" and the "rest of society."[55] The discovery of these records is a chilling reminder of what repressive regimes do in secret and a reaffirmation of the importance of opening such records to society, made possible with funding assistance from Germany, Holland, Switzerland, and Spain, the work of NSA advisors, and consulting from experienced archivist Trudy Peterson, whose work Doyle effuses over, especially her rebuilding the files in order to see how the government covered their crimes. Experienced archivists will understand readily what Peterson was doing, applying traditional archival principles to what had become a vast puzzle of documents. For the public reading this article, however, this is a clear view into what archivists do as well as why such records are so important to preserve and administer.

A prominent theme of this essay is why such revealing records survive, when it seems logical that their creators would seek to destroy them in order to cover their track. As Doyle surmises, those involved in states doing evil things "believe that their institutions will survive forever," creating a "massive paper trail, which cannot be disappeared overnight."[56] Some supporting the current presidential libraries system have invoked the same notion, fearful that strict laws will lead to less documentation. When we examine the cases of repressive regimes or even instances where our own government has sought to act in secret beyond the law, tradition, or commonsense, we still generally find that the records survive the legal, political, and personality battles. Doyle reaffirms the importance of archives, as an entity that "does more than simply confirm his [the citizen] status as victim; it preserves and restores his history."[57] This is an affirmation of what any "archive" means to us. The archive sustains us, provides meaning, and gives us a place in posterity. It can't be secret for this to happen. If it is secret, then the role of the archivist is to recover it and bring it back into the open.

Conclusion: Lessons Learned, Lessons Forgotten, Lessons Learned Again

Archivists have long espoused the notion that government records in democratic regimes should be open and accessible, although their track record in working for and speaking up about such matters has been spotty. John Dirks, in a recent essay, provided this cautionary note: "Archivists must walk a fine line in facilitating the trust of today's governments and organizations so a meaningful record will be created and preserved, while simultaneously ensuring that those records are eventually open to scrutiny, to the arena of history and memory. The task is not easy and requires commitment, professionalism, and resolve."[58]

This gets more complicated when we step outside of the Western paradigm of archives and recordkeeping, just as Anne Gilliland and her colleagues have observed about working with Pacific Rim communities.[59] Archivists acting as advocates for open government and thus open records and information systems might be outside this paradigm. There is an increasing number of international conferences dealing with political implications for government and other archives, with some making substantial contributions to the professional literature.[60]

When we re-read what archivists have had to say about presidential records, federal records classification, national security, and secrecy, we are reminded that we have been wrestling with these and other related issues for a long time and that their resolution still seems elusive. More than thirty years ago, Frank Cook examined the question of the ownership of public officials' personal papers, and in the case of presidential papers, concluded that there has always been a tension between closure and access, with legitimate claims on both sides, while noting that using the "mantle of 'national security' [to hide government activities] must be resisted. Democratic government requires that everyone — citizen and official — respect the delicate balance between premature disclosure and unjustified restriction."[61]

Cook was writing in the midst of the crisis about the ownership and control of the Nixon presidential materials, a topic Montgomery uses as a benchmark in his work. Cook's reactions to such issues reflect the ambivalence of archivists in these matters. He stresses, quite strongly, that archivists have to travel a middle road between researchers and public officials, although he is reluctant to criticize the means by which archivists have sought to manage such records, contending that the "presidential library system is a glorious achievement of the archival profession."[62] Cook could not foresee the tremendous shifts, stresses, and strains in dealing with presidential papers, with increasing discussions about the weaknesses of a system not created by archivists but forced upon them by a president desiring to control his legacy.

A quartet of final observations seems appropriate. First, archivists need to join in the battle over secrecy and accountability in ways they never imagined before. Second, we honestly do not know how history will judge any presidential administration's actions, but it is reasonably certain that archivists need to become more public in their efforts to ensure that government records, on all levels, will be safe, secure, and accessible. Third, there are no good or bad guys in the past decade of challenges to open government; the longer historical view suggests that the temptations to operate in secret are strong and, without exception around the world, human nature seems to be to work behind closed doors. And, fourth, archivists need to bind with others, just as Tim Ericson suggested five years ago, to work to keep government archives open and government accountable. For this to happen, we need a stronger National Archives and to work as closely with the National Security Archive as we can; the two ought not to represent polar extremes but, instead, to be united, with all archivists working for greater openness of government records and information.

Chapter Six

The National Archives Reclassification Scandal

Introduction: A Controversy Erupts

On April 11, 2006, the public learned that the leadership of the National Archives and Records Administration had signed a few years before (March 2002) a secret agreement (later it turned out to be two) with federal intelligence agencies (including the Air Force and CIA) to remove previously declassified records from the shelves of the National Archives.[1] The agreement came to light as the result of a Freedom of Information Act request made by the National Security Archive, an independent watchdog group located at George Washington University. News about the reclassification program, dating back to 1999 as initially reported (actually to 1995 as later learned), had emerged some weeks before, but these revelations were more chilling, at least for those in the records professions.

What was disturbing, at first, was the role of the National Archives in this agreement. It had been signed by Deputy Archivist Michael Kurtz, and the agreement included language seeking to wrap the program in secrecy as long as possible. NARA agreed that "it is in the interests of both [excised] and [itself] to avoid the attention and researcher complaints that may arise from removing material that has already been publicly available." NARA also agreed that the documentation of the removal of the records would hide the reclassification program and "any reason for the withholding of documents." The agreement also stated that NARA would keep the identities of the individuals working on the reclassification secret, including restricting knowledge of the program to NARA staff "who do not have a validated need-to-know." The National Archives revealed the existence of the agreement at a March 14, 2006 House Government Reform subcommittee hearing, where Archivist Allen Weinstein only indicated that the document was "classified." National Security Archive executive director Thomas Blanton, on the release of the memorandum, stated that "This secret agreement reveals nothing less than a covert operation to white-out the nation's history, aided and abetted by the National Archives,"[2] a tragic assessment for both the National Archives and the records community often looking to this institution for leadership. While most archivists decry the increasing secrecy of our Federal Government as antithetical to the archival mission, now archivists learned that their leading program was part of this problem.

The media, not unexpectedly, picked up on the story right away. Associated Press reporters faithfully followed the National Security Archive press release, repeating the details of the secret agreement and providing some comments by Archivist Weinstein about his efforts to investigate the circumstances of the agreement and to ensure everyone that this would not happen again. Weinstein was quoted as saying that "It is an important first step in finding the balance between continuing to protect national security and protecting the right to know by the American public." The AP story also provided comments from others about the incongruity of such an operation occurring at the National Archives. Steven Aftergood, director of the Federation of American Scientists' project monitoring government secrecy, was quoted, "It's baffling. It's basically a covert action taking place at the National Archives." A lawyer for the National Security Archive, Meredith Fuchs, stated of NARA, "It seems odd that they would be so willing to accept this. But NARA was completely complicit in trying to cover it up."[3] The *Washington Post* version of the story likewise played on the ironies of NARA's role in the reclassification mess, starting out with "The National Archives helped keep secret a multi-year effort by the Air Force, the CIA and other federal agencies to withdraw thousands of historical documents from public access on Archives shelves, even though the records had been declassified." The *Post* then described the efforts to obtain a copy of the memorandum, quoted from Blanton, recounted the discovery by historian Matthew Aid of the reclassification program, how many of the previously open records seemed to "pose no conceivable security risk," and commented on Weinstein's pledges to investigate and cease the operation.[4]

Commentators on the unfolding story who were closer to the National Archives also did not mince words about the unpleasantness of the affair. Bruce Craig, of the National Coalition for History, in his analysis of the breaking story, commented on the "disturbing role that NARA played in the multi-year effort by federal agencies to remove thousands of historical documents from public access." Craig had kind words for Weinstein who "applauded the release" of the memorandum, while expressing concerns about the role of his predecessor and other archivists, leading Craig to wonder "why in the first place did the parties to the agreement believe it a necessity to keep the re-review 'secret'" (noting that there had been other public reclassifications). Craig's commentary suggests why the role of NARA in this program seems so troublesome, stating

> An answer to this question may seem baffling, especially to those not "of" the national security establishment. Security agencies generally take the stance that when they have a specific classified program to protect from improper "incidental disclosure," typically they take a firm stance: they insist that all such materials need to be protected under the cloak of classification and secrecy. NARA, on the other hand, generally takes the position that secrecy tends to focus attention on documents that otherwise would not draw any particular attention by researchers, historians, or the press. Often NARA advocates this position in discussions with agencies but finds itself over-ruled by agencies wishing to take a firmer stance. This very public disclosure of a secret re-review program that probably never needed to be classified "secret" in the first place, serves only to raise concerns by the public and Congress alike about excessive secrecy in government.[5]

And, we might add, we should be concerned about the role of NARA in such government secrecy.

Going to the Archivists

On April 14, 2006 (11:35:48 AM EDT) I forwarded the National Security Archive press release to the Archives & Archivists listserv, under the subject line "nara and reclassification." I provided a brief commentary — "Below is another view into the NARA and reclassification case, and this view suggests a serious breach of professional ethics (in my opinion). I do not believe SAA has issued a statement/position on the reclassification, and I urge members of SAA to communicate with SAA leadership to look into this case and take a position." On the day before I had corresponded with Nancy Beaumont, SAA Executive Director, and SAA President Richard Pearce-Moses, about the matter, also forwarding the NSA news release. To Beaumont I wrote, "I think it is time for SAA to stand up and speak about the disgraceful behavior of our National Archives (I know it won't, but until SAA will distance itself from NARA and become a true watch dog of this agency, it will be hard to be serious about a real federal records policy)."[6] My message to President Pearce-Moses was a bit different, as I used the opportunity of his message to individuals about attending a meeting with the National Archives on the topic of new skills for the digital era. I wrote, "You are asking us to participate in a program co-sponsored by NARA at a time when SAA ought to be considering censuring NARA. Obviously, I have no intention of participating."[7] I received no response from either individual. While I received some off-the-record news that there were internal discussions among SAA leadership about a formal response, my sources also suggested that there was great reluctance to go on record, at least until the promised audit materialized.

What then occurred on the Archives and Archivists listserv was an interesting insight into the archival community's interest in the National Archives and government secrecy. Over the course of several days, Maarja Kursten and I posted messages to the list, with hardly anyone else responding. Kursten, a former Nixon records archivist, posted opinions reflecting her insider views about the affair. She commenced with expressing the similarity between about what now seemed to be happening and what transpired three decades before. Kursten reflected, "We have yet to hear a good explanation from NARA about the reclassification matter. Who knows how much NARA will be able to tell the public." She remembered that comments about the Nixon tapes controversy had to be "handled scrupulously, through regulatory channels, in order to protect the overall credibility of NARA's archival screening efforts." Kursten also wonders what SAA should do, responding to my call for that association to take leadership, remembering that "back in 1992-1993, as the Nixon case unfolded, I kept looking for SAA to comment. However, as I read through the court pleadings and deposition transcripts, I came to recognize that not all the NARA players were on the same page." Kursten captured something of the complexity of the older case: "I don't know of anyone from SAA who went to the courthouse in 1992 or 1993 to read through all the stuff I read there, although I suppose they could have done so. Absent an effort to learn what was said under oath, any SAA reaction to the Nixon problems would have been based on second-hand accounts. And SAA hardly was in a position to start picking and choosing among varying positions voiced by NARA employees. Absent an attempt to get into the nitty gritty of the issues buried in the court filings, which would have been complicated but would have served NARA well, all SAA then could do was issue general statements."[8]

The conversation between Kursten and myself continued to dominate the discussion on the listserv. I cautioned about investing too much energy into discussing the Nixon case, instead urging us to look at this particular case. More importantly, I wrote that SAA needs to issue a statement calling for a strong, independent NARA; that SAA needs to be involved in looking at what has actually occurred in this reclassification case and be critical of

NARA if warranted; and finally, that the archival profession needs to call for a stronger NARA as well.[9] Kursten acknowledged that the Nixon experience was a "searing experience" for her, affecting the manner in which she considers all archival issues. More importantly, she worries about how NARA could be strengthened since the Archivist "serves at the pleasure of the President." Kursten also notes that retired Archivists don't even speak up about such controversial issues after they retire, hurting NARA being able to strengthen its role. Kursten then provides this assessment of the NARA reclassification controversy:

> SAA is very limited in what it can do in examining a case that involves national security classification issues. It's not like SAA can subpoena the named and unnamed agencies in the MOU. Or compel anyone involved in this matter to share any information, at all. Consider the present environment, not just at NARA, but elsewhere, regarding these types of issues. Isn't SAA mostly dependent on what others uncover? While I sympathize entirely with your objectives, I think you underestimate the difficulties of SAA independently getting at the facts with these particular players, in the current environment. That is why I cited the Nixon case, where the facts in court filings were unclassified but still never examined by anyone from SAA. That's not to say no one should try. For now, I'm placing my trust in Bill Leonard of NARA's ISOO unit, who sounds as if he is trying to do the right thing under difficult circumstances.[10]

While I clarified that I did not believe that strengthening NARA would be an easy task, I certainly see the point that Kursten has when it comes to archival public policy and politics. My main concern, then and now, was for the SAA to step up to the plate and take a decisive stand: "If our main national professional association refuses to do anything, then we must admit that we have no real leadership, at least in matters of public policy. The closest we come to it is the National Security Archive — perhaps we might consider contributing our membership dues to it."[11]

For a few days Maarja Kursten and myself discussed the reclassification case. Kursten drew in news reports and postings from other listservs, these additional sources all striving to determine an approach for the profession speaking out in a useful fashion about the scandal. Kursten commented, for example, that "SAA probably needs to take a page from the National Security Archive's playbook and start submitting Freedom of Information Act (FOIA) requests to get to the bottom of some issues. It's hard to get at the facts just by talking to NARA officials and press officers — the extent to which they can be candid is really going to vary. FOIA has the force of law behind it. Unfortunately, this is Washington and to get to the bottom of some matters, that is what it sometimes takes."[12]

Kursten's reflections prompted me to assert, "too often, SAA seems to be more a creature of NARA than a watchdog or critic (or supporter when appropriate) of it. What is most interesting to me is that the NSA seems to exist. Perhaps, because of failings of NARA; NARA seems to assume that it is mostly a cultural agency with a generally passive role, when in fact, as a government archives, it ought to function with a focus on matters of government accountability as well." To make my point, I advised listserv members to consider the reclassification in light of NARA's mission statement (found on its Web site), where the federal agency described itself as being a "public trust on which our democracy depends." NARA is pledged to "ensure continuing access to essential evidence that documents" citizens' rights, federal officials' activities, and the "national experience." In this statement NARA identified a variety of values it recognized as important, including being open to change, developing trust, and acting "openly, honestly, and with integrity," being accountable, and so forth. All of this seemed counter to much that seemed to be occurring in the reclassification controversy.[13]

Allen Weinstein Speaks Up

While the discussion on the Archives and Archivists list began to heat up, Archivist Weinstein made his views about the reclassification controversy better known. An interview in the *Federal Times* with Allen Weinstein focused on the case. Weinstein related that he first learned of the reclassification story in an article in the *New York Times*, indicating his unhappiness about learning about this in this manner and contending that he immediately met with Assistant Archivist Michael Kurtz, Director of the Information Security Oversight Office Bill Leonard, and NARA's general counsel. While noting that he immediately stopped the program, Weinstein also depicted his desire for a stronger National Archives: "The archivist may need more authority, in which case we will go to Congress, go to the administration and talk to the folks across the spectrum, including people in the intelligence community and other agencies affected, and try to maintain a serious consensus on this process.... We're not talking about new bureaucracy; we're talking about a process, procedures that would be more acceptable to the general public, to historians, to scholars, and to the intelligence community."[14]

Weinstein expressed hope for improvements, believing that the intelligence community was ready for reforms and hoping to see the internal audit recommend some specific mechanisms for engineering these reforms. It is in the hopeful rhetoric that we would see the archival profession ultimately buy what he was selling. When asked about his vision for NARA, Weinstein first commented on the need for more resources — "Part of my vision is that, when I leave this position, the funding for the Archives will be substantially more in line with our responsibilities and what we're asked to do" — the typical federal bureaucrat's response to any such question, but one that a profession that has seen itself as continuously under-funded would readily accept. And the rest of his vision, "tending to the documents with the greatest care as possible," "education in as many dimensions as possible," and "developing the technology that will allow us to deal with the Archives of the future, the Archives Without Walls, as we like to call it,"[15] all were answers sure to reassure other archivists and historians and other users of the archives, even though they had little to do with the internal lapses of management and fumbling with information policy that the reclassification scandal reflected.

The day after this interview was published, Archivist Weinstein issued a formal statement about the secret memorandum, his pledge that such agreements will be "replaced by thoroughly transparent standards," and a reiteration of NARA's mission. According to Weinstein, "There can never be a classified aspect to our mission. Classified agreements are the antithesis of our reason for being. Our focus is on the preservation of records and ensuring their availability to the American public while at the same time fulfilling the people's expectation that we will properly safeguard the classified records entrusted to our custody. Agencies have the prerogative to classify their requests to the National Archives if disclosure of the reasons why they are asking us to take action would cause identifiable damage to national security. However, what we do in response to such requests, and how we do it, will always be as transparent as possible. If records must be removed for reasons of national security, the American people will always, at the very least, know when it occurs and how many records are affected."[16]

As had been transpiring before the Weinstein official statement, Kursten and myself largely continued the public discussion. I posted a message urging archivists to contact SAA to push that organization to take the lead to see an independent review body established, reminding everyone that the Information Security Oversight Office was an internal NARA body. The crux of my argument derived from a statement issued the day before by Weinstein's successor, John Carlin, indicating that he knew nothing about the reclassification secret agreement, and that he was "shocked by the content, particularly the language that it was in the best interest of the National Archives to keep the public in the dark. I spent most of my tenure stating that NARA is a public trust — this MOU undermines that trust." While Carlin espoused confidence in the efforts by Weinstein, I made the point that Carlin's statement shouldn't cause us to wonder if anyone is in charge of NARA.[17] Kursten expressed the need for caution, suggesting that it may be difficult to find out just what occurred inside the National Archives. She muses, "The Archives' lawyers may claim attorney-client privilege, for example, over the substance of what they advised. However, NARA should be able to tell us whether or not the MOUs were passed through its Office of General Counsel. That type of procedural routing information should not be privileged. Nor do we know what pressure various officials faced. I don't know how much NARA will admit to." Yet, this kind of resistance is precisely why SAA needs to be vigilant in its observations about NARA. Kursten acknowledges this (while expressing some optimism about what Leonard of the ISOO might do), writing, "NARA does not have a strong history of examining thoroughly or candidly problems relating to third party pressure it faces in attempting to open historical records. Or reporting about such findings publicly. In my view, the past failure to do so simply sets the scene for future pressure."[18]

More Private Than Public Messages

For myself, two issues reigned supreme in the reclassification case, the role of NARA leadership and the voice of the profession. Since the problems we were seeing with NARA, in my opinion, had been evident for decades, perhaps all the way back to its creation, it should not be surprising that my hopes rested on seeing the archival community take on a stronger role. Starting in the early-1990s, SAA had been issuing more, as well as more timely, position statements on a number of public and policy issues; so, it could stand to reason that SAA could take on a different role with NARA. Such was not to be the case, however.

With this, I drew on my personal experience. When I was on SAA Council in 1986 to 1989, I had fought from time to time to see SAA take on a different role with NARA. At one point, I even proposed to Council that no NARA employees should be allowed to run for elected office; the point of this proposal, one I had little hope would gain any support, was simply to try to persuade SAA that it needed to take a stronger hand with NARA. After Council, I proposed a censure of the then Archivist of the United States, for his role in a variety of messes, one that included the destruction of materials from a NARA personnel file, and, once again, there was no support (but some anger) from SAA's elected leadership.

And, in fact, as the reclassification case debate continued, we heard nothing from the current SAA leadership. Instead, other than the public postings by myself and Maarja Kursten, what I received as support came only from private, off the record, messages.[19] I received a brief message from a former colleague at a state archives expressing support for my opinions. A longer message came from a former NARA employee, sent to both myself and Kursten, confirming that the National Archives had lost its sense of mission about the role of the Archivist and the public access to federal records. According to this insider, NARA had allowed federal agencies to begin dictating classification and declassification procedures, allowing the Archivist's authority to become diminished. This individual also believes that NARA lost its interest in building a coalition of support, concluding that it would be appropriate for SAA to not only investigate the current reclassification scandal but to lobby for a stronger NARA with greater authority over all Federal archives, including testing some of the current laws, including the Archivist's authority over the declassification of thirty year old federal records vested in Title 44 of the Public Records Act. Maarja Kursten, in this private exchange, agreed with such assessment, but saw, as I did, little hope that SAA leadership was going to take any issue that seemed to oppose NARA and its public statements. For myself, I had witnessed first-hand SAA's unwillingness to confront NARA; however, I also saw in work on earlier writings about NARA and the presidential library system and 2004 Archivist nomination controversy the seeds of NARA weakness buried deeper and longer ago.

Increasing Attention

Although only a few other archivists entered the listserv discussions — Terry Baxter posted on the Advocacy listserv, for example, that "Since this list is intended to solicit actual recommendations for SAA Council, I would be willing to put something together, but I know there are people in this group with a lot more knowledge about the issues than me"[20] — the reclassification case was acquiring increased scrutiny. For example, the *Chronicle of Higher Education* carried a lengthy story about the case, commencing the article with the phrase "hoping to restore its reputation among scholars and members of the public," indicating its view on what was happening. With ample quotations from NARA officials and others, the *Chronicle* recounted the litany of events leading up to the internal audit; in this article I was quoted as stating we needed a stronger, more independent National Archives (building on what I had been posting online for the previous week).[21] It was obvious, then, that no matter what anyone thought of this case or NARA's role in it, that it was going to receive a sustained and critical public media scrutiny.

SAA Finally Speaks Up

On April 18th, SAA finally issued a statement about the NARA reclassification case. One might presume that it took this long for SAA to deliberate and gain the support for its elected officers (when such matters like this develop, SAA works through its Executive Committee with input from other officers), but the tone and content of the final statement suggests that SAA might have been trying to avoid issuing any statement at all.

On this day Richard Pearce-Moses sent to the Archives and Archivists listserv a copy of the letter he had sent, on behalf of SAA, to Archivist Weinstein. Pearce-Moses started the letter reaffirming the idea that archivists believe in open access to government records, as part of a democratic government accountable to its citizens. He also indicated that there are needs to limit access in "interests of national security and to protect individuals' privacy," understanding that the recently reported reclassification efforts "may be an attempt to correct errors of documents mistakenly declassified." Pearce-Moses also expressed concerns that the reclassification program "may have been an effort to restrict access to information for reasons other than national security," concerns generated by the text of the secret memorandum of understanding. The remainder of the letter is a list of actions Weinstein had taken, with Pearce-Moses expressing appreciation for these actions. Pearce-Moses, without making any call for independent auditing or full disclosure, ended his letter with this statement: "The Society believes that only those documents that would pose a genuine security threat if open should be reclassified, that all other documents be left declassified, and that agreements with agencies restricting access to be published."[22] By all ways of examining it, this was a letter that did not position SAA to take any action or to call for a higher standard of accountability.

I expressed my concern about the SAA statement in a public posting to the Archives and Archivists listserv, "that SAA, while urging NARA to continue to reform and strengthen its role in such secret Memoranda of Understanding, does not call for an independent investigatory group to examine what has occurred. It seems that congratulating Archivist Weinstein for his actions to open government and NARA's work is premature until we have additional information about what exactly happened with this reclassification effort and the March 2002 MOU (and whether there might be others). The SAA letter should have focused on asking for a greater accountability. What we have here suggests that the problem has been fixed, long before we have more information about what actually occurred." And as the audit report eventually showed, I think this SAA posture was incorrect. But I also reiterated in this posting my main concern: "The deafening silence from the profession, or at least that portion subscribing to the Archives list, suggests that this is not a serious matter for it. Perhaps, at least later this week we could curtail the endless postings of Friday Funnies as we witness the continuing weakening of our democratic state. A kind of moment of silence. . . ."[23]

As had become the normal routine, Maarja Kursten posted a long, thoughtful response to my message, indicating that we needed to wait until the audit was released before we congratulated NARA and Weinstein. As was her usual perspective, she worried both about NARA's response and about just what NARA really could do to right the ship. And in one of her most telling comments on this controversy, Kursten wrote, "There are people involved in every step of the way in creating and handling records. They can be the weakest or the strongest links in the process. Whatever is in them, ultimately, government records end up at the National Archives. That's the final stop for records of national memory. If NARA can't properly handle them, then we all are in real trouble." Kursten returned to asking some questions about SAA's role: "Until NARA finishes its review, we will not know how much our long-term confidence in the agency should be affected. As does Richard, I wish SAA's statement would have been more nuanced and had reflected greater contextual sophistication. I give SAA credit for putting something out relatively quickly, and hitting some of the important points, but hope yesterday's release does not represent its final word on these complex issues." Unfortunately, it appears that it was SAA's final statement.[24]

Whether it was SAA's statement or my comments about the professional silence about the NARA reclassification matter, more voices began to be heard from on the Archives and Archivists listserv. There was commentary on the *Chronicle* article.[25] However, what concerned me more were the growing number of postings by individuals who were either relying on the messages of Kursten and myself, or who expressed a general lack of understanding of the issues involved. Christina Hostetter perhaps expressed it best, indicating that since she was new to the field that she felt unqualified to express an opinion: "I certainly feel that this is an important matter which is why I have been following it closely but not knowing the details and all of the relationships, not to mention that I don't work for NARA and don't understand all of their policies and operations I feel that I can't comment. Personally, I am worried that NARA may become a puppet of the current administration (which means it could continue to be manipulated by future administrations) and that if we don't act now the whole reason for NARA's existence will be lost on future generations." Hostetter continued, "I also agree that SAA's statement on this issue may have been hasty but I certainly hope that isn't the last word from either SAA or the archival community." Then she attempted to relate her concerns more broadly to the professional community: "I don't think I'm alone in saying that yes, this does matter and it is incredibly important to the profession but the 'silence' on the listserv is not because archivists are not interested or concerned with the topic at hand but rather cannot form opinions or draw conclusions without further information or an understanding of the entities involved. Republican or Democrat doesn't matter in this case. What is most important is that our profession and our existence are not trampled by political bullies trying to change history."[26]

Others basically just lamented that they were too busy with their own responsibilities to devote much effort to learning about the reclassification case issues. As another archivist wrote, "Many of us are interested in NARA as citizens and funding for NHPRC as a means of funding our own projects. However, in addition to finding time to learn about the history of these organizations, many of us have quite a few other things to learn about that have a more immediate impact on our collections. The nature of the profession is such that many of us come to it from different areas of expertise, or even from different types of collections, and we continually try to educate ourselves about how to better care for our own repositories. This leaves little time for other topics."[27]

Some private messages suggested the same views as Hostetter and Hocking, while others joined the public side of the discussion. What was not being questioned was how every archivist might be impacted in their own program if NARA dissolved into a weak, non-descript federal agency and SAA functioned as a weak association afraid to speak out on matters of public policy. Both private and public messages struggled with how to find mechanisms for both determining what had happened at NARA with reclassification as well as how to build a network for strengthening NARA's ability to carry out its mission. For example, one individual suggested that the Society for History in the Federal Government could be a source of support, but others, principally Kursten, worried just what knowledge and level of commitment historians, public or academic, brought to the table.[28] One individual wrote to me privately that they just didn't feel that they knew enough about the case, and, as a result, they were not comfortable posting messages publicly. It prompted me to respond that while I appreciated such an opinion, I thought that "all archivists need to become more vigilant and informed about what is happening in the realm of government secrecy."[29] One who did comment publicly posted a message that, while reasonable, was also chilling. Ariel Lucas thought that some archivists have probably not expressed openly their views because either they were seeking jobs or because they represent their employers:

> The issues are frighteningly Orwellian, smacking of revisionism (of history) at worst or of the suppression of politically embarrassing documents. No matter who we are as archivists, however, I think we are acutely aware that we are expected to represent the interests of our employers, whether they be academic, religious, corporate, or governmental. We are expected as well to respect the interests of other such groups, and there is a different attitude that I have noticed between academic archivists and those who work for corporations, churches, or governments. Academics have been among the most vocal on this issue in favor of the public's right to know, and I think this attitude—that information should be public where it affects the public interest—is characteristic of archivists in academic institutions as well. I think it may not be to my credit in the eyes of some people (I can vividly remember one interview, for instance) that I worked as a project archivist in the Tobacco Control Archives, of which the founding papers were alleged to have been stolen from a tobacco corporation. It was as if I had stolen the papers myself and was expected to give them back![30]

If archivists remained silent, however, just what would be the long-term consequences for them? Lucas herself noted, "Perhaps the feeling is that if we keep quiet and don't get involved in political issues both we and the papers we preserve will be safer. Unfortunately, I doubt this is the case."[31]

And the voices came from all different directions. Well-known consultant Rick Barry, in response to my comment about an independent inquiry, suggested: "The National Coalition for History has been urging much more visible congressional oversight of NARA for a long time and indicates that Allen Weinstein would welcome that. I think it would be in NARA's interest to receive more such high-visibility congressional oversight. So perhaps we should be voicing our interests in NARA's well being to our Congress members and its TTHUD [Transportation, Treasury, and Housing and Urban Development] committee that we were urged to contact in support of NHPRC's budget."[32] Bruce Montgomery, an archivist who has written about federal records issues, suggested that the reclassification controversy should not be seen as "unexpected," contending that NARA has been "transformed into an essentially political (more than cultural) executive branch agency." Montgomery focused on a long and troublesome history, suggesting that "so far it would seem that Allen Weinstein is doing a commendable job of trying to put the Archives on solid footing as an agency that operates with integrity according to its fundamental mission. It's a difficult job and I'm not sure he can do it completely on his own without the support of congressional backing."[33]

No matter how many archivists seemed at this point to be posting messages, it had to be a very small number of those that could. In response to a comment by Kursten about the silence on the list and how few NARA employees there may be subscribed to it, former SAA President Peter Hirtle reported that there were 4399 subscribers with 85, or about two percent, giving "nara.gov" as their email address (out of slightly over three thousand NARA employees).[34] This, and Montgomery's rather bleak assessment of NARA's reform, prompted me to post a lengthy message suggesting that we needed the archival community to make its voice heard. For me, the lack of attention to the reclassification controversy was troubling for the very existence of archivists and their mission: "If we just sit back and allow our government to create a more and more secret regime, is there any point at all in trying to function as archivists? Are we going to sit back and allow the FBI, and other intelligence agencies, come into our archives to shut down our collections in the name of national security and state secrets, such as is happening with the Jack Anderson papers being offered to the George Washington University?" Then I asked, "Why is it that the Smithsonian-Showtime agreement has generated such a quick response, according to Jacqueline Trescott in the April 18th *Washington Post*, when "More than 200 filmmakers and historians asked the Smithsonian Institution yesterday to abandon its production deal with Showtime Networks and reconsider a recently imposed policy that limits access to Smithsonian archives and experts"? It seems to me that the government secrecy issues represented in the reclassification controversy possess far greater implications for us as a nation and profession than the intellectual property concerns that we see in the Smithsonian controversy. Are archivists just too uninterested in the National Archives? Do they merely think that this is business as usual, for both NARA and the Bush administration, so why bother? Or are archivists just too willing to accept, at face value, any explanation coming from Archivist Weinstein and NARA leadership?"[35] Then I listed a number of new books recently appearing on government secrecy and records/information policy.³⁶

The small number of archivists speaking out, along with their professional association's silence, suggested that the NARA case ultimately would fade from the media attention and public profile. Kursten, responding to Arel Lucas, noted that "archivists are not a monolithic group, their views and even their desire (or lack of desire) to speak out are going to vary." She mentioned that whether they would speak out would be affected by where they worked and the circumstances of their employment. "The one thing I hope we all agree on," she wrote, "is that people with power in an archival organization should do their utmost to prevent their employees being placed in positions where they have to knowingly lie to the public." And then she noted the differences between archivists working with government records and those working with other types of records, the former being those where the complicated matter of classification is an issue.³⁷

Looking for Resolution and Compromise

Sooner or later someone was going to emerge who would attempt to identify a reasonable compromise view. Peter Hirtle was this individual. Stating that he wanted a strong National Archives, he also thought that the SAA statement was a "pretty good statement of the archival principles ... at issue in the case." Hirtle reminded readers that the "National Coalition for History, on whose governing Board SAA sits, has called for congressional oversight hearings on NARA. Such hearings would certainly be the best way to learn more about, and testify on behalf, of operations at NARA." Hirtle also urged waiting to see what the ISOO audit has to say about the reclassification affair. And, finally, Hirtle thought we should wait to see what the recently constituted Public Interest Declassification Board (PIDB) has to say about the reclassification, and its hearings would not start until May 9, 2006. Hirtle cautioned the archival profession to "accept at face value" Weinstein's assertions that he would be faithful in resolving the reclassification problems.³⁸

There was a weak link in Hirtle's chain of reasoning. Not only did he wonder about the historic precedent of independent bodies investigating a national archival program, but he worried about why archivists would sign such memoranda of understanding. "My guess," Hirtle speculated, "is that they were doing the same sort of balancing act that all archivists must do when it comes to donations. We sometimes accept a donation with an inappropriate restriction in the deed of gift in the belief that in doing so, we are ensuring the preservation of a record that might otherwise be lost - and we can comfort ourselves with the knowledge that eventually the records will be opened. I suspect that some at NARA felt that if they were not accommodating towards the CIA and the USAF in what is after all a congressionally-mandate re-review process, those agencies might be less willing to turn over historical records to NARA. My impression is that similar sentiments drive NARA's support of classification review by agencies prior to automatic declassification. Supporting agencies in their desire to keep material that should remain classified out of the automatic declassification chain may lead to more agency willingness to turn over material to NARA - and less lobbying to short-circuit automatic declassification. In a perfect world, the Archivist would have the authority to demand that agencies turn over all historical files to the Archives, but I am not predicting a perfect world any time soon."[39]

Hirtle's commentary brought no closure to the reclassification debate. Kursten acknowledged that he made some good points, but questioned the donor analogy "because, unlike in the private sector, we're dealing with statutory authorities" and that part of the text of the MOU chronicled something "antithetical to the way NARA operates or is supposed to operate because it expresses an underlying contempt for the American public." Kursten, drawing on a variety of examples, continued: "When you're negotiating with a donor in the private sector, there is much less at stake than there is in records dealing with governmental actions. The fact that citizens (voters, tax payers) are involved, both in being the potential subjects of and requestors of records, places a different perspective on the matter. Someone has to represent their interests in the proper handling of government records. Since they can't "sit at the table" when NARA is discussing matters with record creating agencies, it is up to NARA to keep their interests in mind. The underlying contempt for the public in the statement about researchers suggests that this was not done sufficiently in the case of the MOUs."[40]

My own disagreement with Hirtle related to his seemingly commonsense approach to allowing other independent bodies, rather than SAA, evaluate NARA. I thought SAA had avoided dealing with NARA for too long, but I especially disagreed with his allusion to the notion that archivists sometimes must place "inappropriate restrictions" on records when donated. I wrote in response, "This is a kind of situational ethics that ought to deeply trouble us, leading to situations such as Janet Malcolm chronicled in her book, *In the Freud Archives*, considering the control of Sigmund Freud papers at the Library of Congress. It is also the kind of argument that has us sitting back and watching the presidential library system spin onward, often bringing in challenges for access to the records and, at the least, the same kind of control of the interpretation of the past as we can see in memoir writers. ... Since archivists are almost always concerned about the protection of records and threats to them, the logical extension of this argument would be to create a rampage of awful access restrictions to collections, frustrating researchers and undermining the mission of archives everywhere." What concerned me more was Hirtle's notion that NARA needed to cave-in from the pressure of the intelligence and other agencies or run the risk of losing historical records. I noted that such views extend back to earlier disputes, such as the PROFS case, asking, "So, where do we go with this? Do we urge having a National Archives with no role in federal records and information policy, just so some records might survive for future historians. In addition to being an archivist, I am a citizen, and I would like to see a strong NARA protecting and defending open government. I am not naïve about that 'perfect world,' but I hope we can agree that it is worth working for a much better world."[41]

It was obvious, even with a weak SAA statement and no groundswell of support from the archival community, that there was a mood to try to bring some sort of resolution to what had happened at NARA, even as we waited for the audit report to appear. Kursten looked to federal auditing standards, with provisions for public statements of operational problems, as a template for new standards for NARA to work within. She argued, "While I understand why NARA faces pressure and struggles with difficult balancing tests, I believe it can and should act forthrightly in discussing these issues. That includes stating up front if there are any factors or internal or external impairments that affect the release of records (be they Federal, Presidential, etc.)." Kursten also noted how the auditing standards don't rely solely on federal managers but can reach for external evidence. NARA, she contends, "must act with integrity in all steps of the process. Unfortunately, there are not enough standards and protocols in place to ensure that this always will happen."[42]

While some archivists sought meaning in and resolution of the reclassification program, the news media continued to run stories about the program, rehearsing all the details that were already well known. As one reads the *New York Times* article of April 18, 2006 it is hard not to sense the incredulity with which the reporter seems to have described the by then well-known events and attitudes expressed by various individuals associated with the program.[43] Indeed, the *Times* editorial the following day seems best to express the shock and curiosity about the National Archives' involvement. The editorial commenced, "Documents wind up missing from public archives for many reasons. Sometimes they're shelved or labeled incorrectly, or lost, and sometimes they're even stolen. But at the National Archives, documents have been disappearing since 1999 because intelligence officials have wanted them to." In other words, right off readers are hit with the notion that the reclassification program is counter to what government archives are supposed to do. After brief discussion of the program and Weinstein's pledge to fix it, the editorial plays with how odd the entire thing seems: "What makes this all seem preposterous is that the agreements themselves prohibit the National Archives from revealing why the documents were removed. They are apparently secret enough that no one can be told why they are secret—so secret, in fact, that the arrangement to reclassify them is also secret. According to the agreement with the C.I.A., employees of the National Archives are also prohibited from telling anyone that the C.I.A. was responsible for removing reclassified documents." And, finally, the *Times* editorializes about the Bush administration's obsession with secrecy and the attack this represents on our ability to know the past: "It's hard for us to imagine why a declassified document from the 1950's—one that has perhaps been read and referenced by many scholars—should suddenly be deemed too sensitive for public access. Unfortunately, given the Bush administration's obsession with secrecy, it's all too easy for us to imagine why that may be true of more recent documents. It's worth remembering, after all, that the contents of the National Archives represent the raw materials of history."[44]

The Debate Begins to Fade

As the discussion continued, some tried to place the reclassification case into a more sweeping set of efforts by the Federal Government to operate in great secrecy. Bruce Montgomery commented on this, arguing that the "White House has vigorously sought to reassert presidential powers that it perceives to have eroded since the Nixon years, Congress has willingly—until more recently—abdicated its authority. The reclassification controversy has occurred within this much larger context." Montgomery believes that "NARA likely was pressured by powerful executive agencies operating under the wider initiative to shut off information across the Federal Government in the wake of 9/11 and because of the administration's larger agenda of reasserting executive powers. You have to remember that NARA is a relatively weak executive agency vis a vis the others, that the U.S. archivist serves at the pleasure of the White House, and that it has no viable political support in Congress to resist executive branch pressure."⁴⁵ While some NARA leaders and staffers might bristle at the thought of SAA and the professional archival community speaking up about its internal problems, seeing these as criticisms, the lack of public discourse only suggests that the Archives should continue to be a federal weakling.

As the traffic died down about the case, some observers again tried to make final assessments of what they were witnessing. Kim Scott, for example, argued that the archival profession's basic mission was in preserving records for them to be used, noting that "regardless of the political fray that marks the current NARA issue, certainly we can boil down our profession's stance by insisting on this basic principle."⁴⁶ Peter Hirtle once again tried to find consensus, thinking that there was "actually a surprising amount of agreement" among the various perspectives represented. Hirtle, perhaps in the understatement of the debate about the affair, wrote, "Everyone wants a strong, independent NARA that does good things - there is just some debate on the best way to get there." Hirtle believed that there might be a revision of the Executive Order governing classification. Still, there were questions. "As I read the record," Hirtle mused, "NARA under first John Carlin and now Allen Weinstein has become a friend of openness and an opponent of inappropriate government secrecy. It makes the existence of the classified MOU all the more bizarre."⁴⁷

The Lull Before the Storm

As the end of April approached, but still before the anticipated April 26, 2006 release of the NARA audit report,⁴⁸ conversation on the Archives and Archivists list died down, except for reporting on the occasional newspaper article or other public discussion about the reclassification program. A *Washington Post* article reported on a speech by National Intelligence Director John Negroponte, noting that he avoided discussing government secrecy and classification, including avoiding mentioning anything about the "intensified efforts to reclassify public documents in the National Archives."⁴⁹ Some archivists, like Michael Tarabulski, filled in the gap by having fun (although there was a serious intent in his observations), in his case writing about "recklessification" and the "memorandumb."⁵⁰

Some of the reports released provided additional information about the reclassification controversy. Jeffrey Young, writing in the *Chronicle of Higher Education*, provided a fuller account of the NARA reclassification project, tracing its origins and subsequent outcomes. Young interviewed a number of individuals, including myself, and added more of the personal touches to the story. Young got Kurtz, the NARA deputy who signed the secret agreement, to discuss how that agreement happened. Kurtz is quoted as saying, "You need to go back in time to about 2000," he said. "We had some concerns here at the archives about the way the CIA was handling some of the records as they were going about their review work," following Clinton's 1995 executive order about declassification. "The thrust of the emphasis of the National Archives in forging an agreement with the CIA was to codify exactly what procedures [would be used] and how records would be properly handled." This was a rare comment by Kurtz on the affair. Kurtz, Young reported, believed that the sentence in the agreement suggesting that the declassification was to be concealed from the public was "inartfully worded." Kurtz did not believe that the National Archives ought to be fooling anyone, but that it did need to "strike a balance ... between protecting national-security information and having the maximum access possible." In general, Kurtz argued that one had to remember that this was in the immediate post-9/11 era: "I kind of dealt with things as I did at the time, and now this is a different perspective. I personally certainly understand the concerns that have been expressed about these agreements and wholeheartedly support the direction of the archivist." Kurtz also recounted that he had briefed Archivist Carlin, but he thought Carlin might not remember it because "it was in the context of dozens of discussions in the immediate aftermath of 9/11 in regards to security — all aspects of it, particularly relating to records security."[51]

The Audit

On April 26, 2006 the ISOO audit report on the reclassification program was released. The audit uncovered two memoranda with intelligence and federal agencies, leading to the withdrawal of over 25,000 records (nearly three times the scope of what the program was thought to have been), extending even into the presidential libraries. Nearly a quarter (24 percent) of the records affected were "inappropriate" reclassifications and another 12 percent were "questionable." The report included comments by NARA General Counsel Meredith Fuchs about the inappropriateness of the reclassification program, quoting her as saying that "Not only did this surreptitious reclassification program draw attention to information that otherwise would likely have remained obscure, but it did so at tremendous cost. I can't imagine that we are any safer today than we would be if this reclassification program had never taken place." The report made specific recommendations for reforming the classification.[52]

Allen Weinstein, upon the release of the audit, made a number of comments focusing on how the National Archives would strive to ensure that such reclassification efforts would not occur again, at least in secrecy. Acknowledging that "more than one of every three documents removed from the open shelves and barred to researchers should not have been tampered with," in this program, Weinstein also noted that many of the actions were counter to NARA's basic mission. For example, in learning that the CIA withdrew unclassified records mostly as a ruse to conceal what they were doing, Weinstein strongly stated that this "undermined NARA's basic mission to preserve the authenticity of files under our stewardship" and "must never be repeated." Most of Archivist Weinstein's comments concerned the actions he would be taking in the future, including meeting with "representatives of the national security agencies and concerned researchers"; implementing a "new protocol" to "ensure that withdrawal of records from public access are rare, are conducted in collaboration with NARA, and take place only when continued public access to a record would cause serious, demonstrable damage to national security"; restoring "documents removed erroneously or improperly from open shelves at the National Archives"; commencing a "pilot National Declassification Initiative"; "appointing a team to undertake a longer-term analysis of how NARA processes the classified material in its custody"; and recommending to "OMB an appropriation to be used to expedite processing of classified files, both paper and electronic, in order to begin reducing the unconscionable backlog of unprocessed documents due to funding shortfalls."[53]

In the release of the report and his comments, Archivist Weinstein ably demonstrated a commitment to repositioning and repairing NARA's reputation and role. And, indeed, many seemed to think that his commitment was both sincere and appropriate. Kursten noted that the report and accompanying comments "strike the right note."[54] Historian Matthew Aid, the individual who initially discovered the reclassification program, had positive comments although he wondered why the moratorium on reclassification was ended before new procedures were established. Steven Aftergood, Director of the Federation of American Scientists' Project on Government Secrecy, also was favorably inclined to what was being done to bring the program into the light, although he thought it was too early to think that the problem was resolved.[55]

Others expressed concerns. Historian Anna K. Nelson, a long-time advocate for strengthened government records policies, upon learning in the audit that over twelve hundred records had been removed from the

Eisenhower, Kennedy, and Bush presidential libraries, retorted, "I think the National Archives cannot be proud of their actions here. I think they cooperated unnecessarily."[56] Surprisingly, there were not more individuals or organizations coming forward to pose questions about the audit report and its conclusions about reclassification and the National Archives.

Deconstructing the Audit Report

Withdrawal of Records from Public Access at the National Archives and Records Administration for Classification Purposes, issued by NARA's Information Security Oversight Office on April 26, 2006, is an unimposing 34-page report. It is loaded, however, with many statements that should cause the public, government officials, NARA researchers, and records professionals to wonder, worry, and wince at what is going on at our nation's premier archives and in the archival community at large.

The audit report concludes that 64 percent of the records "clearly met the standards for continued classification," suggesting a buy-in to the present sense of excessive secrecy (even though it was thought that "insufficient judgment was applied to the decision to withdraw the record from public access").[57] In fact, the report stresses that since Executive Order 12958 in 1995, federal agencies have sped up declassification and that all of the agencies named in this report were cooperative in the analysis of the reclassification program, putting a positive spin on the government classification efforts. The report states that "it is clearly demonstrable that our national security would be at increased risk if the information involved [that found in the records now reclassified] was compromised,"[58] although the report provides no specificity about this. Far more disturbing, of course, is the report's conclusion that "NARA has, at times, acquiesced too readily to the re-review efforts or withdrawal decisions of agencies," as well as it lacking the "necessary resources" to monitor reclassification efforts.[59] There were other comments suggesting problems at NARA, perhaps due to its resources and managerial issues; a comment about the CIA re-review of records suggested that "due to a significant breakdown in communication between an agency reviewer and NARA, some classified records that State and CIA intended for release were withheld while some classified records that they intended to be withheld were released."[60] There are other allusions to such breakdowns, both at NARA and other federal agencies, throughout the report.

At a number of points in the audit report, there are comments made as to how there needs to be additional investigation. For example, it was discovered that in "one re-review conducted by the CIA, unclassified records were withdrawn in order to obfuscate the truly sensitive classified equities the agency was trying to protect. Some of these unclassified records were subsequently the subject of FOIA requests, most of which have been pending for up to four years." The audit report indicates that due to the "complexity of the issues pertaining to this situation" there needs to be "ongoing ISOO oversight."[61] However, one might conclude that it was precisely this kind of behavior, both on the part of the federal agencies and under the noses of NARA administrators, which needed to be primarily investigated. In another place in the report, describing the fact that some agencies can withdraw records simply "because the agency *can* continue classification," it was also noted that "NARA now recognizes that in some instances they acquiesced too readily to some of the re-reviews and withdrawal of some records." This problem is made all the more critical since the report also notes that "in other instances, where NARA resisted, especially at the presidential libraries, agencies would, at times, reconsider and withdraw their request."[62] Such challenges were made all the more obvious by the audit report's conclusion that while federal agencies were putting more resources into classification and re-classification activities that "there has been no corresponding increase in resources available to or otherwise applied by NARA for this activity."[63] The audit report focuses on having NARA consider re-engineering its classification procedures, but the details of what this means and how this fits into other NARA activities and resource concerns are left unexplored.

More interesting in the audit report is the statement concerning the secret agreements made between NARA and various federal agencies. The following statement explains the official perspective on these agreements:

> Because of the many issues associated with the CIA re-review of INR records and the resulting damage to the collection's provenance, NARA sought to establish more effective procedures in the event that any future re-reviews of open records might occur. Along these lines, in 2001, NARA entered into a classified MOU with CIA relating to records among the holdings of the National Archives at College, which was recently declassified. Subsequently, in 2002, USAF and CIA requested that NARA sign a similar classified MOU, to address a particular problem of improper declassification that they had identified. The USAF MOU was modeled directly on the CIA MOU. NARA has indicated that their interest in signing both MOUs was to ensure that the records were properly handled, that the re-review of open records was done expeditiously in order to minimize the burden on researchers, and to minimize the number of records withdrawn.[64]

This reads like a report made internally, and not something from an independent, external group. While there is wording indicating the need for "increased transparency" so that there would be no "perceptions that such efforts are attempts to conceal official embarrassment or to otherwise attempt to 'rewrite history,'"[65] there is no discussion why a deputy archivist signed such important agreements or why the previous or incumbent Archivist seemed to know nothing about them. This may explain why the ISOO Director appended a nearly three page message to the report, indicating that there are many classification, declassification, and reclassification issues that are far greater than the actions of individuals in the various federal agencies and NARA, and calling for renewed attention to addressing and resolving problems with the system and offering assistance in new training in the classification program to federal officials, researchers, and interested members of the public. However, stating that the "integrity of the security classification program is essential to our nation's continued well-being"[66] is one thing, and holding NARA accountable to its professional mission and ethical standards is something very different.

If one was focused only on the issue of government secrecy and the classification issue, what transpired over a couple of months could be seen in a very positive light. A researcher stumbled upon the re-classification program, secret agreements were revealed, the media cast a spotlight on the case, a national professional association spoke out about the situation, the Archivist of the United States pledged that the National Archives would operate transparently and more responsibly in the future, and proposals for reforming the classification of government records were introduced. All of this looks like democratic governance and professional practices at their finest. All of this must be tempered, however, with some comments of more troublesome matters.

Conclusion: Any Lessons Learned?

While it appears that classification concerns have been reasonably addressed, there are other very disturbing conclusions that can be drawn from this case. The conclusions relate to the matter of professional leadership, the persistent problems at NARA, and the condition of the American archival community.

Does the archives and records management community have any leadership? Both SAA and its counterpart association, the Association of Records Managers and Administrators (ARMA), have often looked to NARA for leadership. However, NARA, in recent decades, has seemed uninterested in assuming such a leadership role, and it has often been more combative with the professional records community. At the same time, SAA's reluctance to speak out about NARA circumstances, in this case and others, reflects poorly on this organization's own leadership commitment. ARMA, even more pointedly, made no statement about the NARA reclassification case and the Records Management listserv, often reflecting ARMA interests, featured no discourse on the case. Any archivist or records manager might wonder, then, just whether their professional community has any strong leadership, at least for matters of public policy.

Are these kinds of problems at NARA really new? Historically, they do not seem to be. Thirty years ago, Donald McCoy, in his superb and balanced history of the National Archives, documented how its efforts in declassification may be the source of forthcoming battles that could politicize the federal agency. McCoy assesses how the National Archives' constant negotiating with agencies about access restrictions, secrecy, and declassification could threaten its mission, partly because of the Archivist's reluctance to take a stronger hand in such matters.[67] McCoy predicted well what we have seen play out in recent years and months. We have lived through the litigation of the FBI field case files, the PROFS email, and the Nixon papers, and we have often seen a very weak National Archives at work. The recent reclassification controversy is not a new situation, and it won't be the last scandal or controversial program — at least it won't be until NARA gets stronger leadership and it embraces a true partnership with its various constituency groups (like SAA, assuming this association wakes up to its leadership responsibilities as well).

Finally, is the archives and records management community really engaged in or knowledgeable about the need for a strong National Archives? The discussion about the NARA reclassification scandal suggests that only scattered individuals really have much interest in this federal archives, and, most likely, the National Archives leaders probably view many of these individuals as more troublesome than helpful (I know this is the case for me, since I have been told this directly and personally). When something as important as this case goes largely uncommented by archivists and records managers, one can easily see why the National Archives itself has so little interest in being a professional leader or staking out a stronger public policy role. Who would be there to help the National Archives? Who would advocate for the kind of archives we need? And while we might not be able to expect that archivists in small programs, far removed from the politics of Washington, D.C. would step out to lobby for change, we can wonder why state government archivists, archival educators, and others are conspicuous by their silence.

And the silence we hear may be the eroding of democracy and a profession once known for its efforts to fight for open access to the documents of the past.

Chapter Seven

Archival Ethics: The Truth of the Matter

"The task of the philosopher is neither to belittle truth nor to exalt it, neither to deny it nor to defend it, but to explain why we need the concept and what it is to possess it."[1]

Introduction

We live and work in a time when there are many challenges to the archival mission and the general administration of records. National security, privacy, intellectual property, a fragile digital documentary heritage, and a host of other issues and concerns requires that society's records keepers be vigilant about technical, administrative, legal, and ethical matters. It is all about public trust, and the ethical dimension looms largest when we assume such a bigger perspective. As one commentator on archival ethics codes notes, the purpose of these codes is to buoy public faith in the trustworthiness of archival institutions and the people who work there, and "they [archivists] must be able to make reference to codified ethics in order to proffer a justification for that faith."[2] In many ways, however, the spate of writings in the past decade in the international archival community about matters of recordkeeping and accountability, public policy, and societal issues have occurred apart from the writings about professional ethics. Not only are there reasons for why this has occurred, but there are consequences as well.

Archivists and records managers strive to ply their trade in an ethical manner. Both branches of the records community possess ethics codes, now regularly read about ethics matters in their professional literatures, and attend conference sessions and workshops on this topic. This chapter explores the question of whether records professionals are as aware of the ethical dimensions of their work as they should be. I consider first the historical and professional context of archival ethics, then examine a recent case about business archives involving the author that suggests the need for some renewed attention about professional ethics, and conclude with a discussion about how archivists might reconsider the ethical dimensions of their work. Since there is no clear consensus about the particulars of archival ethics, what I am writing here may be received by some as being controversial, misguided, or even misinformed. It is why archivists and other records professionals must rethink this aspect of their work.

The Background of Archival Ethics

In 1980 the Society of American Archivists (SAA) approved its first official ethics code; since then it has been revised twice (in 1992 and again in 2005).[3] In this sense, the renewed attention on archival ethics was stirring at about the same time as the more broadly defined information professions were grappling with this area.[4] Prior to this code, the National Archives had adopted a document in 1955 called "The Archivist's Code" and it served as the semi-official ethics guide for the North American profession until SAA's efforts.[5] The earliest SAA code seemed to be a document designed for framing and display (like that of its NARA predecessor), while the 1992 code, with an ample commentary, was a code designed for use (or so that was part of the reasoning behind it).[6] The most recent version has removed the commentary, reflecting the SAA leadership's convictions that the code is not enforceable, that it subjects the Society to potential legal liability, and, as Karen Benedict argues, that the code with commentary muddles its meaning and usefulness.[7]

Through these decades of discussion about the archival ethics code, we can discern the general limitations of codes. The Association of Records Administrators and Managers' (ARMA) adoption of a code a decade and a half after the first of SAA's codes suggests something of the weakness of professional association codes. Commentators on ARMA's code blatantly associate the code's value as providing a foundation for or evidence of a stronger professionalism (and as a way of conveying to employers and the public the notion of what their field represents), rather than providing any set of directives that can be monitored or enforced.[8] When it was perceived that in order to claim professional status one of the benchmarks was an ethics codes, the interest in ethics seems to have grown (at least nominally). The general professional literature about ethics reflects some of these attitudes.

Archivists and records managers have been writing about ethical issues for a number of decades, although not very much (at least, until very recently). Richard Lytle, in 1970, called for revising the ARMA ethics code, pointing to the notion that all "mature professions" possess strong codes and that the "maturity and vitality of a profession can be measured by its concern for ethics in this broadest sense."[9] In 1982, Karen Benedict, concluding that "professional ethics is another important topic that has received scant attention" in the business archives area, then noted that "Lytle's was the only article in business archives literature to grapple with these difficult issues, which need additional exploration and definition." She urged that "particular attention should be paid to the subject of ethics for business archivists, because their positions and responsibilities are somewhat different from the rest of the profession and include a higher probability of involvement in protracted litigation."[10] American archivists, beyond discoursing on the general parameters of the SAA ethics code at various times,[11] have also focused their attention on certain aspects of archival functions and their ethical implications or challenges, such as access, processing, and collecting.[12] Archivists, internationally, have also reflected on a variety of ethical issues concerning the formulating of ethics codes[13] as well as their basic functions, such as preservation and access.[14]

By and large, however, the focus on ethics has been on the role that codes play in these professions. Michael Hill, looking more broadly at ethics in the information professions, notes that the codes have "four practical uses," including being an "occasional reminder... that being a member of a profession does entail an obligation to conform to the standards of behavior which are normal among other members," determining "whether a member who behaves in an usual way has offended against the principles of the profession," indicating publicly that the profession is "responsible," and, finally, provides a "basis for defending one's proper actions against outside pressure and interference."[15] While these all sound good, one wonders just how useful they are in practice. Others have, for example, depicted the limitations of codes, with their focus on rules and procedures, in complex and ever-changing environments,[16] or simply alluded to the range of concerns and challenges that extend far beyond what is represented in codes.[17] Obviously, it is far easier to consider the role, content, and use of professional ethics codes than it is to explore the generally murkier matters of ethical practice, failings, and successes (often because most people don't want to discuss these matters openly and place their heads on the chopping block).

Records professionals in the field usually demand more knowledge about computer applications or professional technical standards than about ethical approaches for their entry-level hires. It is very much a professional dilemma, one suggesting that professionals such as archivists and records managers are both unsure about the primacy of ethics codes and the foundations upon which they are built. Yet, we know that in certain kinds of organizational environments that ethical matters play a primary role in shaping the framework for how records are administered. In the midst of a discussion about records retention scheduling in law firms, Barr, Chiaiese, and Nemchek observe, "Unlike many types of corporations and businesses whose recordkeeping practices are regulated by statutes and/or administrative regulations, records retention practices in the legal environment derive from ethical and/or disciplinary rules governing lawyer behavior."[18] As should be obvious from the discussion that follows, it appears that certain kinds of professionals, such as archivists and records managers in corporations, have adopted a market-centric definition of their work that diminishes the role of ethical considerations.

There are challenges with the sometimes murky realm of professional ethics. This struggle might derive from the often slippery sense of defining such concepts as ethics and accountability. For many, for example, ethics implies a philosophical or even religious matter that extends far beyond the mundane practices of archivists and records managers. And we would be wrong to discount the implications of such elements. No one should discount this aspect when they consider that archives, libraries, and museums and their documentary and artifact collections are often targeted for destruction because of their religious, cultural, and other symbolic values.[19] Or, for example, that individuals with strong religious perspectives can provide illuminating insights into ethical and moral challenges.[20] And, especially significant for archivists and records managers, especially those working in corporations, that some forms of financial records are reflective of religious attitudes from centuries ago.[21]

When I use the word ethics or accountability I am focusing on very basic and very applied concepts. When I discuss ethical practice or concerns, I mean choosing right over wrong, recognizing that we can often debate the nuances of what might be right or wrong but that we cannot ignore such aspects in our work (the identification of truth in records or truthful records is a fundamental part of the legacy of archival and records management theory and practice). Anita Allen provides a sense of what I mean by ethics: "Workplace ethics require diligence, excellence, pride of accomplishment, and integrity. The kind of integrity required begins with honesty, respect for the person and property of others, and self-control."[22] This is close to what some have termed ethical thinking, understanding that "human behavior has consequences for the welfare of others," and that there is a "common core of general ethical principles" whereby they acknowledge that it is "morally wrong to cheat, deceive, exploit, abuse, harm, or steal from others, that everyone has an ethical responsibility to respect the rights of others, including their freedom and well-being, to help those most in need of help, to seek the common good and not merely their own self-interest and egocentric pleasures, to strive in some way to make the world more just and humane."[23] This seems like a workable definition. And it is a definition that often captures at least part of the reasons why organizations and individuals must keep and administer their documents and the information contained in them.

What do I mean by accountability? It is a difficult idea to define concisely and some scholars have begun to investigate its elements as a means of gaining more precision.[24] I use accountability to refer to processes related to individuals and organizations answering to a higher authority, the assessment of compliance and carrying-out of required activities and functions, and reporting on the effectiveness of performing certain tasks and responsibilities. Accountability brings together, under one umbrella, notions of responsibility, liability, laws and regulations, and transparency of activities. In terms of archives, records, and information, accountability assumes issues such as explaining the importance of records, working against unwarranted secrecy, the importance of corporate and societal memory, and trust that is necessary between government and its citizens.[25] If there is no accountability, made possible by open access to records and information, then this represents a serious ethical lapse. And since archivists and records managers are well versed in understanding the ways in which their organizations are compliant and the implications of their records and information systems for compliance, one might expect that they would be equally aware of the ethical dimensions.

Corporate Archives and the Ethical Quest

For a while, corporate scandals replaced government ones as the focal point of ethical, legal, and policy controversies in society as well as in the records professions.[26] The Enron/Arthur Andersen scandals and the dramatic stories of the shredding of Enron's records and the collapse of auditing practices have the highest profile because of the extensive media coverage, the writing of insider accounts, and the refurbishing of business management books that had made Enron into the exemplar of the innovative corporate venture.[27] Many observers of corporate America have made telling commentaries on the challenges facing individuals working within these organizations, as well as about other unethical reporting practices (such as the falsification of annual reports).[28] The kinds of professionals that work for these entities, such as archivists and records managers, must consider matters far more complicated than the basic administration of records and information. Practical methods for managing records move from the fore, and far more complicated concerns about why the records are administered begin to crowd into the picture of what archivists and records managers do.

In a recent history of the corporation, two definitions of this entity are offered: "The first is merely as an organization engaged in business: this definition ... includes everything from informal Assyrian trading arrangements to modern leveraged buyouts. The second is more specific: the limited-liability joint-stock company is a distinct legal entity (so distinct, in fact, that its shareholders can sue it), endowed by government with certain collective rights and responsibilities."[29] It is the latter that we are interested in here. The commentators also offer this historical note about the general nature of corporations and ethics: "In general, companies have become more ethical: more honest, more humane, more socially responsible."[30] While indeed some companies have established major ethics programs, such as Lockheed Martin, the results of such programs are "difficult and controversial" to ascertain.[31] And, at this point, there have been no studies of corporations with ethics programs concentrated on records management, except for the ironic descriptions of Enron's stress on both an ethics code and a corporate consulting program for businesses interested in strengthening their workers' sensitivity to ethical matters.

Ethics codes can become useless in the corporate environment that has spun out of control. And records managers and archivists should have plenty of reason to reconsider and recommit themselves to the importance of ethics and accountability, especially as measures to counter such corporate shenanigans (like the Sarbanes-Oxley Act) dictate many new recordkeeping measures potentially transforming what such records professionals do.[32] Although the long-term implications of these scandals and the various legislative and regulatory responses cannot yet be seen, it is clear that they have shone public light on records management practices, such as records destruction, that were not previously well understood.[33] At the least, archivists and records managers are operating in a new kind of environment where ethical conduct, compliance, and accountability are more prominent and more important as factors defining their mission and driving their work.[34]

On the positive side, the importance of corporate ethics or corporate social responsibility (CSR) has intensified greatly. David Vogel notes, for example, that about five years ago he "became aware of a major revival of

CSR," so much so that the topic is a difficult one to get a handle on: "The amount of material in books, scholarly essays and papers, newspaper and magazine articles, reports, and conference proceedings, to say nothing of Web sites, is enormous — far beyond the capacity of anyone to absorb."[35] Vogel defines CSR, although recognizing that there is no firm consensus about its meaning other than the linking of financial goals with social purpose, as "practices that improve the workplace and benefit society in ways that go above and beyond what companies are legally required to do."[36] Has this movement had any impact on corporate archives and their thinking?

There is a dark storm cloud within the silver lining of CSR and corporate ethics. Vogel believes that "in the final analysis, CSR is sustainable only if virtue pays off," and even he believes that there is a "market for virtue" and that it must be acknowledged that there are severe limits to what this market might be. As Brown argues, "CSR is best understood as a niche rather than a generic strategy: it makes business sense for some firms in some areas under some circumstances."[37] Marvin Brown argues, in fact, versus the classic theory of corporate responsibility being something having to do with making a profit, looking at other ways of making a connection with a greater social responsibility. Brown "explores the challenges of corporate integrity from a civic perspective," encountering "shared civic values of meeting human needs and respecting human rights."[38] It is too soon to say what the dramatic financial collapse since 2008 may do to the notion of corporate ethics, but my suspicion is that it will become a lower priority in business activities.

Despite the growth of interest in corporate ethics and social responsibility matters, there is little in the business archives or records management literature that addresses this topic. While the scholarly business archives and records management literature is not extensive, there are a number of substantial essays where one might expect discussion of ethical matters, among the many other issues considered. Yet, despite the obvious ethical challenges corporate archivists face, these professionals seem not to have engaged with this aspect of their work. Prominent business archivist Elizabeth Adkins, in her fine assessment of the development of American business archives just a decade ago, hardly mentions any aspect that might be termed ethical, probably reflecting the general lack of attention to this topic in the literature and profession to that point.[39] A decade before Adkins' effort, overviews of American corporate archives generally included no mention of ethical issues, often trying to make the case about how much of an asset an archives program could be;

as Harold Anderson once wrote, "a business could not have a less expensive asset with a higher potential return than an archives," while focusing exclusively on the value of the program to the corporation.[40] Essays about particular types of corporate archives usually gloss over ethical issues, even when focusing on basic questions and concerns supporting or detracting from archival operations.[41] Acknowledging the concerns many business archivists have with archival programs acquiring business records and the concerns with control felt by some corporate executives, one archivist describing a state historical society's business records acquisition program still did not discuss any potential or real ethical concerns.[42] It should be the case that as corporate archivists have tried to relate their mission to their role in supporting their employing business that they should also identify where there may be ethical and legal problems in taking on such an agenda.

Some observers have hinted at the ethical problems facing corporate archivists and records managers. Historian Duncan McDowall speculates as follows: "one suspects that the litigiousness of our times ... has bred a conscious impulse in many executives to avoid the keeping of any written record of how and why decisions were made. This same impulse, often combined with an abiding instinct for self-preservation *within* the corporation, may explain why so many executives regard archivists and their purpose with suspicion."[43] English archivist Leonard McDonald has written an essay about "ethical dilemmas" confronting corporate archivists, worrying that "in the world of business ... the archivist still tends to adopt the role of the medieval archivist — defending his master's claims to intellectual property against attack by others."[44] McDonald worries, as well, about the perceptions of the archivist, the division in professional cultures, and our clientele. He notes, for example, archivists "tend to look harder at what we regard as ethical responsibilities than does general management. General management, with its expressed intention of responsibility to the shareholder and to the successful continuity of the Company, has its own singleminded sense of priorities and ethical responsibilities."[45] Anne Van Camp, in discussing the ultra sensitive area of access to corporate archives, mentions some of the tensions inherent in this function but does not frame them in the ethical realm.[46] Douglas Bakken, in his overview of American corporate archives in the early 1980s, mentioned then that many corporate lawyers fear that "creating a corporate archives will automatically lead to a series of lawsuits," adding that "One hopes that more executives will weight the advantages of permanently preserving records before ordering their destruction out of fear of litigation."[47] Yet, Bakken does not provide any guidance about how corporate archivists need to approach their ethical responsibilities.

There are even more dangerous signs about how some corporate archivists view their professional role within their employing organizations. Gord Rabchuk, a Canadian corporate archivist, commenting on the many ways that archivists have traditionally not fit into the corporate environment, essentially argues for corporate archivists to adapt and to forget about the usual archival practices and principles: "Much like any smart business proposition, the success of business archives programs is largely dependent upon two fundamental factors: a genuine demand for the services/products offered and the necessary flexibility to streamline these to meet the client's ever-changing requirements. Unfortunately, the presence of such logic has never been obvious in the traditional definition of corporate archives. Historically, the archives package has been advertised to management with a strong focus on the key activities of archival theory and practice — accessioning, appraising, arranging/describing, preserving, and reference — with little ingenuity demonstrated in how these skills can benefit the corporation. To be perfectly frank, who cares?"[48] For archivists to become capitalists and serve their employers' needs seems fine, but what about matters like professional ethics? Certainly business archivists must connect their mission and activities to those of their for-profit employers, and there have been excellent assessments of this relationship[49]; yet, to relegate professional ethics and other public good responsibilities under the financial bottom-line seems foolhardy at best.

Even efforts to generate guidelines for business archives, while acknowledging the importance of matters of service to society and researchers generally avoid ethical concerns, instead stressing the primacy of serving the needs of the corporation first and foremost.[50] Deborah Gardner, commenting on the 1982 cluster of articles on business archives published in the *American Archivist*, does not mention ethics as a concern and glosses over any concept of public service. For her, as for many corporate archivists as well as employers of such professionals, the case for their programs is "keyed to justifications that clearly define the archival function as part of corporate culture and organization," including being an "income-producing center" and relegating the use of the archival resources by scholars and other researchers as being "an important public service" but primarily one as valued as an asset to the corporation itself.[51] Phil Mooney, providing another commentary, also puts the emphasis on "seeking to make their programs more relevant to company needs," with nothing about ethical and other similar matters.[52] Demonstrating the importance of archives and records management programs to the employing corporation is, of course, a necessary and important activity. Yet, does this mean that ethical and other related issues must play a back seat to current processes, profit-making activities, and other such concerns?

The "Sun Mad" Poster Controversy and Archival Ethics

A minor controversy occurred regarding the use of a political poster on the cover of the *American Archivist* that reflects the challenges of archival ethics in the corporate sector and that speaks perhaps generally to the lack of development of the notion of ethics in this field. It is a painful and difficult matter to write about, both because it involves myself and because it is so easily open to misinterpretation. My intent here is not to accuse anyone of unethical conduct, but I do believe that the poster controversy does suggest something of the political, professional, and societal environment that influences how archivists and records managers view ethical matters.

Two letters and an editor's column were published in the Fall/Winter 2004 issue of the *American Archivist* regarding the use of a political poster (originally created in a campaign against the Sun Maid corporation, with the poster redrawing and parodying the well-known corporate logo to be "Sun Mad") on the cover of the Fall/Winter 2003 issue of the same journal.[53] The inside description of the cover illustration reported that the poster was a "striking example of the powerful messages that can be conveyed by political posters" and that it related to Susan Tschabrun's essay considering "many of the issues archivists face in developing and administering poster collections."[54] However, a group of business archivists and another prominent archivist complained that the cover "disturbed" them. Reasons given for this included that it "seems inappropriate for an association whose membership includes both archivists working in corporations or at universities and historical societies whose holdings include business records"; that it "represents an unnecessary legal risk for the Society" and "sends all of the wrong messages to managers who already view the preservation of the historical record as tangential to contemporary business practice"; how the cover "holds the potential to undermine the professional credibility of SAA members who work in business settings"; that the journal was now an "attack ad against corporations"; and that the poster's use "places sensationalism and circulation above all other priorities." The editor provided a reasoned response about the criticisms of the use of the cover. He describes how he had the Society's legal counsel review the use of the poster and rightly points out that the *American Archivist* serves the "whole archival profession," suggesting as a result that disagreement about the journal's content and covers always may be present. The controversy spurred me on to write my own letter to the editor, published in the subsequent issue of the journal, and essentially summarized here.

The problems presented by this case should be obvious, even with a cursory commentary. First, will we have to achieve the complete happiness of every group in the profession when we select a cover illustration, a task sure to lead one to abandon anything other than putting plain covers on every association publication? Is the apparent offense limited only to covers, or would it extend to the content of the journal, and other publications, as well? Publication in the journal, as well as other publications issued by the Society of American Archivists, supports the ongoing development of professional knowledge, and, as part of this professional knowledge there must be room for a diversity of opinions, including even controversial ideas and opinions. Second, just what is the mission of corporate archives? After all, the illustration on the ill-fated *American Archivist* cover was part of an archival collection. Is the mission of corporate archives only to make their organizations look good or to serve a public relations purpose? What about the values of records and their management for purposes such as legal compliance, evidence of activities, and accountability? If a company found such negative documents and artifacts in their possession as the political poster used on the journal cover, would it destroy or bury the objects?

The corporate role in society has always been controversial, and never so much as today. The recent corporate scandals, leading to new efforts to regulate corporate accounting practices as witnessed in the Sarbanes-Oxley Act, are very much concerned with how corporations administer their records, and are but an example of the corporation's complex place in our culture. Moreover, books are pouring out addressing matters ranging from the corporation's not always positive role in a democratic society to their efforts in controlling intellectual property and information to their ethical practices or lack thereof. One cannot read a newspaper on any given day without reading about some corporate scandal, so the idea that the *American Archivist*'s cover may possibly have offended a corporate leader or two seems a bit misplaced; I suspect CEOs have a lot more on their mind these days than an *American Archivist* cover. What intrigues me is how the individual functioning as an archivist or records manager can work in the corporate environment in any realistic way, adhering to any sense of professional ethics or mission, without some serious reflection about the practical implications both of their work and professional codes and standards. These are not easy questions and there are not pat answers, but suggesting that the Society should be overly concerned about the use of a particular political poster is, in my opinion, way off base from the kinds of concerns the records professions ought to be addressing.

Most disturbing to me was the implied threat of litigation due to the use of the illustration. No one will deny such a possibility, but given that any individual or organization might sue the Society of American Archivists over any issue, can such a concern be the primary factor determining how a professional association acts? Worrying about this would preclude the Society of American Archivists from taking any professional stance, issuing any public pronouncement, and, yes, the Society ought to stop publishing its newsletter and the *American Archivist* as well. It ought to get out of the publishing business altogether and close down its operations. At the least, the Society of American Archivists ought to cease the expansion of its publications catalog, out of fear that it will pick some publication that might express an opinion about records management or archives that a few members (or even one member) of the Society might not like. And what a loss this would be.

And what a contradiction this would be as well. Records can be, by their very nature, inherently controversial. They document good and bad actions, the activities of evil and exemplary people and organizations, the decisions by corrupt and stellar government officials and corporate leaders, and the activities of strong and weak university administrators and faculty members. Records show us at our best and worse, and they depict the full spectrum of activities of people, institutions, societies, and humanity, from wonderful humanitarian campaigns to terrorist and genocidal wars. And records inspire debate about the nature of whether we can ascertain the truth of the past, and the debate certainly continues within the records community and the disciplines depending on access to records. And, it might be added, records, due to their power as memory and cultural symbols, inspire strong feelings, just as the blatantly controversial "Sun Mad" poster does. Does this mean that we cannot preserve or use the poster because it elicits emotions or potentially offends someone or some organization? Hopefully, we will affirm that this is not the case, as well as the impossibility of administering any document or embarking on any project in a way that will not generate responses.

None of the individuals involved in this controversy are bad individuals or poor professionals. What this case illustrates, however, is a degree of professional self-censorship, reflecting trends in our society. There seems to be an edginess, an unease, in the swirling contradictions, interpretations, legal suits, and governmental actions presently evident in our post 9/11-era. If archivists and records managers adopt such conservative views, then they may have to rethink, in a serious and fundamental way, the very mission that they have seemed to adhere to over the years. Corporations administering records only to make themselves look good can hardly be said to understand larger questions about their role in the commonweal. Moreover, they will fail if they strive to manipulate their own documentary heritage in such a way. However, the bigger question is where archivists and records managers will be and what they will be doing in organizations with such an agenda.

I was not the only individual concerned about the corporate archivists' response to the use of the political poster. In the same issue of the *American Archivist* publishing my letter, another letter, from a "new member of the Society of American Archivists," was also published. This individual expressed concern with the idea that cover designs must be chosen with "equal sensitivity," by which this was interpreted as "offending no one." This letter writer also questioned the degree of sensitivity we ought to have for corporations in any event, since the "history of business involves conflict" worldwide. This individual concludes, "I hope the editors of the *American Archivist* will continue to choose controversial art for the cover, publish complex articles of professional and general interest, and retain a commitment to the preserving and accessing the breadth and depth of the historical record, in spite of opposition from interested parties. If so, I know I will not have made a mistake in choosing the archival profession as a practice committed to the impartial preservation of our documentary heritage."[55]

Others privately expressed similar concerns about this controversy. In fairness, I also received complaints. As I was leaving the SAA 2005 annual meeting, I was approached by an individual identifying herself as a corporate archivist who stated that my letter to the journal had "maligned the good name of corporate archivists." This was not one of the signatories of the letters that I was responding, and I denied, of course, that I had any such intention. In retrospect, I suspect that my sentence, repeated in this essay, stating "What intrigues me is how the individual functioning as an archivist or records manager can work in the corporate environment in any realistic way, adhering to any sense of professional ethics or mission" is what has fueled the controversy and become the focus of this controversy, rather than the idea that a particular cover design of the *American Archivist* must be carefully scrutinized to ensure that a single individual in the profession is not offended by it. For a while, I regretted writing the letter because of this, but I am now convinced, more than ever, that at the heart of the problem is a fundamental issue relating to archival ethics. This is what I have tried to explain more fully in this essay.

Others will continue to have other perspectives about this matter, as well as about what is entailed in what we think of as professional ethics. Indeed, this was brought home when the immediate past and current SAA president published their thoughts on the cover controversy in another issue of the *American Archivist*. Randall Jimerson and Richard Pearce-Moses acknowledged that the controversy had "raised important questions for professional debate about how archivists define our professional responsibilities," but they also expressed concerns "that it is important to receive expressions of concern from our members with due consideration and respect." Mostly, they opined, that "we should be especially careful to avoid even the appearance of questioning the ethics of an entire segment of our members," and that this is important in respecting the "need for diversity in the archival profession, and it seeks to ensure that all who are interested in protecting the historical record feel welcome."[56] Except for this essay, their letter brings to a close the Sun Mad poster controversy. My only additional comments are that questioning a particular group's reasons in this debate should not be interpreted as reflecting on their motives and ethics, but that there are certainly elements of this debate that reflect ethical challenges.

This controversy provides no evidence, of course, that any corporate archives or records management program is destroying in any deliberate fashion records in order to protect a business or to provide the best face of the corporation. What it reveals is a set of attitudes suggesting that individuals in the field may be ultra-sensitive to the possibility that certain activities may lead to negative press, jeopardizing programs and careers. Making references to not carrying out certain activities out of fear of litigation, in a highly litigious society, is hardly good advice. Whether or not this kind of thinking violates the spirit of the relevant professional ethics codes is a matter others ought to debate, but I submit that, at best, we ought to be troubled about such attitudes. In an environment where we have weak ethics codes, with no enforcement procedures, along with attitudes suggesting that records professionals may operate out of fear of drawing negative attention to their programs, we ought to be concerned whether we can operate effectively in an ethical fashion or, more importantly, that we can build trust with our employers, constituents, and the public.

Conclusion

These are very dangerous (as well as interesting and exciting) times to be an archivist or records manager, all suggested by recent corporate scandals, evil government regimes, the necessary growth of truth commissions, the control of records and information, media distortion, and fabrications of the past — all events and trends that had me writing over the past couple of years essays about their implications for archivists and records managers. And, given what records professionals do and the access to evidence they have, just what are their ethical responsibilities as societal and organizational whistleblowers — individuals who place the welfare of society and its inhabitants over their own? This is an interesting question hardly being addressed within the archival and records management community, but one that will dominate, I think, much of the discussion and debate in the future.

There are many practical ethical issues we could consider that the archivist or records manager might face. Since records professionals work across their organizations and have access to most, if not all, the information being generated, it is logical to assume that they will discover illegal activities, wrongdoing, and ethical lapses as soon as anyone else in their workplace. Archivists and records managers have not really addressed the consequences of such possibilities, instead choosing to focus on the ethics of their own practice — such as providing equal access to all researchers, not acquiring documentary materials of questionable origins and ownership, and not falsely accusing other archival programs and records professionals of unprofessional practice. These are all important concerns, of course, but they are inwardly focused on activities that must seem like arcane professional activity to outsiders, and they hardly address the major ethical matters of the day. In general, archivists and records managers are honest, sincere, hard-working professionals not prone to enter into questionable activities. The real ethical challenges facing archivists and records managers have more to do with the shifting shapes of the roles of governments and other organizations, such as corporations, that create a considerable portion of the records and employ many of the presently working records professionals.

Archivists and records managers generally believe that records are important and that they make a difference in society, although sometimes they seem to waffle as much as any other group about just what this means. They don't want to be seen as clerks or secretaries, so they develop elaborate new justifications for their roles, usually tying into the glitzier aspects of the information or knowledge society while moving them farther from their main responsibility — records. While some of this falls well within the normal range of professional debate and navel-gazing, some of this also weakens archivists and records managers generating a coherent vision and articulating a clear mission. If there are so many ways of looking at archives, how can records professionals expect organizational leaders, policymakers, and the public to comprehend what it is that they do. Yet, these matters are hardly as serious as the question of whether archivists and records managers ought ever to be whistle-blowers, grabbing onto a higher ethical norm that demands their seeking a different role in contributing a public good.

Whistle-blowing — "employees' reporting of illegal, immoral, or illegitimate activities to parties who may be able to take action"[57] — is rising in frequency, but it is an issue that has received little attention by records professionals, despite the fact that archivists and records professionals have responsibilities that give them access to corporate, government, and organizational information that provides a clear window on any improprieties by these institutions and their leaders and staffs. Archivists and records managers, with access to an organization's records and information systems, have access to more evidence of corporate, government, and organizational wrongdoing than any other group. So, why have records professionals not addressed this issue? The obvious answer is, of course, that whistle-blowers destroy their careers and livelihoods, no matter how right they may seem to be in the public's eyes; but this seems too obvious an explanation. More to the point may be that records managers and archivists tend to be loyal to their organizations, and confused by what their societal roles might entail. They are, for example, bombarded by advice about records retention and destruction instructing them to protect their organizations.

Records professionals may be ill equipped at this point to consider the consequences of whistle-blowing, and, indeed, I feel constrained by the immensity of the problem. But the greater explanation may be that records professionals lack self-confidence or believe that they are powerless given their professional status and public profile. It is difficult, of course, to firmly state when someone should go public and threaten themselves with professional self-immolation.

I am not, however, going to offer a precise list of circumstances that would indicate when an archivist or records manager should break ranks and speak out. Not only are there are too many variables at play to attempt this, but I must admit that I have not formed in my own mind a completely satisfactory picture of what is involved. Hopefully what I offer will generate some dialogue, enabling archivists and records managers to understand better their responsibilities in their organizations and society. In some instances, what may need to be involved is no more than revisiting what people have said in the past about ethical issues. For example, when Pemberton and Pendergraft argued nearly two decades ago for an ARMA ethics code that included the "principle of the free flow of and access to information in society as a necessary condition for an informed populace and maintenance of democratic processes" and to "strongly resist, therefore, any pressure or subornation to mishandle or misuse information or records — even when proper handling may have an adverse affect on the organizations for which they work," one can wonder how this relates to some of the issues recently on the minds of some corporate archivists.[58]

In the meantime, the archival and records management community needs to engage in a number of initiatives relating to ethics issues. Despite a fairly steady stream of writing about ethical matters, there is essentially no research on such concerns. For example, some efforts have been made in other sectors of the information professions to determine ethical attitudes since knowing something of this is important for ascertaining "areas of possible contention" and to identify "where policies may be needed to encourage more ethical behavior in the workplace and high standards of practice for the profession."[59] Some surveys of archivists and records managers about ethical concerns would help in future discussions.

Archivists and records managers need to go beyond the business of creating ethics codes, and, instead, they need to begin to consider just what roles they really play within their employing institutions. Historian McDowall, in mulling over the place of the archivist in the corporation, suggests that historians and archivists can "bring a disinterested, fresh, and valuable viewpoint to the work of the corporation. We can be part of the corporation, but not necessarily its creature."[60] He does not offer any practical insights into what such a disinterested role might be, but that is certainly something records professionals need to re-consider, and in earnest.

Chapter Eight

The Archives & Archivists Listserv Controversy[1]

Introduction

Archivists and records managers have wrestled with the implications, theoretical and practical, of electronic records and information systems for several generations. Most of the discussions have focused on the technical aspects of the digital systems, and these discussions, often leading to heated debate, have tended to suggest a Doomsday scenario of the demise of the documentary universe. Of course, archivists and records managers have often disagreed about the implications of these new and emerging systems — as I recently wrote about regarding electronic mail[2], sometimes because of differing professional missions, varying professional cultures, and divergent mandates set by their employers.

It doesn't take a genius to figure out that the unease with the electronic systems generating and maintaining records is about more than technical expertise or insurmountable technical challenges. After all, records professionals have always contended with technical issues, from how to maintain fading engineering blueprints to the latest portable computing devices being used to create and maintain more complex and seemingly more fragile documents. And neither archivists nor records managers have been shy about expressing their opinions about such matters. In the late winter 2007, we gained ample evidence of this when the Society of American Archivists (SAA) leadership matter-of-factly announced that within a couple of weeks it was going to dump the online archives of the Archives and Archivists listserv.

The controversy about this decision started with the lengthy posting on this listserv on March 13, 2007 by SAA Executive Director Nancy Beaumont about SAA Council's decision to destroy the archives of the listserv.[3] In her message she reported that "after seven months of discussion," involving an "appraisal recommendation from SAA's archival repository," the "recommendations of a Task Force," and a "communication from Miami University of Ohio," the SAA Council decided to dispose of the list archives "representing material created from 1993 to 2006." The reasons offered were costs not in line with the "evidential or informational value of the archives," made more complicated by "significant legal and administrative impediments to transferring the archives to another institution for preservation and access" (the host institution, Miami University of Ohio, was not going to support it past the end of March 2007). Beaumont then provided some additional information about the issues involved and the resulting deliberations by Council, including an appraisal assessment concluding that the "listserv possesses no significant value as evidence of SAA's own history, functions, or activities.... In terms of informational value, the content of the listserv is highly uneven, consisting mainly of postings with current value (such as news items, job announcements, product recommendations), opinion pieces reflecting the views of particular individuals, and advice concerning specific practices and procedures;" an evaluation from two archival educators who did not consider the "listserv to be a significant or substantial research resource; and the revealing about disagreement among Council members about the listserv's value, leading to the establishment of a task force to gather additional information, with subsequent differing recommendations about the maintenance of the listserv archives, especially given intellectual property issues (it was noted that "currently there are two requests pending from posters who wish to remove their posts, one of whom is threatening legal action") and financial costs.

Many of the statements made in her message, while certainly not intended to deceive or mislead anyone (indeed, one could argue quite the opposite, that this official message from SAA headquarters minced no words at all and was a remarkably blunt document announcing a major decision affecting the life of the Archives listserv community and providing nearly no time to respond to it), implied that the decision was merely an appraisal decision — something that most archivists do as a routine part of daily operations. But was it a good appraisal process? Much of her message somehow revolved about the notion that this was a "difficult appraisal decision," a conclusion few might question since all appraisal decisions are a challenge. We know there are differences of opinion about appraisal objectives, different methodologies for this function, and a variety of circumstances that can transform the most seemingly straightforward appraisal assignment into a nightmare. Indeed, Beaumont's message alluded to a number of these issues, particularly costs, intellectual property, and technical aspects concerning the list's electronic archives.

Other aspects of the Beaumont message indicated additional fissures in the SAA appraisal effort. For example, the SAA Executive Director reported that the listserv archives included little evidence about SAA's history and that its content is "highly uneven." Was the archives list supposed to reflect the SAA and its activities? And, what does "highly uneven" mean? One might sense that this indicates that there were some difficulties with understanding just what a listserv represents or how it relates to other documentary forms. References to evaluating some products (not cited, however) of the listserv archives for its research value and the use of unnamed educators and the generation of some kind of appraisal report not released in full all contribute to the sense of a closed or secretive process counter to what many archives were seeking to do in their appraisal efforts. It is easy to argue, for example, that what SAA had engaged in was a process contrary with the kind of collaborative, open appraisal methodologies discussed in the past couple of decades.[4]

Does this SAA appraisal decision reflect a continuing unease with dealing with electronic records and information systems? My comparison of how archivists and records managers perceive electronic mail messages indicates such problems. Or, perhaps, the decision underscores poor leadership and the challenges SAA faces with speaking for the entire American archival community, maybe even the difficulties facing professional associations in the digital age where people can come together and work with each without having to be present physically in expensive hotels and cities. Such matters can only be assessed in an in-depth review of listservs and the reaction of the professional community to this decision by SAA leadership.

The first part of this chapter considers the background of listservs and other similar forms of virtual networked communities. The second part examines in greater detail the debate that ensued when the SAA leadership announced its decision. My argument is that while it is difficult to see this appraisal decision or the report of it as a model for appraisal work, that this is not a case merely about appraisal. Nor, for that matter, is this a case concerning difficulties with electronic recordkeeping systems, although it sends poor messages about how well archivists are dealing with such records. This seems to be mostly a lapse in professional leadership that inadvertently conveys serious problems with appraising digital materials. The ease of communicating and collaborating with each other via listservs and other such networked communities is a significant factor in how records professionals now work. The decision by the SAA leadership to destroy the Archives & Archivists listserv archives not only reflects a lack of understanding of the importance of such virtual communities, but it suggests that professional associations need to rethink their role or face challenges that may make them irrelevant in the near future.

The Archives & Archivists Listserv

From its earliest days, the Archives & Archivists listserv assumed an important position in the professional dialogue among archivists and other records professionals. Frank Burke built his presidential address to the Society of American Archivists around a debate on the listserv, beginning on February 14, 1992 and extending over three months, about the relationship between archivists and historians. From a single comment, an intense dialogue ensued. As Burke comments,

> The response that came back from the participants in the LISTSERV created the greatest archival dialogue on a single subject since Ted Schellenberg and Lester Cappon dined together at the Cosmos Club. In this case, by 'great' I mean extensive, not necessarily intellectually superlative. Where else could one have participants from the United States, Canada, England, and other points of the compass continue a discussion for over three months and include directors of federal archival institutions, state archivists, university special collections librarians, rare book librarians, archival and library educators, some of the people who have written the extant archival manuals, graduate students, museum curators, records managers, members of the national or regional professional organizations, and nonmembers who have an interest in the subject? If there was ever a town hall concept in the archival community, this exchange was it.[5]

Burke comprehends the virtual communities that these discussion groups were establishing and fostering. If we ceased with this part of Burke's commentary, then we would have to wonder why fifteen years later the SAA leadership would want to dump the electronic archives of the listserv.

Burke did not stop here. Evaluating the content of the debate, Burke eventually concluded, "This, then, is my legacy to the future: If we must debate on the archival LISTSERV, at least let us stop being sophomoric and instead recognize the family to which we all belong, provide service without feeling servitude, and advance the cause of knowledge and experimentation, inquiry, and doubt, without concern that the icons of the past shall fall."[6] What Burke was expressing was what many have stated about this or any listserv; indeed, I have been on and off the list, variously angered and disappointed by different discussions or lack of attention to serious topics, and I have expressed such sentiments myself. It is easy to understand, then, why the SAA elected officers didn't seem to be fazed in deciding to destroy the evidence of more than fifteen years of debate, discussion, and drifting on the Archives & Archivists listserv. However, how we evaluate the quality of the information and evidence represented by listserv discussions is more complex than what Burke suggests, especially since a substantial virtual community has developed around the list.

Burke's comments generated some response, including an acerbic commentary by Philip Alexander, noting, "The Archives listserv is an open electronic forum for discussion of issues affecting the profession. With over seven hundred current subscribers, it provides a unique opportunity for archivists to meet and develop relationships with colleagues, to pose questions, to share knowledge, and to debate topics of mutual concern. The listserv is a kind of electronic town meeting in which all are welcome and encouraged to express their views."[7] Alexander believes that the discomfort with the listserv was because of its "threat to business as usual. Unlike a regular conference or print vehicle (ordinarily structured to reflect mainstream thinking and favored agendas of the professional leadership), the listserv is broadly inclusive and fosters the expression of a rich diversity of views. Topics for discussion arise not by fiat or decree (what the leadership thinks ought to be discussed) but directly—and, in a sense, organically—out of the concerns and experiences of individual participants (what rank-and-file archivists want to discuss). As each of us lines up from time to time with our virtual documents, all listserv members have pretty much equal access—something quite rare in professional discourse."[8] Alexander irritated many, myself included, but in this statement, he did capture one of the chief characteristics of these online discussion groups, that they challenged other means of normally doing business. And this seems to be one of the primary characteristics of the recent debate about the maintenance of the list's archives.

Listservs carry the seeds of what can make them frustrating, namely, especially when not moderated, that they openly display lots of chaff with the wheat. They are messy. Posters send in jokes, tangential commentaries, and considerable fluff that no one is likely to think is very important, but that add to the character and culture of a list's experience. Burke, an experienced listserv user was "opposed, however, to mixing gossip, social theory, and, yes, even vituperation with professional discussion. When such objections are occasionally raised online, they are often shot down by the ranting of those who appear to have no other mechanism for communicating with the professional world, and so the voices of reason (not to be confused with tradition) often fall silent and turn to other media, thus, lessening the value of the listserv by their absence."[9] It is because of such listservs and the other temptations coming with the now remarkably easy use of email that we have witnessed a growing number of new kinds of etiquette guides.[10] One might add that gossip, vituperation, and professional discourse all can be readily found in most other venues supporting professional debate and conversation, although the ease of composing and posting messages before one's brain kicks into gear is a hallmark of these lists and e-mail in general. Although, it may be for this very reason that both e-mail and listservs can be so instructive or revealing of a wider range of perspectives at play within any professional or other community, a window into the most deeply emotion-laden and contested elements of any social or professional group.

Whatever the theoretical discourse might be about the value and utility of the archives listserv, it was obvious that it built a virtual community and that it was being used from the beginning by instructors with archival courses as a way to orient students to the current issues and debates within the field. Diana L. Shenk and Jackie R. Esposito discuss the early use of the archives list, noting its value to supplement course readings and discussions but indicating that these values are often undermined by many problems of a technical nature. [11] Other studies about the use of listservs in the library and information science field, including the archives listserv, also reveal that these virtual communities are important in professional discourse and can be quite useful in professional education.[12] These problems now, more than a decade later, seem quite quaint. Today, there are essentially no such issues, as students are quite familiar with the mechanics of listservs, blogs, wikis, and a host of other virtual communities; and, in fact, the incoming students often possess a knowledge and confidence in the use of these communications networks that exceed that of the faculty teaching the courses.

The embrace by some educators of the Archives & Archivists listserv ought not to be a surprise, although the assessment by some unnamed educators of the value of the listserv's archives was a little puzzling. For many years now, I have required that archives students monitor the listserv both because it has an uncanny ability to feature a debate about a professional issue that is being discussed in class and because it reveals so many different attitudes and opinions, more than is normally reflected in the professional and scholarly literature guarded by the barriers of peer-review and publishing norms and standards. The controversy about the decision to dump the listserv's archives occurred in the mid-way point of my course on archival appraisal, and as you might imagine it provided grist for considerable discussion about archival appraisal methodology, public dissemination of appraisal decisions, and a variety of other topics related to this course. One of my doctoral students in this class was in the midst of completing research based on the listserv archives for a doctoral seminar, and this raised discussion about the timing of the decision and the responsibility of a professional association like SAA to administer assets like this on behalf of the discipline.

Listservs and Other Professions

We can contrast such perspectives about listservs within the archival community with that of other professional groups. Research on journalists suggests that this professional group has not embraced listservs and other online discussion groups as fully. Thomas Ruggiero concludes, for example, "that the 'informality' of listservs may reflect their perceived ineffectiveness and consequent underutilization by journalists. Because of their conversational and egalitarian tone (and often rambling informality), listservs may be interpreted as a less "serious" ethical channel than journalism reviews, ethical codes, ombudsmen, news councils, and academic journals." Ruggerio sees that journalists believe that "electronic discussion groups are frivolous."[13] In this I hear the echo of what Frank Burke was stating about the archivists list. A study of a listserv supporting those engaged in information science discerned a number of reasons why participants in that community value this forum, seeing five roles: "information dissemination, knowledge exchange, community building and social binding, discussion, and collaboration."[14] One of the listserv participants described its value in the following way: "I think it plays a key role in sharing ideas with each other, so we can avoid duplication of effort. In this way, the occasional queries about a topic serve a nice role. It also plays an important role in communicating what is going on in conferences, jobs, and new things. It probably plays some role in making the IS scholarly community more cohesive by allowing us to communicate ideas, respond to them, and thus come to a consensus on certain issues. The listserv rules, of course, limit this role. But such a discussion can at least be initiated on the listserv. It has a social psychological function—it keeps us from feeling we're alone out there- knowing there are others like us and with similar interests is important. Finally, it plays a role to keep us in touch with others whom we don't know but whom we ought to know because we have similar interests."[15] In these words, I hear the sentiments expressed by

Philip Alexander. These are fairly typical assessments when listserv participants are queried about the value of these discussion groups. One wonders whether such notions of the virtual communities ought to make archivists more eager to preserve and manage their archives as important windows into many different professional and societal groups.

This latter study of an IS listserv had much to offer about issues of its administration, noting that while people were not complaining about the list's management they still had many suggestions to make, including: "make participation more bidirectional (more encouragement to reply to requests and to share request results)"; "encourage fewer cliques and more participation from the entire community"; "encourage more spirited debates on worthwhile scholarly issues—have the list manager or pioneers in the field present questions once a month to discuss"; create a "section to allow for updates of where people have moved - new positions, etc"; and generate "less doctoral students asking for others to do their literature searches for them." These are the kinds of observations that have been made on the archives listserv as well. However, the researchers also note that "whether through policy or intervention, these suggestions are opportunities for the list's management to facilitate more interaction. Nonetheless, a delicate balance must be met between policy and freedom."[16] Might it be that the kinds of fears expressed by Philip Alexander had something to do with the SAA leadership announcing that an archives assembled over a decade and a half would be dumped rather unceremoniously in two weeks time? If nothing, there may have been a misreading of how seriously such a virtual community might be taken because of its seemingly chaotic and free form expressions and discussion threads.

What may be most interesting for the Archives list debate is that the tenth anniversary of another list prompted two "researchers interested in organizational phenomena"[17] to do a study of the list (no such research has emerged in regards to its counterpart in the archives field). As most studies do, this one suggested the formulation of a set of new research questions which could be applied to other listservs, focusing on listserv roles, their relationship to other forms of communication, the mechanisms involved in their operation, how inclusive or exclusive the participation is, and administrative issues.[18] These researchers note, among other things, "Research and design go hand in hand. . . [and] that design should follow research about the community needs and resulting mission of the communication support." These researchers think that the information science "community should support and even experiment with new designs of communication support systems in order to effect new and important streams of research that will ultimately enrich our own and others' community life."[19] Unfortunately, this is a weakness within the archival community, a weakness that is revealed quite dramatically in the SAA leadership's handling of the archives listserv archives. Perhaps rather than seeing the necessity of destroying this listserv archives SAA could have embraced it as an opportunity to experiment with the preservation of the documentation of such virtual communities, giving it an opportunity to take a high profile lead in demonstrating that these kinds of communities are important to be documented.

What is a Listserv?

The *Webopedia*, focused on computer technology, indicates that a listserv is "an automatic mailing list server developed by Eric Thomas for BITNET in 1986. When e-mail is addressed to a LISTSERV mailing list, it is automatically broadcast to everyone on the list. The result is similar to a newsgroup or forum, except that the messages are transmitted as e-mail and are therefore available only to individuals on the list." This source also indicates that a "LISTSERV is currently a commercial product marketed by L-Soft International. Although LISTSERV refers to a specific mailing list server, the term is sometimes used incorrectly to refer to any mailing list server. Another popular mailing list server is Majordomo, which is freeware."[20]

There are other definitions and descriptions about listservs. Zane Berge and Mauri Collins provide this working definition of such online discussion lists: "An 'electronic mailing list', variously referred to as an online forum, a discussion list, a discussion group, as just a 'list', or incorrectly as a LISTSERV®, is a subscription list stored in an email distribution program, (e.g. LISTSERV®, majordomo, listproc, MailMan), to which persons can subscribe using their email address and under conditions set in that particular mailing list's header by the list owner(s). Each time an email post is sent to the list's electronic address, it is distributed to the entire subscription list. Analogous to the subscription list of an email discussion list is the subscription list of various print publications where individuals are represented by their postal name and address."[21]

Although these are rather clinical descriptions of listservs, it is good to remember that they are technical approaches intended to support discussion and deliberation in new ways, breaking down physical barriers and erasing time and place as necessary elements in facilitating meetings. So there are artificial aspects to what these discussion groups experience, some of which encourage odd behavior online and the posting of frivolous messages. Whether the existence of such material minimizes their value to the degree to where archivists ought not to be interested in their preservation may be the essential question involved in such a debate as has occurred with the archives listserv.

The archives list is a much more informal discussion group, populated primarily by working practitioners who use it for a variety of practical and personal reasons. Zane L. Berge and Mauri Collins note that "Scholarly discussion groups (SDG) in general can be likened to at least four types of group gatherings: 1) a library where one gathers information, listens, and thinks, 2) a seminar, meeting, conference, or salon where ideas and findings are discussed informally with colleagues and where 'new' thinking might be found, 3) a roomful of people in which dinner conversation is appropriate, and 4) as a newspaper subscription where 'lurking' is allowed or even encouraged. . . ."[22] The Archives & Archivists listserv probably combines a little of all these elements, although it is certainly more like three and four. It is because this list is a window into the informal chatter making the round of a fairly diverse group of archivists, a group that is probably representative or as representative as one could get of the American archival profession, that its archives deserves to be saved in some form.

There is something particularly interesting about such informal or almost accidental glimpses into the working nature of a profession. Davy Rothbart, the editor of *Found Magazine*, suggests "Found notes and letters open up the entire range of human experience; they offer a shortcut directly into people's minds and hearts. We often feel most alive when we're glimpsing someone at their most honest and raw."[23] This is not to suggest that the kinds of miscellaneous stuff discovered by Rothbart is what ought to go into archives. However, archivists and the users of archival documents also prize the truly spontaneous letter, personal diary entries, and scribbled notes on an important speech. We can reflect, in this manner, on the doodles American presidents have left behind. David Greenberg writes,

> Presidential doodles are intriguing, above all, because they provide us with a glimpse of the unscripted president. They're the antithesis of the packaged persona. Made with neither help from speechwriters nor vetting by a focus group, a doodle is the ultimate private act; its meaning may remain opaque even to the doodler himself. As a result, it renders the president human in ways that a staged family outing cannot. And if we can't make conclusive judgments about what a president's drawings reveal about his innermost fears or fantasies, his

doodles can still be suggestive and provocative. They're of interest *cumulatively*: side by side, the scores of doodles in this book reveal the range and diversity of the styles and mental habits of the men who have led this country. Collectively they help in a benign and inviting way to demystify the office — to build a bridge between citizen and leader.[24]

Listservs are most prone to have these kinds of informal discourse, so why shouldn't they be saved? The archival professional literature, so valuable for documenting the history of the profession and its practice, is akin to the scripted presidential press releases. The Archives & Archivists listserv is unique for its peek into the underbelly of the profession; its messages are like doodles on the official and more formal records of the profession.

Listserv History

The Archives & Archivists list is part of the rapid growth of such lists across disciplines and society. In twenty years, the growth has been phenomenal. In May 1986, there were 41 public listservs and in a year and a half after that the number had grown to 1000. With the commercialization of LISTSERV and enhanced computing possibilities, especially the move from mainframes, the number of such lists grew remarkably.[25] By 1991, there were over 3,000 discussion groups and other electronic communities in operation.[26] By this time the software necessary for supporting such group discussions had been liberated from any proprietary hardware, and the race was on for generating new virtual communities. There were discussion lists before LISTSERV, but it was with this software that easier growth was possible, as Grier and Campbell explain: "Listserv proved to be the lasting legacy of Bitnet. It was more flexible than competing technologies of Usenet, and it could support a wider range of social organizations. Users did not need to have any special software, as all communication through Listserv was conducted through email. In fact, many users of Bitnet Listserv were not directly connected to Bitnet. Listserv could host an email-based open forum, host a moderated discussion group, or publish an electronic periodical. It could archive correspondence and even maintain an electronic library." [27] The ease of using electronic mail facilitated the growth of these discussion groups, just as it also explained why among the useful messages there was always so much dross. Most professionals, like archivists today, now face nearly unlimited choices for joining highly specialized discussion groups and most are probably members of at least half a dozen.

Ironically, as will be seen, it is only with the listserv technology that we have had a chance to document early internet use and the development of online communities. As David Alan Grier and Mary Campbell state,

> Part of the reason for the lack of histories of early network users is the ephemeral nature of network correspondence. The notes transmitted by interactive message commands and the communications distributed by chat programs vanished before the computers that ran those programs were disconnected. The archives of early email, should any remain to this day, are stored on rapidly decaying floppy disks and other media that are sliding toward obsolescence. Only with the appearance of Listserv programs—programs that managed email lists and distributed mass mailings—do we find systematic archives of electronic mail and a coherent picture of the early general user. These record archives chronicle the development of the first network communities.[28]

This suggests that we also ought to reflect on just what else archivists might possess, that is worth preserving, that is similar or superior to the Archives listserv archives. Archivists would take the lead both in documenting these listservs and their own professional community's use of them. This seems not to be the case.

The Power of Listservs

Discussion groups, such as represented by listservs, developed quickly because they enabled groups with common interests and objectives to work together quickly and effectively. Among academics, scholars took to these lists rapidly because they enabled the sharing of ideas, collaboration, and the effective searching and retrieving of information from the postings.[29] Among information professionals, the advantages of listservs seem obvious. One list administrator writes, "The electronic mailing list adds to the library professional's communications arsenal a tool that distinguishes itself in its speed (instantaneous or nearly so), directness (it reaches only those who ask to be reached), and economy both in time (one message written once reaches many people) and in money (no paper or stamp costs)."[30] One study of a listserv suggests that its nature allowed participants, both question askers and respondents, to be more reflective in their messages,[31] an attribute of listservs that is sometimes glossed over in the debates about their utility. It is no surprise, then, that archivists took so quickly to their listservs; many archivists work in one-person archives and in remote locations. The listserv provided the opportunity to link people together, creating a new and very practical sense of community. Now an archivist, far from other archivists and libraries of professional sources, could pose questions, evaluate answers, and debate any professional matter at their convenience and as the need developed.

Each virtual community takes on its own character. Avi Hyman, considering the use of listservs by academics, provides a good sense of the possible variations: "The depth of interactivity varies widely among discussion groups. Some groups are like cocktail parties with many conversations (threads) competing. Some, like formal seminars, focus around specific topics. Some are like notice boards in the local grocery store where messages are pinned and left for others to read and comment on. And some groups merely function as newspapers, disseminating electronic journals or computer programs, advertising conferences or job vacancies. Many people are content to just read and listen, even in the most interactive groups, while a relatively few dominate conversations."[32] This is not the place to try to ascertain what the character of the Archives & Archivists listserv is, but it is not difficult to assert that it supports a group where a core of its subscribers feel loyalty to it, precisely because it has taken on particular characteristics. We can see this is in the subsequent reaction, described below, to the SAA leadership's efforts to destroy the online archives.

Many have commented on the values of listservs. Randall W. Marcinko provides a good sense of the varying utility of these discussion communities, noting, "Just like daytime soaps and gossip at the water cooler, listservs frequently take on a life of their own. Newcomers to listservs are amazed by the flames (epithets from one list member against another) and battles waged over apparent minutiae. If you seek entertainment value in a listserv, then perhaps this makes them more exciting. However, minutes become hours, and in the course of a month, hours become days, spent on the interpersonal dialog of lists. In this world where the Internet already usurps a large percent of our time, if we allow them to, listservs can be extremely wasteful."[33] Anyone involved in the Archives & Archivists listserv can testify to this. On a regular basis, someone will beg for mercy for a frivolous thread of discussion to cease. However, it is often these threads, with little to do directly with archival work, that seem to bind together particular groups of individuals. Is this any different than the groups at professional archival conferences who annually come together to go to baseball games or to indulge in golf matches? The only difference seems to be that the online variations are captured online; all of these are emblematic of work done among archivists (a lot of professional discussion goes on in the baseball and golf outings).

The Managerial and Legal Challenges of Listservs

The virtual community emerging in the past thirty years has generated a wide range of new legal issues, especially for those who administer online discussion groups. Thomas Steele writes, "As a broader segment of society began to use listservs as a method of communication, broader legal concepts became more important. For example, flaming can be construed as a way of defaming another, attaching a response to an original message and retransmitting the original message can be construed as infringing upon the copyright of the original author. Disclosing private facts can be seen as invasions of privacy. Expressing your sexual preference can be seen as pornography, sexual harassment or as discriminatory to groups and individuals with other sexual preferences. Each of these activities can have very real legal consequences."[34] Steele describes a variety of options for administering discussion groups, from avoiding risk by simply getting out of the activity to insuring themselves against risk. His most practical advice comes with the notion of managing risk. Steele states, "Most courts have used a standard for review or test that compares the listserv owner to being like a publisher to being like the post office. That is, if a listserv owner acts as if it controls content, reviews content, or supplies content it will be treated like a publisher. If a listserv owner acts like a passive conveyor or carrier of information without controlling the content, it will be treated like a bookstore or library. The courts have tended to find more liability for those who act like publishers."[35] It is probably in this arena that SAA leadership expressed most of its reasons for concern about the online archives, especially as one individual apparently had requested the removal of many of his or her postings. SAA, like the majority of professional associations, fears litigation of any kind because of its relatively meager financial resources, small professional staffs, and thin voluntary labor pools.

Another way of seeing the challenges of administering listservs is that they reflect the range of normal group behavior that we see in society, and that has been studied in controlled experiments,[36] with new challenges presented by the virtual environment. One study summarizes the problem in this way:

> In virtual groups, social cues to guide newcomer socialization may be minimal due to a lack of physical social environment. Virtual group members may not physically meet their colleagues, or may do so only infrequently. In a virtual setting, the tacit communication of norms, expectations, or standards must be substituted with explicit communication. As dispersion increases, the need for communicating explicitly may also increase as members across different organizations

and locations coordinate their work towards a common goal. Further, this may need to be done through the use of information technology. Although there are other ways for virtual groups to communicate and socialize new members (such as telephone, handbooks/manuals, virtual chats, occasional meetings, desktop videoconferencing systems, virtual private networks, web-centric systems including intranets and extranets, and groupware), due to its inexpensive and pervasive nature, e-mail represents the primary means by which virtual group members ... communicate with one another. In the limited forum provided by electronic mail, it is difficult for information to be related to a context within the group so that a mutual interpretation and understanding can be achieved.[37]

Some of the quirkiness of the Archives & Archivists listserv may be the result of the technological limitations in communication, a trait to be accounted for rather than factored against the listserv when considering its overall value. Nevertheless, the nature of these communications need to be evaluated against whether there are other sources capturing a wide range of opinions from working archivists who tend not to express their thoughts, in documented venues, such as through publishing, presenting conference papers, or maintaining blogs and personal web sites (the latter may be the closest they come).

Online discussion groups such as the Archives and Archivists listserv may face a number of challenges that many have worried about with the advent of new virtual communities. However, there are also many concerns, such as the protection of anonymous voices,[38] which are not factors in such professional discussion groups (where everyone readily identifies themselves). There is little reason for anyone on the archives list to have any advantage in posting anonymously; in fact, it could be a disadvantage, as a poster without name or affiliation could weaken their authority or claim for responses. Such questions and issues also raise a variety of ethical issues, especially as those designing, maintaining, and running networked communities often make decisions based on what they believe to be operational or practical needs of their users that reside on a variety of assumptions that may or may not be true.[39]

Many observers of, participants in, and critics of virtual communities, such as represented by listservs, worry about a variety of legal issues — and they should since the development of the technologies supporting such groups has consistently outpaced the courts in the establishment of legal guidelines and precedents. However, such issues are no different for archivists or records managers dealing with earlier shifts in recording technologies, such as with changes in still and moving images; it is a commonplace that new legal and administrative concerns emerge with every generation of analog and digital technologies, so one might ruminate a bit on whether the degree of such issues is any more complex in online environments. Even if the conclusion that they are is true, and it probably is, these concerns are not out of the realm of ordinary responsibilities for records professionals. Are they so complex or disruptive that they should lead to wholesale destruction of or avoidance in dealing with digital recordkeeping systems?

Intellectual property and copyright issues have become more complicated because of the proliferation of listservs, blogs, and wikis. Tharon Howard, for example, presents a typical challenge about quoting from a posting to a listserv. Assuming that someone was doing research for an article, where the researcher discovers a posting forcing a rethinking of what is being researched, the question emerges as to how to "legally and ethically quote from an e-mail message? Indeed, are you obligated to cite the message since it has had such a profound impact on your own thinking? If so, does anyone own the copyright on the message? Do you need to seek the author's permission? Or, since the message was electronically 'published' by an electronic discussion group, do you need to have the permission of the person(s) who created and operate the discussion group or the university or company which owns the computer that hosts the group?"[40] Howard believes that it would be no problem in citing and quoting, because "it seems more likely that sending an e-mail message to a discussion group would be considered a form of publication, so the author of the e-mail message can't really argue that the work has been upstaged. Indeed, while the exact copyright status of texts sent to and distributed by electronic discussion groups is still unclear and can vary widely from group to group, more and more groups are operating as electronic publications."[41] Despite the broader latitude concerning the use of messages posted to such lists, one still can't post or re-use from that post, legally that is, previously copyrighted material on listservs and other group discussions.[42] As it turns out, the legality of use of messages posted originally to the Archives & Archivists listserv was a major factor in the SAA leadership's concerns about maintaining the electronic archives of that list. It seems, perhaps, an overly cautious perspective held sway among this group.

Such legal, ethical, and just plain commonsense issues extend from the nature of the ease of use of electronic mail, what makes it possible for listservs to exist and function as they do. James Porter captures the dilemma quite clearly:

> Electronic mail by its very discourse nature raises new issues. On the one hand, electronic mail has some features of face-to-face spoken discourse (e.g., a telephone call). On the other hand, it also possesses some characteristics of writing (e.g., it lasts, it can be copied, archived, etc.). Anyone who has used it for any length of time realizes how easy it is to write a *flame* (an offensive, insulting, or sarcastic response to an electronic interlocutor). We sometimes write email as if we were talking to ourselves, as if it were a private journal entry, an immediate reaction-and then it goes out on the network, where it lives on in recorded format, gets redistributed, and maybe ends up in somebody's book. Email by its very discourse nature lives at the borders between speech and writing, between public and private discourse. It invites and encourages spontaneity, which means that our best thoughts, and our worst, can go flying through cyberspace, and outside it, to appear in contexts that we did not imagine when we first wrote them.[43]

Because posters on listservs often post out of anger or frustration, these virtual communities can be valuable forums for learning about the attitudes and feelings of working professionals. From an educational perspective, I like my students to see these outbursts, partly because they can be insightful when discussed in a classroom and partly because they suggest that archivists and other records professionals feel passionate about their work.

Closely connected to the notion of commonsense behavior on listservs is that of free speech in cyberspace. Porter notes how "electronic discussion groups often develop their own acceptable use policies establishing guidelines on, for instance, netiquette, the relevance of message content, and the reproduction or redistribution of messages." Some lists have established no "flaming" policies, although flaming is not always clearly defined, and some civil libertarians and academics have protested that such policies weakens "legitimate discourse" or encourages censorship or unnecessary gatekeeping, the latter precisely what many defenders or advocates of the Web are most keen to promote. Porter argues that "we might see flaming as representing the willingness of writers to speak plainly and bluntly and angrily when the circumstances warrant. Here is where it might be helpful to distinguish between an angry reply and an offensive or insulting reply. An angry or strong response could be warranted, [one] would say, in certain circumstances." Porter believes that "discourse that insults or demeans others is another matter. The personal attack or insult, the offensive 'othering' of individuals on a list, the assault or dismissal that has as its aim the silencing or elimination of others, which constitutes a form of restricting their access, is certainly unethical."[44] Again, examining this as an educator, I prefer the freer form of expression, regardless of the consequences. It is good for students, as well as for others in the profession, to see these strong reactions and, hopefully, to see how archivists and other records professionals resolve their differences and get on with their work. While such behavior may seem to undermine the value of the content of a list such as that of the Archives & Archivists one, it ought to be seen as adding valuable information to the attitudes, trends, and opinions at work in the archival community.

The Debate Begins.

The reaction to SAA's decision to jettison the online listserv archives was swift and nearly uniform in its criticism. The criticism about the decision shifted from its mechanics to the decision reflecting a lack of interest in the full profession by the SAA leadership; some posters even suggested that this decision showed an interest in controlling or censoring the profession (the latter reflecting how strongly feelings ran about this issue). This theme emerged with a vengeance when it became evident that the incoming president of SAA, the individual identified as being the officer to whom to send expressions of concern, was not monitoring the discussion on the Archives & Archivists listserv itself. A number of people posted the messages they sent to Mark Greene on the listserv, compounding the sense of a disconnection between SAA and a large portion of the profession. Despite more than fifteen years experience with the listserv community, and a useful if not comprehensive community about virtual communities, the Society seemed to be acting as if all this was novel to it.

Many posters decried the appraisal decision. Words and phrases like "astounded and dumbfounded," "astounded," a "total hoot," "embarrassing," "stunned," and "short-sighted" were used to characterize what individuals on the list thought of the decision. One of the posters stated that the appraisal decision "boggles the mind," using as one of the reasons for keeping it one of my own "controversial" postings when I was editor of the SAA journal, the American Archivist.[45] Another poster tried to shift the argument in the appraisal realm to declare that since these messages were being used by people subscribed to the list that they were active records, constituting a "knowledge base" for records professionals; this may seem like a stretch, but, at least, it represented an honest debate about a conceptual approach to the listserv archives. Some of the problem from the outset was the limited information being provided by the SAA leadership about its decision. There was incredulity expressed by some of the posters about the supposed demand by individuals to remove old postings to the Archives & Archivists listserv, leading a number to wonder, first, why anyone would want to do this and, second, why SAA would be so easily intimidated by a demand like this.

Many messages appeared about the utility of the listserv archives. One poster indicated that he was about to "mine it" for a conference paper. Another indicated that it was a "remarkable historical resource for the development of the profession in a time of great change," even if it did not reflect the activities of the SAA (something it was established to do). Individuals attested to how, when they were students, they consulted archived discussions to complete assignments. One poster, Heather Crocetto, remarked about how the listserv was a means for lone arrangers, archivists working by themselves, to stay connected to the larger archival community and to have access to good, practical information:

> It is a body of work that contains not only the 'ordinary man's' history of this profession, but also contains vendor recommendations, user policies, reading lists, theoretical discussions of archival principles and practices and so many other topics; these posts are from varied perspectives and can help a lone arranger see the breadth and depth of our profession. Just last year, I went into the listserv archives for discussions regarding scanning fees; I showed these posts to my superiors in support of raising scanning prices in our institution. I have also used the archives for vendor recommendations.[46]

Comments such as these suggest that no matter what degree of chaff there might be in the listserv archives, it was a living and useful entity.

Many of the posters took exception to the tone of the SAA appraisal decision that this listserv archives was not an effective documentary source of the SAA itself. Christine Di Bella summed up this sentiment quite effectively, asserting,

> If we use the broader, and I think more relevant in this case, definition of SAA, as an organization of individuals and institutions united by a common professional framework, then the listserv archives are one of the richest sources available. The listserv archives feature debates on the most significant issues we face as archivists, among them the evolution and adoption of descriptive standards, the changing nature of educational requirements, professional status and pay, performance and productivity metrics, certification, government secrecy and the appointment of the Archivist of the United States. The "postings of current value" like job descriptions and announcements of projects take on greater significance as the years pass, since they document our profession's evolving priorities and expectations. While comment on their use by a broad swath of archivists was not sought by the Task

Force, anecdotal evidence (and likely the web logs for the archives) clearly indicates that the listserv archives are consulted frequently, and for a vast array of purposes, both practical and scholarly.[47]

This astute commentator also indicated how so few wrote letters to the *American Archivist* editor and how few archival blogs exist, suggesting, that even with all the problems with the weakness of content, this was still a rich and unique source. Another poster, in a similar vein, systemically compared what goes on the listserv with the SAA mission statement and, needless to say, discovered that there was considerable compatibility between the two.

Anyone examining the discussion on this list about the fate of the listserv archives would, in my opinion, come to a similar conclusion. I counted, spread from the first full day of discussion on March 14 to the last lingering message on March 30, sixty different participants. Only eleven posted two or more messages in the discussion. These individuals ranged from seasoned veterans to students preparing for careers. They came from seventeen different states and three countries. And those working as archivists were employed in museums, universities, corporations, medical institutions, local governments, historical societies, public libraries, religious archives, and the Federal Government. There were several self-employed consultants also participating. Based on my own more than thirty years of experience, I am hard-pressed to find any archival professional forum reflecting such broad-based conversation. The closest one can come to such participation is at onsite professional conferences, but even there costs, travel requirements, and group dynamics (time constraints, personal characteristics, and sometimes deference to leaders and established experts) work against everyone being able to state a position or opinion.

Despite the legal, administrative, and other problems with the listserv archives, a number of individuals offered their institutions as hosts for the listserv and its archives. One of the posters, a long-time moderator and manager of a professional listserv, mocked the reasons offered by the SAA leadership for wanting to destroy the archives, attributing the explanation as nothing more than a "lack of Internet savvy," a lack of understanding of the legal issues, and a lack of creativity in handling the costs of running the listserv. Still, no one was disputing the fact that there were real and difficult legal issues, well-represented by Edward Sevcik, writing, "In the currently hostile legal environment, when corporations routinely destroy every shred of correspondence and delete e-mails the moment the law allows (and sometimes earlier), this is a course of safety. No one knows what is in all those messages. In addition, it is very likely—I would say certain—that the 1993-2001 messages include thousands of comments and postings by people who did not realize those messages would persist in an easily searchable venue, and who do not want those messages preserved forever, instantly accessible with phone numbers and work addresses, to anyone in the world."[48] Yet, others suggested that if we let the financial implications of litigation and other challenges dictate how we approach appraisal, then the archival community faces other even more serious issues. Fred Leutzenheiser, for example, writes, "Are we going to let liability issues deprive us of important parts of our profession? Where does this stop? In this litigious age there are probably a dozen other things besides people reneging on what they published which could present huge financial liabilities, if we try to imagine them. If we start thinking about the sky falling, we might as well give up on this field altogether, as well as any sort of public life in this country."[49] Other posters suggested that the owners and administrators of listservs and other such virtual discussion venues are generally immune from the threat of litigation, and that this fear of litigation was an unnecessary fear.

There also were observers who expressed sympathy to SAA because of the difficulty in making this appraisal decision, but this was a clear minority of those posting messages. A few comments were made about the fact that SAA never intended this list to be a reflection of its own activities, suggesting that any legal or administrative problems ought to be seen in that light. This indicates, of course, that SAA should not recognize that this was a service provided to a part of the professional community, putting exclusively a rather utilitarian spin on the affair. No matter how small a portion of the posters supported SAA, however, this was not a rabid anti-SAA group of individuals debating the archives listserv decision. Concerns were expressed and disagreements outlined, but the discourse was civil and everyone seemed to accept that this was a group of archivists debating among themselves about some core principles and practices.

The Debate Broadens

Concerned that I had not heard much from archival educators who I was sure had students, like mine, using the listserv archives, I posted a message to the archival educators list. My message was posted after the announcement that SAA had rescinded its decision to destroy this electronic archives, and the message started as follows: "I am sure all will agree that we applaud the SAA Council decision to not destroy the archives of the Archives & Archivists listserv. However, I believe that the archives community, especially those who are SAA members, should not cease pressing SAA leadership about this matter until the task report, cited in the initial announcement about this matter, is made public."[50] I was especially interested in sending this message to archival educators because although they carry an important responsibility to develop and advance the knowledge foundation for archival practice and for preparing the next generation of archival practitioners, they have often been very quiet about professional debates and controversies. In my message I explained my position about the appraisal decision, the lack of information forthcoming from the Society, and the supposed administrative and legal issues.[51]

Meanwhile, on the listserv itself, the conversation about the SAA decision continued, with various proposals introduced and various opinions about these proposals offered. The idea of making the listserv a moderated forum, so as to generate higher quality content in a more consistent fashion, emerged as one topic, although most liked the listserv as it was. More discussion also developed about the problem of individuals wanting to remove posts they submitted, mostly with individuals wondering why someone might want messages they broadcast publicly years later to be removed, for whatever reasons they might articulate. It is a curious feature of the discussion that archivists, professionals who probably more highly value the serendipitous content of correspondence, diaries, and informal notes scribbled on official reports and memorandum, would be uneasy about this in their own communication and documents.

Others considered the ownership of the listserv. SAA was questioning its own right to the messages posted on the listserv, but it was also making a decision to dispose of the listserv archives. Posters questioned why the SAA leadership could even claim the right to destroy the archives. Others were perturbed that the SAA leadership was not even engaging in debate with the participants in the listserv, suggesting that it simply did not value the archives at all as a useful source of professional dialogue, or this element of the archival community. This is a point well-taken, and it is one that never did get resolved. As one who has been battered and bruised in listserv debates, I can well understand the temptation not to engage this way, but I also side with those that see this as indicative of some disengagement by SAA leadership with the professional ranks of archivists.

There was also discussion about just how well SAA was doing in administering the listserv. Some commented on the lack of functionality of the Web-based archives, hoping to see it get better and even wondering if the listserv was moved that perhaps it and its archives wouldn't improve. A segment of this discussion was criticism of SAA's references to an appraisal report, research papers, and other materials used in the appraisal decision

— although none of this material was being shared or perhaps even very effectively summarized. Some also commented on how *good* appraisal must take into account the needs of the records creators or a particular community utilizing the records, suggesting that the unfolding discussion on the archives listserv clearly indicated that this group wanted its archives preserved and maintained in a usable fashion.

The debate also spilled onto other listservs and blogs. Patrick Cunningham posted a sympathetic message on the Records Management listserv concerning the intellectual property, legal, and administrative issues facing SAA, but also noting "My sense is that some insight into the development of an online community will be lost, as will something of a historical snapshot of the profession's evolution during the growth of the Internet. If anything, that is the real loss — not being able to see how archivists and institutions began to come to grips with electronic records and new types of media. Again, purely anecdotal, but still an interesting snapshot."[52] One blog featured a practical account of the debate, noting, "I have always found that you can't understand all the issues related to a technical project (like the preservation of a listserv) until you have a real life case to work on. Even if SAA doesn't think we need to keep the data forever - here is the perfect set of data for archivists to experiment with. Any final set of best practices would be meant for archivists to use in the future - and would be all the easier to comprehend if they dealt with a listserv that many of them are already familiar with."[53] Richard Urban, a doctoral student at the University of Illinois at Urbana-Champaign Graduate School of Library and Information Science, argued in his blog that the "listserv of any professional community is more than 'routine' correspondence. Within those messages are [sic] the history of how a community has developed and changed. What are the major arguments the community went through? What were the issue[s] of the day? Who was talking about them - who was responding?"[54] Another blogger mused, "I understand that a great number (probably a majority) of the posts on the Archives and Archivists List may be off-topic, outdated, or spam-like, but isn't the whole idea of being an archivist based on the recognition that individual documents and pieces of information gain value from being presented in the context of their original creation? And don't we, you know, like to save stuff?" This observer also commented. "Maintaining the archives of the A&A list will allow future researchers of our profession to see how archivists used early listserv technology, not to mention what we think about such hot-button topics as certification, the Patriot Act, and a whole series of appointed Archivists of the United States, not to mention an irreplaceable documentation of changes in best practices in all areas of archival administration."[55] Mark Matiezo, in his blog, added, "I find this to be an embarrassment to the profession. How are we to be trusted with retaining the memory of society if we can't even retain our own?"[56] And Rick Prelinger referred to the SAA leadership's decision to destroy the archives as a "really big mistake. This list contains much valuable information, and is a thick and fascinating record of how a legacy-ridden field responded to the Internet revolution. The irony of an archival organization disposing of its own archives (and the archives of an entire profession) is obvious."[57] Sympathy and advice abounded in these other sources, but it was all built on a firm foundation of criticism for the SAA decision.

A Public Relations Disaster

Apart from all the appraisal and practical issues associated with this case, there is the matter of what SAA leadership thought it was doing when it announced its decision to destroy the online archives. One poster on March 14th states, "On a practical note, when fellow archivists insist they don't join SAA because it 'doesn't give me anything,' I have in the last few years been able to point to the A&A List and its very useful Archives. Obviously, after March I won't be able to make that argument."[58] Some posters eloquently shared comments about how they could not afford to go to SAA meetings, and that the listserv was the closest they could come to a professional community, albeit one that was virtual. The decision by the SAA leadership to destroy the listserv was feeding general negatives of some in the archival community about the responsiveness and relevance of SAA to them.

Messages appeared suggesting how contrary SAA's actions on the listserv archives seem when one considers the other activities and priorities of the association. Comments were made about how SAA's various stances on government transparency ought to carry over to transparency within its own ranks. One poster, Vernon Rood, even connected the action of SAA leadership with the message that it usually tries to convey to society: "As archivists, we often struggle to justify our existence against detractors who claim that our material is rarely used, that saving it has few immediately visible benefits, and that moreover it is expensive. Astonishingly, the archivist's professional organization, the Society of American Archivists (SAA), now appears to take the same viewpoint with respect to the records of its own profession." [59] Few seemed inclined to disagree with such an assertion.

Although there was little actually stated by SAA leadership about the digital nature of the listserv archives having anything to do with its ultimate appraisal decision, many of the listserv posters interpreted this to be an indication of the inability of the main archival association to solve a technical issue. I don't think this was viewed as a technical issue of electronic records management. Nevertheless, it clearly broadcast to the world that this is what it might be about. One commenter, Matt Snyder, provided a good sense of this perspective with this observation:

> Many people in our field are disturbed by the possibility that because so much of our current documentation is being born digital, and because digital information is without a doubt the most endangered and short-lived form information has ever taken, our era is in danger of losing most of its documentation over the long run. In comparison to the vast amounts of digital data being produced all the time by our governments at every level and by industry, the SAA A&A listserv is a small affair. If the Society of American Archivists (an organization whose mission is, in part, to advise our nation on best practices for archival preservation) demonstrates very publicly that it either doesn't care enough to or is practically unable to preserve its own digital archives, why should anyone listen when it advises others to care for and preserve their archives? The same excuses of uselessness and cost can be made by anybody to cover up for actual, more substantial and questionable motives. I am not accusing SAA of having such devious motives, I simply think the organization is being myopic.[60]

Such comments are legitimate. Couldn't anyone at the top of SAA see that this interpretation might occur or understand that this sent a poor message at best?

Perhaps other factors intruded, clouding the ability of SAA to comprehend all of the potential fallout. There is evidence that the SAA leadership, responding to a request by its university host that it no longer wanted to be its host, knew of this situation for nearly a year before springing onto the listserv community itself the news that it was going to dump the archives in a few weeks. A number of posters commented on this, and it certainly did not elevate the SAA's profile no matter what explanation could have been offered. One individual believes that the SAA leadership was acting in "good faith," but he also mused, "The Listserv has become in effect a public utility and questions relating to it should have some public discussion."[61] In other words, this seems a horribly bungled process.

Many of the posts concerned requests to SAA to share more information about its decisions, especially aspects such as the financial costs, legal risks, and, of course, details about the appraisal decision. Rick Barry, a well-known records management consultant, expressed quite well the dangers of considering matters in such an appraisal decision, reflecting "While revealing consulting secrets, I might also add that it has been my experience that organizational attorneys tend too often to be of one of two minds: 1) Keep everything. 2) Get rid of everything as soon as you can. My own observation over the years has been that archivists can be very quick to kow tow if not quickly cave in to the general counsel in such matters, rather than taking the position that no one is better trained to assess preservation options between those two extremes than those who are highly trained and experienced in the venerable profession of the archivist."[62] At the least, there were political mistakes. In one of my favorite comments to the list, a poster states that the whole matter seemed like a "poor political decision that deserves attention from *The Onion*."[63]

Some posters searched the listserv's archives, perhaps in a last use of it before its demise, to build a case against the SAA decision. James Cassedy's letter to Mark Greene provides an example, starting,

> On March 31, 1998, in a rather poignant Archives-L posting announcing his resignation as co-director of the Archives and Archivists Listserv, John Harlan wrote, I have been assured, and I am completely confident, of SAA's commitment to maintain the Archives & Archivists LISTSERV list as the open forum of international professional communication and discourse that it has always been intended to be, and of which it has had various shining moments in its nine year history. I am also confident of SAA's commitment to the continued diversity of the list, and to the list's role in serving the entire archival profession, not just the SAA membership or American archivists. (Mom and I often commented to each other on our mutual pride in the breadth and scope of the list's subscriber base and the discussion that often resulted from that diversity. I have been assured that SAA shares those values and will work to preserve them.)

Obviously, things changed in just a decade.[64] Indeed, Cassedy reminded others that at the time there was a bit of a debate about preserving the list's archives. Cassedy also submitted to Greene as part of his letter a call for a motion to be considered at the forthcoming SAA business meeting, providing some of the history of this SAA commitment to maintaining the listserv and reaffirming its value (and that of its archives) to the profession.[65] Cassedy's motion was additional evidence that the archives listserv was more than an informal community, but that it easily morphed into a lobby group with real coherent discussion and leadership when circumstances merited it. This is a normal characteristic of new virtual communities.

Another indicator of the public relations problems was the reactions of students. Students represent, after all, both future archivists and the dues paying members of the SAA itself. SAA has generally valued these members, authorizing the establishment of SAA student chapters at various schools and offering memberships at reduced rates in order to attract these future members into their fold. One wonders, therefore, whether much thought was given to the impact on this element of the association membership, especially since this demographically younger group is generally more comfortable with online activity (having grown up with it). The University of Maryland SAA student chapter sent a message to Mark Greene protesting both the decision about the electronic archives and the process leading to that decision, noting the listserv's value to the

> community of new archivists, who might otherwise be hard-pressed to determine the concerns of the community and how those concerns have changed over the years. In addition, the List has proven useful as a resource for any kind of scholarly study of American archival practice; the introductory archives course at Maryland examines the list every fall and has generally found it a fascinating window into the workings of the profession."[66] The students at my own school likewise sent a message to the archives listserv, also desiring to see the list's archives maintained and a "full disclosure of the appraisal report regarding the issue." This letter argues, "As new members to the field, we view the list archives as an invaluable reference, which helps to preserve, in detail, the evolving narrative of the archival profession since the rise of digitization."[67]

The Debate Simmers Down

Within a few days into the debate SAA President Elizabeth Adkins posted a message seeking to reassure listserv members that their voices were being heard, suggesting that the association's governing council was planning to reconsider its "appraisal" decision and, perhaps, release the appraisal report that had been referenced in the original posting.[68] Some posters also argued that SAA needs to rethink the listserv message as not being part of its official records, mostly because, in their opinion, this association is supposed to represent the entire archival community. However, this issue of the relationship of the SAA membership to the American archival community seems to be one of the persistent issues in the debate.

Individuals expressed a variety of other issues, mostly minor although still interesting points, as the discussion began to wane. There was some reflection about why SAA might be reacting to a demand by one or more individuals (this matter was never completely clarified) to remove messages, why others could not demand that their messages be maintained and that SAA really did not have the authority to remove them. Such a point, while perhaps seeming to be a stretch, suggests the weakness of building an appraisal decision around a fear of litigation. I wonder that if SAA is timid about the potential of litigation, why it never seems to fear legal action from its own members about such decisions. Functioning in such a manner suggests all kinds of difficulties, not only in archival appraisal but also in all archival functions; for example, would SAA cave in to seek to remove older articles from its print and online publications? While this possibility might seem ridiculous, where does one draw the line about such requests or with litigation threats?

Five days after Adkins' conciliatory message, she posted another to the listserv indicating that the SAA leadership was responding to the comments made by various individuals about the decision to dump the list's archives. On March 21 Adkins reported that the "SAA Council convened via conference call last night to review the feedback on our previously announced decision to dispose of the A&A List archives (1993-2006). We are impressed by, and grateful for, the range and depth of responses to our announcement - particularly as they relate to concern on behalf of the profession. After taking everyone's thoughtful comments into account, we've decided to work with Miami University of Ohio to explore the option of transferring the list archives to another repository." This was, indeed, encouraging news to many concerned about this decision. Adkins reflected continuing concerns by the SAA leadership: "We remain concerned that transferring the list archives raises administrative and legal considerations that must be addressed, but we are willing to work to find ways to address those issues, if at all possible. We have contacted MUO, which has agreed to extend until further notice the date by which the list archives must be taken down to give us more time to work out the details. Should it become necessary, we will arrange for a download of the archives list files that could be used in a transfer to another repository." This assessment indicates, if nothing else, that the listserv discussions serve a useful role in professional community deliberation. Also, as the SAA leaders continued to claim, "Clearly this experience demonstrates that appraisal is something about which good archivists can disagree, and we respect the passionate disagreement of the list community with our original decision. I want to thank all who have expressed their concern, publicly or privately, and for the constructive suggestions that many of you have made to address SAA's concerns."[69] The question lingering is, however, whether this decision or subsequent debate had much to do with archival appraisal.

The Report is Released

After more than two weeks of debate and discussion on the listserv, SAA President Elizabeth Adkins released the frequently referred to but as of until then unseen appraisal report on the listserv archives.[70] Adkins indicated that it had taken this long for SAA leadership to decide about the release of the report for "two reasons": "1) it includes the names of individuals who did not authorize release of their names to the public, and 2) it was intended as guidance to the Council rather than as a public document, it is written more informally than is typical of reports to the Council, and it includes some unguarded language." Adkins argued that since SAA is an advocate for transparency, it was releasing the report — although it was also partially redacted "to remove identifying information about an individual who had privately requested that a post be removed from the list archives." As Adkins states, and no archivist would argue too much with, "As archivists we all strive to balance the need for transparency with the right to privacy." She also indicates that this report was not the only source used for the decision, but "it was one resource that the Council considered when reaching its decision, and it could have been returned to the Task Force for revisions or its plurality recommendation could have been rejected or modified."

The SAA President also reports that the association had "made a successful appeal to Miami University of Ohio to extend its maintenance of the list archives while we work on the legal and administrative issues that must be resolved prior to finding a new home for the archives." This included removing from the listserv archives the "message about which one individual had threatened a credible lawsuit," with another such request being considered. The association was also seeking to clarify the ownership of the list archives and "whether SAA can transfer title to another repository." Adkins indicates, "many details remain to be resolved, but at this point the Council is optimistic that a successful conclusion can be reached."[71]

The report, as it turns out, was nearly anticlimactic after the many days of discussion on the listserv. Entitled "Report: Task Force on Disposition of the Archives and Archivists List Archives" and signed by Mark Greene, the report commences with the charge to "review issues associated with retention of the Archives and Archivists List Archives and prepare a recommendation for the Council's consideration regarding the long-term disposition of the List Archives. The review should take into consideration content analysis, cost maintenance and ongoing study of use of the data." True to this charge, the report considers these issues. The report indicates that there was a division in opinion about whether there was any worth to maintaining the list archives, with particular comments on the matter of off-topic postings, postings of an ephemeral nature, questions about whether the unmoderated or unmanaged nature of the listserv undermined its value, and legal issues regarding the intellectual property of the messages.

One of the disturbing aspects in reading the report is the degree to which the question about the management of the listserv affects the quality of the information represented in its messages. Greene, in his report, summarizes one of the perspectives of a task force member as maintaining that the "list reflects current attitudes toward archival practices and provides evidence of an established online community and culture of the profession. One of the main problems with the list is that it has not been managed as a record. It seems that at a minimum, categories for the list could be established and a records schedule associated with those categories so that announcements and routine communications are not maintained over time. Taking a managed approach to the list may also encourage users to search the 'Archives' more often (currently, searching is an issue) as the search would be on the core content for a period of time." Another task force member made a similar statement: "I think the listserv provides a unique insight into how our profession responded to the new networking technologies. The messages may not be profound — and certainly would have been more profound if we knew they might be saved. Nevertheless, they are what they are." These statements are a bit odd. Archivists acquire records that have not been particularly well managed all the time. Indeed, some would argue, as I certainly would, that the better documentary sources are often those created with no eye on preservation, where people state views and opinions freely and candidly. A more cynical view would argue that this suggests an interest in control by SAA leadership. A more balanced perspective suggests that the value of the listserv ought to be seen in its unregulated, free form conversations. It seems as if the discussion about the listserv archives wanted this to be more like the *American Archivist*, a peer-reviewed journal, but no one could ever argue that such a journal could represent the broad range of views making up the archival community.

Releasing the report did clarify some issues. There were only two individuals requesting messages to be removed, although one had asked for over five hundred messages to be deleted. This prompted Miami University of Ohio to request SAA to take responsibility for the online list archives, leading to the task force, this report, and the initial decision by SAA to dump the archives. The appraisal report was not the only source for the decision about the list archives. SAA had backtracked from its initial decision to destroy, on short notice, the listserv archives. The report reflects that the main emphasis relates to financial, legal, technical, and administrative matters. Drawing on one of the advisory reports, this statement was made: "About the only argument you can come up with out of author 1's paper for saving the list over the long haul is that it somehow captures a sense of the archival 'community,' a point he/she raises more than once. Well maybe, but being one who likes to talk about costs I'm willing to ask a pretty mean spirited question - how much money does SAA want to throw at this on the off chance that somebody, someday, is going to decide to use the list archive as evidence in a paper/article/thesis or whatever about archival 'community,' and, to be even more mean spirited, which part of SAA's mandate directs the Society to worry about documenting the 'community?'" And here we may have the crux of the divide between the SAA leadership and the listserv community, the former truncating its mission in a manner that seems peculiar in light of initiatives like the major census of the profession and the latter seeing the association as representing the profession not just the membership. Or to put the matter in a more personal context, in my more than thirty years of being a member of SAA, even while acknowledging that not every working archivist belongs to this association, it never occurred to me that SAA somehow did not represent this community; I think that one difficulty surfacing in this debate about the listserv archives was the apparent conclusion by SAA leadership that this is wrong, when so many others assumed it was the case.

Releasing the report also possibly confused some issues. Why would SAA leadership involve itself in making a decision about the listserv archives by drawing on a background report never intended to be opened? If the background report was only one component of the information for the ultimate decision about the list archives, what were the other sources and factors leading to the final decision? Were SAA leadership's concerns about intellectual property issues reflecting a much too conservative perspective? One can postulate that if all archivists made appraisal decisions about documentary sources based on such legal concerns, there would be very few records coming into archival repositories. Moreover, while the technical issues raised seem legitimate, and involving some financial costs, they did not seem to be insurmountable, except in relation to issues about the overall value of the listserv archives. And, perhaps more important, there must be questions about whether the report can even be considered an appraisal report of any particular value itself (it is certainly not a model appraisal report in any form or fashion, although since it was never intended to be opened it is clear that no one was thinking that it should be). It is informally written and a bit confusing to follow. None of the reasons presented for not wanting to maintain the list archives are represented in enough detail to merit making a penultimate decision to destroy the archives. And, in addition, the opinions of the task force were quite divided about the various recommendations; this was not a unanimous report, nor was there really any consensus expressed in the report.

20/20 Hindsight?

In the March/April 2007 issue of SAA's newsletter, in the regular column of the association's executive director, Nancy Beaumont tries to bring closure to one of the more difficult episodes she has faced in her work with SAA. In the column, one can sense her frustration and weariness. In reviewing the debate about whether the archives of the Archives and Archivists listserv should be retained, she makes three points. First, she suggests that the debate reflects why professional associations are "so important and valuable: They provide a 'safe' place to discuss and debate professional issues." Second, Beaumont believes that the debate "brought to the surface (not for the first time) some fundamental disagreements within the profession and has pointed out the truism that good archivists can disagree about appraisal — and many other aspects of what they do." Third, and finally, she laments how "many, many hours of volunteer and staff time" was consumed by this debate, leading her to worry about how SAA's various contributions to the profession might be lost or glossed over because of the internecine squabbling about the listserv. To counter this, Beaumont describes nine various actions and activities underway by SAA. Unfortunately, her article ended with her description of the need for a dues increase, another case of bad timing and, in my estimation, poor judgment by the Society's leadership.[72]

There are many reasons why SAA should release the report. Most importantly, there is the matter of its accountability to the archival profession to explain better why the decision was made, and how it was communicated to the profession. Some of these reasons can be discerned from SAA's own public statement of its goals and objectives.[73] Even a cursory reading from these goals and objectives suggest the reasons for making the report public and why SAA leadership should have striven to prepare an appraisal report assumed to be a public document; they include providing "opportunities for professional networking and participation" including the use of "Internet-based communications of these groups"; promoting "standards important to sound archival policy and best practices"; "defining educational foundations for professional archivists through standards, methodologies, ethics, and values"; and informing "policy maker's awareness about the archival perspective, mission, work and role of archivists, especially regarding the role and impact of digitization and technology on archival practice." Even the Society's bylaws[74] seem counter to what had transpired with the listserv archives, offering this statement: "The records of the Society, of Council, and other units of the Society shall be preserved by the officers, councilors, the executive director, and unit chairs, and shall be promptly turned over by them to their successors. Non-current records shall be appraised by direction of the Council upon recommendation of the Society's archivist, and those of continuing value shall be placed for preservation in the Society's official archives, and Council shall determine a policy of access to these records." One can understand why SAA leadership may have had difficulty in determining how the archives of the listserv fit into this statement, but this statement also raises other questions about when and how one might get access to the SAA appraisal report about the listserv archives and whether it would be made readily available, at some future point, in its archives. While one sees a finding aid to the SAA archives held at the University of Wisconsin Milwaukee,[75] there is no public statement that I can find outlining the appraisal criteria used in determining what goes into the archives.

One can even find some irony in the recent brouhaha about the archives of the listserv in a statement about the history of the SAA on its Web site tying our ability to know about the past being dependent on the "surviving record at hand," including "electronic messages," and describing the essential role of the archivist "to collect, preserve, and protect this fragile, constantly changing record of who we are and what we do."[76] We need to practice what we preach with the records of our own profession. SAA needs to be an open organization, and my fear is that the damage done to its public image in this recent discussion is severe, supporting what some have criticized as its elitism and disconnection from the archival community. For the record, I have always advocated that this is a false impression, and I always urge my students to become active members. And

I have tried to be an active member as well (including Council, *American Archivist* editor, and Publications Editor).

Being more open about appraisal decisions is due to the need for establishing some degree of accountability for the archival profession and to seek to provide a better understanding by the public, policymakers, resource allocators or funders of archives, and researchers or users of archival materials. This suggests, of course, a better designed and more formal appraisal report than what emerged in this case. The wavering disagreement among SAA leadership about this appraisal decision suggests a deeper problem than merely that archivists disagree about the particulars of appraisal or its application. Former SAA President Richard Pearce-Moses, who had led the initial discussions about the listserv archives in the previous year before the public debate, also posted a message at the end of the debate, seeking to provide a somewhat richer context for the discussion: "One of the ideas that I hammered last year while I was president of SAA was that archivists need 'new skills' for the digital era. I would often encourage people to get in the trenches and wrestle with the problems of managing electronic records so that they had a very practical understanding of the issues." He adds, "It strikes me that the preservation of the A+A list archives could serve as such an exercise." Pearce-Moses then provides a reasonably detailed assessment of the appraisal, custody, preservation, intellectual property, and costs issues influencing the SAA leadership decision about the list archives confirming, if nothing else, that despite all the chaff that might be on the listserv there were also thoughtful messages about real professional concerns that would be valuable for future archivists to read and reflect on.[77]

Conclusion: Expanding the Ethical Paradigm

The SAA leadership's seeming disregard of the archives community represented by the listserv can be interpreted in many ways, ranging from simple shortsightedness to overt callousness. Somewhere in all this is an ethical dimension. While the SAA has long had an ethics code (and a cadre of archivists writing about the code and ethical issues), it has been increasingly uncertain what to do with it, other than to ensure that it not lead to litigation. There is, also, a lack of creative imagination when it comes to ethical concerns, and that figures prominently in the listserv archives caper.

We can see something of the kind of imagination needed in Luke Eric Lassiter's chapter on ethics in his primer on collaborative ethnography. Lassiter describes the practical ethics code a group of student ethnographers developed in working with a community for a research effort. They recognized responsibility to the community participants and consultants they would be working with, pledged "faithful representations" of the community in their work, and endeavored to have a "good rapport with the community" so that other researchers could follow them. Materials emanating from the project would not be archived without the "participants' consent." As well, open communication about the project was promised, along with sensitivity to divergent perspectives. And, the working code indicated a commitment to finish the project.[78] Can we discern any of this kind of behavior in what the SAA leadership conveyed in its decision about the list's archives and its reactions to the criticism about its decision?

A number of posters delivered very negative assessments of SAA's behavior. Sharon Howe, for example, made public her letter to Mark Greene, commencing with this comment: "As an SAA member, I strongly urge the SAA Council to reconsider its ill-advised decision to refuse to maintain the Archives and Archivist Listserv archives. I consider the decision ill-advised as much because of the process as because of the product. References to an unreleased report and unnamed individuals do not engender confidence in the fairness and honesty of the appraisal and the decision. Furthermore, some of the arguments put forth publicly smell too much of smokescreen." Howe stated that when she became a member of the organization in the 1980s, she found it to be "practically impenetrable except to those who had institutional and/or personal resources," but that over the years "dedicated leaders and administrators made great strides in changing SAA into an activist and at least somewhat more welcoming and inclusive organization." Howe, like others participating in this debate, were worried: "Now, I fear there are signs that we may have forgotten our own history and may be headed back to the bad old days of SAA." And, drawing on basic commonsense, Howe added: "Ever since I have been a member of SAA, the organization has talked and talked and talked some more about how it needs to increase diversity within its ranks. At last, that talk has resulted in making this one of three top goals, but I cannot see how that goal will be achieved, if even in a matter such as the List archives, the Council fails to follow the one cardinal principle that might move us closer to achieving that goal: You must consult with the community of interest."[79] While no one wants to accuse the SAA leadership of unethical behavior, and I am not, its activities regarding the listserv archives were certainly poorly timed and badly executed.

The substance of the debate on the Archives & Archivists listserv about the threat to its own archives countered the notion that the SAA leadership offered that there was little worth saving in these digital communications. In fact, the mass of messages provided many insights into the archival community, how it saw itself, appraisal issues, electronic records management concerns, and, yes, the notion of professional leadership. From my vantage, as I have tried to show here, this was also an excellent case study for teaching purposes. One could argue that the SAA has an ethical responsibility to maintain the listserv archives. One might also question the wisdom of SAA passing the listserv and its archives off to another host. This can be seen as an abrogation of professional responsibility, to state the obvious, even though many posters, in frustration, urged some other institution to take the listserv as a means for preserving the archives. This seems especially to be the case since the membership of the archives listserv rivals the membership of the SAA itself, and only with partial overlap. What appears certain is that it was not merely a disagreement about appraisal or a lack of ease with digital documentation but as much about professional vision, mission, and leadership; the debate was a means for remembering that in carrying out appraisal or seeking to maintain digital information and evidence many other factors intrude.

A generation ago David Gracy speculated that archivists shape their identities by what they keep, but judging by this case study, their identities also can be shaped by what they do *not* keep. Gracy, in urging his compatriots to work to inform society about the importance of archives, reflected, "one of the most fundamental, recurring, and easily seen messages of and lessons in history is that where one is not moving forward, one is moving backward."[80] It seems that in the decision to destroy the listserv archives we have taken a step backward, suggesting to the world that archivists do not care for their own professional memory, community, appraisal accountability, or the digital heritage. None of this was anyone's intentions, but this was a sad and disturbing episode in the history of the Society of American Archivists.

Chapter Nine

The Anthony Clark Case, SAA, and Professional Ethics

Preliminary Note: What follows is a series of postings from my blog, "Reading Archives," originally written and published on February 14 and 19, and March 7, 18, 26, 2009. Only slight editing has been done on these posts, and what I offer here is a kind of historical document, albeit just from my perspective, in the debate about the Anthony Clark case and his difficulties with NARA and the nature of SAA's position on the topic of archival ethics. While I have had discussions with Clark about this, what follows is my opinion, and Mr. Clark endorses none of this.

Introduction

On Wednesday, February 11, 2009, Anthony Clark, a freelance scholar, presented a lecture at my school, entitled "Presidential Libraries: The Last Campaign; How Presidents Rewrite History, Run for Posterity and Enshrine their Legacies." We advertized that Mr. Clark was completing a history of the presidential libraries, a project taking him to every library; evaluating the experiences of visitors to these institutions; interviewing docents, guards, and library staff, including their directors and high-ranking staff at the National Archives; attending public events; working in their public research rooms; and examining the administrative and other files in and about these institutions. I had been in communication with Clark some months before, when he contacted me to discuss some issues about the National Archives and his difficulty in gaining access to the records of the Office of Presidential Libraries for his research. Clark had read my article on presidential libraries published some years before, and since it remains one of the few critical, independent assessments of this system, he hoped to gain some additional insights into the nature, function, and problems of these institutions.

The talk that Clark presented was well documented and quite disturbing, prompting me to write an open (I posted it on the Archives & Archivists listserv) letter to the Society of American Archivists leadership (Frank Boles and Nancy Beaumont). I start the letter by noting that a very serious matter concerning the behavior of the administrators of the U.S. National Archives had been recently brought to light by independent researcher Anthony Clark. I quote from Section VI of SAA's Code of Ethics: "Archivists strive to promote open and equitable access to their services and the records in their care without discrimination or preferential treatment, and in accordance with legal requirements, cultural sensitivities, and institutional policies. Archivists recognize their responsibility to promote the use of records as a fundamental purpose of the keeping of archives. Archivists may place restrictions on access for the protection of privacy or confidentiality of information in the records." I also referenced the Preamble to the Code, stating that it "establishes standards for the archival profession. It introduces new members of the profession to those standards, reminds experienced archivists of their professional responsibilities, and serves as a model for institutional policies. It also is intended to inspire public confidence in the profession." While it acknowledges that the Code only "provides an ethical framework to guide members of the profession" and "does not provide the solution to specific problems," I believe as a long-time SAA member (then 35 years) that the spirit of the Code requires SAA leadership to investigate claims into the unprofessional and blatantly unethical behavior of NARA and its leadership.

I referred SAA to the recording of the lecture available on the Web, indicating that in the lecture Clark presented disturbing evidence about efforts to deny him access to the records of the Office of Presidential Libraries by a number of NARA officials. I believe he has made a very strong case about the unprofessional, unethical, and perhaps illegal behavior of NARA leadership. I indicate that I hope to see SAA take steps to investigate these issues and complaints. I believe the health and reputation of our professional community depends on SAA speaking up about this issue, especially given the steps being taken by President Obama and his administration to open up government and to appoint a new Archivist of the United States. It makes little sense for SAA to list the qualities a new Archivist should possess (as it had recently done as the search for a new Archivist was starting), if it is not willing to be vocal about investigating and speaking out about these serious allegations of activities engaged in by members of our own professional community.

And, from this moment, another debate about the relevance of ethics in the American archival profession had started. My discussion of this incident builds around a series of blog postings I had made on my blog, "Reading Archives," starting on February 14, 2009. I have made changes only to meld them into a narrative of the Anthony Clark case.

NARA, SAA, and Anthony Clark

The issues discussed about NARA's treatment of Anthony Clark and the role of SAA, its code of ethics, and its independent voice in the archival community are much more than about one case. It is about the issue of leadership in the U.S. archival community. It is about the problems of eroding leadership by NARA (especially in the last two decades) and the views of SAA leadership about its code of ethics (we need a code, but we will never refer to it). However, this case does suggest that agitators ought to be seen as advocates; while some view Mr. Clark as a pest, I am sure, his views about the role of NARA and his appeals to SAA suggest he may possess a stronger notion of the archival community's mission and societal role than even elected and appointed leaders in the field at NARA and SAA. I used my blog to share some of my own views about this and to cite, when relevant, some of my own writings on this topic (and related ones). I did this in my blog so as to not irritate unnecessarily those on the Archives & Archivists listserv or in other venues.

When I first entered the archival profession in the early 1970s, I read all I could find and I remember reading the book by H.G. Jones, *The Records of a Nation*, published in 1969 and addressing the need for an independent National Archives (rather than its positioning under the General Services Administration).[1] As is typical of everything that Jones wrote, it is an elegant and beautiful argument for why an independent archives was so critical both to its mission and to the archival and historical professions. Some years later I watched with interest as the movement to gain NARA's independence kicked into full gear (my history master's mentor Walter Rundell was a leader in this), but by then I wondered just what difference it really would make if the National Archives was independent. Would it have a more precise mission and would it carry it out with more authority? Donald McCoy's 1978 book on the National Archives provided many hints that independence was not the real issue; while at one point I viewed his book as an exemplary piece of archival history, I have had occasion to re-examine the book for other reasons related to understanding the National Archives and have seen it as identifying weak parts of the foundation of the archival community. Clarity of mission and stronger leadership seem more important.[2]

My time on SAA Council in the late 1980s, work on an NHPRC-funded project on electronic records starting in the early 1990s, and continuing work in archival circles, such as editor of the *American Archivist*, gave me a unique opportunity to observe both SAA and NARA *and* the relationship between the two. While we worked on the research project about electronic recordkeeping, we witnessed the PROFs case, NARA's strange role in it, and one of my doctoral students, David Wallace, wrote an important study (his dissertation) of that case.[3] At my last SAA Council meeting in 1989 I witnessed leadership from NARA fumble about answering questions why it had sold marketing rights to Philip Morris for the use of the Bill of Rights, ultimately telling SAA that it did *not* care what SAA or the archival community thought about this (or any other) issue. When the 1992 House report on mismanagement at the National Archives appeared, I contacted SAA about the unethical activities of then AUS Don Wilson, but I was told that the ethics code was unenforceable and that in America people were assumed innocent until proved guilty (I pointed out that, while true, this did not deal with individuals confessing or when strong evidence materializes such as with the then startling report — now not so startling).

I also participated in the early 1990s in a meeting of graduate archival educators at NARA to assist it in evaluating its internal training program, and the consensus was that NARA needed to open up this program and align itself with new trends and opportunities in the emergence of stronger education programs (later, it was reported that we had endorsed their program, hardly true, and this was the last time I have ever had an invitation to participate in anything with NARA). The one exception to this occurred a few years ago when I was a candidate for a faculty position at the University of Maryland, and I was invited to a meeting with a high-ranking NARA official where I was told that they didn't want me there because I had been critical of the National Archives (true) and the Maryland program was *their* education program (false), I neglected my masters students in favor of my doctoral students (strange, and just ask my doctoral students if they feel so favored), and that they opposed me because I was a collaborator with David Bearman who they disliked (I had not worked at that point with David for nearly a decade). Such sentiments were clearly residue from my involvement with David on the Pitt electronic records project and some of my writings about ERM that were critical of NARA, leading to some strident criticisms of me in the literature by NARA staff such as Tom Brown and the late Linda Henry[4] — but such debates in the professional literature I always view differently (if you dare to publish, you have to be ready to accept such responses — and they always drive up one's citation counts anyway). I withdrew my application for unrelated reasons, but this was obviously a weird meeting (and one that makes me appreciate all the more the problems faced by Anthony Clark).

As time passed other issues related to the role of the National Archives continued to emerge. Although a considerable portion of my early career seems to have had me connected to some aspect of the National Historical Publications and Records Commission, the small funding arm of NARA, its role in diverting much of its funds to documentary editing projects in traditional approaches and formats seemed counter-intuitive. In the early 1990s a supposedly impartial study about the use of documentary editions was released by the NHPRC, but it mostly seemed to be a thinly veiled rationale or defense of these editions — prompting me to write a critical review of the report.[5] At one time in the late 1990s, the re-authorization of NHPRC seemed to distort even the balance of funds for editing and archiving projects, prompting me to write a critical assessment of the documentary editing projects.[6] While NHPRC has played an important role over the years in many aspects of the archival community, from supporting the publication of basic manuals and various research projects, I also have come to see the annual battle about its small federal allocation to be increasingly out of proportion to the needs of the archival community for a national archival policy and national funding. Advocacy and lobbying for stronger support for the archival mission needs to move beyond this small group buried within NARA (but I digress).

Because NARA is the defacto physical and institutional representation or symbol for so many (the media, scholars such as historians, genealogists and other citizen groups, and school groups) of the archival mission, it is important to watch, comment on, and lobby for change with or about NARA when it either wanders away from this mission or provides us opportunity for supporting it when the federal agency embarks in new and interesting directions. (Let me add here, that I write as both citizen/taxpayer wanting to see his interests represented and a long-time member of the archival profession). So, for example, when NARA announced its intentions to refurbish the display of the Declaration of Independence and other critical seminal documents, I thought this provided an opportunity for NARA to do some different things in representing new challenges (in this case digital documentation) to the archival mission, and I enjoyed writing about this.[7] Likewise, when we witnessed the transition from the Clinton administration to the second Bush one, this prompted me to write an analysis of the role and activities of the presidential library system,[8] mostly because I had become so appalled at the dominance of presidential library insiders in writing about these institutions *and* the complacency of the archival community about these institutions (that is, the complete lack of critical perspective about their strengths and weaknesses).

The second Bush administration, with its remarkable commitment to secrecy, has some watching even more closely the activities of the National Archives and how it would deal with such challenges. And I have found myself writing about a variety of issues about such matters, generally prompted by specific cases. The naming of a new Archivist of the United States in the midst of the Bush era caused me to reflect on the importance of this position.[9] Increasing scrutiny by journalists, scholars, and other commentators on matters of government accountability and secrecy has led me to write reviews of some of their observations.[10] Sadly, some odd activities by NARA itself, such as its involvement in secret arrangements with some federal agencies to reclassify previously open records, also has led to some additional writings.[11] Some of these essays I have folded into some of my books (such as this one), and others will appear in this way in the future. The point here is, in my opinion, NARA has not performed particularly well.

My commentaries on NARA and related topics have been a very minor part of my writings about archival issues in the last two decades. Yet, I worry about the future of the profession because of archival leadership issues, a seeming neglect of ethics and accountability matters, and a sick feeling that most working archivists do not care about NARA (or even SAA for that matter). Personally, I feel that the most important future issues faced by the archival community won't be technology (as the community has assumed for most of the past two decades), but it will be accountability and ethical issues. And apparently, from time to time, SAA leadership seems to think this way as well. In 2006 SAA President Richard Pearce-Moses sent a letter to Archivist of the United States Allen Weinstein expressing concern about the reclassification mess, starting the letter in this way: "Archivists share a passion and professional ethic for open access to government records. We believe that a citizen's right to review public records is a hallmark of democratic government. This right allows citizens to hold their public leaders accountable and to protect their rights and privileges." Pearce-Moses outlined actions they wanted NARA to take, but the main point here is here we have an open reference to a sense of ethics.[12]

I believe, given the evidence Anthony Clark presents, that SAA, through its Ethics and Professional Conduct Committee, should hear both sides — Clark and NARA — and issue a statement criticizing NARA for how it has treated Mr. Clark and restricted access to the records of the Office of Presidential Libraries (I say this because of the evidence Mr. Clark presents). If "Archivists [really] share a passion and professional ethic for open access to government records" and they "believe that a citizen's right to review public records is a hallmark of democratic government," then SAA can take no other action. A year ago I stated that I thought that the National Archives is in ruins, and I hope that the Obama Administration will name a dynamic and energetic individual to be the Archivist of the United States to restore it to what it once was and give it a hope for what it could be (now we have a new Archivist and only time will tell if we have the new leadership needed). SAA needs to step in and become an independent leader and a vigilant watchdog of NARA, not just a bystander expressing little opinion about NARA's troubles, poor leadership, and sometimes unethical activities.

I have served SAA in many capacities. I have published in the *American Archivist* from 1974 to this year, served on Council, been the *American Archivist* editor, been SAA's editor of publications, and been on numerous committees and presented at numerous conference sessions. I believe that to be a strong profession we need a strong professional association, but it is getting harder for me to answer questions posed by my masters' students about *why* they should be a member of this association. And every September when my dues notice comes, it gets a little harder for me to answer the same question for myself.

I have lost friends and colleagues through the years because of my stands on a number of issues, and this hurts me more than I generally let on. I am saddened by the lack of support even today by many of my educator colleagues who won't take a position on such issues as the SAA ethics code or the problems plaguing NARA's leadership, for reasons only known to them. I believe, strongly, that the future of the archival field depends on speaking up about such matters, not remaining silently on the sidelines and merely tending to our own gardens. I will be the first to admit if I am wrong about any of this, and I have made mistakes in the past because I am human, but I believe the silence of so many is a far greater wrong. Help me explain to my students why they should be SAA members and, for goodness sake, why they should heed the call to be archivists.[13]

More About SAA, NARA, and Anthony Clark

What follows is my second round of exchanges with SAA about the Anthony Clark, NARA, and the SAA Code of Ethics situation. I believe this is an unfortunate lapse in SAA leadership. We may be at a crossroads concerning the viability of SAA as a serious professional association, if it abandons its responsibility to speak out about problems at NARA or if it continues to neglect any serious commitment to archival ethics.

Here is my second open letter to Frank Boles, Nancy Beaumont, and SAA leadership:

> Several weeks ago, February 14th to be exact, I wrote to the two of you (Boles and Beaumont) making my concerns known about issues related to researcher Anthony Clark's treatment by the National Archives in seeking to gain access to the records of the Office of Presidential Libraries. Specifically, I cited the SAA Code of Ethics, noting that it "requires SAA leadership to investigate claims into the unprofessional and blatantly unethical behavior of NARA and its leadership."
>
> In a round of emails between Frank Boles and Rand Jimerson, the matter seemed to have been referred to the Code of Ethics and Professional Conduct Committee (although some subsequent comments reported on the Archives and Archivists List suggests this may not have happened and would be considered at the SAA Council meeting held last weekend [this was the last weekend in February 2009]). While I found this confusing, I have waited to see what SAA would do at its Council meeting about this very important case.
>
> In today's "In the Loop," [dated March 7, 2009] sent out to all SAA members, there is a brief report of the "highlights" of the SAA Council meeting, but there is no reference to the Clark case. With this message, I am requesting as an SAA member a brief report about what, if any, action has been taken. I am writing this as a open letter to you and the professional community, sending it to you directly and also posting to the A&A list. I will report on any response I receive.
>
> I would appreciate if I could have a timely response about Council's deliberations and actions.
>
> Thank you.

Here is Frank Boles' response to my second open letter:

> Richard:
>
> Prior to the convening of the SAA Council meeting on February 26 in Washington, I spoke with Anthony Clark by phone to review the history of his contact with NARA and SAA and to gain a better

understanding of his concerns. On February 25 I met with Acting Archivist of the United States Adrienne Thomas and two of her staff members to discuss several topics, including the issue of Mr. Clark's access to records of the Office of Presidential Libraries. During the course of the Council meeting, I reported to the full Council about my conversations with Mr. Clark and Ms. Thomas; the Council did not take up a discussion of the issue. On March 4 I again contacted Mr. Clark by email.

During my conversation with Ms. Thomas it was clear to me that she is aware of the background and many details associated with Mr. Clark's requests and claims. She assured me that she and her staff intend to work quickly — and directly with Mr. Clark — to resolve the matter. People of good will may disagree about whether NARA is acting in good faith and with reasonable speed; however, given new leadership I believe NARA should be given a continued opportunity to meet Mr. Clark's requests and allowed a reasonable period of time for a mutually satisfactory agreement to be reached.

Regarding the SAA Code of Ethics:

The SAA Council, in February 2005, adopted the current Code of Ethics
(http://www.archivists.org/governance/handbook/app_ethics.asp).
Prior to the adoption of this code, the Committee on Ethics and Professional Conduct (CEPC) was charged to draft a revision of the code and to seek member opinion about the draft, which was done via an article in the July/August 2004 issue of *Archival Outlook* and an open forum at the 2004 Annual Meeting in Boston. As the July/August 2004 article states: "On advice of legal counsel, this draft revision eliminates commentary on each principle, as well as guidelines and procedures for interpretation of the code and mediation of disputes..... The proposed code is intended to be aspirational." Earlier, in January 2003, the Council voted to "revoke SAA's code of ethics enforcement procedures." The current Code does not require SAA leaders to investigate claims of unethical behavior.

Unfortunately there is an inconsistency between the Code and the guidelines under which the CEPC operates — an artifact, I believe, of our failure to review the Council Handbook carefully and update it in light of adoption of the new Code. The guidelines for the CEPC allow it to respond to ethical complaints if directed to do so by the president. Should the president invoke this clause, however, she or he would be in violation of at least two Council actions. I will ask Council to rectify this administrative error.

Currently the CEPC is discussing revising the Code to reflect current scholarship and professional discourse regarding archival ethics and the profession's goals and identity. In its recent annual report to the Council, the CEPC indicated that it "plans to engage in further review of the SAA Code of Ethics to make recommendations to the Council and to the SAA membership regarding revising the Code," with some preliminary recommendations to be made by the date of the 2009 Annual Meeting in Austin. Although several SAA members have suggested over the years that the Code be revisited with an eye to creating something that could be used in resolving ethical disputes, as I understand it, the CEPC currently does not recommend such changes, which would entail significant administrative and legal obligations, expenses, and liabilities.

As always, I appreciate your willingness to raise issues that are of concern to you.

Here is My Open Response to Frank Boles:

I am saddened by President Boles's response, for several reasons.

First, there is no "new" NARA leadership. There is an acting Archivist of the United States, pending the nomination and approval of a new AUS. All the individuals in leadership, several named by Anthony Clark in his presentation, have been there many years and are still there — and as I have written elsewhere, the problems with NARA were present before he asked for access to the records of the Office of Presidential Libraries.

Second, I am amazed by the candid response that SAA Council did not discuss the issue at its latest meeting. The reasons seem to be based on procedural issues related to inconsistencies about how or whether the president can refer matters to the Committee on Ethics and Professional Conduct. I guess life in SAA Council meetings have changed since I was on it. Did Council members review the Clark lecture? Was anyone concerned about the broader issues represented about NARA culture and leadership? Did anyone on Council want to talk with Anthony Clark and evaluate the evidence presented by him extending far beyond his own issues of access to records? As Bruce Montgomery [in the Archives & Archivists listserv discussion on this topic] nicely stated, there is a "larger issue" at work here and that "SAA's mission should include making inquiries (or investigating), joining lawsuits, and otherwise taking action in the public interest when larger principles of freedom of information and the public's right to know are involved."

Third, now I realize the mistake I made in invoking the Code of Ethics in the Clark case. I invoked the code because I believe that ethical issues represent perhaps the most important professional matters we will be involved with in the future. I also invoked the code because my responsibility as an educator is to prepare future archivists to work in an increasingly complex world, and this involves teaching about ethics and related matters. However, by doing this I enabled Council to avoid the Clark case and the broader issues reflected by NARA's actions in dealing with him and in other concerns related to its mission. I am naïve. I did not consider that Council would avoid the NARA issues by acknowledging problems with its internal procedures and logistics. I did not realize that an "administrative error" would lead to Council not even discussing what are obvious serious issues (or, if you like, charges that there are serious issues) at NARA. Honestly, this shocks me.

I won't address the matter of whether Mr. Clark is now being treated fairly by NARA or how he feels about his discussion with Frank Boles and SAA's actions (really, lack of activity); he is in the best position to discuss this if he wants. What I now must mull over is whether SAA is the best place to discuss and seek to resolve serious professional issues. Fortunately, I have a number of months before my dues notice arrives, and this gives me the opportunity to see what happens both with the appointment of a new AUS and how NARA responds to Anthony Clark's FOIA and other requests, as well as whether SAA realizes that it cannot just mouth empty rhetoric about ethical matters and it attempts to reaffirm the importance of professional ethics (or, more practically, whether SAA understands that it is long overdue in separating itself from NARA so it can honestly speak up about what the national archives needs to be, whether it uses the word "ethical" or not). In the past, I reflected on this and still written the check; I am not so sure I will do this when faced with the moment again at the end of the summer. [For the record, I have remained a member.]

I have noticed that a lot of SAA energy has been devoted to telling us about the large membership it now has. While I know that it faces tough economic decisions ahead, as every organization does these days, I assume this membership desires SAA to be a leader and that people are not just members to get discounts on meeting registrations and publications, receive a personal copy of the *American Archivist* or the newsletter, or other such benefits. I see a failure here to provide leadership, and I accept the fact, given my own long involvement with SAA, that this is my failure as well; the victim here, the person who should be most concerned, is a citizen like Anthony Clark. It is with people like him that all our high ideals of preserving the documentary record, ensuring government transparency and accountability, and enabling citizens to have access to essential archival sources in order to understand their past will be tested and found working or not working. Whatever the reason, we have failed him, at least for the moment.

Different Perspectives on Presidential Libraries (and More Commentary on the Anthony Clark Situation)

Anthony Clark's recent travails in getting access to the records of the Office of Presidential Libraries at the National Archives is only evidence of one aspect of this system, partly archival in nature and purpose, that ought to trouble archivists and others interested in the archival mission in a democratic society. Anyone who has paid attention to the presidential libraries and the issues related to their history, performance, mission, and controversies ought to acknowledge that this is a highly flawed system and one that is often in conflict with what archivists usually assume to be their role in American society. Indeed, three recent peeks into these institutions reveal continuing, troubling issues that represent the historical and political context for the kinds of problems Clark has encountered.

Susan Jacoby's slim, elegant study about the Alger Hiss case offers insights about the current debates about the nature and role of presidential libraries. Jacoby traces the changing attitudes about the case and Hiss' innocence or guilt about his conviction for spying for the Soviet Union. Acknowledging early on that Hiss looks more guilty because of additional government files declassified, Jacoby does not attempt to draw a conclusion about the merits of the case against Hiss but instead strives to show how the case has been a weathervane for the shifting fortunes of right and left political viewpoints. As she writes, "The contradictory historical scripts about the Hiss case reveal much more about conflicting visions of what America ought to be than about what American Communism actually was — or about who Alger Hiss was."[14]

What does the book have to do with presidential records? For one thing, it places former Archivist of the United States Allen Weinstein and his book on Hiss (*Perjury*, published in 1978) in its context. Weinstein used effectively FOIA to gain access to a greater quantity of documentation about the case, perhaps explaining why he has tried to assist Anthony Clark in his own FOIA efforts to get access to the Office of Presidential Libraries records. Jacoby describes Weinstein's interviewing and working with Hiss and his assessments of what the evidence suggests about the issue of whether Hiss had been a Soviet spy, Weinstein's conclusion being that the evidence did not absolve him of guilt. Subsequent opening of Soviet records after the fall of the Soviet Union seem not to have countered the conclusions offered by Weinstein in his earlier book.

Indeed, Jacoby returns, in her conclusion, to the issue of records and the evidence they offer in resolving the split viewpoints about Hiss. She does not see how any additional evidence could resolve the controversy between right and left since the Hiss case has become a "metaphor for the fundamental dispute about the essence of patriotism that has created a wall of separation between many conservatives and many liberals."[15] Jacoby sees the case as a "powerful argument in favor of maximum, not minimum, civil libertarian safeguards in times of real as well as perceived danger."[16] It is why the problems revealed about the activities of both the SAA and NARA in regards to Anthony Clark's efforts to examine the OPL records are, in my view, so dangerous to the health of the archival mission, a mission that must include the importance of records for holding government officials accountable to the public.

Writer James Traub's recent description of the efforts underway to bring to Southern Methodist University the George W. Bush Presidential Library also ought to give pause to the purpose and viability of these institutions. Traub focuses on the Freedom Institute, the "policy center to be housed alongside his presidential library and museum on the campus of Southern Methodist University," then searching for an executive director.[17] Traub explores the controversy about the Bush library at SMU, and the manner in which he characterizes the substance of the debate ought to give us (the public and the archival community) pause about why we should continue to support such facilities: "But George Bush is not everyone's guy on the S.M.U. campus. Indeed, the prospect of being identified in perpetuity with the Freedom Agenda freezes the blood of some of the university's leading academics. Everything about the planned institute reminds them of what they detested about the Bush administration. It will proselytize rather than explore: a letter sent to universities bidding for the Bush center stipulated that the institute would, among other things, 'further the domestic and international goals of the Bush administration.' And it will hold itself apart from S.M.U.'s own world of academic inquiry, reporting to the Bush Foundation itself rather than to the university president or provost, as academic institutes—even presidential ones—normally do."[18] Is this political agenda really the container we want for preserving and administering archival records?

Traub admits that it might take time for the Bush library to develop into an institution where research and scholarship of the variety normally desired at a university are both welcome and evident. However, he doesn't hide how long this might take: "Even [R. Gerald] Turner, S.M.U.'s president, is hedging his bets. He expects there to be an 'adjustment period' during which the institute may feel a little bit like George Bush's wonderful place but that over time, 'Bush's views will become irrelevant.' That may be; the Hoover Institution eventually outgrew its namesake. But since the process took half a century, and involved some very ugly battles with Stanford, that may not be the most encouraging precedent."[19] That suggests what are well documented, then, about presidential libraries, namely that there are so many political and other agendas that the archival mission is threatened or compromised. Ought archivists not be surprised that the National Archives resists Anthony Clark's requests to have access to the OPL records? Isn't it likely that a lot of the ugliness of these other agendas will be revealed and any role by NARA to have a legitimate stake in preserving such records for purposes such as understanding our political processes, holding government accountable in a democratic system, and supporting reputable scholarship and other research be dashed on the rocks of at least the recent administration's objectives to oppose such higher aims?

Another book provides a clever and interesting examination of the "second lives" (their post-presidency careers) of our chief executives.[20] Authors Benardo and Weiss look at how these individuals earn a living, the political careers and activities they engage in after their time in the Oval Office, new outlets for public service that they discover or pursue, and the rehabilitation agendas that some pursue with great vigor. One of the activities of the ex-presidents they examine (how could they not?) is their presidential libraries. These authors provide the background on the library system — how it developed, arguments for and against it, the costs associated with it, controversies such as influence peddling in order to raise funds to design and build the expensive facilities, and how the system has been transformed. Benardo and Weiss pull no punches. Right at the outset they present what is the real problem with the library system: "In a country bereft of emperors, monarchs, or pharaohs, America's most powerful elected officials have embraced libraries as their personal shrines."[21] Woe to those that question this. Indeed, the authors return to this topic in their general conclusion when they see as a common theme the prevailing interests of these former presidents to be that of controlling their legacy. While many scholars, including some archivists, have pointed out that the formation and preservation of archives has often been tied up with issues of power and control, it is not the public good objective we strive for in most articulations of the archival mission. The manner in which Benardo and

Weiss characterize the nature of these archives cheapens the better objectives that these libraries could engage with and makes many archivists and their primary professional association, the latter seemingly asleep while the more dangerous issues with these institutions pile up and the former quiet and focused on their own institutional challenges, look more like court jesters.

There are, of course, good people who hold different opinions about the presidential libraries. There have been good people who have tried to steer these archives and museums in the right direction. However, I believe that what we are seeing with the case of Anthony Clark ought to demonstrate that this system is not the best way for us to preserve the records of the ex-presidents and their administrations; it creates a rationale for protecting not documenting former presidents, exacerbated by the poor work of the National Archives and the uneven handling by the SAA when it needs to function more as a professional and citizen watchdog of NARA. What Clark has brought to the table is an outsider's perspective armed with substantial evidence of problems with what we used to see as our "ministry of documents" (borrowing from Donald McCoy's thirty-year old history of the National Archives). Anyone trying to write NARA's history since 1968, the cut-off year of McCoy's history, it seems, could be blocked by the archivists themselves (how ironic), perhaps motivated by protecting their own legacy. We ignore this at the peril of destroying our professional ideals. I wonder if the damage may not already be too great.

At the moment, I am not sure where to go with SAA or NARA, partly because Anthony Clark is still laying out one important part of the evidence regarding his treatment. What I do know, is that in the case of the Society, is that the membership rightly expects its leadership to be accountable to it (and there are ways to hold it accountable *if* individual members opt to band together and speak up, something it has not done and is not doing). We certainly are entitled to more than weak explanations revolving around administrative procedures, comments about a vague ethics code, and lame reassurances that NARA's leadership is new and ought to be given time to resolve its internal problems. With regards to NARA, we have many more options available to us as U.S. citizens to voice our concerns. This is something to be discussed in the future.

Not Enforcing Ethics

On March 20, 2009, SAA President Frank Boles issued a statement, "Enforcing Ethics," and in straightforward language he closed the case about how we, members of this association, are to view and use the ethics code. Without any additional inquiry, Boles also indicated how SAA views the NARA situation regarding Anthony Clark, referring, only at the beginning of his statement, about the "alleged ethical shortcomings of some of our colleagues in Washington" and, quite candidly remarking, that it would not "formally investigate the situation" because of a variety of "policy decisions" emanating from "several assumptions." I congratulate Frank Boles, and the SAA leadership, for clarifying the matter for all of us about both the ethics code and its relationship to the National Archives. He also kindly offers a suggestion about "how the Code can be used to good purpose."

There is no reason to reiterate in much detail this statement, since anyone can read it and decide what it all means; indeed, that is the point after all, that the code is aspirational and to be used how any archivist or archival institution sees fit. Boles' reporting on the CEPC's support of only an aspirational ethics code "but one that more clearly reflects recent scholarship and professional discourse regarding archival ethics and the profession's goals and identity," confirms that there is little to be gained for pushing SAA on its perspective about ethics. However, it is worth commenting on the assumptions, stated and unstated, behind the statement. Indeed, I am left wondering about the connection between the issue of the ethics code with that of just how a professional archival association ought to respond to the kind of complaints publicly made about the nation's premier archival institution. Do the procedural and legal concerns about the ethics code really relate to the specifics of this case? Or, as I have mused about in a couple of past comments, did I make an error even invoking the ethics code? Are there approaches SAA could have used to address concerns about NARA or, for that matter, charges made by a researcher about NARA?

My intention is not to provide a detailed response to or critique of the four assumptions raised by Boles, but they are worth some reflection. Actually, as will be obvious by my comments below, I don't understand how the ethics code bars SAA from examining or questioning the conduct of any federal agency vis-à-vis the administration of its records, especially when the agency happens to be the National Archives. In fact, the commentary about the present Council being restricted in how it uses the ethics code by the actions of previous Councils seems somewhat strained since Council has the ability to change any of its decisions (except perhaps those needing to be brought for membership actions, such as changes in bylaws). Moreover, any Council could certainly decide that the allegations and evidence made about the fundamental mission and activities of the

THE ANTHONY CLARK CASE   199

National Archives are serious enough to warrant a public statement about them, whether or not these have anything to do with ethical issues. In other words, is every matter Council might have set before going to be derailed by the fact that nearly everything it does — approving professional standards or guidelines, for example — is aspirational (since anybody can be a member and SAA is not a certification or accreditation body)? Does this mean that about all SAA leadership really can do is set out housekeeping rules for its activities such as publishing, running conferences, and offering workshops?

Boles cites the American Library Association (ALA) and the American Historical Association (AHA) as other associations that lack "an enforcement mechanism." However, there are omissions in this assessment. The historical associations changed their mechanism because they were over-burdened with complaints, something SAA has never faced or probably would face. Even as these associations abandoned this process, some who were involved protested the decision and believe that this has been a mistake for the profession's credibility.[22] Boles quotes from an AHA statement that what it did was not workable, but one might still wonder whether AHA's decision is good for the profession or not. We also need to recognize that AHA made its decision after an effort to hear complaints of fifteen years duration, whereas SAA has not made any such effort. SAA has never pushed the use of its ethics code, except if you count efforts a few decades ago to market an earlier version of the code suitable for framing and display in one's office.

I have not done an analysis of AHA's past experiences with its professional conduct committee other than to read commentaries about it. Of course, the historical profession has been quite facile in how it convenes scholarly conferences and sessions to feature debate about what are seen to be breaches in professional and scholarly inquiry and discourse.[23] However when we consider what AHA has been up to, we ought to realize that we could be comparing apples and oranges when we put its activities alongside that of SAA. How can we compare the complaints of a researcher about his treatment by NARA with that of complaints of plagiarism and other issues of scholarly research that will be given their day in the normal process of reviews and conferences? Certainly, as has been suggested to me, we can prepare essays for publication or papers for conference presentation about Anthony Clark's case, but these won't be very timely in assisting this researcher or even in providing a fair hearing if NARA chooses not to participate (which NARA is prone not to do). Why SAA cannot function as a broker to bring these two parties together, privately or publicly, really is a mystery to me. However, a reading of the evidence being presented by Clark himself on his blog suggests that, instead, some of the SAA leadership seems to have been inclined to help NARA handle the Clark complaints, suggesting that maybe there are other reasons for SAA not wanting to be involved in this case that extend beyond the utility of an aspirational code of ethics (my interpretation not Clark's). As I have commented on in earlier posts, there is a culture of a partnership between SAA and NARA that works against SAA being able to speak up when NARA stumbles (and this is at least a twenty year old problem). So, we need to look for other watchdogs to scrutinize this federal agency.

As for the ALA, it may have an aspirational code, but no one would ever suggest that this organization is bashful about speaking up about issues of misconduct. Frank Boles is correct that the ALA is not in the enforcement business, when ALA states this on its web site: "The ALA does not at this time provide mediation, financial aid, or legal aid in response to workplace disputes. Your employer has an array of sanctions that may or may not be imposed on you, including but not limited to: reassignment, passing you up for promotion, passing you up for raises, denying you tenure, passing you up for the best assignments, and ultimately dismissal. If you decide to speak out on a matter involving professional policy, it will be a matter between you and your employer." Yet, ALA is working to develop its ethics code, stating, "The Council Committee on Professional Ethics shall augment the Code of Ethics by explanatory interpretations and additional statements, prepared by this committee or elicited from other units of ALA." This seems in stark contrast to SAA's recent activities in both the area of professional ethics or advocacy. Maybe I will be proved wrong by future activities undertaken by the SAA; I hope so. However, at the moment, before this statement by SAA's president, the association offered no guidance whatsoever about the ethics code. Moreover, it has been moving in the opposite direction, tearing away at explanations and interpretations, gutting the code from what it once had been in 1992 (then one of the best professional codes in terms of details, although it was true even then that the Society was wary of supporting its use).

When it comes to the mechanics of enforcement, Frank Boles seems to employ commonsense, describing how difficult it would be to develop "rules that are fair and well understood." Actually, I agree. What I don't understand, however, is why SAA cannot examine evidence offered up about professional misconduct or publicly speak up when there seems to be misconduct on the part of archival programs or their leaders or staff (when this misconduct has to do with fundamental archival practice and principles). Why is this different than speaking up when government agencies restrict access to records, illegally destroy records, or seem to violate laws and public policies? SAA does not need to launch an investigation when it does this. Given the amount of evidence being presented by a private citizen and researcher, citing and reproducing records of NARA itself, it seems strange that SAA cannot call into question NARA's conduct or, at the least, suggest that NARA correct its handling of these requests for access to its records. (It does not have to mention individuals or SAA members working at NARA, although given the small number of the latter that seems both unlikely and certainly unnecessary).

SAA does not have to convene a court of inquiry itself. However, there is absolutely nothing to prevent it from calling on Congress or the President to investigate such serious charges, and I believe the amount of evidence presented certainly merits such action. As I have written elsewhere, there is something amiss with the culture of the relationship between SAA and NARA that prevents SAA from being critical of NARA when there seems to be a need to do so. And this is a problem, given NARA's prominent role in government information policy. When I was on SAA Council in the late 1980s I proposed that Council pass a motion that no NARA staff member could hold an elected position within SAA, indicating that there were problems of conflict of interest even then (mirroring the kind of problem Anthony Clark sees in NARA staff answering FOIA requests even when they concern records they created or that concern them). By the way, the motion was never taken seriously. We have had a legacy of conflicts of interests and lack of accountability between SAA and NARA that go back to the origins of both in the mid-1930s. And, if you don't think there is any responsibility of SAA for NARA because one is a professional association and the other a federal agency, then we need to give up on any kind of advocacy about government activities in archives and records management and recommend that all citizen interest groups be shut down as well.

When Frank Boles turns his attention to the legal issues, he connects to the primary reason we have been hearing about the Society's concern with the ethics code, stating "Should a federal court find that an individual was wrongfully harmed, financial penalties can be levied against both the professional organization collectively and the judges individually." I am not a lawyer, and I have never played one on television, but I shake my head at this kind of concern. In America, litigation is as much recreation as anything. Everyone sues each other and organizations for almost anything. It is clear that SAA's concern is legitimate, but how can you function or do anything if the fear of litigation is a determining factor? What is to prevent a group of SAA members from suing the Society because it has not developed a code that could be enforced or used (and I am not suggesting this at all)? Couldn't the Society be sued for comments made by a workshop instructor, a conference speaker, or because of an author's statements in an *American Archivist* article? A half dozen years ago some archivists expressed the opinion that SAA could be liable for its use of a political poster on the AA cover, an illustration discussed in an essay about the management of political poster collections (see chapter seven). So, it seems to me that SAA is always facing the possibility of litigation because of the society we live in, apart from whatever it does or does not do.

President Boles does commend what ALA has done, encouraging its members "to adopt the code as part of each member's workplace policies. In this way, library ethics voluntarily become a part of well-grounded institutional policy — and become the responsibility of each institution to enforce among its employees." To do this, of course, you need a code with some greater specificity than what we have now. And, if this is the case, why does SAA not inquire about whether NARA has done this itself? There is an ethics resources site on the NARA Web site, but it addresses general federal issues and guidelines and has no reference to general professional ethics codes such as promulgated by SAA. Perhaps, there is simply no critical mass of SAA members within NARA leadership who have advocated anything like this, and this suggests another reason, perhaps, why SAA should be a little bolder in asserting itself when it comes to NARA activities (even if it does it in a way that does not cite individuals or invoke the ethics code). What are the bounds for when SAA *will* question NARA activity?

If the above commentary seems muddled, it is because I am struggling, as well, about just what the ethics code means and how it should be used. One conclusion I have reached is that the Society of American Archivists' value is in its role as a membership organization providing a range of services that probably cannot include more serious issues of professional standards and guidelines. What it offers, and these are useful, are conferences, workshops, and publications. Just as in my memberships in the American Automobile Association (AAA) or the American Association of Retired Persons (AARP), as long as I am getting good value for my membership dues, with discounts on these products and services offered with my membership, then there is no reason not to be a member. When Frank Boles refers to the ethics code as a "document of persuasion that is to be studied, discussed, and improved," it may be that this study and discussion has to occur just as much outside SAA as within it. It is just as much the case that this persuasion can be more effective unhooked from the drag of SAA policies, politics, and processes. I know I can get help from AAA when the wheels on my car fall off, but I am not sure I can get help from SAA when the wheels of archival principles and practices blow out in obvious ways.

Where does any of this leave us in terms of Anthony Clark and NARA? If not SAA, who will seek to hold NARA accountable? It may be that we are caught in another conundrum when we seek accountability by SAA because of other disconnects between the Society and NARA. Frank Boles, at the end of his statement, muses, "In the end, the Code of Ethics is for our members to use — and perhaps place in their own work environments — rather than for the Society to enforce." And, maybe, there's the rub. If there are virtually no SAA members in NARA, then the ethics code really isn't applicable in that institution. On the other hand, it seems that you could argue that SAA ought to at least work on that level and suggest to NARA that it ought to encourage its professional staff to be SAA members and endorse the SAA ethics code as an additional resource in guiding ethical conduct. I am sure, however, that there may be a dozen technical and other reasons why this is unlikely to occur.

But when I come to the end in my own statement, I worry about the one researcher, Anthony Clark, who has chosen to speak out and has ample documentation about problems with NARA providing access to government records that any citizen ought to expect to be able to examine. I still struggle with what to say to my students about what the implications of the Clark case are for their future careers. I am comfortable with saying to these students that they adopt a consumer mentality and stick with SAA as long as they get services of use to them for the amount they pay in dues. I am comfortable in referring them to other investigations and discussions about archival ethics that will be going on outside of SAA. I am comfortable in raising these difficult and contentious archival ethics concerns in my course on this topic. It is more difficult to know what to say to Anthony Clark, other than I offer apologies on behalf of my profession in our inability to provide much in the way of assistance to him about what are clearly serious problems in archival practice and general interpretations about access to government records (and to conclude that while the first may be the problematic ethical issue, the latter is more about archival policy and procedure, something that SAA ought to be able to deal with). Unfortunately, Mr. Clark, as an ordinary citizen, will need to seek an airing of his concerns and some form of justice elsewhere; other than as individuals, we are unable to assist him. Something seems wrong here.

Postscript a Year Later. More than a year has passed since this brief controversy. A new Archivist of the United States has arrived, but it is too early to determine just what kinds of leadership changes David Ferrario might make. I hear very positive things about his integrity and commitment, so I am hopeful. Anthony Clark is now a staff member for a member of the U.S. House of Representatives, has closed down his blog on presidential archives, and shelved his plans (at least for a while) to write a book about presidential libraries. While I hope he returns to writing this book, one can assume that he may have more influence on the activities of NARA from this new position. The SAA has once again weathered an archival controversy, with little evidence of any particular damage. Its leadership continues to rotate and its corporate memory seems weak, as it was two decades ago when I was on its governing Council.

Someone might come along and write an analysis of this professional debate, but for now SAA's position is probably best reflected in Rand Jimerson's *Archives Power*.[24] Jimerson, a former SAA president and well-known for taking moderate stances on contentious issues, provides a text that is best left for readers to make their own conclusions about the validity of his arguments (suffice it to say that I disagree with him, and he is careful not to associate with my positions). At least Jimerson has given us some thoughtful scholarship to consider in the years ahead. As for me, I will continue to take on unpopular issues within the archives community, but these, after this book, will be more restricted to my classroom and other essays. I weary, a bit, of the public debates that reflect that most members of the profession are too busy tending to their own gardens (and given the woeful economic condition of our times, who can blame them?) to care about cases questioning the role, leadership, and activities of either NARA or SAA. I can hear the voices of the others in the lifeboat telling me to sit down.

Chapter Ten

Revisiting the Archival Finding Aid

Introduction: Remembrance of Things Past

When I entered the archival profession in the early 1970s, there was little discussion about descriptive standards. I remember a conference in 1973 in which an experienced archivist mused about archival arrangement and description in the most idiosyncratic fashion possible. Each institution had its own traditions, practices, and approaches, and it seemed acceptable and logical that unique manuscripts and archival records would be handled in unique ways from institution to institution. The key, after all, was the archivist's knowledge. The researcher, generally assumed then to be an historian, also would possess immense knowledge about their own field and provide additional context that would be extremely useful in their negotiations with the archivist and in identifying just what records they needed to consult.

I also remember being troubled then by some of the very loose practices. Most of what bothered me I dealt with by developing consistency in how we did things in my own institution, and that seemed to be challenge enough. My first employer was a 130-year old private historical society, so bringing consistent descriptive practice to it was difficult enough. There you could discern particular periods when an individual stamped his own sense of how to do things, and you learned quickly by understanding when a particular finding aid (of every conceivable variety) was done and who was responsible for it. We hired a librarian to work with us in bringing consistency to our internal indexing terminology. Of course, this was happening in the days when we relied on an ink dribbling, hand rolled stenciling device, so the extent of what damage we could do in archival descriptive practice was quite limited. Even with such efforts, I found myself writing a master guide to the finding aids both for staff and researchers, trying to describe the potpourri of various articles, books, card catalogs, loose-leaf binders, and other devices that had been accumulated since the first guide had been published in 1854. When one came across a description reading "located near water bucket in basement," no one panicked; all you did was check to make sure that the box of records was not still there (they were not, but the century old water bucket was).

Today we seem to be in the golden age of archival descriptive standards. Almost thirty years ago, archivists sought to standardize inventories and registers that had been used by the National Archives and the Library of Congress since the 1940s, bringing some order to the kinds of internal finding aids researchers could expect to find (only a small number of archival repositories seemed to publish these kinds of finding aids — and for good reason — since they were more likely to be used by archivists than researchers). Twenty years ago, the US MARC AMC format forced archivists to learn, use, and adapt standardized indexing, thesaurus, and other methods long used by librarians and other information professionals in order to place their descriptions in automated library catalogs and national and international bibliographic utilities. A decade ago the emergence of Encoded Archival Description (EAD) brought the promises of standardizing finding aids for use on the World Wide Web, supplementing the MARC records, so the riches of archival holdings could be more easily discovered.

Generations of Descriptive Practice

Little more than a decade after its emergence, the newest version of archival descriptive standards, Encoded Archival Description, reigns supreme, but reveals some stresses and strains. Each successive generation of standards supporting the production of finding aids, from the formulation of the structure of manuscript registers and archival inventories in the mid-twentieth century to the adoption of the tags and fields of MARC-based records to the reformulation of hypermedia versions of registers and inventories in EAD, has met with quick acceptance. Nevertheless, as with nearly all developments in the standardization of archival description, there have been reservations, from costs and techniques to the implications for users, expressed about the utility of every other descriptive genre. As with every stage of development in archival description, we have moved forward with modest knowledge of the use of archival materials (in the case of EAD, we have little information about users' experiences with online finding aids).[1] Still, experts like Helen Tibbo refer to the "rise of a ubiquitous networked information environment" as a revolution changing "perspective, policy, and practice" in archival description,[2] and studies are emerging suggesting that historians and other heavy users of archival sources are developing new expectations for how they access archives in the Web age.[3] Perhaps the entire past half-century of developments in archival description represents a revolution of sorts, but one that archivists are far too closely involved with to understand or evaluate objectively.

Archivists have tended to prepare their finding aids in a language and manner they are more comfortable with than are the researchers seeking to use archives,[4] and they maintain the same content and format of the finding aids even as they have learned that researchers and their expectations are changing.[5] A new generation of researchers have begun to make statements such as this: "A knowledge of what elements people use to describe their information need and how they structure their requests will make it possible to design better research aids, including automated information retrieval systems, finding aids, and web interfaces, that will guide the user to the information she or he wants";[6] this represents a sea change of thinking about the nature and construction of archival finding aids. It is why institutions adopting EAD may believe that they have created better and more effective finding aids, but that in reality most of the implications of utilizing this latest archival descriptive approach are unknown because archivists have not acquired the depth of needed knowledge about how their researchers use or desire to use documentary sources.[7] It is also why some archivists, using descriptive standards, have determined the need to circumvent accepted rules to serve better particular kinds of researchers.[8] Archivists still have a long way to go in determining how researchers actually are successful in archives, although there are efforts underway to gain a better understanding of this; indeed, some are now openly assessing the means by which to study the ways archival sources and finding aids are used, such as evaluating the prospects of having these researchers maintain diaries for later evaluation.[9]

Studying Users and Finding Aids

Studies about archival users have been illuminating in regards to the effectiveness of archival finding aids. One suggests that a characteristic of the successful archival researcher is knowledge of archives, what they term "archival intelligence," indicating the role archivists must play in educating their researchers. This study notes that finding aids are not well understood, nor, for that matter, are other access tools to archival records.[10] Another study indicates that despite evidence that researchers like historians are using online finding aids, archivists cannot assume that archival resources are more widely available. Helen Tibbo, in this analysis, notes that historians also rely just as much and in many cases more on traditional older aids, concluding that the "message for libraries and archives is clear. They must maintain access to traditional means of locating resources while building easily navigable Web sites that contain useful information."[11]

While some make suggestions for more rigorous archival user education, it is also just as true that the way archivists prepare finding aids ought to be re-examined as well. In the latter study, Tibbo comments that many historians don't know about the online finding aids, and she advocates the need for better publicity: "To accomplish this, repositories must move beyond provision of access and bibliographic instruction. Time and other resources must be allocated to user studies, user education, and especially, outreach within repository budgets. These should not be seen as dispensable add-ons. This is the business of the archival enterprise in the digital age."[12] However, it is just as much the case that archival finding aids, the traditional printed ones and the newer online versions, have not been understood by researchers. Perhaps the real business of postmodern archival enterprise ought to be re-evaluating just what finding aids represent over time, studying them as a documentary source reflecting attitudes and practices of the archival community at various times. At the least, archivists need to recognize that, as Wendy Duff and Catherine Johnson state, "finding information in archives is not an easy task" and that "designing intuitive systems that meet the researchers' needs requires a thorough understanding of the information-seeking behavior of archival users."[13]

Occasionally, some, such as Michelle Light and Tom Hyry, have made more radical pronouncements about archival finding aids. Although acknowledging that finding aids have generally performed an excellent service, especially in providing "important contextual information" about records and in representing the "cohesive nature of records in a collection or record group,"[14] they detect some problems. They think that finding aids "fall short" because they omit some "contextual information," namely the "impact of the processor's work" on bringing order and coherence to the records and in disguising that the finding aid represents "but one viewpoint on a collection."[15] Light and Hyry provide a postmodern spin to their analysis, suggesting that traditional archival finding aids are modernist in their "ways of understanding order and truth."[16] From my vantage you don't need to become so tangled up in philosophical and theoretical perspectives to detect such problems; good old-fashioned commonsense suffices. These archivists argue that more information about the collections, such as their acquisition, needs to be made public, and, more importantly, that we need to construct our online finding aids in a manner that allows others to submit annotations about the documents, their use, and the value of the finding aids.

More issues about finding aids persist, even considering that the motivations for developing EAD were as pure as they come. EAD was hatched because it was a means to make information about archival materials widely available on the Web, providing easy (maybe nearly instantaneous) access. What studies about EAD suggest that this objective has been more a dream than a realization.[17] As one of the pioneers of the EAD approach suggests, EAD was intended to overcome the limitations of earlier archival descriptive standards, such as MARC AMC, where the "generalized descriptions found in AMC records can only lead a researcher to a collection which may have individual relevant items" and where the descriptions are not the full information found in traditional archival finding aids.[18] Few would argue about such aspirations.

Indeed, we seem now to have an ever-shifting target. The greater the possibilities for individuals using the Web for online archival research, the greater the changes may result in how archivists provide assistance to their researchers — if for no other reason than that researchers may feel less need to come in-person to the archives.[19] Yet, this may have more to do with other issues than just technological changes. At various critical junctures in the development of archival descriptive standards, we have tended to focus on technical and process issues rather than in creating mechanisms to help researchers. Some of this may suggest a faith about or over-confidence in archivists' sensitivity to what researchers need, or, and maybe more important, it might imply an interest in the arrangement and description function that supercedes the end goal of enabling researchers to discover what they are looking for.[20]

Twenty years ago Lawrence Dowler noted that it is difficult, among other things, to determine how to shape archival finding aids to meet user needs because we then knew so little about how researchers used archival records, laying out a research agenda to address this professional lacunae.[21] Dowler's essay was part of a flurry of reconceptualizing the notion of archival use at that time that has finally began to pay off with new studies on how archival documentation is used with more specific notions about how any type of finding aids or guides are used.[22] As Jacqueline Goggin wrote two decades ago, "only recently have archivists begun to acknowledge the deficiencies in current archival administrative practices and to argue that they should pay more attention to the users of archival materials."[23] While we could restate this sentiment today, we can at least acknowledge that we know a lot more about the users of archival materials.[24]

At every transitional stage between new modes of finding aids, we seem to learn something about the nature and limitations of these devices. Dennis Meissner, in evaluating the process of transforming traditional archival finding aids into EAD finding aids, notes that the problems that they found were not because these finding aids "were poorly written, or inaccurate, or that their descriptions of collections were incomplete. Rather, the problems lay in the way that they structured, ordered, and presented information. The effect of these problems in frustrating access to collections would be magnified tremendously when the finding aides were delivered over the Web, with no hope of explanation by a staff member."[25] This statement was a reminder that the purpose of EAD finding aids was to take advantage of new computer software and hardware, as well as the availability of the Internet. It is also a remainder that if we discern such problems, what must our research clientele think of these aids?

Archivists have been trying to analyze the use of their finding aids and users' habits in general in order to possess a better understanding of what they need to do in descriptive work. Christopher Prom, in a study about the usefulness of online finding aids, indicates the challenge confronting archival representation: "The representation of archival materials is inherently complex, and researchers' successes in locating materials sometimes seem to show a high dependence on 'strange attractors' or clusters of information that do not at first appear to be logically connected."[26] Acknowledging the great attention devoted to finding aids, descriptive standards, and understanding users' activities, Prom's study reveals that online finding aids are "most efficiently used by either archival and computer experts,"[27] a conclusion suggesting to me the need to rethink what we are doing with finding aids (although Prom believes that archivists need to focus on gaining a "deeper understanding of users").[28] Prom suggests, instead, that the focus remains on the archivist as access mediator, whether the reference process is on the in-person or online reference function. We might ask if the reliance on the archivist as mediator, as a living finding aid, is not also an indictment of the usefulness of our traditional and newer (but really not all that newer in scope and content) finding aids (although in certain situations, such as administrative use of archival records, this might have more to do with the needs of the parent organizations and even their confidence in the archivists working there).[29].

When examining an archival function such as the construction of finding aids and the necessity of descriptive standards, it is often easy to be unfairly critical of present efforts or the recent past. We need to be able to step outside of our own institutional and disciplinary surroundings and re-evaluate where we are, where we are heading, and where we should be. From time to time, outsiders to the archival community have looked at what archivists have been doing in certain of their activities. Historian William C. Binkley, four decades ago, provided a critical assessment of the first three published volumes of the National Union Catalog of Manuscript Collections, concluding that they "constitute the most important step ever taken in this country toward providing concisely and in conveniently available form the basic description and the information most essential to a research worker who is surveying the field and deciding where his source material is most likely to be found."[30] Such efforts are necessary, especially since we have long possessed evidence that archival descriptive efforts often have not been clear to those who we think will use the finding aids as a mean of getting into the archival sources.[31] We also need this external perspective since archivists, looking at themselves and their work, tend to see the finding aids in extremely positive terms. A quarter-of-a-century ago, Mary Jo Pugh writes, "Archivists tend to be too passive and bureaucratic when writing inventories and registers. Inventories, which should be the major intellectual accomplishment of our profession, are too often merely lists of container and file headings."[32] Yet, many archivists continue to point to finding aids as their main priority and their pre-eminent contribution to scholarship.

I believe one might be hard-pressed to sustain an argument that most finding aids are an intellectual accomplishment. In this chapter, I explore three ways archival finding aids might be examined from outside our own professional community. Ultimately, they might be evaluated like museum exhibitions have been by historians, anthropologists, and other scholars, as artifacts defining their particular view of the world. Or, archival finding aids can be studied by those who are experts on design, considering the message they intend to convey to society. And, finally, archival finding aids might be one other means by which archivists are, or could be, held accountable to society. Such perspectives take us far from the burgeoning new scholarship on how individuals find and use archival sources, a new set of research that will provide a much fresher and more balanced view of the purpose and utility of archival finding aids. These are not the only ways we can look at finding aids, but they are a start in stepping outside archival boundaries (getting researchers' feedback is another way of breaking through the boundaries).

Archivists and their colleagues have predicted great breakthroughs in archival representation for many years. David Bearman, considering the AMC format two decades ago, argued that the "challenge of the next century will be to transform archives from repositories to intermediaries. Archivists must ask how they can best position their institution to deliver information in all its richness to the citizens of tomorrow who may learn from, and work with, archives as a primary cultural resource. Information delivery begins with the reexamination of finding tools and access points, but it doesn't end until the information itself is provided directly to patrons, in their own intellectual framework, on their own terms, and wherever they may be."[33] Such pronouncements have galvanized considerable discussion, but they have not necessarily transformed what archivists are actually doing with their finding aids and the provision of access to their holdings. Maybe the problem is that we have not used our imaginations enough to squint into the distance in order to imagine how others see us and our finding aids.

We are learning more, however, as specific research is completed about the use of archives. Elizabeth Yakel, studying how users view archives and archivists in their research process, learned that "users' conceptions of archival access tools varied greatly" and, if nothing else, were substantially different from how archivists thought they might see them.[34] Yakel learned what others had learned, that researchers did not rely on archival finding aids but, instead, used "word of mouth" as well as citations in other studies.[35] Yakel relied on interviews with researchers, and then transformed this into practical advice for educating users, built around finding aids. Yakel writes, "It is in finding aids that users' representations of archives meet archivists' representations of collections. If these two cognitive representations intersect enough, the user is able to locate and utilize the archives and to identify primary sources that may hold the answers to his or her inquiry. If these representations diverge, the access tools are useless for the researcher. Creating finding aids that are true boundary objects is key. Researcher after researcher noted the intricacies of access systems and it is apparent that finding aids are not the transparent tools for users that archivists intend."[36]

While Yakel works in the here and now, dealing with current researchers, my predilection is to take a longitudinal and maybe impractical, but potentially illuminating, perspective. By seeing how other representational devices, such as museum exhibitions, have changed over time, we can adopt a more realistic notion of the value of similar devices, such as the archival finding aid, in our field and time. If there is any practical value in this, it is in adopting a greater openness for how others see us and, perhaps, shift our activities to serve posterity rather than our own perceptions of the present or in seeking to find some kind of "archivally" pure mindset that enables archivists to set themselves off from others.[37]

I hope this chapter adds to the small, but important, reflective literature on archival description. Archivists have been so intent on building new and better systems to assist researchers in finding the documentary sources they need, that they only occasionally pause to be reflective about the progress made or in discerning what they may have learned. For a couple of generations, archivists rushed ahead of researchers, neglecting to study how researchers operate, in designing and building descriptive systems. And when we have paused, sometimes our observations have been sobering. More than a decade ago Ann Pederson observed that "we have not succeeded in unlocking the full value of archival resources," suggesting major limitations with our finding aids and descriptive standards.[38] When will we fulfill this dream?

Learning from Museum Scholarship

If we think of an archival finding aid as a form of exhibition, then we might wonder just why these guides (published and unpublished) do not ever become controversial. Thinking about the history and nature of museum exhibitions causes us to stop thinking how innocent any organization of exhibitions might be and instead to understand how they reflect present ideas and biases. The situation has intensified in the past decade. Steven C. Dubin notes, "Museums and their exhibitions have become controversial sites in a number of respects over the past few years. They no longer merely provide a pleasant refuge from ordinary life, nor are they simply repositories of received wisdom. Museums have moved to the forefront in struggles over representation and over the chronicling, revising, and displaying of the past. Museums today differ greatly from their predecessors."[39] Archives, at least in their major function of representing records through finding aids, have been spared such problems. One might wonder if this will change as they build a more pronounced presence on the World Wide Web. Or, is it because archival finding aids really are not read or engaged in any way that is similar to what happens with museum exhibitions (and their catalogs)?

We might think of the archival finding aid as being like the museum display case. Kevin Walsh provides a useful description of the display case:

"The developing ability to place objects in ordered contexts often implied a unilinear development of progress. Such representations implied a control over the past through an emphasis on the linear, didactic narrative, supported by the use of the object, which had been appropriated and placed in an artificial context of the curator's choosing. This type of display is closed, and cannot be questioned. ... In a way, museums attempt to 'freeze' time, and almost permit the visitor to stand back and consider 'the past before them.' This is the power of the gaze, an ability to observe, name and order, and thus control."[40] In the same fashion archivists freeze time and add control in their description of a records system. In many ways the closing and ordering is more intensive in the archival version, as descriptive standards and traditions in the finding aid have often shifted more with an eye on the archivist than on the use of the archives.

Thinking of the finding aid as being like the museum exhibition, in the latter's traditional or historic role extending order and coherence to the world, also opens up the sense of connecting the archival finding aid to the real world. Chon A. Norriega has commented on the changes wrought by the American museum's need to attract more funding support from the public: "The result has been a drastic change in the way museums approach their audience. Rather than edifying, the museum increasingly plays to the masses in competition with tourist sites, amusement parks, cultural centers, bookstores, and shopping malls. As such, the museum exhibition has become much more event-oriented — in roughly the same way as motion pictures during this period — while the museum itself now offers a wide range of revenue-generating services and activities beyond that of the exhibition proper."[41] One might dismiss any relevance of this to the archival finding aid since the museum exhibition is much more a public device. Yet, the finding aid is intended if not to attract researchers then at least to edify them in a manner that helps them to use the archives. We can go farther, however, in realizing that the archival finding aid also competes with entities such as the World Wide Web in providing or offering information (or better yet, evidence).

Writing effective finding aids is a complicated business, one that often has been blotted from existence by the pragmatic desire to train archivists to be able to produce utilitarian guides to their records. We know that the holdings of an archives possess layers like one finds in an archaeological dig. Paul Collins notes, "To see any library, any bookstore, any archive, is like seeing a city: you are viewing buildings constructed atop the unknown and unknowable cities that once were and once might have been."[42] It is why "discoveries" are always being made in repositories like archives. No matter how complex archival finding aids might become, it seems unlikely that they can represent effectively all the layers, details, nuances, and vagaries that constitute records. To try to achieve the full richness of an archival repository would be to have the ability to see the full text of every document, and while some futurists strive to achieve this objective, it seems unlikely that it will ever happen given the quantity of records, the number of archivists, and the resources available to archivists.

The preparation of archival finding aids also partially transforms the records. Archivists, as they work on describing records, are generally not working with full sets of documents but rather they are examining records already appraised (formally or informally). What archivists sometimes neglect to consider is how they transform the records as they examine them and transform them again as they describe them. Charles Merewether, considering ruins, dredged up an 1896 discussion of ruins by Freud who wondered if ruins should be left as is or excavated, but who concluded that ruins cannot be left as is because they speak. According to Merewether, Freud "concluded that only by digging into the rubble does one reveal the fragments of a larger story or meaning. Yet, when ruins are uncovered they are irrevocably changed: they become part of the present."[43] It is not hard to imagine archival records as ruins, as they are often survivals with all the marks of time's passage; even digital archives can be viewed in this way as they have perhaps faced an even more daunting task of survival, having gone through all the vagaries of hardware and software transformations.

One wonders what archival finding aids are saying to researchers, if language communicates and, as some argue, records speak. Of course, all objects, records included, have language attributed to them, or as Miguel Tamen argues, "the very idea of an object's performing an action is already quite extraordinary. And yet, to speak of talking corporations, communicating lawns, scheming statues and moving icons makes a certain sense, at least in some well-defined contexts."[44] What would be the best context for the archival finding aids? Certainly, finding aids, dating back in the modern sense to the nineteenth century, first existed in print form, then in online catalogs, and more recently on the World Wide Web, and it is the Web that provides the best opportunity for finding aids to speak (literally and figuratively). But, as I have argued before, archivists need to muse about whether the language of finding aids is the same as the language of most of the Web browsers and potential audience for and users of archival records. And, of course, I do not mean this in any literal sense, questioning whether finding aids should be in English or some other language, but in a metaphorical sense — wondering if a finding aid as traditionally conceived of (from inventories and registers to EAD documents) is anything like what someone on the Web might be expecting.

One wonders *what* finding aids are trying to tell us? Steven Conn, in explaining museums in the Victorian era, writes of a "metanarrative of evolutionary progress. A trip through the galleries followed a trajectory from simple to complex, from savage to civilized, from ancient to modern.... Museums functioned as the most widely accessible public form to underscore a positivist, progressive and hierarchical view of the world, and they gave that view material form and scientific legitimacy."[45] In fact, museum exhibitions have displayed from their beginning an impulse to order and categorize. David Benjamin describes Charles Wilson Peale's museum enterprise in the later eighteenth century in the following way: "Peale's representation of the world was clearly structured, and he intended his audience to extend the economic, social, moral, intellectual, and religious lessons of the museum to their daily lives. He selected the categories of exhibits and he chose the systems by which displays were arranged. His 'world in miniature' situated humans at the top of the natural order. Humanity, too, was ordered. Peale provided exemplars of military, political, and intellectual authority, as well as images of the range of human races, the sick and the well, and the moral and criminal. In gridlike, systematic arrangements of animals and artifacts, hierarchical relationships were made to appear natural."[46] Many archivists, seeing strict hierarchical structures in their records accumulations, probably convey something similar, although lacking the more visual, three-dimensional experiences of galleries. What archivists communicate comes through the texts of their printed or online finding aids or catalogues. Still, the actual words conveyed and organized in these finding aids can be interpreted, and mostly what we find is that records have structure and meaning beyond their most basic or rudimentary level of discourse.

When an archivist sits down at his or her computer to compose the final version of the archival finding aid, what is going on in the archivist's mind? Daniel J. Sherman and Irit Rogoff, in describing the role of the museum, note that the "concept of the museum emerges as a field of interplay between the social histories of collecting, classifying, displaying, entertaining, and legitimating."[47] Later, they add, the "museum, in other words, while seemingly representing objectively and empirically located contexts for the object it displays, actually participates in the construction of these categories and in the numerous internal shifts and differentiations they are held to contain."[48] Archivists will likely disagree over the extent to which the act of creating a finding aid presupposes or actually constructs a new order of meaning for the described records. Archivists differ over the concepts of how much order already exists in organizational and, certainly, personal recordkeeping regimes. Yet, every archivist has imposed some order on the records under their control, and the very substance of composing the truncated descriptions (apart from the more routine box and file listings) results in a meaning-laden exercise that is, at its most basic, a public relations exercise (one striving to attract researchers).

I am not sure we can go so far as to see the archival finding aid as an artistic venture, although some archivists have certainly sought to add some artistry to their descriptions, seeking to make their finding aids more than directories. Joshua Taylor, in his classic visual arts handbook, believes that "many centuries ago it was recognized that art, in bringing order to the senses, could serve to temper the mind through a reciprocal interplay: the mind imposed order on the sensuous environment, and the senses, thus well ordered, presented the mind with a tangible paradigm of harmonic perfection."[49] I have seen neat and orderly finding aids that bear little similarity to the records jammed in containers or still wrapped in original storage devices such as ribbons and old wrappers. I have also seen apparently orderly finding aids that do not reflect much of an act of creation or even one of rote copying of the records. In neither case have we witnessed an artistic effort, but most archivists would confess to having little in the way of art as an objective. Many archivists *would* describe their processing work as *art* rather than science, an activity based on their sensibility about what researchers need and their own knowledge of the records being described.

One might wonder why all the fuss about museum classification and exhibition schema, especially since archivists more readily identify with historians than with museum curators. Building on Foucault's concepts about disciplinary knowledge and technologies, Eilean Hooper-Greenwell, considering the emergence of museums, writes, "Through the organization of 'cells,' 'places,' and 'ranks,' the disciplines create complex spaces that are at once architectural, functional, and hierarchical. Spaces fix positions and permit calculations; they mark places and assign values. They individualize things and individuals in a vast table of discrimination and distinction. The division of spaces and bodies entailed the establishment of records: daybooks, ledgers, were all required to document the spatial distribution of bodies and things. Thus, in the eighteenth century, the classificatory table became both a technique of power and a procedure of knowledge."[50] It also reveals that archives have something in common with how museums and libraries classify things. It also suggests a way of reading finding aids.

The Finding Aid as an Artifact of Design

Examining finding aids as similar to what museum curators have done in their work in classifying, organizing, and displaying specimens and artifacts is also to suggest that these archival references are products of design. Donald Norman, one of the widely cited experts on the design of things and systems, provides a couple of illuminating points about the matter of design relevant to what we are discussing here in his most recent work on design principles. Norman asks, "Why must information be presented in a dull, dreary fashion, such as in a table of numbers? Most of the time we don't need actual numbers, just some indication of whether the trend is up or down, fast or slow, or some rough estimate of the value. So why not display the information in a colorful manner, continually available in the periphery of attention, but in a way that delights rather than distracts?"[51] Despite what appears to be continual transformation in archival descriptive standards over the past half-century, especially the past two decades, these standards when applied still amount to lots of lists and often unimaginative ways of trying to communicate to researchers what is available in an archives or a particular archival fonds. Designers, like Norman, often look to nature and other sectors for ideas about design. Norman also mentions, for example, "Many natural systems, from the actions of ants and bees, to the flocking of birds, and even the growth of cities and the structure of the stock market, occur as a natural result of the interaction of multiple bodies, not through some central, coordinated control structure." Norman continues by noting that "modern control theory" has evolved from any "assumption of a central command post" to adopt "distributed control" as a "hallmark of today's systems."[52] Is there anything natural in how archivists construct finding aids, except for the millennia old listing stuff dating back nearly to the beginning of writing?

Those who write about design generally argue that design can only transpire, at least good design, if one knows the intended audience or user of the design. This makes sense. Those who write about systems design argue much the same thing. Who are finding aids intended for? Archivists seeking to connect with the public, trying to communicate the importance of archival records to society and to scholars, often have a large gap to transverse. Steven Lubar, writing about museum exhibitions, explains, "one difference between historians and the general public is the extent of critical distance we put between ourselves and our subjects. We share an interest in history, but the approach we take is different. Our sources are different also; historians want to use archives and objects, the public often turns to memory, personal connections, and family stories."[53] If this is true for museums, how more it is true for archives? We might try to explain archives as being repositories of memory and containing innumerable stories, and there is a certain relevance to this, but we might also blur the sense of archives into being little more than storehouses of stuff, not unlike what we might find at flea markets and secondhand stores. And do finding aids only provide a kind of false order to a pile of stuff, accumulated over time, that rarely has little order except as the product of a collecting or hoarding impulse?

Postmodernists and other scholars have seen the archive as a societal metaphor, with particular emphasis on how it orders things. A study of the conscious design of mapping as part of English imperialism provides an example: "The built environment of the archive and museum has long served as a fundamental metaphor for modern European conceptions of knowledge creation. Data and artifacts can be collected within sturdy walls and there reassembled into meaningful arrangements. Indeed, the walls are overly protective. They physically divorce the collected data and artifacts from the actual contexts of their occurrence and existence. They keep their contents from being harmed and they actively shield them from the confusion and corruption of the world beyond. Within those walls, the archivist or curator constructs an artificial environment within which data and artifacts can be rearranged."[54] One can see in this both the finding aid as a deliberate paper or electronic means of providing meaningful arrangement and how design, with all its artificial ordering, plays a role in the construction of finding aids as well. This particular scholar also considers the post-structuralist archive, commenting that there is "no longer the coherent and ordered archive as it traditionally has been envisioned: it is fractured, ambiguous, duplicitous, and nuanced. The coherency and order of the archive is an ideological myth."[55] And the archival finding aid may be one of the prime means by which to sustain this myth. The archival finding aid might be to records what the university, as Jefferson saw it in his design of this institution in Charlottesville — the "reconciliation" of "regimentation and individual expression, of hierarchical order and relaxed improvising"[56] — is to human knowledge.

Accountability and the Finding Aid

Sometimes archivists and records managers see themselves as powerless, at least in a comparative sense, and, as a result, are placid in the face of controversies, improprieties, and even illegalities. It is easy to see themselves as so ineffective that they lack any responsibilities to speak up and make themselves heard and more visible. This is ridiculous, of course.

As Wendell Berry once put it, "The world is being destroyed, no doubt about it, by the greed of the rich and powerful. It is also being destroyed by popular demand. There are not enough rich and powerful people to consume the whole world; for that, the rich and powerful need the help of countless ordinary people."[57] Are archivists lurking somewhere among these ordinary people and their ordinary products, such as finding aids?

Archivists, in one of their roles as guardians of accountability, are often invisible, perhaps because they have weak links in being held accountable themselves. For example, archivists have only begun to be institutionalized within the university as faculty. Now, I can hear the moans about how unaccountable faculty generally are, as a chorus of critics has slammed higher education for the past decade or more. James Axtell reminds us that "faculty members are constantly and heavily accountable, less to outside authorities than to the high standards of their own profession," and "through the dissertation process, publishing, reviewers, student evaluators, tenure review committees, and the like."[58] The archival community has only begun to place members of its clan into the academy, and the persisting weakness of this aspect of the profession certainly has removed one aspect of critical analysis, as well as visibility, of the archival mission and role. We can extrapolate, however, and note that the nature of accountability of archivists in general is weak, since they often lack authority and influence within their organizations that provide them a visible role, they lack enforceable professional standards or codes such as on ethics, and they are not perceived to be working with essential materials in their organizations given the perceptions of archives as old and dusty records of interest only to a select group of researchers (researchers who themselves often lack any real societal authority). It is not unusual to read in a newspaper an account of some institutional scandal concerning records and information systems and see not a single reference to the archivists who may work in these organizations or to ever hear anything from them about these problems. Archivists may lack the kinds of accountability procedures Axtell is referring to in the academic milieu, or, they may look to other places, outside of their own professional associations and networks, for such accountability.

Our society is one that is constantly beset by controversies, over anything and about nearly anything, so archivists not only need to be prepared for such events but to understand how to prepare finding aids with this as one of many purposes in mind. A recent example concerns a human skeleton, now called Kennewick Man, washed out of a bank on the Columbia River in the mid-1990s. David Hurst Thomas believes that the "pivotal issue at Kennewick is not about religion or science. It is about politics. The dispute is about control and power, not philosophy. Who gets to control ancient American history — governmental agencies, the academic community, or modern Indian people?"[59] What scholars once took for granted, unearthing a skeleton and studying it at leisure, is now fraught with controversies, debates, and legal contests. Documentation, carefully compiled evidence, takes on a much more important role, both the records generated via research and those emanating in the courtroom. And these controversies suggest why the guardians of documentary evidence, in whatever form, need to listen to what is happening in contemporary society. Richard Kurin, in defending the Smithsonian in its actions in the Enola Gay and other controversial exhibitions, argues that "museum curators have to listen to the voices of the represented not only because of political expediency and goodwill. They should actually try to hear those voices, because there may be something insightful and valuable in the substance of what they actually have to say.... It does not mean that curators and scholars give up their responsibilities. But it does mean that they fully and honestly intellectually engage those whom they seek to represent. The presence of those voices should not lead to bad history any more than bad history should be allowed to silence those voices."[60] Of course, historical records, even requiring interpretation and analysis, are voices, indeed usually dead voices, needing to be represented as well. Some of the very controversial interpretations are a result of trying to let those voices speak, in many cases voices that had not spoken because they had not been declassified, discovered, or dissected. This is the nature of records, that they provide accountability and that accountability brings uneasiness in their frankness.

Why accountability has come to be such a vital concern in our age can be seen in Ursula Franklin's assessment of technological entreprenurialship: "You see, if somebody robs a store, it's a crime and the state is all set and ready to nab the criminal. But if somebody steals from the commons and from the future, it is seen as entrepreneurial activity and the state cheers and gives them the concessions rather than arresting them."[61] In such an environment, the temptations are great and the notion of accountability — which must be set and defined — must be both broad and precise enough to hold people and institutions to some sort of higher standard (whether its moral, ethical, or religious might not matter). The increasing number of government regulations concerning records and information systems and court cases invoking fines and penalties for the willful destruction of evidence all attest to the importance of records as part of a society more attuned to the notion of accountability, even if the laws and lawsuits suggest that organizations and individuals are even more determined to make sure that they are not caught up by their records and the exposure of the evidence in them. Are there any implications for the construction of finding aids in this new era? Will archivists be tempted not to report on their records as openly as they have in the past, or will they simply have fewer and less valuable records to describe in the first place?

One of the reasons why the stakes in accountability has been upped in universities, as just one example, is because of the changing relationship between government and other sectors of society. A half century ago, Jacques Barzun wrote, "though it is clearly impossible, the government expects to buy research and ideas in the same way as it buys soap and chairs." The reason Barzun thought it impossible was because "in the end, success comes only out of a happy conjunction of circumstances; it cannot be bought because they cannot be specified."[62] Now, however, universities have grown much more dependent not only on government but on business as well. This can be seen in the proliferation of university-based, government-funded security studies centers, many teetering uneasily between Pentagon extensions and educational research units more likely to be based in the university. Under circumstances such as this, records must be carefully managed and systems of accountability created and maintained. Archivists creating finding aids must think of their audiences, as well as make sure that they provide full disclosure about the nature of the records, their creation, continuing value, content, and relationship to organizational and societal issues and concerns. Why shouldn't archivists be writing finding aids as much as to search for records for legal purposes as for servicing other researchers? Records managers, considering changing information technologies and laws and regulations governing communications systems such as e-mail, seem to be nearly completely focused on the regulatory and compliance aspects of their work. Are archivists so different than records managers?

Universities, long a place where values such as accountability and ethics have been nurtured, have also lost their way in our crass and confusing era. Derek Bok notes, quite simply and bluntly, that "to keep profit-seeking within reasonable bounds, a university must have a clear sense of the values needed to pursue its goals with a high degree of quality and integrity. When the values become blurred and begin to lose their hold, the urge to make money quickly spreads throughout the institution."[63] We have all seen this in a variety of ways. No longer is teaching honored, but how much fame a faculty member brings is the foremost concern. Research is equated with funding rather than as a contribution to knowledge. Compromises in undergraduate and graduate programs are easily and quickly made either if the costs of quality are high or if more profits can be made by focusing on other programs, projects, and prospects. Individuals who are students also join in, becoming more interested in buying a degree rather than in learning anything. The pressures and temptations are so great that the bounds of accountability are loosened and the processes of evaluating, critiquing, and, when necessary, reprimanding people are jettisoned. I mention such contentious matters only because the largest portion of entry-level archivist positions are connected to universities, many located in the university archives, and universities may well be the most documented institution in the United States (if not the world). Have the new academic concerns with accountability, especially to society as the question of the university's traditional claim to be a public good is challenged or revised, extended to the work of archivists in universities? Should they be writing finding aids to help universities locate records to protect them from litigation or to answer difficult queries about their role and functions?

Some worry that the emphasis on open access to government records, in the name of accountability or whatever, leads to fewer and more incomplete documents. Well, that may be. There is another reason. Records need to be accessible in order to counter or support claims made about the government's activities. Noam Chomsky, contentious about every government venture, contends that any topic you pick leads to a skewed version of reality — the "picture of the world that's presented to the public has only the remotest reaction to reality. The truth of the matter is buried under edifice after edifice of lies upon lies."[64] Actually, the truth of the matter is buried under stacks of records, although the continuing philosophical and practical discourses on whether truth is attainable or even desirable certainly make the matter more complicated. What these issues suggest is to make us speculate about what archivists are thinking when they strive to write finding aids. Are these finding aids intended to enable researchers and the public to peer under the stacks of records and to see past the secrecy, firewalls, and screens to enable anyone to understand what an organization, a government, a university, or an individual was doing at some particular moment or in some crucial event? Will finding aids be read at some point in the future as just more documents needing to be deconstructed in order to get at their true meaning or as just another bureaucratic or technocratic interpretation of reality?

Conclusion

Elizabeth Yakel, in part of a series of provocative research articles she has written about archival use and representation, had this to say about the role of the archival finding aid:

> It is in finding aids that users' representations of archives meet archivists' representations of collections. If these two cognitive representations intersect enough, the user is able to locate and utilize the archives and to identify primary sources that may hold the answer to his or her inquiry. If these representations diverge, the access tools are useless for the researcher. Creating finding aids that are true boundary objects is key.[65]

I would argue that we are still a very far distance from seeing these representations come together, at least in terms of the scholarly users of archives. Likewise, Jean-Stéphen Piché suggests how the technology of the Web could enable us to link information from different archival functions (knocking down the internal barriers we create) seamlessly in a way that could benefit researchers and lead to very different kinds of finding aids. Piché contends that the "objective for archives should be to use Internet WWW-related technologies to make archivists' already deep, but often sadly disjointed, knowledge about the context and content of the records available and represented in the infrastructure of internal and external Web sites of archival institutions."[66] Reconsidering such boundaries, often that become barriers, can be done by trying to imagine how scholars and social commentators might look at the archival finding aid on its own merits, as a representation not just of the records by the archivist but also of the archivist and the archives profession.

While the richness of the recent new scholarship about the meaning of the notion of the archive or the function of archiving has both broadened and deepened,[67] mostly the practice of representing archives has been remarkably sterile except for the work, often innovative, on standards and methodologies. Archivists have generally been fixated with the generation of descriptive standards and rather mundane finding aids building on these standards (at least on the ground in common practice and application), despite continuing evidence about the inconsistent use of these devices by researchers, without much of a nod toward the interesting dialogue about the roles and values of archival materials, the nuances of the evidence provided by these sources, or any assessment of a societal mission that encompasses anything broader than providing the raw materials of history. In one major analysis of how Canadian historians use archival materials, the authors write of the "notion of trust, of a trusted professional who provides a service, and of trustworthiness, especially of the records and other types of historical sources. . . ." They note that this "bond of trust is established, in part, by the methods that archivists use in discharging their responsibilities over time. These include deploying the critical and research skills that they share with historians, to which are added knowledge and skill in appraisal, description of sources, exhibition design, reference services, and records management."[68] We might surmise that such trust should also rest, at least partly, on understanding how society and scholars perceive archives. This Canadian study suggests that these historians value highly archival finding aids as a research tool, but, then again, this is not a study about how these guides are really used.

Interpreting, controlling, publicizing, digging through sedimentary layers, transforming records by describing, speaking, artistic expression, designing, accounting, promoting the public good, and building trust — it is not often that archivists discuss such matters when they engage in preparing finding aids or reconsider the fine points of such work. They should talk more like this, if only to try to place their finding aids in a different light.

We live in a world with expectations for instant and easy access, but there is often a price to be paid for this. Matthew Fuller, a few years ago, put it very simply: "The search engine is absolutely unable to treat a word or any collection of symbols entered into it in a contextualized manner."[69] Maybe this is changing, but the point is, is that there are limitations to seeing archival records as matter mainly to be placed in conceptual containers in order for their contents to be quickly searched and harvested. When we think like this, we begin to lose sight of some of the most salient characteristics of an archival record. Sometimes the concentration of energy on descriptive standardization, while certainly important, robs us of the beauty and significance of the documentary record.

Let's put it another way. Poet Luci Shaw writes that the "word story is linked with the word history (from the Greek word historia), the learning that comes from poema, a word that reflects the idea of something being made."[70] And it is really the art of storytelling perhaps that archivists need to be concerned with, as Shaw suggests: "Every time we tell a story or write a poem or compose an essay we give chaos a way of re-integrating back into order; we reverse entropy; pattern and meaning begin to overcome randomness and decay. We find satisfaction in juxtaposition and linkage and succession and resolution as things split and differentiate and flow together again."[71] So, we need a kind of poetics in archival description, or we risk losing what our larger mission is about, as well as something of the joy of our work. As English columnist Michael Bywater writes, "Despite the obsession of our species with organizing, categorizing and making lists ... we have not managed to organize our thinking about loss."[72] Or, in other words, we lose sight of the big picture. When we represent archives, we also represent what has not been saved, the individual archivist's own interest in preserving something of the past, the objectives of the original creators of documents, and society's own sense and value of history. The challenges archivists face in describing archives, or conceptualizing the act of description, may have as much to do with how archivists perceive their calling to the field.

Chapter Eleven

Teaching Unpleasant Things

Introduction

A lot has changed in the graduate archival education programs in North America and worldwide in the past quarter-of-a-century. There are more full-time tenure-stream and tenured faculty, richer course offerings in both depth and breadth, increasing research by faculty and their students, and a growing number of doctoral students preparing for academic careers in archival studies. Although this is not always fully reflected in every graduate program, the scholarship on archival theory and practice encompasses nearly every discipline and provides a much richer orientation to the meaning of archives in society.[1] These changes, to be understood, have to be put within the context of the transformation of higher education, the nature of students attracted to these programs, and vast changes in the kinds of issues faced by the modern archival community.

Higher education has become more corporate-minded, worried about the financial bottom-line, assessments and benchmarks, accreditation, funded research, and the monetary worth of education. New students increasingly enter universities, even in the first of their undergraduate years, with an eye on practical skills and career goals rather than a quest for well-rounded learning. Archival educators are not immune from such matters, even at the graduate level, since archivists are also being challenged by the need to explain in very practical terms their programs and professional missions, as well as to justify the financial implications of their work. Such issues pressure the educators of archivists to stress practical training rather than dealing with the more conceptual or theoretical aspects of archival work. There is a great temptation to stay close to matters that only aid their students to complete tasks such as figuring out how to generate revenue from their holdings rather than to promote fuller access, draw attention to the importance of some holdings for social causes, or deal with testy legal or policy issues such as intellectual property and excessive government secrecy. In other words, basic concerns about practical issues and challenges might tend to overwhelm or squeeze out matters such as ethics, social justice, and equitable access because these are complicated, costly, and generally not captured in formulaic or prescriptive standards. What follows in this chapter is intended to elaborate on such issues.

With this expansion in graduate archival education, the range of topics taught has also grown. Whereas thirty years ago, these programs generally stressed archival descriptive practices and reference services (still considered by many as the core activities for at least entry-level archivists), now many also orient students to functions such as appraisal, advocacy, intellectual property, legal issues, specific documentary forms (such as still and moving images), and other matters that represent challenges both to the new students and the faculty teaching them. However, we still have a distance to go in how we consider archival work. Surprisingly, archival advocacy does not have a place in the most recent professional glossary. The closest we come to it is "outreach": "The process of identifying and providing services to constituencies with needs relevant to the repository's mission, especially underserved groups, and tailoring services to meet those needs." A note suggests, "Outreach activities may include exhibits, workshops, publications, and educational programs."[2] I generally view advocacy to have a more specific aim of affecting a change in support, ranging from increases in resources, strengthened public policy and legislation, reaching new clienteles needing access to archives, and other actions extending beyond just better understanding of archives and the archival mission. The reference to addressing underserved groups perhaps indicates greater access across socio-economic classes, ethnic and diversity barriers, or other social and political matters, but it has just as often meant no more than connecting with groups that have not normally been users of archives. In other words, archival outreach is a public relations process, whereas archival advocacy is a political process, encompassing all of the stresses and strains associated with working for such political aims and teaching about them. Advocacy, therefore, does not always fit comfortably with the developing corporate university seeming to embrace the nature of traditional professional schools stressing skills and credentials, usually in a manner supporting the status quo.

Teaching

Teaching has been likened to a performance, storytelling, and a lot more. A classic discourse on teaching promotes the idea that teaching is an art and a calling, arguing that although teachers master knowledge, they "distinguish knowledge from information." For these commentators, "Information is to knowledge what sound is to music, the unorganized material out of which the structured result is composed. We do not ask teachers to convey information; we seek information from newspapers, the stock market ticker tape, or price tags on items in a store. Instead, we ask teachers to transmit knowledge, that which is organized and formally known about a subject — facts, findings, explanations, hypotheses, and theories accepted for their proven accuracy, significance, beauty, utility, or power."[3] This is not as easy as it sounds, and, as one might surmise, it is a perspective some would disagree with, pointing to other ideas of socially constructed knowledge. The point here is that some of the same issues about knowledge, information, and evidence that provoke debate about the substance of teaching are also issues that could make it simultaneously exciting and exasperating to teach archival students about the nature of their mission and the meaning of archival sources (especially if all these students want is a set of basic tools for practice).

For one thing, students, undergraduate and graduate alike, are not always so receptive to the knowledge part, sometimes because acquiring this is hard work, but more often than not because their attention is on more pragmatic matters (especially in these difficult economic times) and sometimes because they read and believe claims made by universities that their educational programs will equip them for lucrative careers. Jacques Barzun, drawing on more than a half century of his observations about teaching at all levels, makes many astute observations about the challenges of teaching, observing that college students "want education for their souls, training for life, organized social and artistic activities, psychiatric help, and career planning and placement."[4] And sometimes they seem to want this in one course. And, as I have observed, the interests in pragmatic training and skills acquisition only intensifies in graduate programs in professional schools (especially as the prospects for acquiring an entry-level position becomes more competitive and the costs of education rises).

The role of the professor in the university has been challenged, broadened, redefined, and attacked in numerous ways in the last few decades. Classicist James J. O'Donnell suggests that the "real roles of the professor in an information-rich world will be not to provide information but to advise, guide, and encourage students wading through the deep waters of the information flood. Professors in this environment will thrive as mentors, tutors, backseat drivers and coaches."[5] Others, from within the university, still see such clusters of roles as falling far short from what they should be. Jane Tompkins, an English professor, seeks a "holistic" approach to working with students, or, as she explains: "There's too much emphasis on matters related exclusively to the head and not enough attention given to nurturing the attitudes and faculties that make of knowledge something useful and good."[6] Another English professor, writing from the deepest depths of the so-called culture wars, enthusiastically embraces conflicts because of the "deeply contradictory mission" of the university: "The university is expected to preserve, transmit, and honor our traditions, yet at the same time it is supposed to produce new knowledge, which means questioning received ideas and perpetually revising traditional ways of thinking."[7] Those of us in professional schools are more acutely aware of such contradictions, as we face them in the classroom every day (or, at least, so it seems). Such commentators, besides providing evidence of sometimes very contradictory notions about the role of faculty, also provide some hope for academics frustrated by the challenges they find in teaching and advising students. Tompkins's assessment, for example, can be seen as prodding faculty in professional schools to go beyond conveying skills, constructing tools, and disseminating practical information to that of both challenging and consoling students who will face more complicated scenarios in their careers than that encountered by earlier generations.

All of these qualities are necessary when we teach new groups of aspiring archivists, especially when we need to shake them from their preconceptions of archival work to be equipped to advocate for their institutions and their profession in a world with increasingly complex challenges for archival work. We need to be able to deconstruct these students' notions, challenge them by presenting the realities faced in archival work, and then mentor them to a level of confidence so that they can function with success. This is an often-difficult process given the notions of archives and career goals brought by the students to these graduate programs, all the more so given that it is a process often leading to counseling students out of their vocational aims (contrary to the idea of students as customers, so often touted in the corporate university model, shaping their own expectations). While respecting our students and their personal goals, we also need to push them to understand that their perceptions of archival work may be highly flawed.

Professional Schools

There has been a flurry of writing about the emerging corporate nature of the university, with a shift to the primary concern for the bottom financial line rather than higher ideals for educating students and a mission to improve society. Derek Bok, as one example, reviewing the many complaints leveled against the university, argues that these complaints can't be lightly dismissed, although he reminds us just how difficult it can be to present a concise or unified view about the purpose of higher education: "anyone seeking a common purpose must go all the way back to a time before the Civil War, when colleges united around a classical curriculum aimed at mental discipline and character building."[8] Bok traces a shift to vocationalism, the role of teaching writing and speaking, the challenges posed by trying to teach students to think, the issues of focusing on building character or making good citizens, the concern about diversity among students and faculty, the meaning of the global society, and a variety of other compelling and contentious issues.

Vocationalism is at the heart of professional schools located in universities. With complications of high tuition costs and the search for particular skills or credentials, faculty in professional schools must be prepared to explain and justify why they teach what they teach and have thick skins to hear complaints when students fear they are the recipients of impractical theories and ungrounded knowledge. One might believe that introducing students to the realities of archival work would assuage such concerns, yet these realities also can upset students' preconceived notions of archival work and future archival careers. Students often expect that they will be working immediately with archival documents and see the classroom as an extension of an apprenticeship system. They grow impatient when, instead, they are immersed in the philosophical and theoretical dimensions of archival work; instructors understand this is the main opportunity to orient students to the foundation of archival knowledge, but students are not easily mollified by the explanations supporting this approach. Here is where we need to challenge, with sensitivity, students to consider the real fit of the archival mission, and sometimes the controversies about that mission, in the real world.

One might wonder, if there is a leaning to compelling interests in vocations and practical knowledge, why professional schools might not be thriving in universities. Indeed, they are, and that might be the problem when reflecting on how to equip students as future archivists to become better advocates for their discipline and professional mission. Professional schools have had a prominent place in the modern university since the late nineteenth century in the United States. When we consider European versions of professional schools, we can find them dating back to the early nineteenth century and, occasionally, even into the seventeenth century.

They are not new entities at all. And, when we consider the very practical curricular programs of the earlier university or college, we can argue for an even older foundation of these professional programs. Examinations of these schools demonstrate that they were always striving to bring together the university mission of knowledge generation and its application in the real world.

We can even discern these earlier histories of professional education when we look at the history of our own early professional schools for archives. A recent history of France's Ecole des Chartes, widely known by archivists to be the spawning ground for many elements of modern archival theory and practice, demonstrates that many of the ideas developed there were in reaction to political, economic, and social challenges (or realities) of the day. Moore shows how the mission and approach of the Ecole des Chartes shifted a number of times in response to changing governments and political trends, debunking any idea that somehow the origins of the modern archival profession was immune from such influences. In considering their work in classification, inventorying, inspection, and centralization, Moore argues "archives ... were linked with the controlled production of national history, which was seen as essential to political unity and stability."[9] We still see this today, although the archival movements of the disenfranchised, fringe groups, and oppressed speak to how complicated the notion of archives has become.

What professional schools bring to the fore is the tension between the generation of new knowledge, a traditional aspect of the mission of universities, and the training of individuals who desire learning skills and methods and who want a credential for entry into a professional community. Moore's history of the Ecole des Chartes provides a historical case study of this. Although one of the hallmarks of the rise of the modern university in the past century has been the creation of professional schools and the development of disciplines, the professional schools have often had a tenuous, stormy relationship to the university. One of the greatest challenges is a divided loyalty between working practitioners and the demands of the research university, their mission, and the challenges facing them. This has been well documented in studies of some of the preeminent examples of professional schools, such as in education and business.[10] Graduate archival education programs face a bit of a different scenario since these are programs within library and information science schools (or the more recent manifestation of these schools, "I-Schools" or Information Schools); while these schools have existed since the late nineteenth century and have been the topic of much soul-searching about their utility, purpose, and future, they have not received the full-scale study that other professional schools have been given. However, the location of most of the graduate archival programs in such schools, institutions with a heavy emphasis on professional skills and attitudes, may contribute to some of the perspectives new students bring with them.[11]

Many faculty of professional schools struggle with their self-identification as faculty in a university, torn as they are between professions with their own practical agendas and research and publication involving the building of knowledge and theory. If a faculty member engages in building a body of scholarship the very professions they supposedly equip new practitioners to work in may chide them, and if they focus on teaching to prepare these practitioners they may be shunned in their own schools for a lack of productivity. However, it is possible to look at this as a creative challenge. Immersing themselves in the most pressing issues of the present corps of practitioners may lead these faculty members to engage in new forms of scholarship that can press the profession to re-examine its own roots, principles, and assumptions. In my own career, I have found it remarkably interesting to wrestle with such problems, and while it may not win you new friends or have you win popularity contests, such work constantly revitalizes your own teaching and research. The professional school may be a troubling place for some, but it can also be a place of great energy. And, done right, new students with new perspectives can help greatly to energize this process and generate new ideas for the profession itself.

How does this play out in graduate archival programs, most of which are located in professional schools (library and information schools or I-Schools) or function as professional schools when located in other university departments (principally history departments)? There has been a major transformation in graduate archival education in the past quarter-of-a-century in the United States and in a number of other countries, mostly reflected in the growth of full-time, regular faculty members, the proliferation of archival journals, a deepening in research monographs (some the result of the increasing number of dissertations being done in the field), and expansion of the curriculum. What has not fundamentally changed, in any noticeable way, is why students come to the archival programs to prepare for their careers.

Why People Want to Be Archivists

Most individuals come into graduate archival education programs because they love history, old stuff, personal collecting, or have been inundated into the documentary debris of the past because of family and other personal experiences. When I ask my own students to write about why they want to be archivists, I learn about their exposure to reading old family papers or learning to take care of them, personal collecting, diary or now blog writing, and a deep love of history often nurtured by visits to historic sites or even the reading of historical fiction. Some of this is not particularly surprising (if, for no other reason, than that most archival educators can identify with these reasons because they mirror many of their own personal reasons). Students from undergraduate and graduate history programs, for example, have been coming into archives programs for a very long time. Indeed, it is a persistent theme in the archival professional literature, extending back many decades, and at one time was the stimulus for great debate about the location and nature of graduate archival education programs. Now peace reigns about such issues, although there are obvious differences between programs when their course offerings and faculty perspectives are examined.

Many students enter graduate archival education programs because they discovered the profession when seeking an on-campus job as an undergraduate or because of volunteer work done or other part-time paid positions. Many developed interests in the archives field because of varied work experiences, such as the mortgage industry, banking, newspaper reporting and journalistic research, paralegal experience, and social work — as well as in other fields where recordkeeping played a key role and consumed considerable time and energy. I have witnessed a growing number of people who become interested in archives because of visits to historic sites, historic homes, battlefields, and museums, although not all these explicitly proclaim anything about archives or archivists (although some feature exhibitions with archival documents and nurture an interest in the past). Nearly every kind of archives position is represented by such experiences, although, not surprisingly, for the youngest students, academic archives and special collections experiences while undergraduates predominate. These reasons have remained stable over time, as David Wallace's survey of a decade ago affirms.[12] Since we know, very well, that the work of the archivist is not a high profile profession, such experiences may be the predominant means by which individuals discover the field. The interests and experiences we see new students bring with them suggest why it is difficult to teach certain (more complicated and challenging) aspects of archival work, such as advocacy, to these individuals.

The Challenge of Teaching Archives Students

What motivates individuals to become archives students is generally what makes it difficult to teach them about the challenges of archival administration in the present day, especially in matters related to archival advocacy. Those interested in history, for example, will need to learn some disturbing facts, such as the realization that archivists split from professional historians, and there are still scars and open wounds caused by this. In fact, while most users of archives can be said to be doing historical research, it is probably the case that most are not professional historians (they are sociologists, anthropologists, family historians, journalists and others ranging from high school to doctoral levels of education). However, archival studies (or science, as some insist on calling it) are generally seen as an interdisciplinary or multi-disciplinary field, suggesting that there are disciplines with important roles to play as well (try library and information science for starters). Those interested in archives because of interests in historic sites or museums need to learn that while these organizations employ archivists that there are substantial differences between museum, public history, library, and other fields' work with that of what archivists do.

A small portion of individuals entering graduate archival education programs arrive there because they have read something that motivated them to consider archival work as a vocation. My personal favorite, and I see this regularly, is the reference to Nicholson Baker's *Double Fold* book, a literate rant about Baker's perceived concerns and problems about preservation that not only disparaged the value of formal education but is a book that confuses the library and archives fields and their missions;[13] it troubled me enough to write a book-length response.[14] Baker's book still draws more attention to the preservation issue than any other book in recent memory. It is curious to me that some thought that Baker was a professional librarian rather than the novelist and essayist that he is, especially since young students and novice archivists also indicate that they have been influenced by encountering fictional archivists in novels and mysteries, and learning something about what archivists do. The problem with such influences is that they often feed the popular stereotypes young students bring with them, that archives are quiet places for individuals to work, unbothered by the troubles of the world or the challenges of relating to diverse communities and individuals. The archivist's responsibility to work with records today places them directly in the crosshairs of legal challenges, intensive media scrutiny, complex compliance situations, and contentious squabbles over everything from ownership of intellectual property to repatriation battles about documents and artifacts. These are not monastic positions where one withdraws from worldly cares.

It would be unfair if I implied that students come into graduate archival programs totally naïve and uninformed. Some, in fact, bring with them interesting questions and challenging concerns that have also energized debates among experienced archivists and those who are composing theoretical models for archival work or conducting research to refute or endorse older, newer, and emerging frameworks for archival epistemology. One recent group of students at my own program brought with them issues about the changing nature of the document, how to contend with practical archival challenges you are facing in your current places of employment, social and political issues affecting the nature of the archival field and its societal mission, censorship and privacy issues and debates, the relevancy or validity of the claims for a new profession (will we be digital curators in the future rather than archivists?), and the nature of the fiscal management of archival material. As I will suggest shortly, it is easy to engage such students about matters such as archival advocacy, but it is also likely the case that these are in a distinct minority among all the students.

It is the nature of professional schools, as I indicated above, that they draw people who are searching for a livelihood and a credential for pursuing a vocation, focused on practical skills rather than theory and interested in a paycheck for doing something that interests them rather than in some grand societal mission and narrative. These kinds of students offer often honest, candid assessments of preparing for archives positions as a pragmatic means to be able to pursue interests in history, film studies, museums, and rare books and special collections (when getting into these fields may be quite difficult otherwise) and the bigger concern for acquiring food, shelter, and the other basics of survival. These may be the ones who might have the hardest time in grappling with the real challenges archivists and archives are actually now facing today, especially when challenged about such matters early in their educational programs as they must be. And they do not realize how critical theory is to practical issues, as recently considered by Manuel Castells in a book examining the "grounded theory of power in the network society."[15] Castells discusses the nature of power, communication, cognitive issues, the historical context of networks, media and politics, and social movements. And in doing this, Castells makes a case for why theory is important both for research and for subsequent practical action: "By engaging in the cultural production of the mass media, and by developing autonomous networks of horizontal communication, citizens of the Information Age become able to invent new programs for their lives with the materials of their suffering, fears, dreams, and hopes. They build their projects by sharing their experience. They subvert the practice of communication as unusual by squatting in the medium and creating the message. They overcome the powerlessness of their solitary despair by networking their desire. They fight the powers that be by identifying the networks that are. This is why theory, necessarily grounded on observation, is relevant for practice: if we do not know the forms of power in the network society, we cannot neutralize the unjust exercise of power. And if we do not know who exactly the power-holders are and where to find them, we cannot challenge their hidden, yet decisive domination."[16] We need to teach our archives students such principles, especially as the complexity of the world requires conceptual models.

The Reality of Being An Archivist, or the Heart of Archival Advocacy

Most experienced archivists assume the importance of the archival mission in society. They soon encounter the knowledge that society doesn't always comprehend the mission or, if it does, that it does not always support it in very useful ways. Sometimes the lack of understanding can be funny, although archivists do not always see the humor in such matters. For example, in the midst of writing this essay, Laurence Shatkin, author of a book on the *150 Best Low-Stress Jobs*, was quoted on HotJobsYahoo! that the archivist was one of those low-stress jobs. It was reported that this "occupation focuses on planning and overseeing the arrangement of exhibitions of collections, there's a certain degree consistency and low stress levels," because people who control their tasks have lower stress factors. It was also mentioned that only a bachelor's degree in history or library science was required, clearly inaccurate, and that the average salary was over $40,000 (also probably more misleading than a question of inaccuracy).[17] The Archives Next blog, located at http://www.archivesnext.com/, gleaned more information from Shatkin, who revealed that his information was based on statistics available from the U.S. Department of Labor. To no one's surprise, archivists reacted to this assessment in a negative fashion.

My own sense, however, is that many individuals are attracted initially to this field because of notions such as those expressed by Shatkin, and then they discover that there are many more challenges to archival work that they did not anticipate. For example, most students never assume that they will have significant administrative responsibilities, anticipating that they will work quietly with collections, documents and artifacts. The kinds of advocacy activities archivists engage in — from fundraising and other work to gain financial support to lobbying for improved government legislation to jockeying for recognition for archival programs within various institutional settings — are hardly ever in the list of reasons for why individuals arrive at graduate archival education programs to prepare for archival careers. One of the challenges for archival educators is determining how to introduce students to and equip them for the realities of archival work. Another challenge is for archival educators themselves to learn about and develop teaching materials for these realities.

Teaching Unpleasant Things

In my own career as an educator I have evolved in ways I never anticipated when I started two decades ago. When I first began teaching about archival administration, I covered the basic functions of this work, including orienting students to issues about how to advocate on behalf of their programs within their employing institutions and in society in general. In fact, I considered nearly every aspect of what I taught to be a form of archival advocacy because it involved grounding students in how to think more expansively about the responsibilities of archivists than the preconceptions they brought with them.[18] As time has passed, however, I have more fully developed ideas about the archival mission to encompass the importance of evidence in recordkeeping, the role of records for accountability in organizations and governments (extending far beyond archives as just cultural enterprises), and archives as memory institutions (a concept that expands the cultural mission in profound ways). This has required me to be involved in working with others to build new kinds of case studies (for use in the classroom) than the archival community has normally prepared,[19] or to enter into public debates with individuals who have critiqued the archival mission in ways that deserve detailed responses (such as my previously cited response to Nicholson Baker).

Over the past couple of decades, the archival profession has mostly seen digital technologies as its greatest issue, and with good reason. These technologies have threatened both the ability of archivists to preserve records and the basic nature of archival work and identity. Clearly a significant part of dealing with the archival issues of the Digital Era involves more effective advocacy, as archivists build new partnerships, lobby for greater resources to solve these issues, and readjust some of their most basic assumptions (such as physical custody and acquisition of archival materials). For example, archivists' ability to take physical custody of new digital forms of personal archives, such as web sites and blogs, may require that the profession adopt new ways of working with society to ensure the preservation of our documentary heritage, a topic I explore in a recent book.[20] However, I am not convinced that these are the most serious issues facing archivists today. There are indicators of success with digital recordkeeping, and as society becomes more aware of the challenges of the long-term maintenance of digital documents, there will be an increasing array of commercial and other solutions for solving these challenges.

The most prominent problems for the foreseeable future may be more ethical and accountability issues, or, to put it another way, the ways that these new technologies can be utilized to invade personal privacy, erode government and corporate accountability, restrict intellectual property, and cause other problems. All of these kinds of issues involve equipping a new generation of archivists to become more effective advocates for their programs and, working within their professional associations, and into society. Unfortunately, perhaps, an abundance of case studies routinely appear for students to examine and for me to present in class.[21]

These are not easy issues to address, and they are sometimes topics guaranteed to affect (negatively) teaching evaluations. In one particularly tempestuous year, I witnessed a group of students in near revolt, complaining that I was preparing them for how to lose their jobs, by whistle-blowing and other means, even before they had secured their first position. They have a point, and I must admit that teaching advocacy requires fine-tuning performance so that the instructor does not come across as overly critical, obsessed with all the injustices of the world, or just overly depressing about the future of the profession. Fortunately, however, there are always successes to point to when considering the teaching of issues such as these.

In my primary course dealing with the topic of archival advocacy (Archival Access, Advocacy, and Ethics), I have students examine specific cases relating to the broad topics covered by the course. In one recent version of this course, I had students write brief (5 to 10 pages) papers about any two of the three areas, with one of the areas being "some aspect of archival advocacy or public programming." Students were also given the option of building on earlier papers done in the introductory archives course if the topics of these papers meshed with the themes of the later course. A number of fine papers were prepared, and I selected three that were closely related (dealing with the ownership and control of the records of indigenous peoples, the use of government records created as part of the normal procedures of the Supreme Court, and the misadministration of electronic mail messages generated by the George W. Bush White House) to create a mock conference session (Archival Accountability and Ethics in the Real World: Three Cases) to give students the experience of what such sessions are like. I then worked with these students to prepare one essay for publication, part of a special issue of *Library and Archival Security* that appeared in the spring of 2009 and also including other student papers from this course.[22] This exercise led to many interesting discussions about the kinds of issues that archivists need to advocate about and how such advocacy might occur. The bonus is adding to the professional literature that can be drawn on for professional advocacy. The stress on case studies may compensate for one of the major expectations students have in these graduate programs — the desire for practical experience; the process of delving into a real-life case enables students to examine first-hand how archivists work and how archives fare in our modern society.

The other aspect of teaching archival advocacy in some graduate archival education programs occurs in working with doctoral students. Obviously there are two benefits in engaging doctoral students in archival advocacy issues. One, they may develop research and scholarship on archival advocacy that can enrich professional discussions and activities. Most of my own doctoral students have worked on topics related to accountability, memory, archival policy, and access that have made such contributions.[23] Two, these individuals will fill academic positions, mostly as full-time, tenure-stream faculty but perhaps also as adjuncts. Equipping them to teach their students about archival advocacy and to develop research agendas to support such a curriculum will have long-term positive benefits. In schools where there are both masters and doctoral students, doctoral students can often be called upon to teach their cases and to mentor masters' students.

Conclusion: A Richer Context

The last thing to say about teaching archival advocacy and related topics is that the literature supporting this area has grown immensely in the past two decades.[24] Some of it has been written from inside the archival community, but a remarkable array of literature from outside has focused on the nature of archives and recordkeeping, public memory, truth commissions, privacy, intellectual property, digital information, networking, public policy, and many other topics, all raising considerable issues and questions about what archivists do. This literature strengthens and challenges us to deal with how the archival enterprise fits within society, and it certainly makes it easier to engage students in aspects of the field that they have taken for granted. The nature of this literature also orients students to a variety of theoretical approaches to the nature of the archive.

Helen Buss, in an introduction to a collection of essays about using women's archives, gives us an example of this: "Feminist scholarship allows for the special passion we feel for the archives of those close to us, encourages the full revelation of bias and highlights the sophistication of the insightful readings that emotional attachment brings by an attention to theorization."[25] When they leave a graduate archival education program, students should have different ideas about what an archivist does and the problems they face — and why they need to be articulate advocates for the archival mission — than when they came. Otherwise, we have failed to teach them.

There can be a cost for faculty teaching a subject such as this. In one of the best books on teaching in higher education, Ken Bain stresses the need to always have an eye on students' learning and thinking abilities rather than on short-term skills or other approaches (sometimes aimed at little more than generating good teaching evaluations for faculty members).[26] The evolution of this particular course from a focus mainly on reference room activities to one that deals with substantial issues challenging archival work, such as ethical misdeeds or reformulating the nature of the archival mission, has also prompted me to look beyond immediate student evaluations to consider measures such as contributions to the published professional and scholarly literature. Some of the more immediate contentious responses by some students concerning the topics taught in this course are mitigated by a sense of more substantial products created by the students taking the course. Some students complain about the theoretical slant of the course, and this is a complaint posed mostly against what they see as the lack of hands-on experience and before they are exposed to postmodern, feminist, cultural studies, and other theoretical visions of what the archive represents. In this manner, I am teaching something about the nature of archival advocacy by being an advocate myself for a different archival mission, one open to being influenced by forces outside the professional community. My goal is to transform what often are romantic, naïve understandings of archival work into a more dynamic version of the archival mission suitable for the rapidly changing Digital Era.

Chapter Twelve

Arguing About Appraisal in the Age of Forgetfulness

Introduction

Traveling from Phoenix to the South Rim of the Grand Canyon, one cannot help but notice both the change in elevation and the transformed landscape. This experience merely prepares you for the magnificent ragged gash you are about to see, something that one finds difficult, ultimately, to describe. Staring at the deep canyon, with the North Rim far in the distance, reminds me of our profession's decades of discussions about archival appraisal. The trip to appraisal has been interesting (after all, some of our best minds have struggled with the archival function), but the gap from one side of the canyon to the other (the gap between daily practice and academic discourse) represents a vista we struggle to understand. For while we seem to have many more ideas about appraisal, and conceptions about appraisal methodologies, we really must wonder just how much the application of appraisal has changed. And now, perhaps, we also must scratch our heads about whether it all really makes any difference.

Long before and long after anyone struggled with creating and filling archives, or getting anyone to use the stuff residing there, people possessed a memory of themselves and their place. If memory is the beginning of archives, it is also the end. Writer Wendell Berry, in his novels and short stories about the fictional Port William, Kentucky, provides a glimpse into this, perceiving its history as a "living memory of itself," seeming to "have been forever."[1] As far as I can discern, there is no fictional archives in this fictional place, only a deep-seated sense of the past emerging from its every nook and cranny, every conversation between family members and friends, and every action taken by one of the characters.

Even without formal archives, memory serves as a representation of our inherent archival impulse. Science fiction writer Ray Bradbury captures something of this impulse, believing that "Man the problem solver is that only because he is the Idea Keeper."[2] Bradbury's emphasis on technology ought not to be surprising given the themes of his fiction, with gadgets and gizmos prominent in his futurist scenarios (peering off into the opposite direction set by Berry). Even in this digital environment, one that so often seems impermanent, we can detect something of the archival impulse for, as Cornelia Vismann tells us, "the administrations of the Western world, a life without files, without any recording, a life *off the record*, is simply unthinkable."[3]

My intention in this final essay is to reflect on how archivists have considered appraisal, how appraisal has been challenged by forces ranging from mundane changes in recordkeeping technologies to complicated legal, cultural, and ethical issues, and whether appraisal is still relevant as part of our professional and societal mission. Appraisal is getting harder, and dealing with it certainly contributes to the anxiety of archivists.

Looking Backward

There have been so many estimates about the rate of growth of documents and texts, all simply attesting to our inability to keep up, that there is hardly a need to provide any specifics of such estimates or even to worry about whether they are any more than crude approximations. Bill Wasik, one of the architects of flash mobs, notes its ephemeral nature, suggesting that bloggers and others "aren't sitting in their bedrooms spinning out moony personal diaries, hoping that someone will come along and recognize them."[4] Wallace Stegner, long before flash mobs, worried about our society's "rootlessness" threatening communities and traditions, noting their "hungering for the ties of a rich and stable social order."[5] And, yet, given the chance, we want to look at our archives as stable and permanent, housed in substantial neoclassical structures radiating permanence. If we have stopped building government and financial structures to look like neoclassical temples (which we have — now they look like shopping malls), we probably should cease conceptualizing our archives buildings and our programs in this way. Maybe the Internet/Web is the new archival symbol — whatever that might mean.

For a very long time, longer than I care to think about, I have been writing and teaching about the centrality of appraisal to archival work. What we do (or do not do) in our appraisal activities influences what we do or can do in all other archival functions; if we fail in making good appraisal decisions (or for that matter, we fail in making the public understand what appraisal represents) we cannot do very well in any other archival endeavor. I do not believe there is anything revolutionary in any of this, as it supported by the Society of American Archivists' plan for the profession a quarter of a century ago (and today that plan looks as conservative as any professional plan could be).[6]

Appraisal has been a function whose conception has had an ever-changing history. We have seen shifts from just mere acquisition of anything remotely useful as historical evidence to a function that others do to very formal statements of value (evidential and informational) to formal planning and research exercises (documentation strategy and macro-appraisal). Are we anywhere close to figuring it out? The lengthy discussions about the effectiveness of archival appraisal twenty years ago suggest our unease with this archival activity, but it may be even more troublesome a matter now. We may have moved from an age of information to an age of memory.[7] However, we know that when we drift into the realm of memory, other issues emerge such as its malleability and the misuse of evidence.

It is not difficult to identify landmark writings in archival appraisal. T. R. Schellenberg set the stage more than a half-century ago by rejecting Jenkinson's "no appraisal" approach, and others began to build on the former. F. Gerald Ham brought in the social history perspective, Leonard Rapport suggested that older appraisal decisions could be questioned, Boles and Young tried to systematize the decision-making process, and then Helen Samuels, James O'Toole, David Bearman, and Terry Cook (among others) added a chorus of voices for a complete rethinking of archival appraisal.[8] It is difficult to assess how much new thinking has really been offered since Samuels and her compatriots promoted the archival documentation strategy and Terry Cook and his cohort built the intellectual framework for appraisal in the guise of macro-appraisal. However, since the halcyon days of musing about appraisal and its aims, methods, and results, we have had precious little research about its outcomes — both successes and failures.

A quarter-of-a-century ago, we had the beginnings of some massive efforts to struggle with how to document big science, but except for some spin-off projects of archival visionaries like Helen Samuels and a few others, the ideas and collaboration and creativity didn't last for very long (or, at least, it hasn't been reported).[9] Perhaps this may change as a new era of doctoral students examine archival topics such as appraisal. One of my own, Jennifer Marshall, provides some of the best descriptions of appraisal activity written to this point, with a focus on the issue of whether how archivists document their appraisal function enable them to be accountable to society and the users of archives.[10] I hope, over the next decade or two, we will see the development of a rich research literature on appraisal and every archival function and concept.

At the moment, the challenge is that, despite a lively literature on appraisal, most archivists still discourse about it based on the much older definition of determining the value of records, evidential and informational concepts that are more mantra than concrete attributes, and see it as more closely connected to archival representation than it should be.[11] For every word in our appraisal definition, we can formulate a host of questions that we have not fully answered. And this may explain why we have debated *every* notion of appraisal, from whether it is scientific or pragmatic or an objective or subjective activity. The brief tussle between Leonard Rapport and Karen Benedict about the conceptual and practical validity of reappraisal, that is, questioning past appraisal decisions, is just one minor skirmish in the appraisal wars. The debates have always been fun, but whether they have always moved us forward, especially in our ability to maintain a responsible connection to society, is not always clear. Do we really know our audience for appraising records and are we fully vested in the problems posed by historical knowledge (the feel of the past, memory and its implications, the nature of both destruction and survival, societal pressures on what archives and archivists do, the power of records and the powerlessness of archivists, and so forth)? These are, by the way, questions fascinating in their complexity and intellectually engaging, and it is from here that we will see some of our most interesting ideas and productive work in the years ahead.

We need to bear in mind the complexities of how archival sources are viewed. We know that people get information (and evidence) from a remarkable array of sources: books, places, architecture, maps, photographs, monuments, advertising, newspapers, television, movies, people, junk mail, letters, e-mail, magazines, art, music, and the Web. Some might even come to a museum, library, or archives, although they might not really understand the difference between these cultural repositories, except that they comprehend that they are something important for society (explaining why when the mob forms, it seeks to destroy these places). Archivists have often taken it for granted that they, and everyone else, understands, the archive.

Archivists have long made assumptions about the value of government archives, confidently described by pioneers such as Schellenberg and Margaret Cross Norton, but recent events, especially after those of

September 11, 2001, ought to make us take a deep breath. The National Archives has been repeatedly in the news for the wrong reasons, the subject of reports on security breaches and misguided efforts to remove records long ago declassified and involving secret deals, leading to critical editorials in leading newspapers.[12] Who cares about how well they are conducting appraisal when they are involved in such activities? Or, does it even matter how we define appraisal if this kind of stuff is going on? And while it can be argued that the National Archives leadership finds trouble because of the scale of what they do and the environment in which they work, these situations also suggest the societal complexities confronting the fundamental responsibility of making selection decisions. At the least, it means that we need to question our assumptions about what has guided archivists in their thinking of appraisal (once the National Archives was the principal source of appraisal and records management methodology for many decades).

When we turn and consider the reasons organizations, of any kind including government agencies, create and support archives we develop an interesting portrait. Anniversaries and special events, the work of champions or advocates, the influence of professional and technical standards, laws and other factors demanding compliance, crises and disasters, the need of public relations and marketing units, and other factors have all been documented as having some influence on the creation of archives and records management programs.[13] But what do any of these issues have to do with how we appraise records, especially since there have been few efforts to chart the relationship between archival appraisal approaches and records management scheduling (and the latter often takes place with little or no consideration of archival issues despite the notion that records managers believe in the records life cycle concept).

Looking at the Present

Appraising records, if done correctly (or if done at all), ought to get archivists as close as they can come to the pulse of society (and the organizations archivists work for) and all its debates and dissension about the past. Humans are consummate storytellers, constantly crafting a narrative trying to explain their meaning in time.[14] Nearly everyone discovers, at some point, the value of preserving documentation of their past and that of their family and community, even if history is always more messy than anyone can imagine.[15]

There is a good bit of tension concerning how the past is interpreted, and archivists and archives are right in the midst of it all. Marie Tyler-

McGraw reflects, the "challenge for public historians is to negotiate between the 'stakeholders,' persons with some claim to the story being told, and the historic record."[16] Too often archivists have shied away from a good fight about what the historical record represents or engaging in debates about the acquisition of controversial materials or testy subjects (not with themselves — they often discuss such issues at their own conferences — but they don't engage the public very often). They are not alone. William Hogeland recently criticizes what public historians have been doing as well, worrying that their "kind of simplification . . . erases our deepest conflicts."[17] Working in such circumstances, archivists may find it more difficult to negotiate for the preservation of historical sources or to determine just what should be in their repositories (actually and virtually). Too often, we have associated ourselves more with the feel-good heritage industry than with the evidence and accountability mandates of managing records.

Margaret MacMillan warns that we can distort history into a "series of moral tales," losing the nuances and complexities that are the past.[18] When we assume responsibility for administering the Stasi files or in determining what to do with records revealing the illegal or unethical activities of our employers such purposes must be set aside. Archivists are not in business to make people or our society feel good, but to provide critical evidence for understanding our past and how we have gotten to where we are today. Of course, we should not go out of our way to be difficult or to generate controversy; we don't have to — the minute we do our jobs we will find ourselves in political, ethical, and societal dilemmas, and how we approach appraisal is our best tool for defending and explaining our actions.

Archives are a form of monument, and we certainly now understand that monument building is a contentious business because they connect to and reflect societal beliefs about the past and the present.[19] If it is a challenge to determine how we will commemorate the destruction of the World Trade Center, the attack on the Pentagon, or the crash of Flight 93, it is no less difficult to figure out how to appraise records concerning such events. Despite numerous efforts to distance ourselves from the present and to build a kind of objectivity, what ultimately goes into the archives often gets there because of an incalculable number of factors involving power, present uncomfortable attitudes, and efforts to make archives appear neutral (an impossible task). In the same sense, we have become sensitized to the influence or dominance of Western ideas on our basic archival concepts, a process that has both opened up and complicated the values we assign records or even what we perceive to be legitimate ways of creating records or what constitutes a legitimate archival document.[20]

Many archivists are attracted to their field because of their love of the artifact. And, of course, the document as artifact provides considerable evidence, even if this evidence is sometimes buried in our own admiration of the artifact. [21] However, the tactile, romantic notions of documents, however pleasing they may be, are not what drives appraisal. Indeed, if we get sappy about the materials we care for, we lose our way quickly in the value of documents in society. Without question, we must be careful to take into account when the physical attributes of records are factors in why we preserve them, but we need to do this in a manner that does not become an obstacle to reliable appraisal.[22]

Looking Inside the Box

Archivists have been challenged by many societal changes in the past couple of decades, forcing some to rethink their basic activities such as appraisal. Postmodernist concepts push archivists to expanded definitions and views of archival sources. The culture wars and multiculturalism press archivists to rethink the roles of their repositories within particular communities. Political, legal, and ethical issues suggest that archival sources may be much more than quiet historical sources but important and dynamic sources for holding government officials, corporate leaders, and university administrators accountable for their actions. And social computing, in its constantly changing formats, suggests a shift for archivists from maintaining physical repositories to providing virtual advice and services.

Postmodern theories and methodologies have considerably "juiced up" our thinking about how to look at a document, enriching our understanding of what a record should or could be. However, postmodernism also can suck out the significance of text and, hence, the documentary form supporting it. Susan Sontag, nearing the end of her life and commenting on the post-9/11 celebrations and national soul-searching, states, how the "great Lincoln speeches ... in true postmodernist fashion — become completely emptied of meaning."[23] It gets worse. Mary Lefkowitz, describing her own fortunes in debates about Afro-Centrism and evidence in the ancient world, sadly concludes, truth was "less important than achieving social goals" and evidence unimportant.[24] Some will object to this, that truth is a cultural object or that it depends on one's perspective; it is a difficult matter to tease out from the records piled up in the archives, but to toss it aside as unimportant is to mortgage the archival mission.

If it were only postmodernism archivists had to contend with in appraising records, it would amount to only an intellectually engaging challenge. Now we contend with privacy, security, intellectual property, government restrictions and intrusions, the rights of every societal group imaginable (and some we have not yet imagined), the misuse or even worse, the neglect, of archival evidence by even the scholars who have long used such sources, the establishment of competing notions of archival repositories such as those formed by truth commissions, and a marauding media looking for the next abuse to report on the front page or to sprinkle across the Web. Whatever power we might have held may be ebbing.[25]

To be convicted that archives are essential to understanding the past ought to be a reminder that remembering the past is not necessarily a prescription for pain relief or societal solace. Truth commissions, operating around the world, are committed to seeing that history is not lost.[26] Records, by their very nature can make us uncomfortable because they provide a glimpse into the unpleasantness of the past, hold us accountable for our actions, challenge what our memories (societal and individual) trick us into thinking about the past, are not always conclusive in what they tell us about previous events, and dredge up aspects in our lives, communities, and institutions that are often contested as to their veracity or significance.[27]

One Damned Thing After Another

When we think of emerging challenges, we tend to reflect on the rapidly changing and increasingly complex web of technologies. I guess there is nothing wrong with this, since archivists do face a lot of compelling and confusing technical issues; after all, we have fussed with this for a very long time, sometimes scaring the hell out of ourselves in discussing digital technologies by predicting the end of us.

To reduce our challenges to an array of technological issues would be problematic, since archives are becoming more and more the domain of not just us, the professionals, but the many communities who create records. The number of citizens creating archives is on the rise, and there are some graphic representations of this. A person leaving stuff at the Vietnam Veterans Memorial is a particularly poignant example, "inspiring a collection that literally makes itself."[28] Although this transforms any notion of archival appraisal, it is certainly not the *most* typical of what we will see in the future in terms of citizen archivists (after all, there is a federal program supporting a repository for the materials left behind, from motorcycles to letters to military medals). Buoyed by a remarkable range of reasonably inexpensive and heavily marketed portable information technologies, personal information management has emerged as an important area of new interdisciplinary research and scholarship (although archives has not been represented very well yet in such research).[29]

The most difficult aspect of this impact on archival work may be the need for archivists to readjust how they conceive of their societal mission, not the technical issues generated, and this re-evaluation requires examining a number of other issues such as professional ethics. I have been a subject of ethics discussions, since speaking up about ethical breaches reverses the focus backward. The Society of American Archivists has a long history with ethics and a code dating back to 1980, but what do ethics have to do with archival appraisal? Everything, given that archivists will be working increasingly with records that are contested by issues of intellectual property, ownership, control, personal privacy, and, well, where does it end? What I consider to be the prickly reaction of some corporate archivists to the "Sun Mad" *American Archivist* cover a few years ago is but a modest indication of difficult issues we will face with every effort to identify and preserve portions of our documentary heritage. However, in a professional association with a toothless code, it will be incumbent on archivists to be much more careful in how they are appraising, especially in publicly documenting their aims, accessions, and activities.

It may also be a reason why others than archivists assume archival responsibilities for their own documentary materials. We live in an age when corporations, governments, and universities — and politicians, CEOs, and university boards — do outrageous things usually captured in their records, but records not always making their way to the archives. We know, for example, that at the end of the Second World War the Nazis were rapidly seeking to destroy the records about the concentration camps, often using the camps' victims for the destruction (who were also secretly trying to save as much as they could);[30] nothing really has changed today — those in power try to control the archives, including their unlawful or immoral destruction when they reveal too much.

Working against being sensitive to the ethical and related matters of archival appraisal is the tendency of many archivists to assign values to certain records (and artifacts), a kind of yard sale mentality. Scholarly inquiry into collecting is voluminous, and it reveals collecting as a kind of semi-irrational marketplace activity working against rational planning, careful documentation, efforts to identify benchmarks for determining success, and even ethical understanding of the role and power of archives in society. We can develop all kinds of psychological and sociological explanations for collecting, but the real challenge may be trying to extend collecting, as much about fetishism of the material object, to the virtual world of future recordkeeping. Not only does digital recordkeeping suggest all kinds of different approaches for the work of the archivist (technician, policymaker, facilitator, teacher, resource, advocate), this recordkeeping, as Verne Harris reminds us, is really about justice and ethical matters.[31] For archivists to believe that their work is essential to society and not deal with the ethical implications of their appraisal and other work is to make everything pointless.

Speculating About the Future of Archival Appraisal

As much as anyone I have pushed, prodded, and pinched both archival appraisal theory and its applications. Some of my questions remain, but I now believe we need to go much further in our appraisal practice. First, if archivists are not actually doing appraisal — passively acquiring stuff without much serious reflection on what it represents or competing for the good stuff, then they need to restructure their program for doing real appraisal. This may be the easiest task ahead, although perhaps not so easy for us to admit how sloppy we may have been in filling our repositories.

Even more critical is that archivists document their own appraisal activities in order to explain to the public what archives and the archival mission are all about, that these are not just places acquiring old *Life* magazines, scouring flea markets, and building places to entertain antiquarians and hobbyists. Of course, this requires that we understand ourselves and have a clearer sense of what our objectives are in appraising records. We might want to immerse ourselves in the developing, rich literature on public memory in order to understand how we are memory builders and what this means for our self-perception (and to understand how others see us).

We need to collaborate in new ways. Decades ago I worried about archivists being more interested in competing with each other, but now the greatest opportunity may be working with citizens in equipping them to become personal archivists, that is, to give them some basic tools for caring for their own records, especially those in digital form. Historian Antoinette Burton remarks, "that we are, effectively, all archivists now."[32] We can move well beyond this, to restate without reference to the public perception of history, to encompass all the shiny new gadgets designed to enable us to manage our private documents in both portable and digital form. These wonderful devices will generate archival questions as individuals more easily lose stuff or see it corrupted — giving archivists great new possibilities in conveying a sense of the archival mandate (and not one tied to esoteric concepts of historiography or law or accountability but one connected to the practical maintenance of personal and family documents).

Let's bury the old fossils, mimicking what Schellenberg said about Jenkinson (except that now we can place Schellenberg in that category as well). Our students need to be introduced to these pioneers, but they also need to be enlightened about their limitations. Schellenberg, for example, broadly sketched out the idea of evidential and informational values, but not in a fashion that can be used precisely. If we state these values in a courtroom, the lawyers will demand much more detail as they should, discovering that these concepts are a bit blurry. We need to expand these archival values to encompass notions such as accountability, societal and institutional memory, community significance, an understanding of records and the powers associated with them, and personal privacy.[33] Thinking about such issues extends the idea of appraisal into documentary planning, naturally following on the discussions of the past two decades, but with greater emphasis on matters such as memory and accountability.

When I started working on this essay as a conference address I assumed I would end with a plea for a renewed emphasis of appraisal concepts and practices for accountability carried out in an ethical manner. I still believe that these are intensely important issues, substantially moving the archival profession from a passive cultural discipline to one that stands in the center of our society's concerns for accurate information. Like journalists, an endangered profession, archivists provide accountability of the past to the present (think of records unearthed about Nazis and the looting of art and other Holocaust victims' assets). I would argue that for archivists to be engaged in additional values, for want of a better term, such as accountability which may be far more relevant in the digital era, they need to be much more strongly committed to their own ethical sensibilities.

But Do Archivists Agree?

I believe, more strongly than ever, that the digital information technologies are pressing us to jettison older models of appraisal and beckoning us to start over in developing realistic appraisal strategies. Let me take just one example. The move from film to digital images in photography, both still and moving, has created malleable images[34] and images more as information than symbolic conquering of time.[35] If digital images are fundamentally different from film images, does it not stand to reason that the process of appraising images, especially in the past when we appraised to accession them physically into repositories, must be reformulated? When we move from the old archives of film negatives to laptops full of digital images, from the photographer carefully selecting an image or images to maintain while storing stacks of negatives to the photographer rapidly taking great quantities of images that he or she will just as quickly delete or lose sometime in the near future, then we have the need for a new appraisal framework and a different documentary objective. Somehow the notion of the repository is different (and maybe that of the archivist as well).

But what does the community of archivists tell us about such issues? Any interpretive community shares and uses rules.[36] For archivists, however, the rules are changing (whether they know it or not). Sue Myburgh reminds us that information and communication technologies have changed "all three of the basic pillars upon which the information professions rest: the containers of information, i.e. the documents themselves, the means by which they can be communicated and the tools used to manage them." Myburgh lashes out about too much emphasis on "document management and the management of warehouses of documents." For Myburgh, however, the emphasis of the traditional information professions on their information artifacts has led to their irrelevance in modern society.[37] So, do archivists want to be part of this community?

Others have expressed somewhat similar arguments, although with very different conclusions. Carol Chosky, writing from one particular branch of the records management world, argues, "records management is concerned with concepts rather than artifacts. ... Records management is focused on the organization — corporate, non-profit, or government — not its heritage."[38] Chosky decouples archives and records management, undermining any notion of the standard view of the records life cycle or any idea that records managers when they schedule records are doing anything like archival appraisal (and vice versa). But let's take a gander at another perspective, that of archivist Terry Cook, who examines the difficulties in the relationship between historians and archivists and suggests, the "major act of determining historical meaning — perhaps *the* major act — occurs not when the historian opens the box, but when the archivist fills the box and, by implication, through the process of archival appraisal, destroys the other 98 or 99 per cent of records that do not get into that or any other archival box."[39] While many historians don't see or acknowledge this crucial role of the archivist, Cook certainly reconnects archivists to their crucial societal role.

Maybe the archival process isn't so invisible. The number of studies about document forms is on the rise, and these studies, while not concentrating on archivists, do reveal something about why certain records are preserved. David Gerber, studying the letters of British immigrants to North America in the nineteenth century, comments on the issue of the survival of these letters, how they got into public repositories, and were passed from generation to generation.[40] Not only do we get a sense that some scholars are edging closer to studying archivists, we ought to see a kind of invitation for us to contribute to such scholarship. It moves us back to the kind of intellectual infrastructure Terry Cook argued years ago that appraisal requires, and it opens the door for archivists to see (perhaps) that research leading to wise or defensible appraisal decisions are their main scholarly contribution (not finding aids).

This is not a new idea, although it may not be widely practiced. Barbara Reed, one of our more articulate commentators on the relationship between archives and records management, writes, "records have to be able to tell the story of exactly what has happened to them during the course of their existence," providing details about what this means.[41] For this to happen, we need to have archivists who are sensitive to these aspects of recordkeeping, who are, in other words, studying records and recordkeeping systems and not just placing them on shelves or backing them up in digital repositories.

Conclusion: Refiguring the Archive

Confronted by the rapid expansion of exotic and increasingly portable digital technologies and buoyed by postmodern and other philosophies peering into the files and records of organizations and private citizens, archivists today have mostly accepted the notion of a changing archive.[42] It is easy to accept this idea, of course, but it is more difficult to believe it when pursuing the archival mission in practical ways. For instance, what does this mean for archival appraisal? It means nothing if we just unintelligently add stuff to the archival repository, taking it as it comes. It means a lot, if we are pursuing specific documentary objectives such as ensuring that there is sufficient information about a particular event to allow it to be deciphered and understood or if we are desiring to hold certain evidence to keep some organization or public official accountable or if we are sensitive to protecting some aspects (competitive advantage, proprietary information, privacy and confidentiality, to name a few) of a records creator.

Contemplate for a moment just a sample of the documentary forms and technologies that have nearly disappeared in a short time (my lifetime, if not yours): the typewriter, the mimeograph, the personal letter, an eraser

— all with long, leisurely histories and produced in a manner giving us ample opportunity to figure out what they mean. As one commentator argues, time has lost its meaning for us because of intensity of its pace: "We barely have time to reach maturity before our past has become history, before our individual histories belong to history writ large. ... History is on our heels, following us like our shadows, like death."[43] What does such a notion, and the loss (potential and real) of so many documentary forms, do to how we think about appraisal?

Archivists could bury their heads in the sands and appraise backwards, fixating on old documentary forms they are comfortable with that are left behind in attics, basements, closets, landfills, safe deposit boxes, and off-storage bins. I am not arguing that we should think that we won't find valuable stuff in those places, we have too much testimony that we will and have, but this suggests a terrific problem about the documentary forms and systems created in the last half century and especially in the past decade or two. Ignoring these newer records and information systems negates our societal mission, obliterates any sense of being involved in appraising contemporary documentation, and makes us look somewhat irrelevant. The challenge now is when we examine something like appraisal is to realize that our not using this archival function may be not as much about technical challenges, our own knowledge, or even our resources but a collective lack of interest.

There are two other issues, what we have to say to the public and how we define our own mission and, as well, the societal and community backups that support what we do or do not do in appraising for archival records. As I have already stated, we live in a culture where records and information technologies are rapidly impacting what kinds of documentary sources continue to possess viability (and not all will). We could review dozens of such vanishing sources, but let me just offer up one as an example — the printed newspaper. Daily and weekly printed newspapers have begun to vanish in recent years with serious implications both for the present and the understanding of the past. Newspapers have become the victim of the Web, online news, blogs, declining advertising revenue, and a host of other factors. Even though it is plainly obvious that the producer of most real news reporting featured on the Web remain newspapers and their reporters, various factors are conspiring to eliminate the number of journalist positions and the newspapers employing them. The specter of such a loss is serious for a democratic society, threatening the end of real accountability news, a commitment to reporting the truth, and the verification of such news sources that promote an open society and a government responsible to its citizens.[44]

The same may apply to archivists, that is, figuring out how to define our mission in society and what it may evolve to as the basis of archival sources changes. Alex Jones, in assessing the loss of printed newspapers, wonders what the impact will be on their accountability role. Archivists, while some also see an accountability role, also cling to many other roles as well. Rand Jimerson, in his work on archives and memory, accountability, and social justice, argues for a professional model accommodating traditional and many other perspectives, a model affirming the need to encompass ethical, accountability, and justice roles while not upsetting any particular group represented in the archival community or using archival sources.[45]

Appraisal is acknowledged to be a critical function for archivists, but the message of Jimerson is not about issues such as appraisal. His message is that there is considerable power residing in the archival mission and in the repositories assembling the records and that archivists won't abuse this power. He stresses the archival community's honoring of diversity (meaning political and other perspectives as well as race, ethnicity, and sexual orientation), especially as he turns to consider some of the ethical debates and quagmires afflicting the archival community.[46]

There are problems. Jimerson states, "No one should be denounced for following the call of justice in professional work, nor for rejecting it. Traditional archival practices and principles still provide valuable social benefits."[47] Not only is this statement problematic because of the manner in which he treats some of the cases he explores, leaving out some details,[48] but it is problematic because of the societal importance and power space archives occupy and which he spends considerable effort demonstrating. From my vantage, archivists, especially via the appraisal function, need to open up how they identify records with archival value and, in fact, I question whether the traditional approaches are still valid (at least for very long). And I believe it is a problem for archivists to reject issues like justice.

With all the technologies challenging the continuing viability of certain documentary forms, what archivists are about has stayed out of the public mainstream and debates within journals of public scholarship. As new digital technologies have impinged upon traditional book publishing, there have been many debates about the future of the printed book and about the different digital forms of books that might be in our future.[49] Yet, there is little of such a literature about archival sources, something I believe is the extension of the lack of intellectual inquiry supporting the study of records for the purpose of appraising records and an archival education enterprise still too focused on teaching skills not building knowledge (please give me the secret formula for appraisal, and don't make me think about it). We know, for example, that archives are often targeted (in the form of museums, libraries, and historic sites — that is, highly visible places holding archival collections) because of their symbolic value to communities, ethnic and religious groups, and nation states.[50] We even know that in efforts to protect cultural heritage during times of warfare and strife, archives often come up short.[51]

Sometimes I wonder if there really is anything left to say that is innovative regarding a topic like archival appraisal. It's not as if anyone outside of the archival profession really understands it or knows anything about the debates within the profession about appraisal or what they might reveal. Glossing over issues like the matter of the Native American Archives Protocol or the implications of archival ethics codes in the travails of researcher Anthony Clark's efforts to obtain reasonable access to the records of the Office of Presidential Libraries because these records had not been "appraised," not only sends wrong signals about our archival mission but undermines our role in society. And here is where things get interesting. My sense is that particular communities, indigenous peoples or others sensing disenfranchisement, will band together, create their own archival principles and practices, and teach us some new things that our traditional principles can't stretch to accommodate. Jimerson's efforts to distinguish between different kinds of memory, including a distinctive archival memory, may only be significant within the archival repositories where archivists stand on the barricades. We need, perhaps, a new kind of archival appraisal that brings archivists around the table with other interested (or even uninterested) partners and incorporates their concerns. Otherwise, these groups will build their archives and not quibble about whether they are in the archives, history, evidence, or memory business. We will be on the sidelines, perhaps where we belong. But, then, maybe I am obsolete, soon to be replaced by a machine transmitting signals over the Web giving you the answers in a few slides with a few bullets — so why listen to me?

Conclusion

Introduction

There was a time, not too many years ago, when I was accused of holding a progressive view of all matters archival; that is, when I wrote about any topic I tended to see everything as getting better over time, that the more recent was better than what was done in the past. This is a temptation for all professionals, especially those working in the information disciplines where the claims for the Information Age are buttressed by the remarkable changes in the technologies and the declining costs for more powerful retrieval and increasing capabilities for storage. The criticism was generally justified, as I was often both writing and working to make our professional mission stronger, clearer, and better known — tasks that all archival educators adhere to in one form or another. Today, however, I am more likely to be told that I am cynical, pessimistic, or negative, as I have become increasingly skeptical about the Information Age and the condition of the university. More importantly, I have become anxious about the archival profession itself, especially its leadership (of which I have been part and therefore can share the blame for its inadequacies). I suspect that the essays in this book may affirm the latter view, even though my aim is to wrestle with issues, controversies, and trends either needing to be resolved or reflecting the growing pains of an important societal function in order to strengthen the archival profession. We live in difficult times, and being successful requires more effort and a tough-mindedness that many never anticipated when they responded to a call to enter the field.

For the record, there is much that is better in our archival community. We have many stronger graduate education programs. One can find nearly anywhere, including online, basic training programs on every aspect of archival labor. Research within the field (and by a number of scholars outside the field as well) is both deeper and broader. There is a new generation emerging of archival educators who are carrying out innovative research and creating imaginative approaches in teaching based on that research. Scholars from outside the field are studying records and recordkeeping, archival repositories, and, yes, even archivists, and creating a deeper level of understanding about all these and other areas within the archival community (the change in just three or four decades in what one can read about archives, archivists, and archival work is so immense as to be nearly unfathomable). The archival community is networked in ways unimaginable to those who entered it a few decades ago, with news and commentary on news traveling worldwide in what seems like mere seconds. While at one time archivists struggled to get reports, studies, copies of conference papers, and internal policies and procedures — what was once part of the challenges of grey literature, now with a few simple searches these kinds of materials, on any given subject, are located and downloaded. And I could go on describing the many positive changes.

Nevertheless, from time to time, there is a great outpouring of anger and angst by students, young archivists, and even experienced old hands about the state of the archival profession and its future prospects. Sometimes the grief is great and the tone conspiratorial. Here is an example. As I was putting the finishing touches on this book, an outburst of post-Society of American Archivists "howling" briefly occurred on the blog "Derangement and Description," the "world's first . . .webcomic about archives, digital preservation, and metadata." The author of the blog, Rebecca Goldman, the digital archives technician at the Drexel University Archives, attended the SAA annual conference and expressed her anger and frustration about the poor employment prospects, education programs, SAA priorities, and other issues that resulted in an outpouring of over sixty posts and responses within a week (you can view the original message and responses, starting August 16, 2010, at http://derangementanddescription.wordpress.com/2010/08/16/post-saa-howl/).

In my own response I note that some of these problems and challenges are evident in other fields as well, and that this is the result of the worst economic downturn since the Depression. But mostly I expressed concern about the tone of many of the postings being conspiratorial, as if the education programs are deceiving students or that SAA has not done enough for them, while many students come into these programs without having evaluated employment prospects or even with an idea of the nature of archival work. Have some students been given false promises or hopes, possibly, but I doubt it is a profession-wide scandal (besides, what is said to a student has an awful lot to do with the skills and other attributes of that particular student).

The purpose of this final essay is to explore, briefly, some practical steps that the archival community (mostly my focus is on the community in the United States) can take to fulfill the essential need to manage archival materials (note that the purpose is not to secure the archival profession's future, for who cares if it has a future if it is not doing the right things). What do archivists need to do to eliminate their anxiety?

Do the Right Things

Attract the Right People into the Profession (for the Right Reasons). As I write this, our graduate programs are bursting at the seams with new recruits, at a time when there are fewer positions. No wonder we sense so much anxiety in our classrooms, at the conferences, and in our repositories where we have brought together veteran archivists with part-time archivists working at underpaid and often soft-funded positions. How can there not be friction at all these places? We need to develop stronger admission standards to the masters level archival studies programs that favor those individuals who have experience and some knowledge of the nature of archival work. When I say the right people, this conjures up all kinds of negative images about a closed and elitist profession, the last impression I want to give. However, we need individuals who have a working sense of what archivists can and should do, so that they can appreciate what is taught in the relatively brief programs. It is no secret that the archival community has tended to have a very broad or loose definition of who an archivist is and how someone becomes an archivist, while at the same time being concerned about the level of salaries, the quality of benefits, and the availability of positions. The twenty-year-old certification of individual archivists (by the Academy of Certified Archivists) has done little to resolve such matters.

We cannot afford to allow our class sizes to continue to grow (this only adds to the dissatisfaction felt by many students), and we certainly cannot lengthen the masters programs in the time necessary to complete them (we have long since passed the cost threshold when someone can recoup the money laid out for education with the salaries offered in entry-level positions, especially when many graduates face the prospects of considerable delay into real positions). While, in my opinion, the quality of graduate education has improved immensely (even if not uniformly), the profession needs to rethink how it attracts the people who genuinely can attest to hearing a call to form the next generation of archivists. This is, of course, much more complicated than it sounds. While it is commendable to push graduate programs to be more comprehensive and rigorous, essential if some are also to support the education of the next generation of archival faculty and to be intellectually sophisticated enough to have a place in the university, it is probably time to recognize that a portion of the graduate programs have missions far beyond equipping individuals to be archival technicians, orienting individuals to skills best learned on the job.

Sending the Right Message About the Archival Mission. For a long time, through most of the twentieth century, individuals were drawn to the archival community because of an interest in the past (and as I describe earlier in this book, I confess to being one of these people). Possessing such an interest has not always provided the right compass for steering individuals into this field or through their careers. Archivists also are essential to providing accountability and evidence services that can often be far from the historical and cultural aspects of their work. The profession must develop a more complete message attracting new and young professionals to become archivists and records managers, and we especially need a diversified body of knowledge and skills transcending those gained by studying history. This is not only an essential task, but it is a task that is competitive since other professions also will be seeking to attract new workers to their fields as well. After all, the archival mission is so essential in our society that someone, even if not archivists, will support it. How do we grab and hold the attention of the next generation who will become archivists? How do we develop a substantial and comprehensive mission to guide records professionals? How do we stay relevant? And how do we keep the archival mission in the public's eye?

Archivists are no stranger to developing mission statements or planning how to accomplish them. The SAA spent much of the 1980s and 1990s doing this, alongside the National Historical Publications and Records Commission pushing statewide historical records plans. But I am not arguing for continued, large-scale profession-wide planning (although I am not arguing against it either). What we need to do is to encourage individuals to develop long-term professional goals, rather than short-term objectives, enabling them, first, to understand that their initial education is just a foundation for their subsequent careers, and, two, that this education enables them to shift through handling ever larger responsibilities and increasingly more complicated challenges (even if individuals become archivists by first being enamored with old paper and media, they need to be able to grow to deal with new digital recordkeeping). Far from doting on basic skills and practice, graduate archival education ought to feed the novice archivists' intellectual curiosity and orient them to the growing knowledge base supporting archival work (where they can understand that practice is one part of that knowledge but not its sum).

Promote a Reasonable Holistic Approach to Managing Records. Over the past several generations, we have witnessed the splintering of the profession between archivists and records managers, between records and other information professionals, and between archivists working with various documentary forms (such as visual media and moving images, and sometimes these splits seeming to morph into new disciplinary approaches, most notably, data or digital curation). We can add to this the division between archivists actively engaged in professional conferences and those who seem cut off, for a variety of reasons, from any form of professional engagement. Now, we have virtual means (such as listservs, blogs, and Twitters) to keep us connected, but not everyone is comfortable with these ways to communicate (nor should they necessarily be). We can attribute this kind of growth to many external factors, such as the dynamic nature of information technologies and a greater diversity of institutions hiring individuals to be archivists or some other form of information professional, so we need to be careful in critiquing this aspect of the field.

None of this is necessarily a problem. These trends, natural to any profession, result in new ideas, partnerships, the advancement of knowledge, the diversification of professional and scholarly literature, and other attributes making our professional lives richer, even if more complex in how we define or perceive ourselves. However, this professional richness also makes our work more complex and certainly more expensive as we sort out professional memberships, balance our reading, and decide which conferences to attend — all with an aim of identifying how we can discover ideas and approaches to improve the work of our repositories, especially in this era of diminishing financial resources. This has led some, most recently SAA president Peter Gottlieb in his address to the 2010 SAA annual meeting, to propose a re-unification of the profession by consolidating professional associations (you can hear his remarks at http://vimeo.com/channels/127627#14245218). To use an old Ozark expression, this is like pissing in the wind, but, more importantly, it misses at least one important point. What is needed is not some super professional association, especially one that would be expensive to support; what we need is a clear, simple message (and accompanying set of principles) about the archival mission that the public, policymakers, and, dare I say, archivists can comprehend and support. Despite the long-term existence of such notions as the records life-cycle, provenance, and respect des fonds, all principles that many archivists do not readily accept or, at least, question in light of new technologies, there is little evidence that these pull together archivists in a common agenda. Indeed, there is as much evidence that there are considerable differences between archivists preventing them from coming together in any structural mechanism; whether they would join together for campaigns to build greater public awareness of their work and purpose is another matter. At the present, it appears that what unites them are common concerns and complaints about professional status, funding, and public recognition. And what may enable archivists, despite a proliferation of agendas and missions, to work together is their increasing use of social networking.

Strengthen and Support Graduate Education. The growth in breadth and depth in graduate archival education has been remarkable, but this transformation has occurred without much assistance from professional associations. The SAA maintains an education directory, and other than regular sessions and those of the Archival Educators Round Table at its annual meetings, that is about it. SAA has been careful not to make distinctions between programs featuring a course or two taught by adjuncts and those with many courses and regular faculty appointments, preferring to let the marketplace dictate what programs succeed or not. SAA plays to but often does not always lead its membership, and most seem content to have it that way. The field has supported education to the extent that archival programs require some sort of graduate degree with a focus on archival studies. Other professional associations, such as the Association of Records Managers and Administrators (ARMA), focus on education below the graduate level. One has the sense that the profession holds mixed reactions to graduate education, especially evident when there is an outburst of concerns about an issue such as the job market when many blame, at least partially, graduate education programs for such problems. And, generally, these education programs have emerged and evolved because particular schools have seen an opportunity and market, they have hired faculty, and these faculty have advocated for their programs usually with the result of expanded curriculum and additional faculty hires.

My agenda is not to argue that organizations such as SAA should intensify their support for graduate education, and I certainly do not believe that SAA should be involved in accrediting these programs. SAA is a membership-based organization that often plays to what the core of the membership wants (or what it thinks the membership wants), and the result can be mixed at best (but that is the nature of such organizations). Although SAA and the archival community often seem to believe that archival faculty work for them, they actually work for their universities and for themselves. The faculty must establish their programs and themselves within their schools, and this requires a commitment to scholarship (and by this, I mean via research/publication and teaching) that often seems at odds with the stress on a practice-based approach (although it is not at odds, since archival knowledge is built on practice, theory, and methodology). This is why not every education program or archival professor should be involved in distance or continuing education, since it seems to be played out mostly as part of offering basic training (it has potential to be more, of course, but it will take a long time to see how this education delivery mode will evolve).

We need to take graduate education to the next level, rather than being content with what we have. We need to teach as if there is a greater public good and students are responding to a calling, rather than teaching archival topics as if they were just part of a craft or a set of techniques (there is certainly some of that, of course). However, we are not going to achieve such goals through the political processes of professional associations. This is going to happen through the individual and collective efforts of archival educators, and we can see that this is happening. The Archival Education Research Institute (read all about it at http://aeri.gseis.ucla.edu/) has in 2009 and 2010 brought together in a week-long gathering eighty individuals, equally divided between educators and doctoral students, to share research about archives, discuss the nature and needs of graduate archival education, and, most importantly, mentor the next generation of archival faculty. While much of this research has considerable value for basic practice, especially since a good portion is either collaborative with archivists in the field or studying what goes on in archival repositories, a lot of it has no immediate benefit; but, it is necessary because it deepens archival knowledge and strengthens the place of graduate education programs within the modern research university. By design, for these reasons, this effort is operating as independently as it can, with the freedom to focus on issues crucial to having a home in the modern university.

Get Passion Back into the Professional Community. As we have become more committed to professional standards and best practices, archivists have become more business-like. This may be the cost of success. We have considerable need for more creativity and imagination about what we do and how we respond to how others see us. Too often when an archivist appears in a mystery or a film, archivists become hypercritical about how they are portrayed and lose opportunities to engage with the public about their work. Of course, when we do this, archivists usually debate it among themselves anyway. We tend not to produce self-reflective literature about our work, careers, or missions (like what we can find in other fields, such as history, literary studies, and librarianship) that has any prospects for being read outside of our own community or for generating debate and discussion (except for that by archivists in their listservs, blogs, and hotel bars at conferences). Do we lack such writings because we are not passionate about our work? Because we are just doing something that was a second or third level career choice, the best we could do in getting close to our real interests? While it would be wrong to make statements that are too broad, since there are many dedicated archivists working out there, there is still a sense that there is a malaise affecting our professional community.

Our repositories are full of documents and collections telling powerful and engaging stories, but it is hard to tell that by how archivists sometimes act. A portion of the archival community has discovered the power of archival records as well as the power that produces and preserves these documentary materials. Scholars outside the field, such as historians and literary scholars, have begun to probe into the factors creating and maintaining records. Yet, many archivists still try to convey that they are impartial observers, neutral partners to their researchers, or, worst of all, meek civil servants quietly managing storerooms full of records that may or may not be used. Archivists need to let the power of records — evidence about the past, information to keep public officials and others accountable, support for the value of cultural heritage affirmations that memory is important in the present, and the nature of structures creating and maintaining sources sometimes for reasons of control — shine through the finding aids, in the reading rooms, on the Web sites, and through the barriers necessarily created for security and protection of the valuable holdings. The power of archivists, for as much as they feel the need to think about power, comes from their records not from anything they say or do. There should be something liberating in this.

We need to rediscover the joy of reading and using archives (recapturing the original reasons why so many of us became archivists in the first place), especially as we see more scholars who were former users of archives making use of other kinds of sources in their research (the Web is a siren for them, calling to them, and driving them away from the repositories built across the centuries and guarding the treasures of past cultures). This requires greater commitment by archivists to advocating about their programs and to using every means, including social media, to breaking down barriers and expanding access to their holdings (especially as our potential users become more fluent with digital media, expecting more and more of what they need to be accessible online). Where at one time we made assumptions that any form of research about the past or about contemporary issues requiring some historical context would draw researchers to visiting archival repositories, now we should make the assumption that these researchers will go to the Web or to the digital resources administered by university and other libraries. Now we need to discover a new joy and excitement in reading archival materials, digitally born and digitized, online, and this will require a major rethinking of how we build Web sites and participate in virtual communities.

Don't Back-off From Critical or Controversial Issues

Informal conversation with working archivists suggests that many feel overwhelmed by their responsibilities in their own institutions and opt not to become involved in profession-wide issues or controversies. While a commitment to one's own employing institution is admirable, ignoring these other matters threatens to undermine both professional knowledge and performance. Moreover, it is essential for the profession to contend with critical or high profile issues if the archival community wishes to have a presence in our society. If archivists sit idly by, while concerns about complicated matters such as intellectual property play out in the public forum and, in this case, the courts, they will pay ultimately the price in their own institutions (and in their own careers). We need to do things that enable us to sleep at nights, the right things, even if doing so puts us in an uncomfortable position.

A number of essays in this book provide fuller descriptions of these and other issues. Let me re-iterate about one such matter just to re-emphasize why being connected to and monitoring complicated and contentious issues is so important. Again, even though many individuals enter into the profession with clear antiquarian predilections rather than interests in public policy matters or any understanding of records for purposes beyond the cultural values (such as accountability), it is necessary for archivists to follow events, laws, and debates affecting access to their records. For example, it is no question that government archivists, especially those working in the federal level, operate in an increasingly secret environment. This is an issue that cannot be ignored, because it is antithetical to the archival mission (at least for archives in democratic societies). While it would be nice to have a strong, vigilant national archival leadership monitoring this area (we have had uneven attention, sometimes good and sometimes not very useful), it is really the responsibility of individual archivists to speak up. With growing numbers of blogs and listservs to post such concerns, and a media always ready to report on secret government operations that have been exposed, closed access to government records and information, and the interference of elected officials and civil servants — all topics at the heart of journalists' modus operandi, individual archivists and other records professionals have the means available to them to be watchdogs about government secrecy. It does no one any good, or the archival community, to have a National Archives advocating the importance of historical records for the public good if it is learned that it is unnecessarily restricting access to records that should be open. It does not do the archival community any good to have a national professional association lacking courage to speak up, clearly, strongly, consistently, and courageously, when one of the core tenets of the value of archival records is ignored or trampled upon.

Being engaged in such matters is particularly important since we need new leadership and, as I mentioned earlier, new heroes in the archival community that inspire people to want to be archivists and that make the profession prominent enough to be noticed by people contemplating career possibilities. Some recent debates have led more to calls for archivists to be civil to each other, but civility without conviction or passion is not very useful (or interesting) — and it certainly doesn't get us anywhere. We also need to be open for more dialogue with other professions with an interest in or commitment to archives, a perspective more conceptual than practical. While we have had such relationships throughout our history, it is also obvious that we have been competitive as well (as debates about basic education in history or library and information science programs, still flaring up from time to time, suggest). Sometimes the competitiveness with other disciplines is so ridiculous that archivists refuse to read research about records and record keeping appearing in other disciplines' journals because they don't perceive the practical value; while other disciplines studying archives and archivists may just be beginning to read our own literature, we short-change ourselves if we do not read everything we can to deepen our own knowledge about the nature of the documents we work with, how they have evolved and been managed or mismanaged, and how they are presently evolving.

Separate the Archival Impulse from the Professional Community

Some, perhaps many, archivists associate the state of the archival perspective with the condition of the profession. There is always a lot of handwringing about how journalists confuse archivists with librarians, or, worse, don't refer to archivists in any meaningful way. Archivists associate their often-understaffed programs, usually lower than expected salaries, and sometimes their lack of administrative clout with the idea that the archival mission is threatened or weak. This is a natural conclusion, but it is not

CONCLUSION   269

necessarily true or particularly relevant. Is the archival impulse alive and well in our digital era? Probably. Perhaps a better way to state what I am getting at is to argue that humanity's impulse to preserve materials from its past is an inherent trait extending far beyond the recent development of the modern archival profession.

Everywhere we turn, people are creating and maintaining archives, even if they don't understand that they are doing archival work. They are creating blogs at an astounding rate. Web sites with personal information appear every second. Digital photography is the de facto photographic standard, and people are waking up to some of the challenges in maintaining these images as part of digital scrapbooks. People are immersed in Facebook with the expectation that this material will be archived in some fashion. Twittering is the hot digital communication, and now efforts are being made to archive these messages. Commercial storage services for digital materials are developing, suggesting an alternative archival paradigm. Underlying all such activities is a societal commitment to the archival function, the importance of historical evidence, and the notion of societal memory. Every citizen can be an archivist, albeit an amateur one, and the work of the professional archivist expands in new and potentially positive ways. We can no longer view professions as medieval guilds, closed and secret, but now we must see that professions have a responsibility to be open about their expertise and share it as broadly as possible.

Such concerns accentuate the need for a new kind of archival leadership, one that is more inclusive and innovative. There have been some exemplary efforts by the SAA, such as its long-term diversity efforts, its embracing of training Native Americans to be tribal archivists, and establishing student chapters, to identify just a few examples. However, it has not gone far enough. The SAA leadership has dragged its feet on the controversial Native American Archives Protocols, whereby it would encourage archivists to develop new ways of managing the archival materials of the indigenous peoples, including the return of some archival sources acquired under suspicious circumstances as well as the obvious looting of others. There are honest differences of opinions among well-meaning and informed people, but there needs to be some movement to openly resolve the issues of ownership and access in ways satisfying all groups (archivists, the tribal communities, and scholars). The profession also has just heard about the idea of empowering members of the public to be citizen archivists, but it is doubtful that it will accept this with enthusiasm, reluctant to give up its traditional approaches to acquiring documents for their real physical spaces. We need new voices articulating new ideas with new chances for success. The more we wrestle publicly with such matters, the stronger our lot in society will be.

Not too many years ago, some within the profession, scanning across the new landscape of digital record keeping, predicted the disappearance of the archival profession and professional archivists. We love to predict the future, of course, and usually such predictions either involve dire consequences or the rosiest scenario possible (and, mostly they are wrong). Again, whether archivists disappear or not, people holding positions with that title may not be important at all. What is critical is that the archival function is embedded in the systems creating records and in the institutions important to our society. So, the real issue may be how we ensure this happening. I don't think it will occur through business as usual, leaving us with the matter of how, and whether, it will happen. And here we have reasons for more anxiety, especially since whatever we do must be done in ways keeping us accountable to society (and to each other).

Conclusion

Anyone making it to this final essay may walk away with different reactions. Some will be happy and surprised (for I don't always provide such endings) that I have tried to summarize actions the archival community and individual archivists ought to take to strengthen itself for its future in what are uncertain times. At one time, such uncertainties were attributed to more powerful and complex digital information technologies. Then some, myself included, added ethical and legal issues that can make the technological ones look mild (as I discuss in this book). More recently, the global economic collapse has added another set of reasons for anxiety, although since archives have been traditionally underfunded and undersupported we might be better able to deal with these (assuming we also can develop some innovative, even if more risky, approaches to running our archives).

Others will be quite unhappy with the topics I selected to conclude my thoughts about the state of the archival profession. My emphasis on education, the definition of the mission, ethics, and other related matters could be seen as being far from the daily demands on the working archivist. And they are certainly correct in coming up with other issues that may merit attention. But I have faith that there are others out there who will lift their voices, including a new archival generation to come. Novelist and screenwriter Larry McMurtry, in the second volume of his memoir, writes, "Seeing my books reminds me that, in a modest way at least, I'm part of literature and its whole complicated cultural enterprise that is literature. ...

CONCLUSION

Sitting with the immortals does not make one an immortal, but the knowledge that they're around you on their shelves does contribute something to one's sense of what one ought to try for. An attitude of respect for all the sheer work that's been done since scribes first began to scratch on clay tablets is a good thing to cultivate."[1] I feel the same way. There are many other essays and books about archives out there or yet to be written that may have more and better ideas to offer than in the ones I have written, including this one. I hope, however, that what I have presented here may help move the discussion forward, even if there are many who disagree with what I have stated.

Endnotes

Notes on the Introduction

[1] Mike Rose, *Why School? Reclaiming Education for All of Us* (New York: New Press, 2009), p. 166.
[2] David A. Hackema, "Is There An Ethicist in the House? How Can We Tell?" in Elizabeth Kiss and J. Peter Euben, eds., *Debating Moral Education: Rethinking the Role of the Modern University* (Durham: Duke University Press, 2010), p. 253.

Notes on Chapter 1
The Archival Calling

[1] Consider, for example, G. Kim Dority, *Rethinking Information Work: A Career Guide for Librarians and Other Information Professionals* (Westport, Conn.: Libraries Unlimited, 2006).
[2] See Stephen Miller, *Conversation: A History of a Declining Art* (New Haven: Yale University Press, 2006), especially the last few chapters.
[3] See, for example, Jean-Noël Jeanneney's assessment of the future of librarians in his *Google and the Myth of Universal Knowledge*, translated by Teresa Lavender Fagan (Chicago: University of Chicago Press, 2006), p. 23.
[4] John C. Maxwell (with Stephen R. Graves and Thomas G. Addington), *Life@Work: Marketplace Success for People of Faith* (Nashville: Nelson Business, 2005), pp. 75, 125, is a good example.
[5] William M. Sullivan, *Work and Integrity: The Crisis and Promise of Professionalism in America*, 2nd ed. (San Francisco: Jossey-Bass, 2005), p. 38. There are other negative ways to consider professionalism, such as, "One of the central legacies of the professionalization of librarians has been the mechanization, automation, and routinization of library work to the extent that much of the traditional intellectual tasks once performed by librarians – collection development, cataloguing, and reference and readers' advisory services – have been delegated to clerical and paraprofessional staff or outsourced to third-party vendors in the name of

efficiency and cost-effectiveness"; Juris Dilevko, *The Politics of Professionalism: A Retro-Progressive Proposal for Librarianship* (Duluth, MN: Library Juice Press, 2009), p. 53.

[6] Ken Dychtwald, Tamara J. Erickson, and Robert Morison, *Workforce Crisis: How to Beat the Coming Shortage of Skills and Talent* (Boston: Harvard Business School Press, 2006), p. 72.

[7] Ibid, p. 12.

[8] Ibid., p. 27.

[9] Ibid., p. 117.

[10] Witold Rybczynski, examining Andrea Palladio and the role of the architect, provides a good glimpse into how things have changed. He notes that when Palladio came on the scene in the sixteenth century there was "no period of formal training or apprenticeship. In that sense, to be an architect did not mean to be a professional; it meant, rather to hold a position." Palladio changed this by developing a "simple set of architectural elements (vocabulary) and straightforward rules (grammar) that inspired and were used by succeeding generations of architects." Witold Rybczynski, *The Perfect House: A Journey with the Renaissance Master Andrea Palladio* (New York: Scribner, 2002), pp. 9, 164.

[11] Dychtwald, Erickson, and Morison, p. 9.

[12] This and the earlier quotation can be found in ibid., p. 208.

[13] For example, when I was preparing the original version of this essay, I came across the "Microsoft Records Management Team Blog," an engaging reading about that company's efforts to incorporate records management capabilities into its software offering. Many of the topics being discussed, while focused on software engineering issues, are mirroring many of the discussions and debates featured in the records community's literature and conferences. This blog can be found at http://blogs.msdn.com/recman/default.aspx.

[14] English professor John Ellis, dissecting the decline (according to some) and the vociferous debates (and with this, few would disagree) in literary studies, argues that the theory-heavy humanities have created a language that very few can decipher: "Those who have learned the language demonstrate their mastery of theoryese in titles of conference papers that are full of verbal tricks and gyrations." Ellis adds, "this also draws the attention and the well-deserved derision of the general public." John M. Ellis, *Literature Lost: Social Agendas and the Corruption of the Humanities* (New Haven: Yale University Press, 1997), p. 201.

[15] The book in question is The Nelson Mandela Foundation's *A Prisoner in the Garden* (New York: Viking Studio, 2006); I wrote about it in the October 2006 issue of RIMR in the essay "Empty Temples: Challenges for Modern Government Archives and Records Management."

[16] Parker J. Palmer, *Let Your Life Speak: Listening for the Voice of Vocation* (San Francisco: Jossey-Bass, 2000), p. 55.

[17] Wendy Lesser, *The Amateur: An Independent Life of Letters* (New York: Vintage Books, 1999), p. 105.

[18] The *Oxford English Dictionary* provides a broader, commonly used notion of profession to be "Any calling or occupation by which a person habitually earns his living," the origins of the word extending far back to a more profound religious meaning: "The declaration, promise, or vow made by one entering a religious order; hence, the action of entering such an order; the fact of being professed in a religious order" and "Any solemn declaration, promise, or vow." This is from the online version of the *OED*, at http://www.oed.com/ and accessed September 21, 2006.

[19] Alice W. Flaherty, *The Midnight Disease: The Drive to Write, Writer's Block, and the Creative Brain* (Boston: Houghton Mifflin Co., 2004), p. 57.

[20] Dorothy L. Sayers, *Letters to a Diminished Church: Passionate Arguments for the Relevance of Christian Doctrine* (N.P.: W Publishing Group, 2004), p. 10. Her essays were originally published in the Second World War.

[21] Mihaly Csikszentmihalyi, *Good Business: Leadership, Flow, and the Making of Meaning* (New York: Viking, 2003), p. 175.

[22] Russell Muirhead, *Just Work* (Cambridge: Harvard University Press, 2004), pp. 11, 28, 39.

[23] Ibid., pp. 105-106.

[24] James J. O'Donnell, *Avatars of the Word: From Papyrus to Cyberspace* (Cambridge, MA: Harvard University Press, 1998), p. 25.

[25] George Weigel, *The Cube and the Cathedral: Europe, America, and Politics Without God* (New York: Basic Books, 2005), p. 172.

[26] See the chapter on the disciplined mind in Howard Gardner's *Five Minds for the Future* (Boston: Harvard Business School Press, 2006).

[27] See, for example, David Denby, *American Sucker* (New York: Back Bay Books, Little, Brown, and Co., 2004), p. 8.

[28] Robert B. Reich, *I'll Be Short: Essentials for a Decent Working Society* (Boston: Beacon Press, 2002), pp. 11-13.

[29] Bruce W. Dearstyne, "Records Management of the Future: Anticipate, Adapt, and Succeed," *Information Management Journal* 33 (October 1999): 4-6, 8, 10-12, 14, 16-18 (quotation, p. 12). In another essay, Dearstyne again stresses how important formal education is to a field that seems to be rapidly changing, but he also notes that because of this fluidity it is often difficult to have a sense of just what that formal education ought to be; see "Information Education in the 21st Century," *Information Management Journal* 36 (January/February 2002): 50, 52-54.

[30] Csikszentmihalyi, *Good Business*, pp. 11-12.

[31] Benjamin R. Barber, *An Aristocracy of Everyone: The Politics of Education and the Failure of America* (New York: Ballantine Books, 1992), p. 99.

[32] Richard Sennett, *The Culture of the New Capitalism* (New Haven: Yale University Press, 2006), p. 4.
[33] Ibid., p. 44.
[34] Ibid., p. 105.
[35] Ibid., p. 181.
[36] Derek Bok, *Our Underachieving Colleges: A Candid Look at How Students Learn and Why They Should Be Learning More* (Princeton: Princeton University Press, 2006), p. 286.
[37] See, for example, Richard A. Lanham, *The Economics of Attention: Style and Substance in the Age of Information* (Chicago: University of Chicago Press, 2006), chapter 7.
[38] John Polkinghorne, *Belief in God in an Age of Science* (New Haven: Yale University Press, 1998), p. 83.
[39] See, for example, Magia Ghetu, "Two Professions, One Goal," *Information Journal* 38 (May/June 2004): 62-66.
[40] David Smythe, "Facing the Future: Preparing New Information Professionals," *Information Management Journal* 33 (April 1999): 44, 46-48.
[41] Anne E. Pemberton, J. Michael Pemberton, Jeanine M. Williamson, and John W. Lounsbury, "RIM Professionals: A Distinct Personality?" *Information Management Journal* 39 (September/October 2005): 54, 56-58, 60 (quotation, p. 54).
[42] John T. Phillips, "Professional Certification: Does It Matter?" *Information Management Journal* 38 (November/December 2004): 64-67 (quotation, p. 64).
[43] Information about the SAA mentoring program can be found at http://www.archivists.org/membership/mentoring.asp, accessed October 19, 2006.
[44] This can be seen at http://www.arma.org/join/benefits.cfm, accessed October 19, 2006.
[45] Sue Myburgh, "Records Management and Archives: Finding Common Ground," *Information Management Journal* 39 (March/April 2005): 24-26, 28-29.
[46] José Van Dijck, "Composing the self: of diaries and lifelogs." *Fibreculture: Internet+Theory+culture+research* 3 (2004), available at http://journal.fibreculture.org/issue3/issue3_vandijck.html.
[47] Derek Bok, *Higher Learning* (Cambridge: Harvard University Press, 1986), p. 6.
[48] Typical of the extreme view about the corporate university is Henry A. Giroux and Susan Searls Giroux, *Take Back Higher Education: Race, Youth, and the Crisis of Democracy in the Post-Civil Rights Era* (New York: Palgrave Macmillan, 2004). The Giroux argue that the "corporate model fails to recognize that the public mission of higher education implies that knowledge has a critical function; that intellectual inquiry that is unpopular or debunking should be safeguarded and treated as an important social asset; and that faculty in higher education are more than merely functionaries of the corporate order" (p. 265).

[49] I have written about the challenges of professional education in the corporate university in my *The Demise of the Library School: Personal Reflections on Professional Education in the Modern Corporate University* (Duluth, MN: Library Juice, 2010).

[50] Eric Gould, *The University in a Corporate Culture* (New Haven: Yale University Press, 2003), pp. x, 22.

[51] David Labaree's study of the position of education schools in the university suggests the challenges of this relationship. Labaree examines their poor reputation, lack of respect, a divided loyalty between working practitioners and the demands of the research university, their mission, and the challenges facing them – all relating to issues faced by other professional schools (such as in library and information science) with responsibility for educating archivists and records managers. David Labaree, *The Trouble with Ed Schools* (New Haven: Yale University Press, 2004).

[52] John A. Fleckner, "'Dear Mary Jane': Some Reflections on Being an Archivist," *American Archivist* 54 (Winter 1991): 9.

[53] Ibid., p. 11.

[54] Ibid., p. 12.

[55] Ibid., p. 13.

[56] Jacques Barzun, *Begin Here: The Forgotten Conditions of Teaching and Learning* (Chicago: University of Chicago Press, 1992), p. 204.

[57] Berenika M. Webster, "Records Management: From Profession to Scholarly Discipline," *Information Management Journal* 33 (October 1999): 20, 22, 24-30.

[58] Bruce Dearstyne, "The Right Stuff," *InfoPro* 2 (December 2000): 46, 48-52 (quotation p. 46).

[59] Bruce W. Dearstyne, "Education for the Future of the RIM Profession," *InforPro* 2 (March 2000): 22-24, 26 (quotation p. 22).

[60] James M. Banner, Jr., and Harold C. Cannon, *The Elements of Teaching* (New Haven: Yale University Press, 1997), p. 9.

[61] The guidelines may be found at http://www.archivists.org/prof-education/ed_guidelines.asp, accessed December 2, 2006.

[62] Barzun, *Begin Here*, p. 157. This is not far afield from the continuing debate about the value of theory versus that of practice in the records professions. A group of authors considering the impact of the market on undergraduate education provides a very good idea of what the public expects of faculty in the classroom: "The public wants more than a diploma. Generally, Americans expect students to gain workplace skills along with knowledge, maturity, organizational skills, communication skills, technological competence, the ability to get along with others, and the capacity to solve problems"; Frank Newman, Laura Courturier, and Jamie Scurry, *The Future of Higher Education: Rhetoric, Reality, and the Risks of the Market* (San Francisco, CA: Jossey-Bass, 2004), p. 71. Not only is this relevant to the typical graduate program in professional schools in the university, this statement reads very much like the typical job advertisement for an archivist or records

manager position or the set of questions I am often asked in giving a reference for one of my graduate students.

[63] Richard Klumpenhouwer, "The MAS and After: Transubstantiating Theory and Practice into an Archival Culture," *Archivaria* 39 (1995): 94-95.

[64] Banner and Cannon, *The Elements of Teaching*, p. 9.

[65] Eric Lott, *The Disappearing Liberal Intellectual* (New York: Basic Books, 2006), p. 131.

[66] Paul Woodruff, *First Democracy: The Challenge of an Ancient Idea* (New York: Oxford University Press, 2005), p. 161.

[67] Oliver Leaman, "Who Guards the Guardians?" in Chris Scarre and Geoffrey Scarre, eds., *The Ethics of Archaeology: Philosophical Perspectives on Archaeological Practice* (Cambridge: Cambridge University Press, 2006), p. 237.

[68] Leo Groarke and Gary Warrick, "Stewardship Gone Astray? Ethics and the SAA," in Chris Scarre and Geoffrey Scarre, eds., *The Ethics of Archaeology: Philosophical Perspectives on Archaeological Practice* (Cambridge: Cambridge University Press, 2006), p. 170.

[69] Newman, Courturier, and Scurry, *The Future of Higher Education*, p. 73.

Notes on Chapter 2
Public Memory Meets Archival Memory: The Interpretation of Williamsburg's Secretary's Office

[1] Appreciation is expressed to the staff of the Colonial Williamsburg Foundation Archives and John D. Rockefeller Library, Colonial Williamsburg, especially Donna Cooke and Del Moore, for their assistance at their repositories. This essay was originally prepared for a presentation at the Second International Conference on the History of Archives and Records, held in Amsterdam, Netherlands in September 2005.

[2] Anders Greenspan, *Creating Colonial Williamsburg* (Washington, D.C.: Smithsonian Institution Press, 2002), p. 41.

[3] Marcus Whiffen, *The Public Buildings of Williamsburg Colonial Capital of Virginia: An Architectural Library* (Williamsburg, VA: Colonial Williamsburg, 1958), p. 131.

[4] The building was called by both names in the past century, but it has been known as the Secretary's Office for at least the last two decades. As this essay suggests, the Public Records Office designation seems to have been a temporary creation of the early interpretation of the building, the name intending to be an explicit means for indicating the structure's purpose.

[5] J. G. De Roulhac Hamilton, "Three Centuries of Southern Records, 1607-1907," *Journal of Southern History* 10 (February 1944): 3-36.

[6] Ernst Posner, *American State Archives* (Chicago: University of Chicago Press, 1964), p. 9.

[7] Charles B. Hosmer, Jr., *Preservation Comes of Age: From Williamsburg to the National Trust, 1926-1949* (Charlottesville, VA: Published for the Preservation Press, National Trust for Historic Preservation in the United States, by the University Press of Virginia, 1981), I, pp. 65, 67.

[8] *A Guidebook for Williamsburg, Virginia* (Williamsburg, VA: Colonial Williamsburg, 1935), p. 33.

[9] *Colonial Williamsburg Official Guidebook* (Williamsburg, VA: Colonial Williamsburg, 1964), pp. 7-8.

[10] "The Public Records Office," Department of Research and Record, Colonial Willamsburg, Inc., September 23, 1938, 1937-38 Block 17, no. 12 Clerk's Office file, Colonial Williamsburg Foundation Archives (hereafter cited as CWF Archives).

[11] The initial archaeological excavations were completed in 1938. "Public Records Office (Block 17, Building 12) Archaeological Report," Colonial Williamsburg, Inc., Architectural Department, February 28, 1942, John D. Rockefeller Library, Colonial Williamsburg Foundation is the final report. The 1938 archaeological report is in the Special Collections at the Rockefeller Library, filed under Public Records Office, Archaeology Block 17, Building 12.

[12] A. Lawrence Kocher, "The Public Records Office (Secretary's Office of the Colony of Virginia)," Department of Architecture, Colonial Williamsburg, September 22, 1945, CWF Archives.

[13] The exhibition in the Secretary's Office was one of four exhibitions around the restored capitol, with the old public records building used to display Revolutionary War period maps; "Williamsburg Exhibits Mark Bicentennial Year, Fiftieth Anniversary of Restoration," January 20, 1976, CW press release, CWF Archives.

[14] R. E. Graham to P. L. Epley, September 14, 1976, 1948... Block 17, no. 12 PRO file, CWF Archives.

[15] "Williamsburg Antiques Forum Reflects Its Own Character," December 6, 1977, CW press release; "Antiques Forum Features Exhibition of Portraits," January 9, 1978, CW press release; "Westover Drawings to Be Shown at Antiques Forum," January 17, 1979, CW press release; "Two Special Antiques Forum Exhibitions Open to Public," January 30, 1980, CW press release, CWF Archives.

[16] These were drawings completed for the Historic American Buildings Survey; "Architectural Drawings Are Displayed in Williamsburg," February 20, 1979, CW press release, CWF Archives.

[17] "Calendar of Events – December-February 1981-82," November 2, 1981, CW press release, CWF Archives.

[18] Mary R. M. Goodwin to Dr. Riley, February 5, 1974, 1948... Block 17, no. 12 PRO file, CWF Archives.

[19] Lester J. Cappon Papers, Diaries, June 19, 1969, College of William and Mary.

[20] Peter A. G. Brown to Mr. Short, February 12, 1976; E. M. Riley to Peter A. G. Brown, April 8, 1976, 1948... Block 17, no. 12 PRO file, CWF Archives.

[21] Louis H. Manarin, "A building ... for the preservation of the Public Records," *Virginia Cavalcade* 24 (Summer 1974): 22-31.

22 Vicki Kelly, "Archival Drawings of CW Buildings to be Exhibited," *Virginia Gazette*, January 17, 1979, in Westover Exhibit folder, CWF Archives. The drawings were part of the Historic American Buildings Survey project.
23 "Pew Freedom Trust Fund to Assist Proposed CW Citizenship Activity," September 8, 1982, CW press release, CWF Archives.
24 "Colonial Williamsburg Completes Courthouse Research," December 16, 1986, CW press release, CWF Archives.
25 Howard Gill, Jr., "Preserving the Public Records: A Building to Withstand the 'Flames and Injuries of Time,'" *Colonial Williamsburg* 9 (Spring 1987): 16-18 (quotation, p. 17).
26 George Humphrey Yetter, *Williamsburg Before and After: The Rebirth of Virginia's Colonial Capital* (Williamsburg, VA: Colonial Williamsburg Foundation, 1988), pp. 78-79.
27 Cary Carson to Dennis O'Toole and Members of the Educational Administrators Group, March 28, 1988, Public Records Office file, Special Collections, John D. Rockefeller Library, Colonial Williamsburg Foundation.
28 "Colonial Williamsburg Programs Explore 18th-Century Courtship and Marriage," December 11, 1996, CW press release, CWF Archives.
29 "Capitol Tells Citizenship Story," *Colonial Williamsburg News*, March 19, 1998, CWF Archives.
30 Even the visitors' guide to monthly events marks the location of the Secretary's Office as a location for "Tickets, Treasures and Books"; *Colonial Williamsburg June 2005 Guide to Dining and Shopping*.
31 *Official Guide to Colonial Williamsburg*, new ed. (Williamsburg, VA: Colonial Williamsburg Foundation, 1998), pp. 29-30, 66-67 (quotation, p. 66). The guidebook is available in all the shops in the restored district and local bookstores.
32 Jefferson's reflections were cited as long ago as 1941 in Helen Duprey Bullock, "The Papers of Thomas Jefferson," *American Archivist* 4 (1941): 243-44 and later by Silvio A. Bedini, *Thomas Jefferson and His Copying Machines* (Charlottesville: University Press of Virginia, 1984), p. 2. Jefferson reflected on this copying, with specific reference to the Secretary's Office, in his May 9, 1798 letter to St. George Tucker, now published in Barbara G. Oberg, ed., *The Papers of Thomas Jefferson* (Princeton: Princeton University Press, 2003), p. 342.
33 Morgan P. Robinson to Helen Bullock, November 16, 1938; Helen Bullock to Mr. Geddy, November 19, 1938, 1937-38 Block 17, no. 12 Clerk's Office file, CWF Archives.
34 Manarin, "A building," p. 31.
35 Mrs. Rutherford Goodwin to Morris L. Radoff, August 30, 1950, Research Queries File, John D. Rockefeller Library, Colonial Williamsburg Foundation. It is likely that Radoff was working on what became his *Buildings of the State of Maryland at Annapolis* (Annapolis: Hall of Records Commission, 1954), trying to ascertain whether Maryland had, in fact, the oldest public records structure in North America. There had been a repository authorized in 1729 and some documentary

evidence that it was used, and it may be that the old structure on the State Circle near the capitol building known as the "old treasury building" may be the building originally built for storing public records. The problem may be that the identification of the structure is far less certain than it is for the old public records office in Williamsburg, making the latter's claim for the oldest extant records repository the more certain.

[36] Mrs. Rutherford Goodwin to John Melville Jennings, July 1, 1954, Research Queries File, John D. Rockefeller Library, Colonial Williamsburg Foundation.

[37] John D. Krugler, "Behind the Public Presentations: Research and Scholarship at Living History Museums of Early America," *William and Mary Quarterly*, 3rd series, 48 (July 1991): 365.

[38] Philip Kopper, *Colonial Williamsburg*, 2nd rev. ed. (New York: Harry N. Abrahams, Inc., in association with the Colonial Williamsburg Foundation, 2001), pp. 203-04, 246.

[39] Edward M. Riley, "The Virginia Colonial Records Project," *National Genealogical Society Quarterly* 51, no. 2 (1963): 81-89, and John T. Kneebone, "The Virginia Colonial Records Project," *Perspectives: American Historical Association Newsletter* 30, (September 1992): 15-16, 18, 20.

[40] Eric Gable and Richard Handler, "The Authority of Documents at Some American History Museums," *Journal of American History* 81 (June 1994): 119-136 (quotation, p. 121). They ultimately published a fuller study, *The New History in an Old Museum: Creating the Past at Colonial Williamsburg* (Durham: Duke University Press).

[41] Cary Carson, "Lost in the Fun House: A Commentary on Anthropologists' First Contact with History Museums," *Journal of American History* 81 (June 1994): 139.

[42] Carson, "Lost in the Fun House," p. 141.

[43] Barbara Franco, "The Communication Conundrum: What Is the Message? Who Is Listening?" *Journal of American History* 81 (June 1994): 152.

[44] Franco, "The Communication Conundrum," pp. 162-163.

[45] Stuart D. Hobbs, "Exhibiting Antimodernism: History, Memory, and the Aestheticized Past in Mid-Twentieth-Century America," *Public Historian* 23 (Summer 2001): 59.

[46] Gable and Handler, "The Authority of Documents," p. 129.

[47] See, for example, H. G. Jones, *For History's Sake: The Preservation and Publication of North Carolina History 1663-1903* (Chapel Hill: University of North Carolina Press, 1966).

Notes on Chapter 3
Public and Private History in Colonial Williamsburg: A Memoir of a Half-Century and a View to a Calling

[1] James M. Banner, Jr., and John R. Gillis, eds., *Becoming Historians* (Chicago: University of Chicago Press, 2009) provides a group of memoirs, often about graduate education in the 1960s and early 1970s, and the embarking by individuals into history careers. Rhys Isaac describes, for example, getting his first exposure to archives at the Colonial Williamsburg research center and comments on working on the Carter diary and his discovery of the importance of stories.

[2] Richard J. Cox, "A History of the Calvert Papers, MS. 174," *Maryland Historical Magazine* 68 (Fall 1973): 309-22; "Public Records in Colonial Maryland," *American Archivist* 37 (April 1974): 263-75; and "The Historical Development of the Manuscripts Division of the Maryland Historical Society," *Maryland Historical Magazine* 69 (Winter 1974): 409-17.

[3] This led to an edited collection of his essays, *Lester J. Cappon and the Relationship of History, Archives, and Scholarship in the Golden Age of Archival Theory* (Chicago: Society of American Archivists, 2004). After the diaries opened, I made numerous visits to the College of William and Mary, and I am presently working on another book about Cappon as a pioneer public historian.

[4] April 12, 1960, Lester J. Cappon Diaries, College of William and Mary.

[5] March 14, 1958, Cappon Diaries.

[6] July 29, 1981, Cappon Diaries.

[7] January 27, 1955, Cappon Diaries.

[8] Lester Jesse Cappon, ed., *The Adams-Jefferson Letters: The Complete Correspondence between Thomas Jefferson and Abigail and John Adams*, 2 vols. (Chapel Hill, N.C: Published for the Institute of Early American History and Culture at Williamsburg, Va., by the University of North Carolina Press, 1959).

[9] William Hogeland, *Inventing American History* (Cambridge: A Boston Review Book, MIT Press, 2009), p. xiv.

[10] See Chapter two for this essay and the subsequent references.

[11] Arthur C. Clarke, *Childhood's End* (New York: Ballantine Books, 1990; org. published 1953), p. 62.

[12] Kathleen Norris, *Acedia & Me: A Marriage, Monks, and a Writer's Life* (New York: Penguin, 2008), p. 41.

[13] Norris, *Acedia & Me*, p. 185.

Notes on Chapter 4
Empty Temples: Challenges for Modern Government Archives and Records Management

[1] Henry Petroski, *Success Through Failure: The Paradox of Design* (Princeton: Princeton University Press, 2006), p. 163.

[2] Mark Danner, *The Secret Way to War: The Downing Street Memo and the Iraq's Buried History* (New York: New York Review Books, 2006), p. 80.

[3] See, for example, Mark Lewis Taylor, *Religion, Politics, and the Christian Right: Post-9/11 Powers and American Empire* (Minneapolis: Fortress Press, 2005).

[4] Scott Shane, "Increase in the Number of Documents Classified by the Government," *New York Times*, July 3, 2005, p. 12.

[5] John Wertman, "Bush's Obstruction of History," *Washington Post*, 26 February 2006, B07.

[6] The National Security Archive posted its report, "CIA Removes 50 Year Old Documents from Open Stacks at National Archives," on its Web site, www.nsarchive.org, on February 21, 2006.

[7] This statement, "The National Archives Responds to Reclassification of Documents," was issued by the National Archives on February 22, 2006 at 1:29 PM.

[8] Benjamin Hufbauer, *Presidential Temples: How Memorials and Libraries Shape Public Memory* (Lawrence: University Press of Kansas, 2005), p. 1.

[9] Hufbauer, *Presidential Temples*, p. 7.

[10] Hufbauer, *Presidential Temples*, p. 8.

[11] Hufbauer, *Presidential Temples*, p. 198.

[12] Hufbauer, *Presidential Temples*, pp. 117-118.

[13] Another recent book on this topic is Bruce P. Montgomery, *Subverting Open Government: White House Materials and Executive Branch Politics* (Lanham, MD: Scarecrow Press, Inc., 2006), stressing how presidents have continued to strive to manipulate and control their records.

[14] Hufbauer, *Presidential Temples*, p. 24.

[15] Hufbauer, *Presidential Temples*, p. 31.

[16] Hufbauer, *Presidential Temples*, p. 57.

[17] Hufbauer, *Presidential Temples*, p. 67.

[18] Hufbauer, *Presidential Temples*, p. 29.

[19] Hufbauer, *Presidential Temples*, p. 32.

[20] Hufbauer, *Presidential Temples*, p. 37.

[21] Hufbauer, *Presidential Temples*, pp. 32-33.

[22] Hufbauer, *Presidential Temples*, p. 70.
[23] Hufbauer, *Presidential Temples*, p. 101.
[24] Hufbauer, *Presidential Temples*, pp. 139-140.
[25] Hufbauer, *Presidential Temples*, p. 89.
[26] Hufbauer, *Presidential Temples*, p. 140.
[27] Hufbauer, *Presidential Temples*, p. 35.
[28] Hufbauer, *Presidential Temples*, p. 39.
[29] Hufbauer, *Presidential Temples*, p. 41.
[30] Hufbauer, *Presidential Temples*, p. 150.
[31] Hufbauer, *Presidential Temples*, p. 172.
[32] Hufbauer, *Presidential Temples*, p. 173.
[33] Hufbauer, *Presidential Temples*, p. 187.
[34] Hufbauer, *Presidential Temples*, p. 199.
[35] Alasdair Roberts, *Blacked Out: Government Secrecy in the Information Age* (New York: Cambridge University Press, 2006), pp. 14, 15.
[36] Roberts, *Blacked Out*, p. 48.
[37] Roberts, *Blacked Out*, p. 79.
[38] Roberts, *Blacked Out*, p. 214.
[39] Roberts, *Blacked Out*, p. 152.
[40] Roberts, *Blacked Out*, p. 99.
[41] Roberts, *Blacked Out*, p. 111.
[42] Roberts, *Blacked Out*, p. 117.
[43] Roberts, *Blacked Out*, pp. 112-113.
[44] The Nelson Mandela Foundation, *A Prisoner in the Garden* (New York: Viking Studio, 2006), p. 23.
[45] *A Prisoner*, p. 35.
[46] *A Prisoner*, p. 45.
[47] *A Prisoner*, p. 52.
[48] *A Prisoner*, p. 65.
[49] *A Prisoner*, p. 69.
[50] *A Prisoner*, p. 83.
[51] *A Prisoner*, p. 116.
[52] *A Prisoner*, p. 203.
[53] David S. Allen, *Democracy, Inc.: The Press and Law in the Corporate Rationalization of the Public Sphere* (Urbana: University of Illinois Press, 2005), pp. 2, 55.

Notes on Chapter 5
Secrecy, Archives, and the Archivist

[1] Howard Zinn, "Secrecy, Archives, and the Public Interest," *Midwestern Archivist* 2, no. 2 (1977): 25.
[2] William S. Price, Jr., "N.C. v. B.C. West, Jr.," *American Archivist* 41 (January 1978): 21-24 and Thornton W. Mitchell, "Another View of the West Case," *Georgia Archive* 9, no. 2 (Fall 1991): 19-30.
[3] Julian P. Boyd, "'These Precious Monuments of ... Our History,'" *American Archivist* 22 (April 1959): 180.
[4] Timothy L. Ericson, "Building Our Own 'Iron Curtain': The Emergence of Secrecy in American Government," *American Archivist* 68 (Spring/Summer 2005): 18-52.
[5] Robert M. Pallitto and William G. Weaver, *Presidential Secrecy and the Law* (Baltimore: Johns Hopkins University Press, 2007).
[6] Ted Gup, *Nation of Secrets: The Threat to Democracy and the American Way of Life* (New York: Doubleday, 2007).
[7] Alasdair Roberts, *The Collapse of Fortress Bush: The Crisis of Authority in American Government* (New York: New York University Press, 2008).
[8] Bruce P. Montgomery, *The Bush-Cheney Administration's Assault on Open Government* (Westport, Connecticut: Praeger, 2008) and *Subverting Open Government: White House Materials and Executive Branch Politics* (Lanham, MD: Scarecrow Press, 2006).
[9] Athan G. Theoharis, "The FBI and the FOIA: Problems of Access and Destruction," *Midwestern Archivist* 5, no. 2 (1981): 61.
[10] Joan Hoff-Wilson, "Access to Restricted Collections: The Responsibility of Professional Historical Organizations," *American Archivist* 46 (Fall 1983): 441-447.
[11] Sigmund Diamond, "Archival Adventure Along the Freedom of Information Trail: What Archival Records Reveal About the FBI and the Universities in the McCarthy Period," *American Archivist* 12, no. 1 (1987): 41.
[12] Dwayne Cox, "*Title Company v. County Recorder*: A Case Study in Open Records Litigation, 1874-1918," *American Archivist* 67 (Spring/Summer 2004): 46-57 and "The Rise of Confidentiality: State Courts on Access to Public Records During the Mid-Twentieth Century," *American Archivist* 68 (Fall/Winter 2005): 312-332 charted the increasing acceptance of the right to access public records, leading to, by the 1960s, a balance of the right to know with that of confidentiality.
[13] Pam Hackhart-Dean, "A Hint of Scandal: Problems in Acquiring the Papers of U.S. Senator Herman E. Talmadge – A Case Study," *Provenance* 13 (1995): 80. In fact, sometimes archivists have worked to avoid controversy; see, for example, Karen M. Lamoree, "Documenting the Difficult or Collecting the Controversial," *Archival Issues* 20, no. 2 (1995): 149-153. Others have expressed very different perspectives, such as Julie Herrada in her description of the decision by the University of Michigan to acquire the personal papers of Ted Kaczynski (the

Unabomber): "A little controversy about our collections is better than whitewashing social history"; Herrada, "Letters to the Unabomber: A Case Study and Some Reflections," *Archival Issues* 28, no 1 (2003-04): 45. See also, Frank Boles, "'Just a Bunch of Bigots': A Case Study in the Acquisition of Controversial Material, " *Archival Issues* 19, no. 1 (1994): 53-66, chronicling the public reception by Central Michigan University's decision to purchase records of the Ku Klux Klan.

[14] Elena S. Danielson, "The Ethics of Access," *American Archivist* 52 (Winter 1989): 53. The Lowenheim case is well-documented in Herman Kahn, "The Long-Range Implications for Historians and Archivists of the Charges Against the Franklin D. Roosevelt Library," *American Archivist* 34 (July 1971): 265-275 and Richard Polenberg, "The Roosevelt Library Case: A Review Article," *American Archivist* 34 (July 1971): 277-284, a case in an era when archivists seemed to be more fearful of historians' displeasure than issues such as government secrecy and accountability.

[15] James Gregory Bradsher, "Researchers, Archivists, and the Access Challenge of the FBI Records in the National Archives," *Midwestern Archivist* 11, no. 2 (1986): 95-110 and Susan D. Steinwall, "Appraisal and the FBI Files Case: For Whom Do Archivists Retain Records?" *American Archivist* 49 (Winter 1986): 52-63.

[16] H. G. Jones, "Presidential Libraries: Is There a Case for a National Presidential Library?" *American Archivist* 38 (July 1975): 325-328; "The Records of Public Officials: Final Report of the Forty-Eighth American Assembly," *American Archivist* 38 (July 1975): 329-336; David Bearman, "The Implications of *Armstrong v. Executive of the President* for the Archival Management of Electronic Records," *American Archivist* 56 (Fall 1993): 674-689.

[17] Marie Elwood, "The Discovery and Repatriation of the Lord Dalhousie Collection," *Archivaria* 24 (Summer 1987): 108-116; Jeannette Allis Bastian, "A Question of Custody: The Colonial Archives of the United States Virgin Islands," *American Archivist* 64 (Spring/Summer 2001): 96-114.

[18] Lisa K. Speer, "Mississippi's 'Spy Files': The State Sovereignty Commission Records Controversy, 1977-1999," *Provenance* 17 (1999): 101-117.

[19] Eleanor S. Danielson, "Privacy Rights and the Rights of Political Victims: Implications of the German Experience," *American Archivist* 67 (Fall/Winter 2004): 170-193.

[20] William G. Rosenberg, "Politics in the (Russian) Archives: The 'Objectivity Question,' Trust, and the Limitations of Law," *American Archivist* 64 (Spring/Summer 2001): 79. See also George Bolotenko, "Frost on the Walls in Winter: Russian and Ukrainian Archives Since the Great Dislocation (1991-1999)," *American Archivist* 66 (Fall/Winter 2003): 271-302. For another case study see Joel A. Blanco-Riveria, "The Forbidden Files: Creation and Use of Surveillance Files Against the Independence Movement in Puerto Rico," *American Archivist* 68 (Fall/Winter 2005): 297-311.

[21] Harold L. Miller, "Will Access Restrictions Hold Up in Court: The FBI's Attempt to Use the Braden Papers at the State Historical of Wisconsin," *American Archivist* 52 (Spring 1989): 180-190.

²² Loretta L. Hefner, "Lawrence Berkeley Laboratory Records: Who Should Collect and Maintain Them?" *American Archivist* 59 (Winter 1996): 62-87.
²³ Michael Isikoff, "Papers? I Don't See Any Papers," *Newsweek*, October 29, 2007, pp. 37-38.
²⁴ Cornelia Vismann, *Files: Law and Media Technology*, translated by Geoffrey Winthrop-Young (Stanford, CA: Stanford University Press, 2008), p. 103.
²⁵ Vismann, p. 113.
²⁶ Vismann, p. 147.
²⁷ Pallitto and Weaver, p. 8.
²⁸ Pallitto and Weaver, p. 5. Later commentators would go farther with such assessments. Garry Wills, *Bomb Power: The Modern Presidency and the National Security State* (New York: Penguin Press, 2010) traces the growth of power held by the President to wage war and classify documents since the Manhattan Project in the 1940s to the present. Wills contends that most of what has occurred violates the Constitution. Here is an example of his assessment: "Accountability is the essence of democracy. If people do not know what their government is doing, they cannot be truly self-governing. But the National Security State assumes that government's secrets are too important to be shared, that only those in the know can see classified information, that only the President has all the facts, that we must simply trust that our rulers are acting in our interest" (p. 99).
²⁹ Pallitto and Weaver, p. 3.
³⁰ Pallitto and Weaver, p. 69.
³¹ Pallitto and Weaver, pp. 191-192.
³² Pallitto and Weaver, p. 37.
³³ Gup, p. 17.
³⁴ Gup, p. 20.
³⁵ Gup, pp. 205-206.
³⁶ Alasdair Roberts, *Blacked Out: Government Secrecy in the Information Age* (Cambridge: Cambridge University Press, 2006), p. 15.
³⁷ Roberts, 2006, p. 19.
³⁸ Roberts, 2006, p. 238.
³⁹ Roberts, 2008, p. 18.
⁴⁰ Roberts, 2008, p. 23.
⁴¹ Roberts, 2008, p. 132.
⁴² Roberts, 2008, p. 139.
⁴³ Roberts, 2008, p. 167.
⁴⁴ Bruce P. Montgomery, "Nixon's Legal Legacy: White House Papers and the Constitution," *American Archivist* 56 (Fall 1993): 587. There is also the *other* Nixon controversy concerning his tax deduction for his other papers before becoming President, recounted in Matthew G. Brown, "The *First* Nixon Papers Controversy: Richard Nixon's 1969 Prepresidential Papers Tax Deduction," *Archival Issues* 26, no. 1 (2001): 9-26.

⁴⁵ Bruce P. Montgomery, "Archiving Human Rights: The Records of Amnesty International, USA," *Archivaria* 39 (Spring 1995): 108-131.
⁴⁶ Montgomery, 2006, p. vii.
⁴⁷ Montgomery, 2006, p. 24.
⁴⁸ Montgomery, 2006, pp. 28, 31.
⁴⁹ Montgomery, 2008, p. vii.
⁵⁰ Montgomery, 2008, p. 4.
⁵¹ Montgomery, 2008, p. 36.
⁵² Read the Summer 2006 issue of the *Public Historian* entitled "Programs, Policies, and the Public Interest" for the best recent assessment of these institutions. This special issue of the *Public Historian* does not constitute the typical laudatory or uncritical assessment of presidential libraries that we have seen published in different venues through the years.
⁵³ Montgomery, 2008, p. 48.
⁵⁴ Kate Doyle, "The Atrocity Files: Deciphering the Archives of Guatemala's Dirty War," *Harper's* 315 (December 2007): 52-62.
⁵⁵ Doyle, p. 58.
⁵⁶ Doyle, p. 64.
⁵⁷ Doyle, p. 64.
⁵⁸ John M. Dirks, "Accountability, History, and Archives: Conflicting Priorities or Synthesized Strands?" *Archivaria* 57 (Summer 2004): 46.
⁵⁹ Anne Gilliland, Sue McKemmish, Kelvin White, Yang Lu, and Andrew Lau, "Pluralizing the Archival Paradigm: Can Archival Education in Pacific Rim Communities Address the Challenge?" *American Archivist* 71 (Spring/Summer 2008): 90.
⁶⁰ For example, see Margaret Procter, Michael Cook, and Caroline Williams, eds., *Political Pressure and the Archival Record* (Chicago: Society of American Archivists, 2005).
⁶¹ J. Frank Cook, "'Private Papers' of Public Officials," *American Archivist* 38 (July 1975): 318.
⁶² Cook, p. 313.

Notes on Chapter 6
The National Archives Reclassification Project

¹ The National Security Archive press release, Tuesday, April 11, 2006 3:18 PM, entitled "Secret Agreement Reveals Covert Program to Hide Reclassification from Public." Thanks to Toni Carbo for forwarding this message to me.
² Ibid.
³ Frank Bass and Randy Herschaft, "Archives Ok'd Removing Records, Kept Quiet," Associated Press, April 12, 2006.

4 Christopher Lee, "Archives Kept a Secrecy Secret: Agencies Removed Declassified Papers from Public Access," *Washington Post*, April 12, 2006, p. A6.
5 Bruce Craig, "NARA Releases Redacted Version of 'Classified or Sensitive' Records Memo," *NCH Washington Update* 12 (April 14, 2006).
6 R. J. Cox to Nancy Beaumont, April 13, 2006, 9:59:55 PM EDT.
7 R. J. Cox to Richard Pearce-Moses, April 14, 2006, 7:56:50 AM EDT.
8 Maarja Krusten to Archives & Archivists Listserv, April 14, 2006.
9 Richard J. Cox to Archives & Archivists Listserv, April 14, 2006 1:57:49 PM EDT.
10 Maarja Krusten to Archives & Archivists Listserv, April 14, 2006 2:31:39 PM EDT.
11 Richard Cox to Archives & Archivists List, April 14, 2006 3:38:55 PM EDT. Kursten posted a nice message thanking me for my "thoughtful and courageous" perspective; Maarja Kursten to Archives & Archivists List, April 14, 2006 3:55:38 PM EDT.
12 Maarja Kursten to Archives & Archivists List, April 17, 2006 8:28:48 AM EDT.
13 Richard Cox to Archives & Archivists List, April 17, 2006 9:00:14 AM EDT.
14 "Archivist Pushes to Widen Access to Nation's Records," *Federal Times*, April 16, 2006, interview with Allen Weinstein on April 14, 2006.
15 Ibid.
16 This statement, issued from NARA at 11:26 AM on April 17 also was posted on the Archives & Archivists list on that day at 5:11:16 PM EDT.
17 Richard Cox to Archives & Archivists List, April 18, 2006 7:59:03 AM EDT.
18 Maarja Kursten to Archives & Archivists List, April 18, 2006 10:48:30 AM EDT
19 To maintain confidentiality, I have not included any citations regarding these private messages.
20 Terry D. Baxter to advocacy@lists.archivists.org, April 17, 2006 1:17:04 PM EDT.
21 Jeffrey R. Young, "National Archives Will Stop Letting Agencies Secretly Withdraw Documents," *Chronicle of Higher Education*, 19 April 2006, Volume 52, Issue 34, Page A44.
22 Richard Pearce-Moses to Archives & Archivists List, April 18, 2006 12:57:00 PM EDT.
23 Richard J. Cox to Archives & Archivists List, April 18, 2006 6:00:24 PM EDT.
24 Maarja Kursten to Archives & Archivists List, April 19, 2006 7:55:08 AM EDT.
25 Rebecca Hankins to Archives & Archivists List, April 19, 2006 9:26:34 AM EDT; Maarja Kursten to Archives & Archivists List, April 19, 2006 11:10:48 AM EDT.
26 Christina Hostetter to Archives and Archivists listserv, April 19, 2006, 10:57:40 AM.
27 Linda Hocking to Archives & Archivists, April 20, 2006 10:50:36 AM EDT expressed such ideas, even suggesting that SAA might be reluctant to do anything

that might seem critical of NARA because of the efforts to generate support for the funding of the National Historical Publications and Records Commission, the funding arm of NARA. Maarja Kursten to Archives & Archivists List, April 20, 2006 3:43:53 PM EDT thought that Hocking's interpretation of why SAA may be hesitant to speak out was incorrect, as I do, and then commented on the difficulties of NARA taking any sort of independent or strong role as long as it operated with the Archivist being a presidential appointee.

[28] Carol Nowicke to Archives & Archivists, April 20, 2006 4:33:45 PM EDT; Maarja Kursten to Archives & Archivists, April 20, 2006 5:08:38 PM EDT.

[29] Richard Cox to unnamed archivist, April 21, 2006, 11:41:29 AM EDT.

[30] Ariel Lucas to Archives & Archivists list, April 21, 2006 12:40:29 PM EDT.

[31] Ibid. One reason for speaking up was a response to Lucas that the employers of government archivists are the public, wondering why more had not been made of the "outsourcing of the reclassification review to a major military defense contractor. Does it bother anyone that public access policy determinations are being contracted out? I wonder what the metrics, or performance measures, of such a contract would be." Dwight Wallis to Archives & Archivists list, April 21, 2006 1:34:21 PM EDT. Kursten clarified that it was not NARA hiring contractors but the various intelligence agencies that were doing this. And she pointed out that contractors are not prepared to handle all the problems that government employees, like those at NARA, are trained to deal with. As she pointed out, "government employees -- permanent civil servants -- receive ethics training and sometimes save their agencies from terrible problems by courageously speaking out, internally, about emerging issues." Maarja Kursten to Archives & Archivists List, April 21, 2006 2:01:22 PM EDT.

[32] Rick Barry to Archives & Archivists List, April 19, 2006 12:33:42 PM EDT.

[33] Bruce Montgomery to Archives & Archivists, April 19, 2006 4:03:15 PM EDT.

[34] Peter Hirtle to Archives & Archivists, April 19, 2006 2:02:46 PM EDT.

[35] Richard J. Cox to Archives & Archivists List, April 20, 2006 1:40:13 AM EDT.

[36] Here are the publications I listed: Richard J. Cox, *Ethics, Accountability, and Recordkeeping in Troubled Times* (London: Facet, 2006); Mark Danner, *The Secret Way to War: The Downing Street Memo and the Iraq War's Buried History* (New York: NYRB, 2006); Verne Harris, *Archives and Justice: A South African Perspective* (Chicago: Society of American Archivists, 2006); [Verne Harris and others], *The Nelson Mandela Foundation, A Prisoner in the Garden* (New York: Viking Studio, 2006); Benjamin Hufbauer, *Presidential Temples: How Memorials and Libraries Shape Public Memory* (Lawrence: University Press of Kansas, 2005); Bruce Montgomery, *Subverting Open Government: White House Materials and Executive Branch Politics* (Metuchen, NJ: Scarecrow Press, 2005); Margaret Proctor, et al, *Political Pressure and the Archival Record* (Chicago: Society of American Archivists, 2006); and Alasdair Roberts, *Blacked Out: Government Secrecy in the Information Age* (New York: Cambridge University Press, 2006).

[37] Maarja Kursten to Archives & Archivists, April 21, 2006 1:32:14 PM EDT.

[38] Peter Hirtle to Archives & Archivists, April 20, 2006 5:43:24 AM EDT.
[39] Ibid.
[40] Maarja Kursten to Archives & Archivists, April 20, 2006 7:42:55 AM EDT.
[41] Richard J. Cox to Archives & Archivists, April 20, 2006 9:42:42 AM EDT.
[42] Maarja Kursten to Archives & Archivists, April 20, 2006 10:09:13 AM EDT.
[43] Scott Shane, "National Archives Pact Let C.I.A. Withdraw Public Documents," *New York Times*, April 18, 2006.
[44] "Putting the Cat Back in the Bag," *New York Times*, April 19, 2006.
[45] Bruce Montgomery to Archives & Archivists List, April 20, 2006 8:15:04 PM EDT.
[46] Kim Scott to Archives & Archivists List, April 21, 2006 1:57:40 PM EDT.
[47] Peter Hirtle to Archives & Archivists List, April 22, 2006 11:46:16 AM EDT.
[48] On April 24, 2006 the National Archives announced that it was having a press conference two days later to announce the Information Security and Oversight Office audit results.
[49] Dana Milbank, "He Could Tell You, But Then He'd Have to Kill You," *Washington Post*, April 25, 2006, p. A2.
[50] Michael Tarabulski to Archives and Archivists listserv, April 25, 2006, 4:21:12.
[51] Jeffrey R. Young, "How the National Archives Struck a Secret Deal on Documents With the CIA," *Chronicle of Higher Education*, April 25, 2006, Volume 52, Issue 35, Page A43.
[52] The National Security Archive provided a compact analysis of the audit report, released on April 26, 2006 at 1:21 PM entitled "ISOO Audit Report Exposes Abuse of Classification System," available at http://www.nsarchive.org.
[53] "Next Steps from Archivist of the United States Allen Weinstein," posted at the National Archives Web site, April 26, 2006, and available as http://www.archives.gov/isoo/reports/weinstein-remarks.html.
[54] Maarja Kursten to Archives and Archivists List, April 26, 2006, 2:58:00 PM.
[55] Christopher Lee, "Some Archives Files Wrongly Kept Secret," *Washington Post*, April 27, 2006, A25.
[56] Jeffrey R. Young, "National Archives Audit Finds Many Reclassifications of Documents Were 'Inappropriate,'" *Chronicle of Higher Education*, April 27, 2006, Volume 52, Issue 35, Page A1.
[57] NARA Information Security Oversight Office, *Withdrawal of Records from Public Access at the National Archives and Records Administration for Classification Purposes* (Washington, D.C.: National Archives and Records Administration, April 26, 2006), pp. 1, 2.
[58] Ibid., p. 6.
[59] Ibid., p. 2.
[60] Ibid., p. 8.
[61] Ibid., pp. 19-20.
[62] Ibid., p. 20.
[63] Ibid., p. 22.

ENDNOTES

⁶⁴ Ibid., p. 23.
⁶⁵ Ibid., p. 24.
⁶⁶ Quoted from page 3 of the ISOO director's message appended to the report.
⁶⁷ Donald R. McCoy, *The National Archives: America's Ministry of Documents 1934-1968* (Chapel Hill, University of North Carolina Press, 1978), 132-133, 134, 373.

Notes on Chapter 7
Archival Ethics: The Truth of the Matter

¹ Michael Dummett, *Truth and the Past* (New York: Columbia University Press, 2004), p. 116.
² Unfortunately, this commentator suggests that while the codes do well in providing guidance they are not much assistance in helping the public understand better archival work and mission and are weakened even more by the lack of any enforcement mechanisms. Glenn Dingwall, "Trusting Archivists: The Role of Archival Ethics in Establishing Public Faith," *American Archivist* 67 (Spring/Summer 2004): 20.
³ For the original SAA code see [SAA] Code of Ethics Task Force, "A Code of Ethics for Archivists," *American Archivist*, 43 (Summer 1980): 414-418.
⁴ Martha Montague Smith, "Information Ethics," *Annual Review of Information Science and Technology* 21, ed. Martha E. Williams (Medford, N.J.: Published for the American Society for Information Science by Information Today, 1997): 339-366.
⁵ Donald R. Lennon, "Ethical Issues in Archival Management," *North Carolina Libraries* 51 (Spring 1993): 18. This early code was published in the *American Archivist* 18 (July 1955): 307-308.
⁶ Lennon, "Ethical Issues," provides a detailed commentary on the elements of the 1992 code.
⁷ Karen Benedict, "An Evolution in a Code of Ethics: The Society of American Archivists," paper presented at the International Congress on Archives, August 2004, and available at http://64.233.179.104/search?q=cache:tfthhBqK4U0J: www.ifai.org.mx/ica/presentaciones/21.pdf+archival+ethics+SAA+code&hl=en, accessed May 10, 2005.
⁸ J. Michael Pemberton, "Toward a Code of Ethics: Social Relevance and the Professionalization of Records Management," *Records Management Quarterly* 32 (October 1998): 51-56 and "Who Cares About Records Management? Social Relevance and Professional Standing," *Records Management Quarterly* 30 (October 1996): 52-57.
⁹ Richard H. Lytle, "Ethics of Information Management," *Records Management Quarterly* (October 1970): 5. Lytle was worried about the changing nature of information technologies and their implications for intrusion into individual lives and abuse by the creators and holders of documentation, arguing, among other

things, that the ARMA code must include a statement "specifically recognizing the moral dimensions of records management" (p. 8).

[10] Karen Benedict, "Business Archives Literature," *American Archivist* 45 (1982): 314. The next decade led to some more writings on archival ethics, but none focusing on the corporate area.

[11] David Horn, "The Development of Ethics in Archival Practice," *American Archivist* 52 (Winter 1989): 64-71.

[12] Ronald L. Becker, "The Ethics of Providing Access," *Provenance* 11, nos. 1 & 2 (1993): 57-77; Virginia J. H. Cain, "The Ethics of Processing," *Provenance* 11, nos. 1 & 2 (1993): 39-55; Elena S. Danielson, "The Ethics of Access," *American Archivist* 52 (Winter 1989): 52-62 and "Ethics and Reference Services, in *Reference Services for Archives and Manuscripts*, ed. Laura B. Cohen (New York: Haworth Press, 1997); Harold L. Miller, "Will Access Restrictions Hold Up in Court: The FBI's Attempt to Use the Braden Papers at the State Historical Society of Wisconsin," *American Archivist* 52 (Spring 1989): 180-90; and Thomas Wilsted, "Observations on the Ethics of Collecting Archives and Manuscripts," *Provenance* 11, nos. 1 and 2 (1993): 25-37.

[13] Anne Cooke, "A Code of Ethics for Archivists: Some Points for Discussion," *Archives and Manuscripts* 15 (November 1987): 95-104; E. W. Russell, "Archival Ethics," *Archives and Manuscripts* 6 (February 1976): 226-234.

[14] A. D. Baynes-Cope, "Ethics and the Conservation of Archival Documents," *Journal of the Society of Archivists* 9 (October 1988): 185-87; Heather MacNeil, "Defining the Limits of Freedom of Inquiry: The Ethics of Disclosing Personal Information Held in Government Archives," *Archivaria* 32 (Summer 1991): 143-44.

[15] Michael W. Hill, "Facing Up to Dilemmas: Conflicting Ethics and the Modern Information Professional," *Aslib Proceedings* 50 (April 1998): 74.

[16] See, for example, Robert G. Wengert, "Some Ethical Aspects of Being an Information Professional," *Library Trends* 49 (Winter 2001): 486-509.

[17] Thomas J. Froehlich, "Ethical Considerations of Information Professionals," *Annual Review of Information Science and Technology*, 27, ed. Martha E. Williams (Medford, N.J.: Published for the American Society for Information Science, 1992), pp. 291-324.

[18] Jean Barr, Beth Chiaiese, and Lee R. Nemchek, *Records Management in the Legal Environment: A Handbook of Practice and Procedure* (Lenexa, KS: ARMA International, 2003), p. 266.

[19] Rebecca Knuth, *Libricide: The Regime-Sponsored Destruction of Books and Libraries in the Twentieth Century* (Westport, Conn.: Praeger, 2003) and James Raven, ed., *Lost Libraries: The Destruction of Great Book Collections Since Antiquity* (New York: Palgrave Macmillan, 2004).

[20] See, for example, Jimmy Carter, *Our Endangered Values: America's Moral Crisis* (New York: Simon and Schuster, 2005).

[21] For example, James Aho, *Confession and Bookkeeping: The Religious, Moral, and Rhetorical Roots of Modern Accounting* (Albany: State University of New York Press, 2005).

[22] Anita L. Allen, *The New Ethics: A Guided Tour of the Twenty-first Century Moral Landscape* (New York: Miramax Books, 2004), p. 111.

[23] Richard Paul and Linda Elder, *The Miniature Guide to Understanding the Foundation of Ethical Reasoning* (Dillon Beach, CA: The Foundation for Critical Thinking, 2003), p. 2.

[24] For example, Albert Meijer writes, "In spite of its significance for democratic societies, accountability is not a well-defined term and passed into ordinary language only relatively recently. Although there is no generally accepted definition, six elements of accountability can be distinguished: there is an event that triggers the accountability process, a person or organization that is accountable, an action or situation for which the person or organization is accountable and a forum to which the person or organization is accountable. Furthermore, there are criteria to judge the action or situation and, if necessary, there are sanctions which can be imposed on the person or organization"; Albert Meijer, "Anticipating Accountability Processes," *Archives and Manuscripts* 28 (May 2000): 53.

[25] Richard J. Cox and David A. Wallace, eds., *Archives and the Public Good: Accountability and Records in Modern Society* (Westport, Conn.: Quorum Books, 2002).

[26] Increasing government secrecy, the seeming eroding of civil liberties, the misuses of information technologies, the growth in the classification of government documents, pressures by the government and other public figures for various forms of censorship and self-censorship, increasingly complex government policies and regulations, and government-sponsored genocide and terrorism are typical of the kinds of problems being generated in our era. See, for example, Michael F. Brown, *Who Owns Native Culture?* (Cambridge: Harvard University Press, 2003); Nancy Chang and the Center for Constitutional Rights, *Silencing Political Dissent: How Post-September 11 Anti-Terrorism Measures Threaten Our Civil Liberties* (New York: Seven Stories Press, 2002); Priscilla B. Hayner, *Unspeakable Truths: Facing the Challenge of Truth Commissions* (New York: Routledge, 2002); and Richard C. Leone and Greg Anrig, Jr., eds., *The War on Our Freedoms: Civil Liberties in an Age of Terrorism* (New York: Public Affairs, 2003). Occasionally, we have witnessed government-sponsored efforts at opening records, such as related to the Holocaust victims' assets, which reflects the power of government to take the lead in innovative public access; see, for example, Stuart Eisenstadt, *Imperfect Justice: Looted Assets, Slave Labor, and the Unfinished Business of World War II* (New York: Public Affairs, 2003).

[27] Robert Bryce, *Pipe Dreams: Greed, Ego, and the Death of Enron* (New York: Public Affairs, 2002); David O. Stephens, "Lies, Corruption, and Document Destruction," *Information Management Journal* 36 (September/October 2002): 23-26, 28, 30; Barbara Ley Toffler, with Jennifer Reingold, *Final Accounting: Ambition, Greed, and the Fall of Arthur Andersen* (New York: Broadway Books, 2003).

[28] Richard Sennett, *The Corrosion of Character: The Personal Consequences of Work in the New Capitalism* (New York: W.W. Norton and Co., 1998); A. Larry Elliott and Richard J. Schroth, *How Companies Lie: Why Enron is Just the Tip of the Iceberg* (New York: Crown Business, 2002).

[29] John Micklethwait and Adrian Woolridge, *The Company: A Short History of a Revolutionary Idea* (New York: Modern Library, 2003), p. xvi.

[30] Micklethwait and Woolridge, *The Company*, p. xx.

[31] Daniel Terris, *Ethics at Work: Creating Virtue in an American Corporation* (Waltham, MA: Brandeis University Press by University Press of New England, 2005), p. 4.

[32] See, example, Bob Tillman, "Who's Afraid of Sarbanes-Oxley? Accountability Legislation Creates Additional Document Retention Requirements and Responsibilities for Records Managers," *Information Management Journal* 36 (November-December 2002): 16-20; Joseph P. Messina and Daniel B. Trinkle, "Document Retention Policies After *Andersen*," *Boston Bar Journal* (September/October 2002) available at http://www.bostonbar.org/members/bbj/bbj0910_02/analysis_docretention.htm; David C. Reeves, "What Enron/Andersen Taught Us About Records Retention," *Journal of Transportation Law, Logistics and Policy* 69 (Spring 2002): 327-344.

[33] Steven Lubet, "Document Destruction After Arthur Andersen: Is It Still Housekeeping or Is It a Crime?" *Journal of Appellate Practice and Process* 12 (Fall 2002): 323-329.

[34] Nikki Swartz, "Six Months That Changed the Face of Information Management: It Was a One-Two Punch from Which the United States May Never Fully Recover," *Information Management Journal* 36 (July-August 2002): 18-23.

[35] David Vogel, *The Market for Virtue: The Potential and Limits of Corporate Social Responsibility* (Washington, D. C.: Brookings Institution Press, 2005), pp. ix, x.

[36] Vogel, *The Market for Virtue*, pp. 2, 11-12.

[37] Vogel, *The Market for Virtue*, pp. 2-3, 3.

[38] Marvin T. Brown, *Corporate Integrity: Rethinking Organizational Ethics and Leadership* (New York: Cambridge University Press, 2005), p. ix.

[39] Elizabeth W. Adkins, "The Development of Business Archives in the United States: An Overview and Personal Perspective," *American Archivist* 60 (Winter 1997): 8-33. For another overview also short-changing discussion on ethical and related issues, see David R. Smith, "An Historical Look at Business Archives," *American Archivist* 45 (1982): 273-278.

[40] Harold P. Anderson, "Business Archives: A Corporate Asset," *American Archivist* 45 (1982): 265.

[41] Edwin Green, "Multi-National, Multi-Archival: The Business Records of HSBC Group," *American Archivist* 60 (Winter 1997): 72-87.

[42] James E. Fogerty, "Archival Brinkmanship: Downsizing, Outsourcing, and the Records of Corporate America," *American Archivist* 60 (Winter 1997): 44-55. See also Ellen G. Gartrell, "Some Things We Have Learned…: Managing Advertising Archives for Business and Non-Business Users," *American Archivist* 60 (Winter

1997): 56-71, describing the acquisition and subsequent administration of the J. Walter Thompson Company Archives by Duke University, also with no serious discussion of ethical concerns.

[43] Duncan McDowall, "'Wonderful Things': History, Business, and Archives Look to the Future," *American Archivist* 56 (Spring 1993): 352.

[44] Leonard McDonald, "Ethical Dilemmas Facing an Archivist in the Business Environment: The Constraints on a Business Archivist," *Journal of the Society of Archivists* 10 (October 1989): 169.

[45] McDonald, "Ethical Dilemmas," p. 171.

[46] Anne Van Camp, "Access Policies for Corporate Archives," *American Archivist* 45 (Summer 1982): 296-298.

[47] Douglas A. Bakken, "Corporate Archives Today," *American Archivist* 45 (1982): 285.

[48] Gord Rabchuk, "Life After the Big Bang: Business Archives in an Era of Disorder," *American Archivist* 60 (Winter 1997): 39. For a similar perspective, see Jim Coulson, "Our Professional Responsibility," *Records Management Quarterly* 27 (April 1993): 20-25.

[49] George David Smith, "Dusting Off the Cobwebs: Turning the Business Archives into a Managerial Tool," *American Archivist* 45 (1982): 287-290 remains one of the best examples of this.

[50] See, for example, Linda Edgerly, "Business Archives Guidelines," *American Archivist* 45 (1982): 267-272.

[51] Deborah S. Gardner, "Commentary II," *American Archivist* 45 (1982): 294-295.

[52] Philip F. Mooney, "Commentary I," *American Archivist* 45 (1982): 292.

[53] The letters were published in the *American Archivist* 67 (Fall/Winter 2004): 152-154. In the same issue, the editor, Philip B. Eppard, published a response, "Judging a Book by Its Cover," pp. 156-160.

[54] Susan Tschabrun, "Off the Wall and Into a Drawer: Managing a Research Collection of Political Posters," *American Archivist* 66 (Fall/Winter 2003): 303-324.

[55] Philip J. Ashdown to the Editor, *American Archivist* 68 (Spring/Summer 2005): 12.

[56] Published in the *American Archivist* 68 (Fall/Winter 2005): 202-203.

[57] Marcia P. Miceli and Janet P. Near, "Individual and Situational Correlates of Whistle-Blowing," *Personnel Psychology* 41 (Summer 1988): 267.

[58] Pemberton and Pendergraft, "Toward a Code of Ethics," p. 6.

[59] Mary Prior, Simon Rogerson, and Ben Fairweather, "The Ethical Attitudes of Information Systems Professionals: Outcomes of an Initial Survey," *Telematics and Informatics* 19 (2002): 32.

[60] McDowall, "'Wonderful Things,'" p. 356.

Notes on Chapter 8
The Archives & Archivists Listserv Controversy

[1] My doctoral research assistant, Joel Blanco, helped in some of the research for the essays on the Archives & Archivists listserv controversy.
[2] Richard J. Cox, "Two Sides of the Coin: Archivists and Records Managers Consider Electronic Mail; The Records Managers Speak," *Records & Information Management Report* 23 (May 2007): 1-14; "Two Sides of the Coin: Archivists and Records Managers Consider Electronic Mail; The Archivists Speak," *Records & Information Management Report* 23 (June 2007): 1-14.
[3] Nancy Beaumont to the Archives & Archivists List, March 13, 2007, 11:38:37.
[4] See, for example, my own *No Innocent Deposits: Forming Archives By Rethinking Appraisal* (Lanham, Md.: Scarecrow Press, Inc., 2004) describing some of these debates and discussions.
[5] Frank G. Burke, "Letting Sleepy Dogmas Lie," *American Archivist* 55 (Fall 1992): 531.
[6] Ibid., pp. 536-537.
[7] Philip N. Alexander, "Frank G. Burke on the Archives Listserv – A Response," *American Archivist* 57, no. 1 (Winter 1994): 4.
[8] Ibid., pp. 5-6.
[9] "Frank G. Burke on the Archives Listserv: A Response," *American Archivist* 57 (Winter 1994): 7.
[10] David Shipley and Will Schwalbe, *Send: The Essential Guide to Email for Office and Home* (New York: Alfred A. Knopf, 2007).
[11] Diana L. Shenk and Jackie R. Esposito, "Integrating Archival Management and the ARCHIVES Listserv in the Classroom: A Case Study," *American Archivist* 58, no. 1 (Winter 1995): 72.
[12] B.M. Wildemuth, Lisa Crenshaw, William Jenniches, and J. Christine Harmes, "What's Everybody Talking About? Message Functions and Topics on Electronic Lists and Newsgroups in Information and Library Science," *Journal of Education for Library and Information Science* 38, no. 2 (Spring 1997): 137-156.
[13] Thomas E. Ruggiero, "Electronic Mail and Listservs: Effective Journalistic Ethical Fora?," *Journal of Mass Media Ethics* 16, no. 4 (2001): 301.
[14] Dov Te'eni and Andrew Schwarz, "Communication in the IS Community: A Call for Research and Design," *Communications of AIS* 2004, no. 13 (2004): 528.
[15] Ibid., p. 529.
[16] Ibid., p. 535.
[17] Ibid, p. 538.
[18] Ibid., p. 539.
[19] Ibid., p. 540.
[20] "Listserv," *Webopedia*, http://www.webopedia.com/TERM/L/Listserv.html, accessed May 10, 2007.

21 Zane L. Berge and Mauri P. Collins, "Perceptions of E-Moderators about Their Roles and Functions in Moderating Electronic Mailing Lists," *Distance Education* 21, no. 1 (2000): 83-84.
22 Zane L. Berge and Mauri Collins, "The Founding and Managing of IPCT-L: A Listowners' Perspective," *Interpersonal Computing and Technology: An Electronic Journal for the 21st Century* 1 (April 1993), available at http://www.emoderators.com/papers/founding.html, accessed May 19, 2007.
23 Davy Rothbart, *Found: The Best Lost, Tossed, and Forgotten Items From Around the World* (New York: Simon and Schuster, 2004), p. 2.
24 *Presidential Doodles: Two Centuries of Scribbles, Scratches, Squiggles & Scrawls from the Oval Office* (New York: Basic Books, 2006), p. 24.
25 "History of LISTSERV," 1996, available at http://www.lsoft.com/products/listserv-history.asp, accessed May 10, 2007.
26 David A. Grier and Mary Campbell, "A Social History of Bitnet and Listserv, 1985-1991," *IEEE Annals of the History of Computing* 22, no. 1 (April-June 2000): 39.
27 Grier and Campbell, p. 35.
28 Grier and Campbell, p. 35.
29 Zane L. Berge, "Electronic Discussion Groups," *Communication Education* 43, no. 2 (April 1994): 102-111.
30 Karin B. Borei, "The Rewards of Managing an Electronic Mailing List," *Library Trends* 47, no. 4 (Spring 1999): 696.
31 See Carol Wilkinson and Todd R. Pennington, "The USPE-L Listserv: A Forum for Reflective Discourse?," *Physical Educator* 59, no. 3 (Fall 2002): 158-169.
32 Avi Hyman, "Twenty Years of ListServ as an Academic Tool," *Internet and Higher Education* 6, no. 1 (2003): 21.
33 Randall W. Marcinko, "Listservs: The Good News and the Bad News," *Searcher* 6, no. 10 (Nov./Dec. 1998): 34-39.
34 Thomas M. Steele, "Risk Management for Listserv Moderators and Operators," in *National Online Meeting Proceedings – 1996*, p. 368.
35 Ibid., p. 369.
36 Bibb Latané and Martin Bourgeois, "Experimental Evidence for Dynamic Social Impact: The Emergence of Subcultures in Electronic Groups," *Journal of Communication* 46, no. 4 (December 1996): 35-47.
37 Manju K. Ahuja and John E. Galvin, "Socialization in Virtual Groups," *Journal of Management* 29, no. 2 (2003): 165.
38 See, for example, Victoria S. Ekstrand, "Unmasking Jane and John Doe: Online Anonymity and the First Amendment," *Communication Law and Policy* 8, no. 4 (Fall 2003): 405-427.
39 See, for example, James E. Porter, "Legal and Ethical Issues in Cyberspace," in *Rhetorical Ethics and Internetworked Writing* (Greenwich, Conn.: Ablex Pub., 1998), pp. 101-131.

⁴⁰ Tharon Howard, "Who 'Owns' Electronic Texts?" In Patricia Sullivan & Jennie Dautermann (Eds.), *Electronic Literacies in the Workplace: Technologies of Writing* (Urbana, IL: NCTE and Computers and Composition), p. 179.
⁴¹ Ibid, p. 193.
⁴² See Pamela Samuelson, "Copyright's Fair Use Doctrine and Digital Data," *Communications of the ACM*, 37, no. 1 (1994): 21-27.
⁴³ Porter, "Legal and Ethical Issues in Cyberspace," p. 109.
⁴⁴ Ibid., p. 130.
⁴⁵ For short quotations like this, where I am merely characterizing the tone of the debate, I have not made specific citations. Where I have quoted more extensively, I have cited the specific message, assuming these to be published commentaries available for such references.
⁴⁶ Heather Crocetto posting, Wed, 14 Mar 2007 13:34:14 –0400.
⁴⁷ Christine Di Bella posting, Wed, 14 Mar 2007 11:35:48 –0400.
⁴⁸ Edward Sevcik posting, Wed, 14 Mar 2007 16:10:32 –0600.
⁴⁹ Fred Leutzenheiser posting, 15 Mar 2007 15:24:40 –0400.
⁵⁰ Richard J. Cox to the Forum for Archival Educators, March 22, 2007 2:33:32 AM EDT.
⁵¹ Ibid.
⁵² Patrick Cunningham posting, 14 Mar 2007 13:56:52 –0700.
⁵³ "The Archives and Archivists Listerv: Hoping for a Stay of Execution," *Spellbound Blog*, posted March 14, 2007, http://www.spellboundblog.com/2007/03/14/the-archives-and-archivists-listserv-hoping-for-a-stay-of-execution/.
⁵⁴ "Archivists Pitch 'Archives'," *Inherent Vice*, http://www.inherentvice.net/?p=75.
⁵⁵ "Ironic Appraisal," *booktruck.org: squeaky wheels in the information world*, March 14, 2007, http://booktruck.wordpress.com/2007/03/14/ironic-appraisal/.
⁵⁶ Mark Matienzo, "Throwing Out the Baby, the Bathwater, and the Bathtub: The Sad State of the Archives and Archivists Listserv," *thesecretmirror.com*, March 13, 2007. http://thesecretmirror.com/archives/saa-listserv.
⁵⁷ Rick Prelinger, "Society of American Archivist Decides to Nuke its Listserv Archives," *Prelinger Library Blog*, March 13, 2007, http://prelingerlibrary.blogspot.com/2007/03/society-of-american-archivists-decides.html.
⁵⁸ Stephen E. Novak posting, Wed, 14 Mar 2007 09:14:21 –0400.
⁵⁹ Vernon Rood posting, 15 Mar 2007 19:00:27 –0400.
⁶⁰ Matt Snyder posting, 15 Mar 2007 10:25:09 –0400.
⁶¹ Bob Shuster posting, 14 Mar 2007 11:04:39 –0500.
⁶² Rick Barry posting, 14 Mar 2007 12:34:02 EDT.
⁶³ Daniel Alonzo posting, Wed, 14 Mar 2007 16:05:31 –0500.
⁶⁴ James Cassedy posting, 18 Mar 2007 03:02:21 –0000.
⁶⁵ Ibid.
⁶⁶ Evelyn Khoo posting, 19 Mar 2007 21:49:07 –0400.
⁶⁷ Robert Presutti posting, on behalf of the University of Pittsburgh SAA Student Chapter, 21 Mar 2007 20:46:07 -0400.

⁶⁸ Elizabeth W. Asking posting, 16 Mar 2007 12:27:48 –0000.
⁶⁹ Nancy Beaumont, on behalf of Elizabeth Adkins, 21 Mar 2007 15:35:09 –0500.
⁷⁰ The quotations from Adkins's message and the appraisal report are from her posting, 30 Mar 2007 22:01:29 –0000.
⁷¹ Ibid.
⁷² Nancy Beaumont, "The Way Things Go," *Archival Outlook*, March/April 2007, pp. 4, 29.
⁷³ These can be found at http://www.archivists.org/governance/goalstatement.asp; accessed March 22, 2007.
⁷⁴ These can be found at http://www.archivists.org/governance/handbook/section1.asp, accessed March 22, 2007.
⁷⁵ See http://www.uwm.edu/Libraries/arch/findaids/uwmmss172/index.html, accessed March 22, 2007.
⁷⁶ This statement can be found at http://www.archivists.org/governance/handbook/app_i.asp, accessed March 22, 2007.
⁷⁷ Richard Pearce-Moses posting, 26 Mar 2007 06:08:10 -0700.
⁷⁸ Luke Eric Lassiter, *The Chicago Guide to Collaborative Ethnography* (Chicago: University of Chicago Press, 2005), p. 83.
⁷⁹ Sharon Howe posting, 15 Mar 2007 09:50:29 –0700.
⁸⁰ David B. Gracy, "Archivists, You Are What People Think You Keep," *American Archivist* 52 (Winter 1989): 78.

Notes on Chapter 9
The Anthony Clark Case, SAA, and Professional Ethics

¹ H. G. Jones, *The Records of A Nation: Their Management, Preservation, and Use* (New York: Atheneum, 1969).
² Donald R. McCoy, *The National Archives: America's Ministry of Documents 1934-1968* (Chapel Hill, University of North Carolina Press, 1978). My review was published as "Donald R. McCoy's National Archives and American Archival History," *Manuscripts* 31 (Fall 1979): 302-08.
³ David A. Wallace, "The Public's Use of Federal Record Keeping Statutes to Shape Federal Information Policy: A Study of the PROFS Case," Ph.D. dissertation, University of Pittsburgh, 1997.
⁴ Tom Brown, "Myth or Reality: Is There a Generation Gap Among Electronic Records Archivists?" *Archivaria* 49 (Spring 1990): 140–160; Linda J. Henry, 'Schellenberg in Cyberspace," *American Archivist* 61 (Fall. 1998): 309-327.
⁵ Richard J. Cox, "Archivists and the Use of Archival Records: Or, A View from the World of Documentary Editing," *Provenance* 9 (1991 [1992]): 89-110.
⁶ Richard J. Cox, "Messrs. Washington, Jefferson, and Gates: Quarreling about the Preservation of the Documentary Heritage of the United States," *First Monday* 2 (August 1997).

[7] Richard J. Cox, "Declarations, Independence, and Text in the Information Age," *First Monday* 4 (June 1999).

[8] Richard J. Cox, "America's Pyramids: Presidents and Their Libraries," *Government Information Quarterly* 19, no. 1 (2002): 45-75.

[9] Richard J. Cox, "Why the Archivist of the United States is Important to Records Professionals and America," *Records & Information Management Report* 20 (October 2004): 1-14.

[10] Richard J. Cox, "Empty Temples: Challenges for Modern Government Archives and Records Management," *Records & Information Management Report* 22 (October 2006): 1-13, included as chapter four, and, "Secrecy, Archives, and the Archivist: A Review Essay (Sort Of)," *American Archivist* 72 (Spring/Summer 2009): 213-230, included as chapter five.

[11] Richard J. Cox, "The National Archives Reclassification Scandal," *Records & Information Management Report* 22 (November 2006): 1-13, included here as chapter six.

[12] The full text of this letter is available at the SAA web site at http://www.archivists.org/statements/reclassification.asp.

[13] My primary efforts to deal with ethics and accountability issues, in addition to the present volume, are, with David Wallace, *Archives and the Public Good: Accountability and Records in Modern Society* (Westport, Conn.: Quorum Books, 2002); *Archives and Archivists in the Information Age* (New York: Neal-Schuman, 2005); and *Ethics, Accountability and Recordkeeping in a Dangerous World* (London: Facet, 2006).

[14] Susan Jacoby, *Alger Hiss and the Battle for History* (New Haven: Yale University Press, 2009), p. 29.

[15] Jacoby, *Alger Hiss*, p. 218.

[16] Jacoby, *Alger Hiss*, p. 221.

[17] James Traub, "The Academic Freedom Agenda," *New York Times Magazine*, March 15, 2009, p. 40.

[18] Traub, "The Academic Freedom Agenda," p. 42.

[19] Traub, "The Academic Freedom Agenda," p. 43.

[20] Leonard Benardo and Jennifer Weiss, *Citizen-in-Chief: The Second Lives of the American Presidents* (New York: William Morrow, 2009).

[21] Benardo and Weiss, *Citizen-in-Chief*, p. 72.

[22] See Peter Charles Hoffer (a former member of the AHA professional division), *Past Imperfect* (New York: Public Affairs, 2004) as one example.

[23] Such as the January 2002 issue of the *William and Mary Quarterly* reporting the results of a conference on charges of sloppy and deliberately inaccurate work by Michael Bellesiles regarding his book, *Arming America: The Origins of a National Gun Culture* (New York: Vintage, 2001).

[24] Randall Jimerson, *Archives Power: Memory, Accountability, and Social Justice* (Chicago: Society of American Archivists, 2009).

Notes on Chapter 10
Revisiting the Archival Finding Aid

[1] See, example, Christopher J. Prom, "The *EAD Cookbook*: A Survey and Usability Study," *American Archivist* 65 (Fall/Winter 2002): 257-275.

[2] Helen R. Tibbo, "Primarily History in America: How U.S. Historians Search for Primary Materials at the Dawn of the Digital Age," *American Archivist* 66 (Spring/Summer 2003): 10. Similarly, Elizabeth Yakel – in her "Thinking Inside and Outside the Boxes: Archival Reference Services at the Turn of the Century," *Archivaria* 49 (2000): 140-160 – suggests that archivists need to embrace knowledge management approaches enabling them to take advantage of the networked environment in order to empower archivists with their researchers in a way for generating new knowledge about their holdings and the retrieval of information and evidence from them.

[3] See, for example, Ian G. Anderson, "Are You Being Served? Historians and the Search for Primary Sources," *Archivaria* 58 (Fall 2004): 81-129.

[4] Wendy Duff and Penka Stoyanova, "Transforming the Crazy Quilt: Archival Displays from a Users' Point of View," *Archivaria* 45 (Spring 1998): 44-79.

[5] Wendy M. Duff and Catherine A. Johnson, "Where Is the List with All the Names? Information-Seeking Behavior of Genealogists," *American Archivist* 66 (Spring/Summer 2003): 79-95. Indeed, we have known this for a long time, as just the little amount of research about the implications of placing archival descriptions into library bibliographic databases suggests that archivists need to rethink their notion of what they knew about how researchers used archives; see Avra Michelson's "Description and Reference in the Age of Automation," *American Archivist* 50 (Spring 1987): 192-208.

[6] Wendy M. Duff and Catherine A. Johnson, "A Virtual Expression of Need: An Analysis of E-mail Reference Questions," *American Archivist* 64 (Spring/Summer 2001): 44.

[7] See, for example, Jennifer A. Marshall, "The Impact of EAD Adoption on Archival Programs: A Pilot Survey of Early Implementers," *Journal of Archival Organization* 1, no. 1 (2002): 35-55.

[8] See Victoria Lemieux, "RADical Surgery: A Case Study in Using RAD to Produce a Thematic Guide," *Archivaria* 39 (Spring 1995): 51-69, describing an effort to create a guide that works for genealogists.

[9] Elaine G. Toms and Wendy Duff, "'I spent 1 1/2 hours sifting through one large box. . . .': Diaries as Information Behavior of the Archives Users; Lessons Learned," *Journal of the American Society for Information Science and Technology* 53 (December 2002): 1232-1238.

[10] Elizabeth Yakel and Deborah A. Torres, "AI: Archival Intelligence and User Expertise," *American Archivist* 66 (Spring/Summer 2003): 51-78.

[11] Tibbo, "Primarily History in America," p. 28.

[12] Ibid., p. 29.
[13] Wendy M. Duff and Catherine A. Johnson, "Accidentally Found on Purpose: Information-Seeking Behavior of Historians in Archives," *Library Quarterly* 72, no. 4 (2002): 472.
[14] Michelle Light and Tom Hyry, "Colophons and Annotations: New Directions for the Finding Aid," *American Archivist* 65 (Fall/Winter 2002): 216.
[15] Ibid., p. 217.
[16] Ibid., p. 218.
[17] Helen R. Tibbo and Lokman I. Meho, "Finding Finding Aids on the World Wide Web," *American Archivist* 64 (Spring/Summer 2001): 61-77.
[18] Daniel V. Pitti, "Encoded Archival Description: The Development of an Encoding Standard for Archival Finding Aids," *American Archivist* 60 (Summer 1997): 268-283 (quotation, p. 272).
[19] Helen R. Tibbo, "Interviewing Techniques for Remote Reference: Electronic Versus Traditional Environments," *American Archivist* 58 (Summer 1995): 294-310 is an early assessment of such issues.
[20] Clay Redding, for example, has indicated that archivists in using EAD had become more focused on the presentational qualities than in standardizing content so that information interchange can be achieved. See his "Reengineering Finding Aids Revisited: Current Archival Descriptive Practice and Its Effect on EAD Implementation," *Journal of Archival Organization* 1, no. 3 (2002): 35-50.
[21] Lawrence Dowler, "The Role of Use in Defining Archival Practice and Principles: A Research Agenda for the Availability and Use of Records," *American Archivist* 51 (Winter and Spring 1988): 74-86.
[22] A variety of miscellaneous and quite divergent archival user studies began to appear by the early 1980s and early 1990s, such as Clark A. Elliott, "Citation Patterns and Documentation for the History of Science: Some Methodological Considerations," *American Archivist* 44 (Spring 1981): 131-142; Fredric Miller, "Use, Appraisal, and Research: A Case Study of Social History," *American Archivist* 49 (Fall 1986): 371-392; Paul Conway, "Research in Presidential Libraries: A User Survey," *Midwestern Archivist* 11, no. 1 (1986): 35-56; Jacqueline Goggin, "The Indirect Approach: A Study of Scholarly Users of Black and Women's Organizational Records in the Library of Congress Manuscript Division," *Midwestern Archivist* 11, no. 1 (1986): 57-67; Diane L. Beattie, "An Archival User Study: Researchers in the Field of Women's History," *Archivaria* 29 (Winter 1989-90): 33-50; and Barbara C. Orbach, "The View From the Researcher's Desk: Historians' Perceptions of Research and Repositories," *American Archivist* 54 (Winter 1991): 28- 43. Many of these studies played off from Paul Conway, "Facts and Frameworks: An Approach to Studying the Users of Archives," *American Archivist* 49 (Fall 1986): 393-407 and earlier or contemporary expressions of concern about a lack of understanding about archival users, such as Richard H. Lytle, "Intellectual Access to Archives: I. Provenance and Content Indexing Methods of Subject Retrieval," *American Archivist* 43 (Winter 1980): 64- 75 and "II.

Report of an Experiment Comparing Provenance and Content Indexing Methods of Subject Retrieval," *American Archivist* 43 (Spring 1980): 191-207; Mary Jo Pugh, "The Illusion of Omniscience: Subject Access and the Reference Archivist," *American Archivist* 45 (Winter 1982): 33-44; Elsie Y. Freeman, "In the Eye of the Beholder: Archives Administration from the User's Point of View," *American Archivist* 47 (Spring 1984): 111-123; William J. Maher, "The Use of User Studies," *Midwestern Archivist* 11, no. 1 (1986): 15-26; Roy C. Turnbaugh, "Archival Mission and User Studies," *Midwestern Archivist* 11, no. 1 (1986):27-33, a study focusing on the limitations of user studies for planning for programs, as well as the limitations of generating new finding aids to attract new researchers; Bruce W. Dearstyne, "What Is the *Use* of Archives? A Challenge for the Profession," *American Archivist* 50 (Winter 1987): 76-87; Richard J. Cox, "Archivists and the Use of Archival Records; Or, A View from the World of Documentary Editing," *Provenance* 9 (Spring/Fall 1991): 89-110; and Richard J. Cox, "Researching Archival Reference as an Information Function: Observations on Needs and Opportunities," *RQ* 31 (Spring 1992): 387-397.

[23] Goggin, "The Indirect Approach," p. 57.

[24] There has been a burst of new research on archival users generated by Wendy Duff, Helen Tibbo, and Beth Yakel who in their academic posts have made this an important part of their research agendas. The references in this essay include many to these three intrepid researchers. We are also seeing the published results of their students' work as well, such as Kristin E. Martin, "Analysis of Remote Reference Correspondence at a Large Academic Manuscripts Collection," *American Archivist* 64 (Spring/Summer 2001): 17-42.

[25] Dennis Meissner, "First Things First: Reengineering Finding Aids for Implementation of EAD," *American Archivist* 60 (Fall 1997): 375.

[26] Christopher J. Prom, "User Interactions with Electronic Finding Aids in a Controlled Setting," *American Archivist* 67 (Fall/Winter 2004): 234.

[27] Ibid., p. 263.

[28] Ibid., p. 265.

[29] See, for example, Elizabeth Yakel and Laura L. Bost, "Understanding Administrative Use and Users in University Archives," *American Archivist* 57 (Fall 1994): 596-615.

[30] William C. Binkley, "A Historian Looks at The National Union Catalog of Manuscript Collections," *American Archivist* 28 (July 1965): 407.

[31] See, for example, Robert P. Spindler and Richard Pearce-Moses, "Does AMC Mean 'Archives Made Confusing'? Patron Understanding of USMARC AMC Cataloguing Records," *American Archivist* 56 (Spring 1993): 330-347.

[32] Mary Jo Pugh, "The Illusion of Omniscience: Subject Access and the Reference Archivist," *American Archivist* 45 (Winter 1982): 42.

[33] David Bearman, "Archives and Manuscripts Control with Bibliographic Utilities: Challenges and Opportunities," *American Archivist* 52 (Winter 1989): 39.

[34] Elizabeth Yakel, "Listening to Users," *Archival Issues* 26, no. 2 (2002): 117.

35 Ibid., p. 118.
36 Ibid., p. 122.
37 See, for example, Elizabeth Diamond, "The Archivist as Forensic Scientist- Seeing Ourselves in a Different Way," *Archivaria* 38 (Fall 1994): 139-154. At one point, Diamond notes how archivists are often frustrated in "dealing with researchers who do not read the introduction to finding aids before they start to search. She suggests this is because they want "instant access and are frequently too impatient to realize that they also need the contextual background" (p. 143). While I certainly don't want to downplay the importance of contextual information for archival research, I do believe that the lack of use of finding aids may suggest other more profound problems with archivists and their assumptions about how researchers work or should work.
38 Ann Pederson, "Unlocking Hidden Treasures Through Description: Comments on Archival Voyages of Discovery," *Archivaria* 37 (Spring 1994): 51.
39 Steven C. Dubin, *Displays of Power: Controversy in the American Museum from the Enola Gay to Sensation!* (New York: New York University Press, 2001), p. 5.
40 Kevin Walsh, *The Representation of the Past: Museum and Heritage in the Post-modern World* (London: Routledge, 1992), pp. 31-33.
41 Chon A. Noriega, "On Museum Row: Aesthetics and the Politics of Exhibition," *Daedalus* 128 (Summer 1999): 64.
42 Paul Collins, *Sixpence House: Lost in a Town of Books* (New York: Bloomsbury, 2003), pp. 205-206.
43 Charles Merewether, "Traces of Loss," in Michael S. Roth with Claire Lyons and Charles Merewether, *Irresistible Decay: Ruins Reclaimed* (Los Angeles: Getty Research Institute for the History of Art and the Humanities, 1997), p. 25
44 Miguel Tamen, *Friends of Interpretable Objects* (Cambridge: Harvard University Press, 2001), p. 117.
45 Steven Conn, *Museums and American Intellectual Life, 1876-1926* (Chicago: University of Chicago Press, 1998), p. 5.
46 David R. Benjamin, *Public Culture in the Early Republic: Peale's Museum and Its Audience* (Washington, D.C.: Smithsonian Institution Press, 1995), p. 145.
47 Daniel J. Sherman and Irit Rogoff, eds., *Museum Culture: Histories, Discourses, Spectacles* (Minneapolis: University of Minnesota Press, 1994), p. x.
48 Ibid., p. xi.
49 Joshua C. Taylor, *Learning to Look: A Handbook for the Visual Arts*, 2nd ed. (Chicago: University of Chicago Press, 1981), p. 150.
50 Eilean Hooper-Greenwell, *Museums and the Shaping of Knowledge* (London: Routledge, 1992), p. 170.
51 Donald A. Norman, *Emotional Design: Why We Love (or Hate) Everyday Things* (New York: Basic Books, 2004), p. 101.
52 Ibid., p. 202.

[53] Steven Lubar, "Exhibiting Memories," in Amy Henderson and Adrienne L. Kaeppler, eds., *Exhibiting Dilemmas: Issues of Representation at the Smithsonian* (Washington, D.C.: Smithsonian Institution Press, 1999), p. 16.
[54] Matthew H. Edney, *Mapping an Empire: The Geographical Construction of British India, 1765-1843* (Chicago: University of Chicago Press, 1999), p. 39.
[55] Ibid., p. 41.
[56] Garry Wills, *Mr. Jefferson's University* (New York: National Geographic, 2002), p. 17.
[57] Wendell Berry, *Sex, Economy, Freedom, and Community: Eight Essays* (New York : Pantheon Books, 1993), p. 32.
[58] James Axtell, "What's Wrong – and Right – with American Higher Education?" *Virginia Quarterly Review* 79 (Spring 2003): 189-298 (quotation p. 203).
[59] David Hurst Thomas, *Skull Wars: Kennewick Man, Archaeology, and the Battle for Native American Identity* (New York : Basic Books, 2000), p. xxv.
[60] Richard Kurin, *Reflections of a Culture Broker: A View from the Smithsonian* (Washington, D.C. : Smithsonian Institution Press, 1997), p. 77.
[61] Ursula Franklin, *The Real World of Technology* (Toronto: House of Anansi Press, 1998), p. 123.
[62] Jacques Barzun, *House of Intellect* (New York: Harper Perennial Modern Classics, 2002), pp. 212, 213.
[63] Derek Bok, *Universities in the Marketplace: The Commercialism of Higher Education* (Princeton, N.J.: Princeton University Press, 2003), p. 6.
[64] Noam Chomsky, *Media Control: The Spectacular Achievements of Propaganda*, 2nd ed., org. pub. 1991 in *Open Media Collection: 9-11, Media Control, Acts of Aggression* (New York: Quality Paperback Book Club, 2003), p. 37.
[65] Elizabeth Yakel, "Listening to Users," *Archival Issues* 26, no. 2 (2002): 122.
[66] Jean-Stéphen Piché, "Doing What's Possible with What We've Got: Using the World Wide Web to Integrate Archival Functions," *American Archivist* 61 (Spring 1998): 120.
[67] This literature is growing so rapidly that it would be challenging to capture its nature in an explanatory footnote that is not longer than the text of this essay. However, one can get a sense of the nature of this scholarship by perusing Francis X. Blouin Jr. and William G. Rosenberg, eds. *Archives, Documentation, and Institutions of Social Memory: Essays from the Sawyer Seminar* (Ann Arbor: University of Michigan Press, 2006).
[68] Wendy Duff, Barbara Craig, and Joan Cherry, "Finding and Using Archival Resources: A Cross-Canada Survey of Historians Studying Canadian History," *Archivaria* 58 (Fall 2004): 54.
[69] Matthew Fuller, *Behind the Blip: Essays on the Culture of Software* (Brooklyn, New York: Autonomedia, 2003), p. 71.
[70] Luci Shaw in Jennifer Holberg, ed., *Shouts and Whispers: Twenty-one Writers Speak About Their Writing and Their Faith* (Grand Rapids, MI: William B. Eerdmans Pub. Co., 2006), p. 203.

[71] Ibid., p. 205.
[72] Michael Bywater, *Lost Worlds: What Have We Lost, & Where Did It Go?* (London: Granta Books, 2004), p. 3.

Notes on Chapter 11
Teaching Unpleasant Things

[1] Richard J. Cox, Elizabeth Yakel, David Wallace, Jeannette Bastian, and Jennifer Marshall, "Archival Education in North American Library and Information Science Schools," *Library Quarterly*, 71, no. 2 (2001): 141-194.
[2] Richard Pearce-Moses, *A Glossary of Archival and Records Terminology* (Chicago: Society of American Archivists, 2005), available online at http://www.archivists.org/glossary/.
[3] J. M. Banner, Jr. and H. C. Cannon, *The Elements of Teaching* (New Haven: Yale University Press, 1997), p.9.
[4] Jacques Barzun, *House of Intellect* (New York: Harper Perennial Modern Classics, 2002), p. 157.
[5] James J. O'Donnell, *Avatars of the Word: From Papyrus to Cyberspace* (Cambridge, MA: Harvard University Press, 1998), p. 156.
[6] Jane Tompkins, *A Life in School: What the Teacher Learned* (Cambridge, MA: Perseus Books, 1996), p. 206.
[7] Gerald Graf, *Beyond the Culture Wars: How Teaching the Conflicts Can Revitalize American Education* (New York: W.W. Norton and Co, 1992), p. 7.
[8] Derek Bok, *Our Underachieving Colleges: A Candid Look at How Students Learn and Why They Should Be Learning More* (Princeton: Princeton University Press, 2006), p. 24.
[9] L. J. Moore, *Restoring Order: The Ecole des Chartes and the Organization of Archives and Libraries in France, 1820-1870* (Duluth, MN: Litwin Books, LLC., 2008), p. 195.
[10] R. Khurana, *From Higher Aims to Hired Hands: The Social Transformation of American Business Schools and the Unfulfilled Promise of Management as a Profession* (Princeton: Princeton University Press, 2007) and David Labaree, *The Trouble with Ed Schools* (New Haven: Yale University Press, 2004).
[11] See, for example, A. Dillon and A. Norris. "Crying Wolf: An Examination and Reconsideration of the Perception of Crisis in LIS Education," *Journal of Education for Library and Information Science*, 46, no. 4 (2005): 280-298; M. Gorman, "What Ails Library Education? *The Journal of Academic Librarianship*, 30, no. 2 (2004): 99-101; and R. P. Holley. "The Ivory Tower as Preparation for the Trenches," *College and Research Libraries News* 64, no. 3 (2003): 172-175.
[12] David A. Wallace, "Survey of Archives and Records Management Graduate Students at Ten Universities in the United States and Canada," *American Archivist* 63, no 1 (2000): 284-300.

[13] Nicholson Baker, *Double Fold: Libraries and the Assault on Paper* (New York: Random House, 2001).
[14] Richard J. Cox, *Vandals in the Stacks? A Response to Nicholson Baker's Assault on Libraries* (Westport, Conn: Greenwood Press, 2002).
[15] Manuel Castells, *Communication Power* (New York: Oxford University Press, 2009), p. 5.
[16] Castells, *Communication Power*, p. 431.
[17] V. Salemi. "Relax: Find a Low-stress Job with High Potential," 2008, available at http://hotjobs.yahoo.com/career-articles-relax_find_a_low_stress_job_with_high_potential-516, accessed September 24, 2008.
[18] Richard J. Cox, "Advocacy in the Graduate Archives Curriculum: A North American Perspective. *Janus*, no. 1 (1997): 30-41.
[19] Richard J. Cox and David Wallace, eds., *Archives and the Public Good: Accountability and Records in Modern Society*. (Westport, Conn.: Quorum Books, 2002).
[20] Richard J. Cox, *Personal Archives and a New Archival Calling: Readings, Reflections and Ruminations*. (Duluth, Minnesota: Litwin Books, LLC, 2009).
[21] See, for example, my *Ethics, Accountability, and Recordkeeping in Troubled Times* (London: Facet, 2006).
[22] In the subsequent version of this course, a number of papers were prepared about ethical issues in archival practice and these were assembled into a special double issue of the *Journal of Information Ethics*, published in the Spring 2010 issue. The essays concerned archives and indigenous peoples, film preservation, professional and scholarly scandals, personal papers, and archival administration and policy.
[23] These are Jennifer A. Marshall, "Appraising for Accountability: A Comparative Case Study of Appraisal Documentation at the National Archives and Records Administration, the National Archives of Canada, and the National Archives of Australia," (PhD dissertation, University of Pittsburgh, 2006); DongHee Sinn, "Records and the Understanding of Violent Events: Archival Documentation, Historical Perception, and the No Gun Ri Massacre in the Korean War," (PhD dissertation, University of Pittsburgh, 2007); David A. Wallace, "The Public's Use of Federal Recordkeeping Statutes to Shape Federal Information Policy: A Study of the Profs Case," (PhD dissertation, University of Pittsburgh, 1997); and Tywanna Whorley, "The Tuskegee Syphilis Study: Access and Control over Controversial Records," (PhD dissertation, University of Pittsburgh, 2006).
[24] Rather than trying to provide a list of such literature, I refer readers to my blog, "Reading Archives," http://readingarchives.blogspot.com/) that I compiled for two and a half years (ending it in April 2009).
[25] H. M. Buss and M. Kadar, eds. *Working in Women's Archives: Researching Women's Private Literature and Archival Documents* (Waterloo, Ontario: Wilfrid Laurier University Press, 2001), p. 4.
[26] Ken Bain, *What the Best College Teachers Do* (Cambridge, MA: Harvard University Press, 2001).

Notes on Chapter 12
Arguing About Appraisal in the Age of Forgetfulness

[1] Wendell Berry, *Jayber Crow: A Novel* (New York: Counterpoint, 2000), p. 3.
[2] Ray Bradbury, *Zen in the Art of Writing* (Santa Barbara, Calif.: Joshua Odell Editions, 1996), p. 105.
[3] Cornelia Vismann, *Files: Law and Media Technology*, translated by Geoffrey Winthrop-Young (Stanford, CA: Stanford University Press, 2008), p. xii.
[4] Bill Wasik, *And Then There's This: How Stories Live and Die in Viral Culture* (New York: Viking, 2009), p. 11.
[5] Wallace Stegner, *Where the Bluebird Sings to the Lemonade Springs: Living and Writing in the West* (New York: Modern Library, 2002), pp. 72-73.
[6] *Planning for the Archival Profession* (Chicago: Society of American Archivists, 1986), p. 8.
[7] That could be reassuring for archivists, since, as Anne Whitehead tells us, "From the very outset, ... remembering is intimately bound to figures of writing and inscription." Anne Whitehead, *Memory* (London: Routledge, 2009), p. 14. She charts the present interest in memory rising from massive migrations, growth of interest in nostalgia, discourse about virtual memory, prosthetic memory, computer digital memory, popular memory, and the scholarly and other interests in ordinary people (p. 2).
[8] Rather than offer an extensive bibliographic essay here, I refer people to my *No Innocent Deposits: Forming Archives by Rethinking Appraisal* (Metuchen, N.J.: Scarecrow Press, 2004) for these and other citations.
[9] The first of these are worth citing -- Clark A. Elliot. *Understanding Progress as Process: Documentation of the History of Post-War Science and Technology in the United States*. Final Report of the Joint Committee on Archives of Science and Technology (Chicago IL: SAA, 1983) and Joan K. Haas, Helen Willa Samuels, and Barbara Trippel Simmons. *Appraising the Records of Modern Science and Technology: A Guide* (Cambridge, Massachusetts: Massachusetts Institute of Technology Press, 1985) – because they promised so much and stimulated so much re-thinking of appraisal; again, refer to my *No Innocent Deposits* for a fuller consideration of the seminal books.
[10] Jennifer A. Marshall, "Accounting for Disposition: A Comparative Case Study of Appraisal at the National Archives and Records Administration in the United States, Library and Archives Canada, and the National Archives of Australia," Ph.D. dissertation, University of Pittsburgh, 2007.
[11] This is the definition from the 1974 glossary, published as "A Basic Glossary for Archivists, Manuscript Curators, and Records Managers," compiled by Frank B. Evans, Donald F. Harrison, and Edwin A. Thompson. Edited by William L. Rofes, *American Archivist* 37 (July 1974): 415-433. This glossary draws mostly from the work of Schellenberg dating back a quarter-of-a-century before the publication of this glossary.

[12] *New York Times* editorial, April 19, 2006.

[13] I examined such issues in my *A Minor Nuisance Spread Across the Organization: Factors Leading to the Establishment and Support of Records and Information Management Programs* (Pittsburgh, PA: ARMA International Educational Foundation, October 2005).

[14] Poet Luci Shaw explains, "Every time we tell a story or write a poem or compose an essay we give chaos a way of re-integrating back into order; we reverse entropy; pattern and meaning begin to overcome randomness and decay." Luci Shaw in Jennifer Holberg, ed., *Shouts and Whispers: Twenty-one Writers Speak About Their Writing and Their Faith* (Grand Rapids, MI: William B. Eerdmans Pub. Co., 2006), p. 203.

[15] As bell hooks observes, "Now that I have witnessed the deep pain and grief that can be caused by loss of memory, through illness, dementia and Alzheimer's . . ., I can acknowledge the value of documentation for a future time. I know firsthand what a blessing it is to have a record – a way to remember that goes beyond the mind." bell hooks, *Belonging: A Culture of Place* (New York: Routledge, 2009), pp. 185-186.

[16] Marie Tyler-McGraw, "Southern Comfort Levels: Race, Heritage, Tourism, and the Civil War in Richmond," in James Oliver and Lois E. Horton, eds., *Slavery and Public History: The Tough Stuff of American Memory* (New York: The New Press, 2006), p. 166.

[17] William Hogeland, *Inventing American History* (Cambridge, MA: MIT Press, 2009), p. xiii.

[18] Margaret MacMillan, *Dangerous Games: The Uses and Abuses of History* (New York: Modern Library, 2009), p. 114.

[19] Kirk Savage, *Standing Soldiers, Kneeling Slaves: Race, War, and Monument in Nineteenth-Century America* (Princeton, NJ: Princeton University Press, 1997), p. 210.

[20] See, for example, Anne Gilliland and Kelvin White, "Perpetuating and Extending the Archival Paradigm: The Historical and Contemporary Roles of Professional Education and Pedagogy," *InterActions: UCLA Journal of Education and Information Studies* 5, Issue 1, Article 7 (2009), http://repositories.cdlib.org/gseis/interactions/vol5/iss1/art7

[21] Kitty Burns Florey, *Script and Scribble: The Rise and Fall of Handwriting* (Brooklyn, New York: Melville House Publishing, 2009), pp. 125, 128, 129.

[22] Sherry Turkle suggests that the emergence of digital objects "engage us in new and compelling ways," requiring us to develop new stories about our selves and society. Sherry Turkle, ed., *Evocative Objects: Things We Think With* (Cambridge: MIT, 2007), pp. 325, 326.

[23] Paolo Dilonardo and Anne Jump, eds., Susan Sontag, *At the Same Time: Essays and Speeches* (New York: Farrar Straus Giroux, 2007).

[24] Mary Lefkowitz, *History Lesson: A Race Odyssey* (New Haven: Yale University Press, 2008), pp. 2, 132.

[25] Elizabeth Buchanan in Tomas A. Lipinski, ed., *Libraries, Museums, and Archives: Legal Issues and Ethical Challenges in the New Information Era* (Lanham, Maryland: Scarecrow Press, 2002), p. 221.

[26] Priscilla B. Hayner, *Unspeakable Truths: Facing the Challenge of Truth Commissions* (New York: Routledge, 2002).

[27] We can gain a sense of this by reflecting on Douglas Blackmon's compelling argument that slavery in our nation did not end until 1945, not 1865 with the conclusion of the Civil War. While a reporter for the *Wall Street Journal*, Blackmon wondered, "What would be revealed if American corporations were examined through the same sharp lens of historical confrontation as the one then being trained on German corporations that relied on Jewish slave labor during World War II and the Swiss banks that robbed victims of the Holocaust of their fortunes?" (p. 3). At first he was stymied by a lack of records, then he discovered all sorts of documentary evidence, although African-American voices were often absent from the official records. He found a "great record of forced labor across the South," and the legacy of this record was not one of providing a soothing sense of the past: "Most profoundly," Blackmon concludes, "the evidence moldering in county courthouses and the National Archives compels us to confront this extinguished past, to recognize the terrible contours of the record, to teach our children the truth of the terror that pervaded much of American life, to celebrate its end, to lift any shame on those who could not evade it." (p. 402). Douglas A. Blackmon, *Slavery by Another Name: The Re-Enslavement of Black Americans from the Civil War to World War II* (New York: Anchor Books, 2009).

[28] Kristin Ann Hass, *Carried to the Wall: American Memory and the Vietnam Veterans Memorial* (Berkeley: University of California Press, 1998), p. 22.

[29] Here is the definition: "Personal information management (PIM) is the practice and study of the activities people perform to acquire, organize, maintain, and retrieve information for everyday use. PIM is a growing area of interest as we all strive for better use of our limited personal resources of time, money, and energy, as well as greater workplace efficiency and productivity. Good research on the topic is being done in several disciplines, including human-computer interaction, database management, information retrieval, and artificial intelligence." Used in a call for papers for the 2008 PIM Conference; Jacek Gwizdka posting on Asis-l, September 28, 2007 1:48:18 PM EDT.

[30] See, for example, Georges Didi-Huberman, *Images in Spite of All: Four Photographs from Auschwitz*, translated by Shane B. Lillis (Chicago: University of Chicago Press, 2008).

[31] Or as Michael Sandel puts it, "to ask whether a society is just is to ask how it distributes the things we prize. ... A just society distributes these goods in the right way; it gives each person his or her due." Michael J. Sandel, *Justice: What's the Right Thing to Do?* (New York: Farrar, Straus, and Giroux, 2009), p. 19.

[32] Antoinette Burton, *Dwelling in the Archive: Women Writing House, Home, and History in Late Colonial India* (New York: Oxford University Press, 2003), p. 139.

[33] Hundreds of suitcases left behind by the patients at Willard State Hospital in New York State and discovered after the hospital was shut down reveal remarkable things about mental health care, the lives of these patients, and our own society that are difficult to neatly categorize within a template of evidential, informational, and other values. Their stories mostly have been lost. Darby Penney and Peter Stastny, *The Lives They Left Behind: Suitcases from a State Hospital Attic* (New York: Bellevue Literary Press, 2008), p. 45. The hospital closed in 1995 and there was a discovery of 427 suitcases. The curators picked 10 patients, and the New York State Museum mounted an exhibit in 2004.

[34] D. N. Rodowick, *The Virtual Life of Film* (Cambridge, MA: Harvard University Press, 2007), p. 151.

[35] Rodowick, *The Virtual Life of Film*, p. 175.

[36] Howard S. Becker, *Telling About Society* (Chicago: University of Chicago Press, 2007), p. 69.

[37] Sue Myburgh, *The New Information Professional: How To Thrive in the Information Age Doing What You Love* (Oxford, England: Chandos Publishing, 2005).

[38] Carol E. B. Chosky, *Domesticating Information: Managing Documents Inside the Organization* (Lanham, MD: Scarecrow Press, 2006), p. 43.

[39] Terry Cook, "The Archive(s) Is a Foreign Country: Historians, Archivists, and the Changing Archival Landscape," *Canadian Historical Review* 90 (September 2009): 511-512.

[40] David A. Gerber, *Authors of Their Lives: The Personal Correspondence of British Immigrants to North America in the Nineteenth Century* (New York: New York University Press, 2006), pp. 5, 201.

[41] Barbara Reed in Sue McKemmish, Michael Piggott, Barbara Reed, and Frank Upward, eds., *Archives: Recordkeeping in Society*, Topics in Australasian Library and Information Studies, No. 24 (Wagga Wagga, New South Wales: Center for Information Studies, Charles Sturt University, 2005), p. 128.

[42] Carolyn Hamilton, Verne Harris, Jane Taylor, Michele Pickover, Graeme Reid, and Razia Saleh, eds., *Refiguring the Archive* (Dordrecht: Kluwer Academic Publishers, 2002).

[43] Marc Augé, *Non-Places: An Introduction to Supermodernity*, 2nd ed. (New York: Verso, 2008), p. 23. He explains his concern about time this way: "For a number of intellectuals, time today is no longer a principle of intelligibility. The idea of progress, which implied an afterwards explainable in terms of what had gone before, has run aground, so to speak, on the shoals of the twentieth century, following the departure of the hopes or allusion that had accompanied the ocean crossing of the nineteenth. To tell the truth, this reassessment refers to several observations that are distinct from one another: the atrocities of the world wars, totalitarianisms and genocidal policies, which (to say the very least) do not indicate much moral progress on the part of humanity, but did not succeed, along with the deviation or obliteration of the political systems officially based on some of them; in sum, a doubt as to whether history carries any meaning" (p. 20).

[44] Alex S. Jones, *Losing the News: The Future of the News That Feeds Democracy* (New York: Oxford University Press, 2009), p. 200.
[45] Randall C. Jimerson, *Archives Power: Memory, Accountability, and Social Justice* (Chicago: Society of American Archivists, 2009), pp. 189, 213.
[46] Jimerson, *Archives Power*, p. 297.
[47] Jimerson, *Archives Power*, p. 340.
[48] Jimerson leaves out crucial details about the Raisingate debate, namely that some archivists questioned as problematic the reproduction of a labor poster, accompanying an essay on political posters, as undermining the worth of corporate archives (this started the debate and led to my now infamous statement – one sentence in a five page letter – not some high-minded discussion about ethics in the corporate environment); see my "Archival Ethics: The Truth of the Matter," *Journal of the American Society for Information Science and Technology* 59, no. 7 (2008): 1128-1133, incorporated into chapter seven of this book.
[49] A recent issue of the *Wilson Quarterly* features three essays concerning the future of the book. Christine Rosen, "In the Beginning was the Word," *Wilson Quarterly* 33 (Autumn 2009): 48-53 thinks the printed book has life in it yet and worries that the manner in which we now interact with the written word is not to learn from others but rather to share our opinions. Tyler Cowen, "Three Tweets for the Web," pp. 54-58 reflects on the nature of our use of the Web, placing it in the longer view of how we normally react to new technologies and is optimistic about the new digital texts. Alex Wright, "The Battle of the Books," pp. 59-64 gives us a history lesson about the book and sees new and more useful forms of it growing from the Web and other digital delivery systems.
[50] Ron E. Hassner, *War on Sacred Grounds* (Ithaca: Cornell University Press, 2009) provides a good sense of this, writing, "Conflicts over sacred places are particularly difficult to resolve because sacred sites pose an indivisibility problem: they cannot be shared" (p. 3). Sacred sites often "are the largest and most massive structures erected by a community. Many temples, mosques, churches, and monasteries were designed to protect a community's most valuable treasures and relics" (p. 60).
[51] A recent study about the Allied soldiers' efforts to save art and artifacts in Italy in the Second World War indicated that some well-known archivists were involved (such as Hilary Jenkinson and Roger Ellis), but that these archivists often complained that the archival materials were given secondary importance. As the author points out, "In addition to vandalism and retaliation, the many humble ways in which people, often uneducated and illiterate, used paper – to wrap fish or cheese, for instance – made the written records of the country's history extremely vulnerable in wartime." Ilaria Dagnini Brey, *The Venus Fixers: The Remarkable Story of the Allied Soldiers Who Saved Italy's Art During World War II* (New York: Farrar, Straus and Giroux, 2009), p. 209.

Notes on the Conclusion

[1] Larry McMurtry, *Literary Life: A Second Memoir* (New York: Simon & Schuster, 2010), p. 157.

List of Works Cited

Adkins, Elizabeth W. "The Development of Business Archives in the United States: An Overview and Personal Perspective," *American Archivist* 60 (Winter 1997): 8-33.

Aho, James. *Confession and Bookkeeping: The Religious, Moral, and Rhetorical Roots of Modern Accounting* (Albany: State University of New York Press, 2005).

Ahuja, Manju K. and John E. Galvin. "Socialization in Virtual Groups," *Journal of Management* 29, no. 2 (2003): 161-185.

Alexander, Philip N. "Frank G. Burke on the Archives Listserv – A Response," *American Archivist* 57, no. 1 (Winter 1994): 4-6.

Allen, Anita L. *The New Ethics: A Guided Tour of the Twenty-first Century Moral Landscape* (New York: Miramax Books, 2004).

Allen, David S. *Democracy, Inc.: The Press and Law in the Corporate Rationalization of the Public Sphere* (Urbana: University of Illinois Press, 2005).

Anderson, Ian G. "Are You Being Served? Historians and the Search for Primary Sources," *Archivaria* 58 (Fall 2004): 81-129.

Anderson, Harold P. "Business Archives: A Corporate Asset," *American Archivist* 45 (Summer 1982): 264-266.

"Archivist Pushes to Widen Access to Nation's Records," *Federal Times*, April 16, 2006, interview with Allen Weinstein on April 14, 2006.

Augé, Marc. *Non-Places: An Introduction to Supermodernity*, 2nd ed. (New York: Verso, 2008).

Axtell, James. "What's Wrong – and Right – with American Higher Education?" *Virginia Quarterly Review* 79 (Spring 2003): 189-298.

Bain, Ken. *What the Best College Teachers Do* (Cambridge, MA: Harvard University Press, 2001).

Baker, Nicholson. *Double Fold: Libraries and the Assault on Paper* (New York: Random House, 2001).

Bakken, Douglas A. "Corporate Archives Today," *American Archivist* 45 (Summer 1982): 279-286.

Banner, James M., Jr., and Harold C. Cannon. *The Elements of Teaching* (New Haven: Yale University Press, 1997).

Banner, James M., Jr., and John R. Gillis, eds. *Becoming Historians* (Chicago: University of Chicago Press, 2009).

Barber, Benjamin R. *An Aristocracy of Everyone: The Politics of Education and the Failure of America* (New York: Ballantine Books, 1992).

Barr, Jean, Beth Chiaiese, and Lee R. Nemchek. *Records Management in the Legal Environment: A Handbook of Practice and Procedure* (Lenexa, KS: ARMA International, 2003).

Barzun, Jacques. *Begin Here: The Forgotten Conditions of Teaching and Learning* (Chicago: University of Chicago Press, 1992).

Barzun, Jacques. *House of Intellect* (New York: Harper Perennial Modern Classics, 2002).

Bass, Frank and Randy Herschaft. "Archives Ok'd Removing Records, Kept Quiet," Associated Press, April 12, 2006.

Bastian, Jeannette Allis. "A Question of Custody: The Colonial Archives of the United States Virgin Islands," *American Archivist* 64 (Spring/Summer 2001): 96-114.

Baynes-Cope, A. D. "Ethics and the Conservation of Archival Documents," *Journal of the Society of Archivists* 9 (October 1988): 185-87.

Bearman, David. "Archives and Manuscripts Control with Bibliographic Utilities: Challenges and Opportunities," *American Archivist* 52 (Winter 1989): 26-39.

Bearman, David. "The Implications of *Armstrong v. Executive of the President* for the Archival Management of Electronic Records," *American Archivist* 56 (Fall 1993): 674-689.

Beattie, Diane L. "An Archival User Study: Researchers in the Field of Women's History," *Archivaria* 29 (Winter 1989-90): 33-50.

Beaumont, Nancy. "The Way Things Go," *Archival Outlook*, March/April 2007, pp. 4, 29.

Becker, Howard S. *Telling About Society* (Chicago: University of Chicago Press, 2007).

Becker, Ronald L. "The Ethics of Providing Access," *Provenance* 11, nos. 1 & 2 (1993): 57-77.

Bedini, Silvio A. *Thomas Jefferson and His Copying Machines* (Charlottesville: University Press of Virginia, 1984).

Bellesiles, Michael. *Arming America: The Origins of a National Gun Culture* (New York: Vintage, 2001).

Benardo, Leonard and Jennifer Weiss. *Citizen-in-Chief: The Second Lives of the American Presidents* (New York: William Morrow, 2009).

Benedict, Karen. "Business Archives Literature," *American Archivist* 45 (Summer 1982): 312-314.

Benedict, Karen. "An Evolution in a Code of Ethics: The Society of American Archivists," paper presented at the International Congress on Archives, August 2004, and available at http://64.233.179.104/search?q=cache:tfthhBqK4U0J:www.ifai.org.mx/ica/presentaciones/21.pdf+archival+ethics+SAA+code&hl=en, accessed May 10, 2005.

Benjamin, David R. *Public Culture in the Early Republic: Peale's Museum and Its Audience* (Washington, D.C.: Smithsonian Institution Press, 1995).

Berge, Zane L. "Electronic Discussion Groups," *Communication Education* 43, no. 2 (April 1994): 102-111.

Berge, Zane L. and Mauri Collins. "The Founding and Managing of IPCT-L: A Listowners' Perspective," *Interpersonal Computing and Technology: An Electronic Journal for the 21st Century* 1 (April 1993), available at http://www.emoderators.com/papers/founding.html, accessed May 19, 2007.

Berge, Zane L. and Mauri P. Collins. "Perceptions of E-Moderators about Their Roles and Functions in Moderating Electronic Mailing Lists," *Distance Education* 21, no. 1 (2000): 81-100.

Berry, Wendell. *Sex, Economy, Freedom, and Community: Eight Essays* (New York: Pantheon Books, 1993).

Berry, Wendell. *Jayber Crow: A Novel* (New York: Counterpoint, 2000).

Binkley, William C. "A Historian Looks at The National Union Catalog of Manuscript Collections," *American Archivist* 28 (July 1965): 399-407.

Blackmon, Douglas A. *Slavery by Another Name: The Re-Enslavement of Black Americans from the Civil War to World War II* (New York: Anchor Books, 2009).

Blouin, Francis X., Jr. and William G. Rosenberg, eds. *Archives, Documentation, and Institutions of Social Memory: Essays from the Sawyer Seminar* (Ann Arbor: University of Michigan Press, 2006).

Bok, Derek. *Higher Learning* (Cambridge: Harvard University Press, 1986).

Bok, Derek. *Universities in the Marketplace: The Commercialism of Higher Education* (Princeton, N.J.: Princeton University Press, 2003).

Bok, Derek. *Our Underachieving Colleges: A Candid Look at How Students Learn and Why They Should Be Learning More* (Princeton: Princeton University Press, 2006).

Boles, Frank. "'Just a Bunch of Bigots': A Case Study in the Acquisition of Controversial Material, " *Archival Issues* 19, no. 1 (1994): 53-66.

Borei, Karin B. "The Rewards of Managing an Electronic Mailing List," *Library Trends* 47, no. 4 (Spring 1999): 686-698.

Boyd, Julian P. "'These Precious Monuments of . . . Our History,'" *American Archivist* 22 (April 1959): 147-180.

Bradbury, Ray. *Zen in the Art of Writing* (Santa Barbara, Calif.: Joshua Odell Editions, 1996).

Bradsher, James Gregory. "Researchers, Archivists, and the Access Challenge of the FBI Records in the National Archives," *Midwestern Archivist* 11, no. 2 (1986): 95-110.

Brey, Ilaria Dagnini. *The Venus Fixers: The Remarkable Story of the Allied Soldiers Who Saved Italy's Art During World War II* (New York: Farrar, Straus and Giroux, 2009).

Brown, Marvin T. *Corporate Integrity: Rethinking Organizational Ethics and Leadership* (New York: Cambridge University Press, 2005).

Brown, Matthew G. "The *First* Nixon Papers Controversy: Richard Nixon's 1969 Prepresidential Papers Tax Deduction," *Archival Issues* 26, no. 1 (2001): 9-26.

Brown, Michael F. *Who Owns Native Culture?* (Cambridge: Harvard University Press, 2003).

Bryce, Robert. *Pipe Dreams: Greed, Ego, and the Death of Enron* (New York: Public Affairs, 2002).

Bullock, Helen Duprey. "The Papers of Thomas Jefferson," *American Archivist* 4 (1941): 243-44.

Burke, Frank G. "Letting Sleeping Dogmas Lie," *American Archivist* 55 (Fall 1992): 530-537.

Burton, Antoinette. *Dwelling in the Archive: Women Writing House, Home, and History in Late Colonial India* (New York: Oxford University Press, 2003).

Buss, H. M. and M. Kadar, eds. *Working in Women's Archives: Researching Women's Private Literature and Archival Documents* (Waterloo, Ontario: Wilfrid Laurier University Press, 2001).

Bywater, Michael. *Lost Worlds: What Have We Lost, & Where Did It Go?* (London: Granta Books, 2004).

Cain, Virginia J. H. "The Ethics of Processing," *Provenance* 11, nos. 1 & 2 (1993): 39-55.

Carson, Cary. "Lost in the Fun House: A Commentary on Anthropologists' First Contact with History Museums," *Journal of American History* 81 (June 1994): 137-150.

Cappon, Lester J., Papers. College of William and Mary. Williamsburg, Virginia.

Cappon, Lester J., ed. *The Adams-Jefferson Letters: The Complete Correspondence between Thomas Jefferson and Abigail and John Adams*, 2 vols. (Chapel Hill, N.C: Published for the Institute of Early American History and Culture at Williamsburg, Va., by the University of North Carolina Press, 1959).

Carter, Jimmy. *Our Endangered Values: America's Moral Crisis* (New York: Simon and Schuster, 2005).

Castells, Manuel. *Communication Power* (New York: Oxford University Press, 2009).

Chang, Nancy and the Center for Constitutional Rights. *Silencing Political Dissent: How Post-September 11 Anti-Terrorism Measures Threaten Our Civil Liberties* (New York: Seven Stories Press, 2002).

Chomsky, Noam. *Open Media Collection: 9-11, Media Control, Acts of Aggression* (New York: Quality Paperback Book Club, 2003).

Chosky, Carol E. B. *Domesticating Information: Managing Documents Inside the Organization* (Lanham, MD: Scarecrow Press, 2006).

Clarke, Arthur C. *Childhood's End* (New York: Ballantine Books, 1990; org. published 1953).

Collins, Paul. *Sixpence House: Lost in a Town of Books* (New York: Bloomsbury, 2003).

Colonial Williamsburg. *A Guidebook for Williamsburg, Virginia* (Williamsburg, VA: Colonial Williamsburg, 1935).

Colonial Williamsburg. *Colonial Williamsburg Official Guidebook* (Williamsburg, VA: Colonial Williamsburg, 1964).

Colonial Williamsburg. *Official Guide to Colonial Williamsburg*, new ed. (Williamsburg, VA: Colonial Williamsburg Foundation, 1998).

Colonial Williamsburg Foundation Archives, Williamsburg, Virginia.

Conn, Steven. *Museums and American Intellectual Life, 1876-1926* (Chicago: University of Chicago Press, 1998).

Conway, Paul. "Facts and Frameworks: An Approach to Studying the Users of Archives," *American Archivist* 49 (Fall 1986): 393-407.

Conway, Paul. "Research in Presidential Libraries: A User Survey," *Midwestern Archivist* 11, no. 1 (1986): 35-56.

Cook, J. Frank. "'Private Papers' of Public Officials," *American Archivist* 38 (July 1975): 299-324.

Cook, Terry. "The Archive(s) Is a Foreign Country: Historians, Archivists, and the Changing Archival Landscape," *Canadian Historical Review* 90 (September 2009): 497-534.

Coulson, Jim. "Our Professional Responsibility," *Records Management Quarterly* 27 (April 1993): 20-25.

Cowen, Tyler. "Three Tweets for the Web," *Wilson Quarterly* 33 (Autumn 2009): 54-58.

Cox, Dwayne. "*Title Company v. County Recorder*: A Case Study in Open Records Litigation, 1874-1918," *American Archivist* 67 (Spring/Summer 2004): 46-57.

Cox, Dwayne. "The Rise of Confidentiality: State Courts on Access to Public Records During the Mid-Twentieth Century," *American Archivist* 68 (Fall/Winter 2005): 312-332.

Cox, Richard J. "A History of the Calvert Papers, MS. 174," *Maryland Historical Magazine* 68 (Fall 1973): 309-22.

Cox, Richard J. "Public Records in Colonial Maryland," *American Archivist* 37 (April 1974): 263-75.

Cox, Richard J. "The Historical Development of the Manuscripts Division of the Maryland Historical Society," *Maryland Historical Magazine* 69 (Winter 1974): 409-17.

Cox, Richard J. "Donald R. McCoy's National Archives and American Archival History," *Manuscripts* 31 (Fall 1979): 302-08.

Cox, Richard J. "Archivists and the Use of Archival Records: Or, A View from the World of Documentary Editing," *Provenance* 9 (1991 [1992]): 89-110.

Cox, Richard J. "Researching Archival Reference as an Information Function: Observations on Needs and Opportunities," *RQ* 31 (Spring 1992): 387-397.

Cox, Richard J. "Messrs. Washington, Jefferson, and Gates: Quarrelling about the Preservation of the Documentary Heritage of the United States," *First Monday* 2 (August 1997).

Cox, Richard J. "Advocacy in the Graduate Archives Curriculum: A North American Perspective. *Janu*s, no. 1 (1997): 30-41.

Cox, Richard J. "Declarations, Independence, and Text in the Information Age," *First Monday* 4 (June 1999).

Cox, Richard J. "America's Pyramids: Presidents and Their Libraries," *Government Information Quarterly* 19, no. 1 (2002): 45-75.

Cox, Richard J. *Vandals in the Stacks? A Response to Nicholson Baker's Assault on Libraries* (Westport, Conn: Greenwood Press, 2002).

Cox, Richard J. "Why the Archivist of the United States is Important to Records Professionals and America," *Records & Information Management Report* 20 (October 2004): 1-14.

Cox, Richard J. *No Innocent Deposits: Forming Archives By Rethinking Appraisal* (Lanham, Md.: Scarecrow Press, Inc., 2004).

Cox, Richard J. *Archives and Archivists in the Information Age* (New York: Neal-Schuman, 2005).

Cox, Richard J. *A Minor Nuisance Spread Across the Organization: Factors Leading to the Establishment and Support of Records and Information Management Programs* (Pittsburgh, PA: ARMA International Educational Foundation, October 2005).

Cox, Richard J. *Ethics, Accountability, and Recordkeeping in Troubled Times* (London: Facet, 2006).

Cox, Richard J. "The National Archives Reclassification Scandal," *Records & Information Management Report* 22 (November 2006): 1-13.

Cox, Richard J. "Two Sides of the Coin: Archivists and Records Managers Consider Electronic Mail; The Records Managers Speak," *Records & Information Management Report* 23 (May 2007): 1-14; "Two Sides of the Coin: Archivists and Records Managers Consider Electronic Mail; The Archivists Speak," *Records & Information Management Report* 23 (June 2007):1-14.

Cox, Richard J. "Secrecy, Archives, and the Archivist: A Review Essay (Sort Of)," *American Archivist* 72 (Spring/Summer 2009): 213-230.

Cox, Richard J. *Personal Archives and a New Archival Calling: Readings, Reflections and Ruminations*. (Duluth, Minnesota: Litwin Books, LLC, 2009).

Cox, Richard J. *The Demise of the Library School: Personal Reflections on Professional Education in the Modern Corporate University* (Duluth, MN: Library Juice, 2010).

Cox, Richard J., Elizabeth Yakel, David Wallace, Jeannette Bastian, and Jennifer Marshall. "Archival Education in North American Library and Information Science Schools," *Library Quarterly*, 71, no. 2 (2001): 141-194.

Cox, Richard J. and David A. Wallace, eds. *Archives and the Public Good: Accountability and Records in Modern Society* (Westport, Conn.: Quorum Books, 2002).

Craig, Bruce. "NARA Releases Redacted Version of 'Classified or Sensitive' Records Memo," *NCH Washington Update* 12 (April 14, 2006).

Csikszentmihalyi, Mihaly. *Good Business: Leadership, Flow, and the Making of Meaning* (New York: Viking, 2003).

Danielson, Elena S. "The Ethics of Access," *American Archivist* 52 (Winter 1989): 52-62.

Danielson, Elena S. "Ethics and Reference Services, in *Reference Services for Archives and Manuscripts*, ed. Laura B. Cohen (New York: Haworth Press, 1997).

Danielson, Elena S. "Privacy Rights and the Rights of Political Victims: Implications of the German Experience," *American Archivist* 67 (Fall/Winter 2004): 170-193.

Danner, Mark. *The Secret Way to War: The Downing Street Memo and the Iraq's Buried History* (New York: New York Review Books, 2006).

Dearstyne, Bruce W. "What Is the *Use* of Archives? A Challenge for the Profession," *American Archivist* 50 (Winter 1987): 76-87.

Dearstyne, Bruce W. "Records Management of the Future: Anticipate, Adapt, and Succeed," *Information Management Journal* 33 (October 1999): 4-6, 8, 10-12, 14, 16-18.

Dearstyne, Bruce W. "Education for the Future of the RIM Profession," *InforPro* 2 (March 2000): 22-24, 26.

Dearstyne, Bruce. "The Right Stuff," *InfoPro* 2 (December 2000): 46, 48-52.

Dearstyne, Bruce W. "Information Education in the 21st Century," *Information Management Journal* 36 (January/February 2002): 50, 52-54.

Denby, David. *American Sucker* (New York: Back Bay Books, Little, Brown, and Co., 2004).

Diamond, Elizabeth. "The Archivist as Forensic Scientist- Seeing Ourselves in a Different Way," *Archivaria* 38 (Fall 1994): 139-154.

Diamond, Sigmund. "Archival Adventure Along the Freedom of Information Trail: What Archival Records Reveal About the FBI and the Universities in the McCarthy Period," *Archival Issues* 12, no. 1 (1987): 29-41.

Didi-Huberman, Georges. *Images in Spite of All: Four Photographs from Auschwitz*, translated by Shane B. Lillis (Chicago: University of Chicago Press, 2008).

Dilevko, Juris. *The Politics of Professionalism: A Retro-Progressive Proposal for Librarianship* (Duluth, MN: Library Juice Press, 2009).

Dillon, A. and A. Norris. "Crying Wolf: An Examination and Reconsideration of the Perception of Crisis in LIS Education," *Journal of Education for Library and Information Science*, 46 , no. 4 (2005): 280-298.

Dingwall, Glenn. "Trusting Archivists: The Role of Archival Ethics in Establishing Public Faith," *American Archivist* (Spring/Summer): 2004: 11-30.

Dirks, John M. "Accountability, History, and Archives: Conflicting Priorities or Synthesized Strands?" *Archivaria* 57 (Summer 2004): 29-49.

Dority, G. Kim. *Rethinking Information Work: A Career Guide for Librarians and Other Information Professionals* (Westport, Conn.: Libraries Unlimited, 2006).

Dowler, Lawrence. "The Role of Use in Defining Archival Practice and Principles: A Research Agenda for the Availability and Use of Records," *American Archivist* 51 (Winter and Spring 1988): 74-86.

Doyle, Kate. "The Atrocity Files: Deciphering the Archives of Guatemala's Dirty War," *Harper's* 315 (December 2007): 52-62.

Dubin, Steven C. *Displays of Power: Controversy in the American Museum from the Enola Gay to Sensation!* (New York: New York University Press, 2001).

Duff, Wendy and Penka Stoyanova. "Transforming the Crazy Quilt: Archival Displays from a Users' Point of View," *Archivaria* 45 (Spring 1998): 44-79.

Duff, Wendy M. and Catherine A. Johnson. "A Virtual Expression of Need: An Analysis of E-mail Reference Questions," *American Archivist* 64 (Spring/Summer 2001): 43-60.

Duff, Wendy M. and Catherine A. Johnson. "Accidentally Found on Purpose: Information-Seeking Behavior of Historians in Archives," *Library Quarterly* 72, no. 4 (2002): 472-296.

Duff, Wendy M. and Catherine A. Johnson. "Where Is the List with All the Names? Information-Seeking Behavior of Genealogists," *American Archivist* 66 (Spring/Summer 2003): 79-95.

Duff, Wendy, Barbara Craig, and Joan Cherry. "Finding and Using Archival Resources: A Cross-Canada Survey of Historians Studying Canadian History," *Archivaria* 58 (Fall 2004): 51-80.

Dummett, Michael. *Truth and the Past* (New York: Columbia University Press, 2004).

Dychtwald, Ken, Tamara J. Erickson, and Robert Morison. *Workforce Crisis: How to Beat the Coming Shortage of Skills and Talent* (Boston: Harvard Business School Press, 2006).

Edgerly, Linda. "Business Archives Guidelines," *American Archivist* 45 (1982): 267-272.

Edney, Matthew H. *Mapping an Empire: The Geographical Construction of British India, 1765-1843* (Chicago: University of Chicago Press, 1999).

Eisenstadt, Stuart. *Imperfect Justice: Looted Assets, Slave Labor, and the Unfinished Business of World War II* (New York: Public Affairs, 2003).

Ekstrand, Victoria S. "Unmasking Jane and John Doe: Online Anonymity and the First Amendment," *Communication Law and Policy* 8, no. 4 (Fall 2003): 405-427.

Elliott, Clark A. "Citation Patterns and Documentation for the History of Science: Some Methodological Considerations," *American Archivist* 44 (Spring 1981): 131-142.

Elliott, Clark A. *Understanding Progress as Process: Documentation of the History of Post-War Science and Technology in the United States.* Final Report of the Joint Committee on Archives of Science and Technology (Chicago IL: SAA, 1983).

Elliott, A. Larry and Richard J. Schroth. *How Companies Lie: Why Enron is Just the Tip of the Iceberg* (New York: Crown Business, 2002).

Ellis, John M. *Literature Lost: Social Agendas and the Corruption of the Humanities* (New Haven: Yale University Press, 1997).

Ellwood, Marie. "The Discovery and Repatriation of the Lord Dalhousie Collection," *Archivaria* 24 (Summer 1987): 108-116.

Eppard, Philip B. "Judging a Book by Its Cover," *American Archivist* 67 (Fall/Winter 2004): 156-160.

Ericson, Timothy L. "Building Our Own 'Iron Curtain': The Emergence of Secrecy in American Government," *American Archivist* 68 (Spring/Summer 2005): 18-52.

Evans, Frank B., Donald F. Harrison, and Edwin A. Thompson. "A Basic Glossary for Archivists, Manuscript Curators, and Records Managers," *American Archivist* 37 (July 1974): 415-433.

Flaherty, Alice W. *The Midnight Disease: The Drive to Write, Writer's Block, and the Creative Brain* (Boston: Houghton Mifflin Co., 2004).

Fleckner, John A. "'Dear Mary Jane': Some Reflections on Being an Archivist," *American Archivist* 54 (Winter 1991): 8-13.

Florey, Kitty Burns. *Script and Scribble: The Rise and Fall of Handwriting* (Brooklyn, New York: Melville House Publishing, 2009).

Fogerty, James E. "Archival Brinkmanship: Downsizing, Outsourcing, and the Records of Corporate America," *American Archivist* 60 (Winter 1997): 44-55.

Franco, Barbara. "The Communication Conundrum: What Is the Message? Who Is Listening?" *Journal of American History* 81 (June 1994): 152-163.

Franklin, Ursula. *The Real World of Technology* (Toronto: House of Anansi Press, 1998).

Freeman, Elsie Y. "In the Eye of the Beholder: Archives Administration from the User's Point of View," *American Archivist* 47 (Spring 1984): 111-123.

Froehlich, Thomas J. "Ethical Considerations of Information Professionals," *Annual Review of Information Science and Technology*, 27, ed. Martha E. Williams (Medford, N.J.: Published for the American Society for Information Science, 1992), pp. 291-324.

Fuller, Matthew. *Behind the Blip: Essays on the Culture of Software* (Brooklyn, New York: Autonomedia, 2003).

Gable, Eric and Richard Handler. "The Authority of Documents at Some American History Museums," *Journal of American History* 81 (June 1994): 119-136.

Gardner, Deborah S. "Commentary II," *American Archivist* 45 (Summer 1982): 294-295.

Gardner, Howard. *Five Minds for the Future* (Boston: Harvard Business School Press, 2006).

LIST OF WORKS CITED

Gartrell, Ellen G. "Some Things We Have Learned…: Managing Advertising Archives for Business and Non-Business Users," *American Archivist* 60 (Winter 1997): 56-71.

Gerber, David A. *Authors of Their Lives: The Personal Correspondence of British Immigrants to North America in the Nineteenth Century* (New York: New York University Press, 2006).

Ghetu, Magia. "Two Professions, One Goal," *Information Journal* 38 (May/June 2004): 62-66.

Gill, Howard, Jr. "Preserving the Public Records: A Building to Withstand the 'Flames and Injuries of Time,'" *Colonial Williamsburg* 9 (Spring 1987): 16-18.

Gilliland, Anne and Kelvin White. "Perpetuating and Extending the Archival Paradigm: The Historical and Contemporary Roles of Professional Education and Pedagogy," *InterActions: UCLA Journal of Education and Information Studies* 5, Issue 1, Article 7 (2009).

Gilliland, Anne, Sue McKemmish, Kelvin White, Yang Lu, and Andrew Lau. "Pluralizing the Archival Paradigm: Can Archival Education in Pacific Rim Communities Address the Challenge?" *American Archivist* 71 (Spring/Summer 2008): 84-114.

Giroux, Henry A. and Susan Searls Giroux. *Take Back Higher Education: Race, Youth, and the Crisis of Democracy in the Post-Civil Rights Era* (New York: Palgrave Macmillan, 2004).

Goggin, Jacqueline. "The Indirect Approach: A Study of Scholarly Users of Black and Women's Organizational Records in the Library of Congress Manuscript Division," *Midwestern Archivist* 11, no. 1 (1986): 57-67.

Gorman, M. "What Ails Library Education? The Journal of Academic Librarianship, 30, no. 2 (2004): 99-101.

Gould, Eric. *The University in a Corporate Culture* (New Haven: Yale University Press, 2003).

Gracy, David B. "Archivists, You Are What People Think You Keep," *American Archivist* 52 (Winter 1989): 72-78.

Graff, Gerald. *Beyond the Culture Wars: How Teaching the Conflicts Can Revitalize American Education* (New York: W.W. Norton and Co, 1992).

Green, Edwin. "Multi-National, Multi-Archival: The Business Records of HSBC Group," *American Archivist* 60 (Winter 1997): 72-87.

Greenberg, David. *Presidential Doodles: Two Centuries of Scribbles, Scratches, Squiggles & Scrawls from the Oval Office* (New York: Basic Books, 2006).

Greenspan, Anders. *Creating Colonial Williamsburg* (Washington, D.C.: Smithsonian Institution Press, 2002).

Grier, David A. and Mary Campbell. "A Social History of Bitnet and Listserv, 1985-1991," *IEEE Annals of the History of Computing* 22, no. 1 (April-June 2000): 32-41.

Gup, Ted. *Nation of Secrets: The Threat to Democracy and the American Way of Life* (New York: Doubleday, 2007).

Haas, Joan K., Helen Willa Samuels, and Barbara Trippel Simmons. *Appraising the Records of Modern Science and Technology: A Guide* (Cambridge, Massachusetts: Massachusetts Institute of Technology Press, 1985).

Hackbart-Dean, Pam. "A Hint of Scandal: Problems in Acquiring the Papers of U.S. Senator Herman E. Talmadge – A Case Study," *Provenance* 13 (1995): 65-80.

Hamilton, Carolyn, Verne Harris, Jane Taylor, Michele Pickover, Graeme Reid, and Razia Saleh, eds. *Refiguring the Archive* (Dordrecht: Kluwer Academic Publishers, 2002).

Hamilton, J. G. De Roulhac. "Three Centuries of Southern Records, 1607-1907," *Journal of Southern History* 10 (February 1944): 3-36.

Harris, Verne. *Archives and Justice: A South African Perspective* (Chicago: Society of American Archivists, 2006).

Hass, Kristin Ann. *Carried to the Wall: American Memory and the Vietnam Veterans Memorial* (Berkeley: University of California Press, 1998).

Hassner, Ron E. *War on Sacred Grounds* (Ithaca: Cornell University Press, 2009).

Hayner, Priscilla B. *Unspeakable Truths: Facing the Challenge of Truth Commissions* (New York: Routledge, 2002).

Heffner, Loretta L. "Lawrence Berkeley Laboratory Records: Who Should Collect and Maintain Them?" *American Archivist* 59 (Winter 1996): 62-87.

Henderson, Amy and Adrienne L. Kaeppler, eds. *Exhibiting Dilemmas: Issues of Representation at the Smithsonian* (Washington, D.C.: Smithsonian Institution Press, 1999).

Herrada, Julie. "Letters to the Unabomber: A Case Study and Some Reflections," *Archival Issues* 28, no 1 (2003-04): 35-46.

Hill, Michael W. "Facing Up to Dilemmas: Conflicting Ethics and the Modern Information Professional," *Aslib Proceedings* 50 (April 1998): 71-78.

"History of LISTSERV," 1996, available at http://www.lsoft.com/products/listserv-history.asp, accessed May 10, 2007.

Hobbs, Stuart D. "Exhibiting Antimodernism: History, Memory, and the Aestheticized Past in Mid-Twentieth-Century America," *Public Historian* 23 (Summer 2001): 39-62.

Hoffer, Peter Charles. *Past Imperfect* (New York: Public Affairs, 2004).

Hoff-Wilson, Joan. "Access to Restricted Collections: The Responsibility of Professional Historical Organizations," *American Archivist* 46 (Fall 1983): 441-447.

Hogeland, William. *Inventing American History* (Cambridge: A Boston Review Book, MIT Press, 2009).

Holberg, Jennifer, ed. *Shouts and Whispers: Twenty-one Writers Speak About Their Writing and Their Faith* (Grand Rapids, MI: William B. Eerdmans Pub. Co,, 2006).

Holley, R. P. "The Ivory Tower as Preparation for the Trenches," *College and Research Libraries News* 64, no. 3 (2003): 172-175.

Hooks, bell. *Belonging: A Culture of Place* (New York: Routledge, 2009).

Hooper-Greenwell, Eilean. *Museums and the Shaping of Knowledge* (London: Routledge, 1992).

Howard, Tharon. "Who 'Owns' Electronic Texts?" In Patricia Sullivan & Jennie Dautermann (Eds.), *Electronic Literacies in the Workplace: Technologies of Writing* (Urbana, IL: NCTE and Computers and Composition),

Horn, David. "The Development of Ethics in Archival Practice," *American Archivist* 52 (Winter 1989): 64-71.

Hosmer, Charles B., Jr. *Preservation Comes of Age: From Williamsburg to the National Trust, 1926-1949* (Charlottesville, VA: Published for the Preservation Press, National Trust for Historic Preservation in the United States, by the University Press of Virginia, 1981).

Hufbauer, Benjamin. *Presidential Temples: How Memorials and Libraries Shape Public Memory* (Lawrence: University Press of Kansas, 2005).

Hyman, Avi. "Twenty Years of ListServ as an Academic Tool," *Internet and Higher Education* 6, no. 1 (2003): 17-24, 19. 29.

Isikoff, Michael. "Papers? I Don't See Any Papers," *Newsweek*, October 29, 2007, pp. 37-38.

Jacoby, Susan. *Alger Hiss and the Battle for History* (New Haven: Yale University Press, 2009).

Jeanneney, Jean-Noël. *Google and the Myth of Universal Knowledge*, translated by Teresa Lavender Fagan (Chicago: University of Chicago Press, 2006).

Jimerson, Randall. *Archives Power: Memory, Accountability, and Social Justice* (Chicago: Society of American Archivists, 2009).

Jones, Alex S. *Losing the News: The Future of the News That Feeds Democracy* (New York: Oxford University Press, 2009).

Jones, H. G. *The Records of A Nation: Their Management, Preservation, and Use* (New York: Atheneum, 1969).

Jones, H. G. "Presidential Libraries: Is There a Case for a National Presidential Library?" *American Archivist* 38 (July 1975): 325-328.

Kahn, Herman. "The Long-Range Implications for Historians and Archivists of the Charges Against the Franklin D. Roosevelt Library," *American Archivist* 34 (July 1971): 265-275.

Khurana, R. *From Higher Aims to Hired Hands: The Social Transformation of American Business Schools and the Unfulfilled Promise of Management as a Profession* (Princeton: Princeton University Press, 2007).

Kiss, Elizabeth and J. Peter Euben, eds. *Debating Moral Education: Rethinking the Role of the Modern University* (Durham: Duke University Press, 2010).

Klumpenhouwer, Richard. "The MAS and After: Transubstantiating Theory and Practice into an Archival Culture," *Archivaria* 39 (1995): 88-95.

Kopper, Philip. *Colonial Williamsburg*, 2nd rev. ed. (New York: Harry N. Abrahams, Inc., in association with the Colonial Williamsburg Foundation, 2001).

Kneebone, John T. "The Virginia Colonial Records Project," *Perspectives: American Historical Association Newsletter* 30, (September 1992): 15-16, 18, 20.

Krugler, John D. "Behind the Public Presentations: Research and Scholarship at Living History Museums of Early America," *William and Mary Quarterly*, 3rd series, 48 (July 1991): 347-386.

Knuth, Rebecca. *Libricide: The Regime-Sponsored Destruction of Books and Libraries in the Twentieth Century* (Westport, Conn.: Praeger, 2003).

Kurin, Richard. *Reflections of a Culture Broker: A View from the Smithsonian* (Washington, D.C.: Smithsonian Institution Press, 1997).

Labaree, David. *The Trouble with Ed Schools* (New Haven: Yale University Press, 2004).

Lamoree, Karen M. "Documenting the Difficult or Collecting the Controversial," *Archival Issues* 20, no. 2 (1995): 149-153.

Lanham, Richard A. *The Economics of Attention: Style and Substance in the Age of Information* (Chicago: University of Chicago Press, 2006).

Lassiter, Luke Eric. *The Chicago Guide to Collaborative Ethnography* (Chicago: University of Chicago Press, 2005).

Latané, Bibb and Martin Bourgeois. "Experimental Evidence for Dynamic Social Impact: The Emergence of Subcultures in Electronic Groups," *Journal of Communication* 46, no. 1 (December 1996): 35-47.

Lee, Christopher. "Archives Kept a Secrecy Secret: Agencies Removed Declassified Papers from Public Access," *Washington Post*, April 12, 2006, p. A6.

Lee, Christopher. "Some Archives Files Wrongly Kept Secret," *Washington Post*, April 27, 2006, A25.

Lefkowitz, Mary. *History Lesson: A Race Odyssey* (New Haven: Yale University Press, 2008).

Lemieux, Victoria. "RADical Surgery: A Case Study in Using RAD to Produce a Thematic Guide," *Archivaria* 39 (Spring 1995): 51-69.

Leone, Richard C. and Greg Anrig, Jr., eds. *The War on Our Freedoms: Civil Liberties in an Age of Terrorism* (New York: Public Affairs, 2003).

Lesser, Wendy. *The Amateur: An Independent Life of Letters* (New York: Vintage Books, 1999).

Light, Michelle and Tom Hyry. "Colophons and Annotations: New Directions for the Finding Aid," *American Archivist* 65 (Fall/Winter 2002): 216-230.

Lipinski, Tomas A., ed. *Libraries, Museums, and Archives: Legal Issues and Ethical Challenges in the New Information Era* (Lanham, Maryland: Scarecrow Press, 2002).

Lott, Eric. *The Disappearing Liberal Intellectual* (New York: Basic Books, 2006).

Lubet, Steven. "Document Destruction After Arthur Andersen: Is It Still Housekeeping or Is It a Crime?" *Journal of Appellate Practice and Process* 12 (Fall 2002): 323-329.

Lytle, Richard H. "Ethics of Information Management," *Records Management Quarterly* (October 1970): 5-8.

Lytle, Richard H. "Intellectual Access to Archives: I. Provenance and Content Indexing Methods of Subject Retrieval," *American Archivist* 43 (Winter 1980): 64- 75 and "II. Report of an Experiment Comparing Provenance and Content Indexing Methods of Subject Retrieval," *American Archivist* 43 (Spring 1980): 191-207.

McCoy, Donald R. *The National Archives: America's Ministry of Documents 1934-1968* (Chapel Hill, University of North Carolina Press, 1978).

McDonald, Leonard. "Ethical Dilemmas Facing an Archivist in the Business Environment: The Constraints on a Business Archivist," *Journal of the Society of Archivists* 10 (October 1989): 168-172.

McDowell, Duncan. "'Wonderful Things': History, Business, and Archives Look to the Future," *American Archivist* 56 (Spring 1993): 349-356.

McKemmish, Sue, Michael Piggott, Barbara Reed, and Frank Upward, eds. *Archives: Recordkeeping in Society*, Topics in Australasian Library and Information Studies, No. 24 (Wagga Wagga, New South Wales: Center for Information Studies, Charles Sturt University, 2005).

MacMillan, Margaret. *Dangerous Games: The Uses and Abuses of History* (New York: Modern Library, 2009).

McMurtry, Larry. *Literary Life: A Second Memoir* (New York: Simon & Schuster, 2010).

MacNeil, Heather. "Defining the Limits of Freedom of Inquiry: The Ethics of Disclosing Personal Information Held in Government Archives," *Archivaria* 32 (Summer 1991): 138-151.

Maher, William J. "The Use of User Studies," *Midwestern Archivist* 11, no. 1 (1986): 15-26.

Manarin, Louis H. "A building . . . for the preservation of the Public Records," *Virginia Cavalcade* 24 (Summer 1974): 22-31.

Marcinko, Randall W. "Listservs: The Good News and the Bad News," *Searcher* 6, no. 10 (Nov./Dec. 1998): 34-39.

Marshall, Jennifer A. "The Impact of EAD Adoption on Archival Programs: A Pilot Survey of Early Implementers," *Journal of Archival Organization* 1, no. 1 (2002): 35-55.

Marshall, Jennifer A. "Appraising for Accountability: A Comparative Case Study of Appraisal Documentation at the National Archives and Records Administration, the National Archives of Canada, and the National Archives of Australia." PhD dissertation, University of Pittsburgh, 2006.

Martin, Kristin E. "Analysis of Remote Reference Correspondence at a Large Academic Manuscripts Collection," *American Archivist* 64 (Spring/Summer 2001): 17-42.

Maxwell, John C., with Stephen R. Graves and Thomas G. Addington. *Life@Work: Marketplace Success for People of Faith* (Nashville: Nelson Business, 2005).

Meijer, Albert. "Anticipating Accountability Processes," *Archives and Manuscripts* 28 (May 2000): 53-63.

Meissner, Dennis. "First Things First: Reengineering Finding Aids for Implementation of EAD," *American Archivist* 60 (Fall 1997): 372-387.

Messina, Joseph P. and Daniel B. Trinkle. "Document Retention Policies After *Andersen*," *Boston Bar Journal* (September/October 2002) available at http://www.bostonbar.org/members/bbj/bbj0910_02/analysis_docretention.htm.

Miceli, Marcia P. and Janet P. Near. "Individual and Situational Correlates of Whistle-Blowing," *Personnel Psychology* 41 (Summer 1988): 267-281.

Michelson, Avra. "Description and Reference in the Age of Automation," *American Archivist* 50 (Spring 1987): 192-208.

Micklethwait, John and Adrian Woolridge. *The Company: A Short History of a Revolutionary Idea* (New York: Modern Library, 2003).

Milbank, Dana. "He Could Tell You, But Then He'd Have to Kill You," *Washington Post*, April 25, 2006, p. A2.

Miller, Fredric. "Use, Appraisal, and Research: A Case Study of Social History," *American Archivist* 49 (Fall 1986): 371-392.

Miller, Harold L. "Will Access Restrictions Hold Up in Court: The FBI's Attempt to Use the Braden Papers at the State Historical of Wisconsin," *American Archivist* 52 (Spring 1989): 180-190.

Miller, Stephen. *Conversation: A History of a Declining Art* (New Haven: Yale University Press, 2006).

Mitchell, Thornton W. "Another View of the West Case," *Georgia Archive* 9, no. 2 (Fall 1991): 19-30.

Montgomery, Bruce P. "Nixon's Legal Legacy: White House Papers and the Constitution," *American Archivist* 56 (Fall 1993): 586-613.

Montgomery, Bruce P. "Archiving Human Rights: The Records of Amnesty International, USA," *Archivaria* 39 (Spring 1995): 108-131.

Montgomery, Bruce P. *Subverting Open Government: White House Materials and Executive Branch Politics* (Lanham, MD: Scarecrow Press, Inc., 2006).

Montgomery, Bruce P. *The Bush-Cheney Administration's Assault on Open Government* (Westport, Connecticut: Praeger, 2008).

Mooney, Philip F. "Commentary I," *American Archivist* 45 (Summer 1982): 291-293.

Moore, L. J. *Restoring Order: The Ecole des Chartes and the Organization of Archives and Libraries in France, 1820-1870* (Duluth, MN: Litwin Books, LLC., 2008).

Muirhead, Russell. *Just Work* (Cambridge: Harvard University Press, 2004).

Myburgh, Sue. "Records Management and Archives: Finding Common Ground," *Information Management Journal* 39 (March/April 2005): 24-26, 28-29.

Myburgh, Sue. *The New Information Professional: How To Thrive in the Information Age Doing What You Love* (Oxford, England: Chandos Publishing, 2005).

NARA Information Security Oversight Office, *Withdrawal of Records from Public Access at the National Archives and Records Administration for Classification Purposes* (Washington, D.C.: National Archives and Records Administration, April 26, 2006).

Nelson Mandela Foundation, *A Prisoner in the Garden* (New York: Viking Studio, 2006).

Newman, Frank, Laura Courturier, and Jamie Scurry. *The Future of Higher Education: Rhetoric, Reality, and the Risks of the Market* (San Francisco, CA: Jossey-Bass, 2004).

Noriega, Chon A. "On Museum Row: Aesthetics and the Politics of Exhibition," *Daedalus* 128 (Summer 1999): 57-81.

Norman, Donald A. *Emotional Design: Why We Love (or Hate) Everyday Things* (New York: Basic Books, 2004).

Norris, Kathleen. *Acedia & Me: A Marriage, Monks, and a Writer's Life* (New York: Penguin, 2008).

O'Donnell, James J. *Avatars of the Word: From Papyrus to Cyberspace* (Cambridge, MA: Harvard University Press, 1998).

Oliver, James and Lois E. Horton, eds., *Slavery and Public History: The Tough Stuff of American Memory* (New York: The New Press, 2006).

Orbach, Barbara C. "The View From the Researcher's Desk: Historians' Perceptions of Research and Repositories," *American Archivist* 54 (Winter 1991): 28-43.

Pallitto, Robert M. and William G. Weaver. *Presidential Secrecy and the Law* (Baltimore: Johns Hopkins University Press, 2007).

Palmer, Parker J. *Let Your Life Speak: Listening for the Voice of Vocation* (San Francisco: Jossey-Bass, 2000).

Paul, Richard and Linda Elder. *The Miniature Guide to Understanding the Foundation of Ethical Reasoning* (Dillon Beach, CA: The Foundation for Critical Thinking, 2003).

Pearce-Moses, Richard. *A Glossary of Archival and Records Terminology* (Chicago: Society of American Archivists, 2005), available online at http://www.archivists.org/glossary/.

Pemberton, Anne E., J. Michael Pemberton, Jeanine M. Williamson, and John W. Lounsbury. "RIM Professionals: A Distinct Personality?" *Information Management Journal* 39 (September/October 2005): 54, 56-58, 60.

Pemberton, J. Michael. "Who Cares About Records Management? Social Relevance and Professional Standing," *Records Management Quarterly* 30 (October 1996): 52-57.

Pemberton, J. Michael. "Toward a Code of Ethics: Social Relevance and the Professionalization of Records Management," *Records Management Quarterly* 32 (October 1998): 51-56.

Penney, Darby and Peter Stastny. *The Lives They Left Behind: Suitcases from a State Hospital Attic* (New York: Bellevue Literary Press, 2008).

Petroski, Henry. *Success Through Failure: The Paradox of Design* (Princeton: Princeton University Press, 2006).

Phillips, John T. "Professional Certification: Does It Matter?" *Information Management Journal* 38 (November/December 2004): 64-67.

Piché, Jean-Stéphen. "Doing What's Possible with What We've Got: Using the World Wide Web to Integrate Archival Functions," *American Archivist* 61 (Spring 1998): 106-122.

Pitti, Daniel V. "Encoded Archival Description: The Development of an Encoding Standard for Archival Finding Aids," *American Archivist* 60 (Summer 1997): 268-283.

Polenberg, Richard. "The Roosevelt Library Case: A Review Article," *American Archivist* 34 (July 1971): 277-284.

Polkinghorne, John. *Belief in God in an Age of Science* (New Haven: Yale University Press, 1998).

Porter, James E. "Legal and Ethical Issues in Cyberspace," in *Rhetorical Ethics and Internetworked Writing* (Greenwich, Conn.: Ablex Pub., 1998), pp. 101-131.

Posner, Ernst. *American State Archives* (Chicago: University of Chicago Press, 1964).

Price, William S., Jr. "N.C. v. B.C. West, Jr.," *American Archivist* 41 (January 1978): 21-24.

Prior, Mary, Simon Rogerson, and Ben Fairweather. "The Ethical Attitudes of Information Systems Professionals: Outcomes of an Initial Survey," *Telematics and Informatics* 19 (2002): 21-36.

Proctor, Margaret, Michael Cook, and Caroline Williams, eds. *Political Pressure and the Archival Record* (Chicago: Society of American Archivists, 2005).

Prom, Christopher J. "The *EAD Cookbook*: A Survey and Usability Study," *American Archivist* 65 (Fall/Winter 2002): 257-275.

Prom, Christopher J. "User Interactions with Electronic Finding Aids in a Controlled Setting," *American Archivist* 67 (Fall/Winter 2004): 234-268.

Pugh, Mary Jo. "The Illusion of Omniscience: Subject Access and the Reference Archivist," *American Archivist* 45 (Winter 1982): 33-44.

"Putting the Cat Back in the Bag," *New York Times*, April 19, 2006.

Rabchuk, Gord. "Life After the Big Bang: Business Archives in an Era of Disorder," *American Archivist* 60 (Winter 1997): 34-43.

Raven, James, ed. *Lost Libraries: The Destruction of Great Book Collections Since Antiquity* (New York: Palgrave Macmillan, 2004).

Redding, Clay. "Reengineering Finding Aids Revisited: Current Archival Descriptive Practice and Its Effect on EAD Implementation," *Journal of Archival Organization* 1, no. 3 (2002): 35-50.

Reeves, David C. "What Enron/Andersen Taught Us About Records Retention," *Journal of Transportation Law, Logistics and Policy* 69 (Spring 2002): 327-344.

Reich, Robert B. *I'll Be Short: Essentials for a Decent Working Society* (Boston: Beacon Press, 2002).

Riley, Edward M. "The Virginia Colonial Records Project," *National Genealogical Society Quarterly* 51, no. 2 (1963): 81-89.

Roberts, Alasdair. *Blacked Out: Government Secrecy in the Information Age* (New York: Cambridge University Press, 2006).

Roberts, Alasdair. *The Collapse of Fortress Bush: The Crisis of Authority in American Government* (New York: New York University Press, 2008).

Rodowick, D. N. *The Virtual Life of Film* (Cambridge, MA: Harvard University Press, 2007).

Rose, Mike. *Why School? Reclaiming Education for All of Us* (New York: New Press, 2009).

Rosen, Christine. "In the Beginning was the Word," *Wilson Quarterly* 33 (Autumn 2009): 48-53.

Roth, Michael S. with Claire Lyons and Charles Merewether. *Irresistible Decay: Ruins Reclaimed* (Los Angeles: Getty Research Institute for the History of Art and the Humanities, 1997).

Rothbart, Davy. *Found: The Best Lost, Tossed, and Forgotten Items From Around the World* (New York: Simon and Schuster, 2004).

Ruggiero, Thomas E. "Electronic Mail and Listservs: Effective Journalistic Ethical Fora?," *Journal of Mass Media Ethics* 16, no. 4 (2001): 244-304.

Rybczynski, Witold. *The Perfect House: A Journey with the Renaissance Master Andrea Palladio* (New York: Scribner, 2002).

Salemi, V. (2008) "Relax: Find a Low-stress Job with High Potential," available at http://hotjobs.yahoo.com/career-articles-relax_find_a_low_stress_job_with_high_potential-516, accessed September 24, 2008.

Samuelson, Pamela. "Copyright's fair use doctrine and digital data," *Communications of the ACM*, 37, no. 1 (1994): 21-27.

Sandel, Michael. *Justice: What's the Right Thing to Do?* (New York: Farrar, Straus, and Giroux, 2009).

Savage, Kirk. *Standing Soldiers, Kneeling Slaves: Race, War, and Monument in Nineteenth-Century America* (Princeton, NJ: Princeton University Press, 1997).

Sayers, Dorothy L. *Letters to a Diminished Church: Passionate Arguments for the Relevance of Christian Doctrine* (N.P.: W Publishing Group, 2004).

Scarre, Chris and Geoffrey Scarre, eds. *The Ethics of Archaeology: Philosophical Perspectives on Archaeological Practice* (Cambridge: Cambridge University Press, 2006).

Sennett, Richard. *The Corrosion of Character: The Personal Consequences of Work in the New Capitalism* (New York: W.W. Norton and Co., 1998).

Sennett, Richard. *The Culture of the New Capitalism* (New Haven: Yale University Press, 2006).

Shane, Scott. "Increase in the Number of Documents Classified by the Government," *New York Times*, July 3, 2005.

Shane, Scott. "National Archives Pact Let C.I.A. Withdraw Public Documents," *New York Times*, April 18, 2006.

Shenk, Diana L. and Jackie R. Esposito. "Integrating Archival Management and the ARCHIVES Listserv in the Classroom: A Case Study," *American Archivist* 58, no. 1 (Winter 1995): 66-72.

Sherman, Daniel J. and Irit Rogoff, eds. *Museum Culture: Histories, Discourses, Spectacles* (Minneapolis: University of Minnesota Press, 1994).

Shipley, David and Will Schwalbe. *Send: The Essential Guide to Email for Office and Home* (New York: Alfred A. Knopf, 2007).

Sinn, DongHee. "Records and the Understanding of Violent Events: Archival Documentation, Historical Perception, and the No Gun Ri Massacre in the Korean War," PhD dissertation, University of Pittsburgh, 2007.

Smith, David R. "An Historical Look at Business Archives," *American Archivist* 45 (1982): 273-278.

Smith, George David. "Dusting Off the Cobwebs: Turning the Business Archives into a Managerial Tool," *American Archivist* 45 (1982): 287-290.

Smith, Martha Montague. "Information Ethics," *Annual Review of Information Science and Technology* 21, ed. Martha E. Williams (Medford, N.J.: Published for the American Society for Information Science by Information Today, 1997): 339-366.

Smythe, David. "Facing the Future: Preparing New Information Professionals," *Information Management Journal* 33 (April 1999): 44, 46-48.

Society of American Archivists Code of Ethics Task Force, "A Code of Ethics for Archivists," *American Archivist*, 43 (Summer 1980): 414-418.

Society of American Archivists. *Planning for the Archival Profession* (Chicago: Society of American Archivists, 1986).

Sontag, Susan; Paolo Dilonardo and Anne Jump, eds. *At the Same Time: Essays and Speeches* (New York: Farrar Straus Giroux, 2007).

Spindler, Robert P. and Richard Pearce-Moses. "Does AMC Mean 'Archives Made Confusing'? Patron Understanding of USMARC AMC Cataloguing Records," *American Archivist* 56 (Spring 1993): 330-347.

Steele, Thomas M. "Risk Management for Listserv Moderators and Operators," in *National Online Meeting Proceedings – 1996*.

Speer, Lisa K. "Mississippi's 'Spy Files': The State Sovereignty Commission Records Controversy, 1977-1999," *Provenance* 17 (1999): 101-117.

Stegner, Wallace. *Where the Bluebird Sings to the Lemonade Springs: Living and Writing in the West* (New York: Modern Library, 2002).

Steinwall, Susan D. "Appraisal and the FBI Files Case: For Whom Do Archivists Retain Records?" *American Archivist* 49 (Winter 1986): 52-63.

Stephens, David O. "Lies, Corruption, and Document Destruction," *Information Management Journal* 36 (September/October 2002): 23-26, 28, 30.

Sullivan, William M. *Work and Integrity: The Crisis and Promise of Professionalism in America*, 2nd ed. (San Francisco: Jossey-Bass, 2005).

Swartz, Nikki. "Six Months That Changed the Face of Information Management: It Was a One-Two Punch from Which the United States May Never Fully Recover," *Information Management Journal* 36 (July-August 2002): 18-23.

Tamen, Miguel. *Friends of Interpretable Objects* (Cambridge: Harvard University Press, 2001).

Taylor, Joshua C. *Learning to Look: A Handbook for the Visual Arts*, 2nd ed. (Chicago: University of Chicago Press, 1981).

Taylor, Mark Lewis. *Religion, Politics, and the Christian Right: Post- 9/11 Powers and American Empire* (Minneapolis: Fortress Press, 2005).

Te'eni, Dov and Andrew Schwarz. "Communication in the IS Community: A Call for Research and Design," *Communications of AIS* 2004, no. 13 (2004): 520-543.

LIST OF WORKS CITED

Terris, Daniel. *Ethics at Work: Creating Virtue in an American Corporation* (Waltham, MA: Brandeis University Press by University Press of New England, 2005).

Theoharis, Athan G. "The FBI and the FOIA: Problems of Access and Destruction," *Midwestern Archivist* 5, no. 2 (1981): 61-74.

Thomas, David Hurst. *Skull Wars: Kennewick man, Archaeology, and the Battle for Native American Identity* (New York : Basic Books, 2000).

Tibbo, Helen R. "Interviewing Techniques for Remote Reference: Electronic Versus Traditional Environments," *American Archivist* 58 (Summer 1995): 294-310.

Tibbo, Helen R. "Primarily History in America: How U.S. Historians Search for Primary Materials at the Dawn of the Digital Age," *American Archivist* 66 (Spring/Summer 2003): 9-50.

Tibbo, Helen R. and Lokman I. Meho. "Finding Finding Aids on the World Wide Web," *American Archivist* 64 (Spring/Summer 2001): 61-77.

Tillman, Bob. "Who's Afraid of Sarbanes-Oxley? Accountability Legislation Creates Additional Document Retention Requirements and Responsibilities for Records Managers," *Information Management Journal* 36 (November-December 2002): 16-20.

Toffler, Barbara Ley with Jennifer Reingold. *Final Accounting: Ambition, Greed, and the Fall of Arthur Andersen* (New York: Broadway Books, 2003).

Tompkins, Jane. *A Life in School: What the Teacher Learned* (Cambridge, MA: Perseus Books, 1996).

Toms, Elaine G. and Wendy Duff. "'I spent 1 1/2 hours sifting through one large box. . . .': Diaries as Information Behavior of the Archives Users; Lessons Learned," *Journal of the American Society for Information Science and Technology* 53 (December 2002): 1232-1238.

Traub, James. "The Academic Freedom Agenda," *New York Times Magazine*, March 15, 2009, pp. 40-43.

Tschabrun, Susan. "Off the Wall and Into a Drawer: Managing a Research Collection of Political Posters," *American Archivist* 66 (Fall/Winter 2003): 303-324.

Turkle, Sherry. ed. *Evocative Objects: Things We Think With* (Cambridge: MIT, 2007).

Turnbaugh, Roy C. "Archival Mission and User Studies," *Midwestern Archivist* 11, no. 1 (1986): 27-33.

Van Camp, Anne. "Access Policies for Corporate Archives," *American Archivist* 45 (Summer 1982): 296-298.

Van Dijck, José. "Composing the Self: Of Diaries and Lifelogs." *Fibreculture: Internet+Theory+culture+research* 3 (2004), available at http://journal.fibreculture.org/issue3/issue3_vandijck.html.

Vismann, Cornelia. *Files: Law and Media Technology*, translated by Geoffrey Winthrop-Young (Stanford, CA: Stanford University Press, 2008).

Vogel, David. *The Market for Virtue: The Potential and Limits of Corporate Social Responsibility* (Washington, D. C.: Brookings Institution Press, 2005).

Wallace, David A. "The Public's Use of Federal Record Keeping Statutes to Shape Federal Information Policy: A Study of the PROFS Case," Ph.D. dissertation, University of Pittsburgh, 1997.

Wallace, David A. "Survey of Archives and Records Management Graduate Students at Ten Universities in the United States and Canada," *American Archivist* 63, no 1 (2000):284-300.

Walsh, Kevin. *The Representation of the Past: Museum and Heritage in the Post-modern World* (London: Routledge, 1992).

Wasik, Bill. *And Then There's This: How Stories Live and Die in Viral Culture* (New York: Viking, 2009).

Webster, Berenika M. "Records Management: From Profession to Scholarly Discipline," *Information Management Journal* 33 (October 1999): 20, 22, 24-30.

Weigel, George. *The Cube and the Cathedral: Europe, America, and Politics Without God* (New York: Basic Books, 2005).

Wengert, Robert G. "Some Ethical Aspects of Being an Information Professional," *Library Trends* 49 (Winter 2001): 486-509.

Whitehead, Anne. *Memory* (London: Routledge, 2009).

Whorley, Tywanna. "The Tuskegee Syphilis Study: Access and Control over Controversial Records." PhD dissertation, University of Pittsburgh, 2006.

Whiffen, Marcus. *The Public Buildings of Williamsburg Colonial Capital of Virginia: An Architectural Library* (Williamsburg, VA: Colonial Williamsburg, 1958).

Widemuth, B.M., Lisa Crenshaw, William Jenniches, and J. Christine Harmes. "What's Everybody Talking About? Message Functions and Topics on Electronic Lists and Newsgroups in Information and Library Science," *Journal of Education for Library and Information Science* 38, no. 2 (Spring 1997): 137-156.

Wilkinson, Carol and Todd R. Pennington. "The USPE-L Listserv: A Forum for Reflective Discourse?," *Physical Educator* 59, no. 3 (Fall 2002): 158-169.

Wills, Garry. *Mr. Jefferson's University* (New York: National Geographic, 2002).

Wills, Garry. *Bomb Power: The Modern Presidency and the National Security State* (New York: Penguin Press, 2010).

Wilsted, Thomas. "Observations on the Ethics of Collecting Archives and Manuscripts," *Provenance* 11, nos. 1 and 2 (1993): 25-37.

Woodruff, Paul. *First Democracy: The Challenge of an Ancient Idea* (New York: Oxford University Press, 2005).

Wright, Alex. "The Battle of the Books," *Wilson Quarterly* 33 (Autumn 2009): 59-64.

Yakel, Elizabeth. "Listening to Users," *Archival Issues* 26, no. 2 (2002):

Yakel, Elizabeth. "Thinking Inside and Outside the Boxes: Archival Reference Services at the Turn of the Century," *Archivaria* 49 (2000): 140-160.

Yakel, Elizabeth and Laura L. Bost. "Understanding Administrative Use and Users in University Archives," *American Archivist* 57 (Fall 1994): 596-615.

Yakel, Elizabeth and Deborah A. Torres. "AI: Archival Intelligence and User Expertise," *American Archivist* 66 (Spring/Summer 2003): 51-78.

Yetter, George Humphrey. *Williamsburg Before and After: The Rebirth of Virginia's Colonial Capital* (Williamsburg, VA: Colonial Williamsburg Foundation, 1988).

Young, Jeffrey R. "National Archives Will Stop Letting Agencies Secretly Withdraw Documents," *Chronicle of Higher Education*, 19 April 2006, Volume 52, Issue 34, Page A44.

Young, Jeffrey R. "How the National Archives Struck a Secret Deal on Documents With the CIA," *Chronicle of Higher Education*, April 25, 2006, Volume 52, Issue 35, Page A43.

Young, Jeffrey R. "National Archives Audit Finds Many Reclassifications of Documents Were 'Inappropriate,'" *Chronicle of Higher Education*, April 27, 2006, Volume 52, Issue 35, Page A1.

Zinn, Howard. "Secrecy, Archives, and the Public Interest," *Midwestern Archivist* 2, no. 2 (1977): 14-26.

Index

9/11. *See* September 11th.

A

accountability in the archival field, 132
Adkins, Elizabeth, SAA president, 135, 173, 174, 175
Aid, Mathew, and National Security Archive, 69
American Archivist journal, 139, 140, 141, 251
American Archivist, cover of. *See* controversy, American Archivist cover.
American Association of State and Local History (AASLH), 56, 58
American Historical Association (AHA), 199
American Library Association (ALA),199, 200
Anthony, Clark,
  denial of access to NARA, 184
  SAA's role in case of, 185, 187, 190
appraisal methodology, 153, 172
appraisal of archives, xi, xii, 148-49, 153, 164, 165, 174, 180, 225, 251-52
  application of, 243
  effectiveness of, 245
  future of, 252
  literature on, 245-46
appraisal
  accountability in, 180
  ethics of, 251
  importance of, 244
  legal concerns, 174
  of digital documentation, 182
apprenticeship system, 16
  classroom as extension of, 231
archival advocacy, 228, 237-38
  literature on, 240-41
  teaching of, 239-40
  vs. archival outreach, 229. *See also* outreach advocacy.
archival description
  poetics of, 225-26
  loose practices in, 205
  standardizing of, 206, 218
archival ethics, 129-45
archival field
  dialogue with other professions, 268
  preconceptions of, 230, 231
  progress in, 259
archival functions, basic, 16
"archival intelligence," 207
archival profession
  anger about, 260
archival research
  Web-based, 209
archival studies
  programs in, 261
archival users
  studies on, 207, 212
archival, graduate education, 228, 229
Archives & Archivists Listserv
  background of, 150, 152, 156
Archives and Archivists listserv controversy, 147-50, 164
  resolution of, 167-68, 173
  responses to, 169-73, 181

Richard Cox response to, 167-68
  student response to, 173
Archives and Archivists listserv, and NARA reclassification controversy, 112, 113-14, 116
Archives and Archivists listserv
  appraisal of, 149, 164, 165, 167, 173
  appraisal report, 174, 175-78
  ownership of, 168
archives students
  use of listservs, 152-53, 154
archives,
  as monument, 248
  created by citizens, 239, 250, 252
  perceptions of, 12, 246
  value of, ix, 148, 213, 246, 249, 268
Archivist of the United States (AUS), x, 70, 85, 93, 111, 121, 126, 165, 184, 186, 188, 189, 191, 192, 194, 204
  Ferrario, David, 204
  Weinstein, Allen, 70, 104, 105
  Wilson, Don, 186
archivists
  accountability to society, 220
  identities of, 182
  mission of, 237, 240
  reality of being a, 237
  recruiting, 261
  role of in society, 6, 143, 265
  stereotypes of, 234, 265
  training of, xii, 16, 28, 227, 229, 259, 265, 269
  tribal, 269
  utility of, 1
  voice of, 267-68
ARMA International, 22, 23, 127, 130, 145, 264
Arthur Andersen scandal, 133

Association of Records Managers and Administrators (ARMA). *See* ARMA International.
AUS. *See* Archivist of the United States.

B
Bain, Ken
  on teaching in higher education, 241
Barry, Richard
  on appraisal decisions, 172
Barry, Rick
  response to NARA and reclassification case, 116
Barzun, Jacque, 27, 29, 222, 229
Bearman, David, 186, 212, 246
Beaumont, Nancy, Executive Director of SAA
  on listserv controversy, 147-49, 178
Bitnet Listserv, 157
Blair, Tony, Prime Minister, 68
Blanton, Thomas, National Security Archive executive director, 104
blogs, 5, 8, 21, 24, 152, 161, 162, 166, 169, 238, 256, 263, 266, 267, 269
  as archival work, 269
  "Derangement and Description," 260
  "Reading Archives," 183, 185
Bok, Derek, Harvard President, 19, 25, 222, 231
Boles, Frank, SAA President, 184, 190, 192, 193, 197-203, 245
Braden, Carl and Anne
  papers of, 90
Bullock, Helen, 47
Burke, Franke, SAA President,
  on Archives & Archivists listserv, 150-51
Bush, George H., President. *See* Bush-Wilson agreement.

INDEX 347

Bush, George W.,
  administration of, 68, 79, 88, 91, 94-96, 98, 99, 117, 120, 188, 195
  and presidential libraries, 69, 70, 77, 98, 124, 195-96
  Executive Orders of, 69, 79, 97, 98, 99
  former U.S. president, 91, 239
Bush-Wilson agreement, 97
business archives, xi, 130, 131, 135, 137

C

calling
  to archival field, vii, 5, 226
  changing nature of, 13
  importance of, 6
  information professionals, 5
  ocational, 3-16
Calvert Family papers, 60
Cappon, Lester J., 43, 60-65, 66, 150
Carson, Cary
  Director of Research, Secretary's Office, 44-45, 49-51
Castells, Manuel
  on power, 236-37
Central Intelligence Agency (CIA), 69, 103, 104, 118, 122, 123, 124, 125
  Memoranda of Understanding, 125-26
Cheney, Dick, 88, 91, 96
  and Energy Task Force documentation, 96, 98
Chomsky, Noam, 224
CIA. *See* Central Intelligence Agency (CIA).
Clark, Anthony, xi, 66
  case of, 183-85, 187, 189, 189-93, 194, 195
  interactions with author, 183-84
  lecture on presidential libraries, 183-84
  response to case, 194

Clark, William
  diaries of, 87
Clarke, Arthur, 66
Clinton, Bill, former U.S. President
  Executive Orders of, 70, 122, 124
Clinton, Hilary
  book on, 90
Code of Ethics, SAA, 184, 190, 191-92, 193
collecting, reasons for, 251-52
Colonial Williamsburg,
  archives of, 43, 48, 49, 60
  archivists of, 47
  place, vii, 38-66
Colonial Williamsburg Educational Administrators Group, 45
Colonial Williamsburg Foundation, 49, 59
conferences, 22-24, 101, 153, 159, 166, 199, 202, 263
  as continuing education, 23-24, 29
continuing education, viii, 23-24, 265
controversy
  American Archivist cover, x, 138-39, 140, 142, 202, 251
  American Archivist cover, response to, 138, 139, 142, 251
  NARA reclassification, 103-28
  responding to, 248, 267-68
conversation
  technology and, 2
Cook, Frank
  on ownership of personal papers, 101
corporate archives
  and ethics, 133-38
  literature on, 131
  mission of, 139-40
corporate archivist
  profession, x, 131, 135-37, 141, 145, 251
  role of, 137, 143

corporate ethics, 134-37
corporate university model, vii, 230, 231
corporate university, and archival advocacy, 229
Cox, Richard
    blog of, 183, 185
    college years of, 56-57
    early professional life, 185, 206
    letters to SAA concerning Anthony Clark, 184, 190-94
    master's thesis, 60
    reaction to NARA reclassification controversy, 104
    response to Archives and Archivists listserv controversy, 167-68
    SAA council, 186, 189
    wife of (Lynn), 58-59, 60, 66
Craig, Bruce
    on reclassification of government records, 104
Csikszentmihalyi, Mihaly, 14, 18
CSR (corporate social responsibility). *See* corporate ethics.
CW. *See* Colonial Williamsburg.

D
Danner, Mark
    on secrecy and war, 68
Dearstyne, Bruce
    on vocation, 18, 28
"Derangement and Description," 260
destruction of records, 142, 246
diaries and journals
    10, 58, 62, 65, 168, 234, 245,
    digital, 25, 234
digital curators, 236
digital documentation
    and appraisal, 182
Digital Era, 2, 90, 96, 241
    archival issues in, 238
    role of archives in, 269-70

skills for, 106, 180
digital materials
    appraisal of, 149
digitization, and leaking of information, 95
Director of Research, Secretary's Office, 44-45, 49-51
Dirks, John
    on archivist and government, 100-01
disciplines
    other, relating to archives, 9
discussion groups, 158
documents, federal
    classifying of, 68
    declassifying of, 70, 103. *See also* Executive Order 12958.
doodles, presidential, 156-57
Dowler, Lawrence
    on finding aids, 209
Doyle, Kate
    on Guatemalan National Police archives, 99-100
Drexel University, 260
Duke of Gloucester Street, 38, 39, 55, 57, 65

E
Ecole des Chartes, 232
education
    as entry point, 17
    ease of, 2
    graduate programs, 260, 264-65
    professional, 229
    of archivists, 186, 228
electronic information systems, 7, 25, 147, 149
e-mail, 24
employee satisfaction, 4
employment, first place of, 16
Encoded Archival Description (EAD), 206, 207, 209, 210
engagement, 8

INDEX 349

Enola Gay exhibition, defenses of, 221
Enron scandal, 133, 134
Ericson, Tim, SAA President, 87-88

ethics, x-xi, 3, 105, 118, 129
  and the archival field, 132, 143
  archival, 129-145
  corporate, 135
  in professional schools, xv, 228
  in records management, 8
  in the workplace, 132-3
Ethics and Professional Conduct Committee of SAA, 189
ethics codes
  archival, 130, 145
  archival, background of, 130-32
  ARMA, 130, 145
  use of, 131
  ethics code, SAA, 130
etiquette
  in online professional resources, 152
executive orders, 69, 70, 79, 91, 97, 98, 99, 121, 122, 124
  Executive Order 12958, 70, 122, 124
  Executive Order 13233, 69, 79, 92, 97, 99
  Executive Order 13292, 98

F
FBI, secrecy of, 88
feminist, approaches to archives, 241
Ferrario, David, SAA President, 204
finding aids
  as artifact of design, 218
  as artistic venture, 217
  analyzation of, 210
  and contextual information, 208
  and relation to museum exhibitions, 213-14
  as form of accountability, 211, 219-23
  as source of studies, 211, 212, 215-16, 218-19
  digitization of, 210
  evaluation of, 211, 213-17
  language used in, 207, 215
  online, 206, 208, 210
  online, studies on, 210
  preparation of, 215, 216
  reading of, 217
fire
  records destroyed by, 44, 47, 53
  threat of, 39
Flaherty, Alice W.,14
flash mobs, 244
Fleckner, John A., SAA President
  letters to Mary Jane, 26-27
FOIA. *See* Freedom of Information Act (FOIA).
Franco, Barbara, on Museum exhibitions, 50-51
free speech in cyberspace, 163
Freedom of Information Act (FOIA), 78, 88, 89, 90, 91, 93, 98, 103, 108, 125, 193, 194, 201
Freud, Sigmund
  on ruins, 215
  papers of, 119

G
Gable, Eric, and Richard Handler
  on history museums, 49-50, 52
Gardner, Deborah
  on corporate archives, 137
Gardner, Howard
  on discipline, 15
George W. Bush Presidential Library and Museum. *See* Bush, George W., and presidential libraries.
Goldman, Rebecca, 260
Goodwin, Mary R. M.
  on Secretary's Office building, 43

Gottlieb, Peter, SAA president, 263

Gould, Eric
  on modern universities, 26
government documents,
  disappearance of, 120
government secrecy
  90, 103
  and national security, 91
  books on, 88
government
  accountability of, 112, 195
government, threats to archival practices, 67
Gracy, David
  on archivist identity, 182
graduate programs in archival studies, 228
Greene, Mark
  and Archives and Archivists listserv, controversy of, 164, 172, 173
Guatemalan National Police Files, 99-100
Gup, Ted
  on secrecy in governments documents, 92-94

H
Hackeman, David A., 77
Harvard University
  president of, Derek Bok, 25
  restrictions on official records, 94

higher education, corporate nature of, 228
Hirtle, Peter, SAA President, 116, 117, 118, 119, 121
Hiss, Alger, case of, 194-95
historians
  academically trained, 64
  as researchers, 205, 208, 218
historic preservation movement, American, 40
historical societies
  Maryland Historical Society, 60
  Minnesota Historical Society, 51
history museums, 49, 50, 51
history
  destruction of, 104
  distortion of, 248
  public, 62, 64, 235
Hobbs, Stuart
  on history museums, 51
Hogeland, William, 64, 248
Hosmer, Charles
  on historic preservation movement, 41
Hufbauer, Benjamin
  on presidential libraries, 71

I
indigenous peoples
  archives of, 239, 269
Information Age, x, 2, 237, 259
information organization
  holistic approach to, 263
information professionals
  value of, 6
Information Schools, 232
Information Security Oversight Office (ISOO), 70, 92, 108, 110, 124
information technologies, 17
information
  overload of, 2
Intellectual property, 34, 99, 136, 139, 148, 162, 176, 228
interdisciplinary studies, 20, 235
Internet
  as archival symbol, 244

J
Jack Anderson papers, 117
Jacoby, Susan
  on Alger Hiss, 194-95
Jamestown, Virginia, 55
Jefferson, Thomas
  archival efforts of, 47, 65
Jennings, John Melville

INDEX

on Secretary's Office, 48
John Prentis House, 65

K
Kean, Thomas H.
  on terrorism, 69
Kennewick Man, 220-21
Kissinger, Henry, 96-97
knowledge
  creation of, 219
  control of, 1
Krugler, John
  on research, 48
  on controversial museums exhibits, 221
Kursten, Maarja
  on NARA reclassification controversy, 106-08, 118, 119
  on Richard Nixon records, 106
Kurtz, Michael, Deputy Archivist at National Archives, 103, 108

L
Lassiter, Luke Eric
  on ethics, 180-81
Library of Congress
  and Sigmund Freud papers, 119
Library of Congress Manuscripts Department, 94
library
  as personal shrine, 196
listserv
  challenges of, 160-64
  definition of, 155-56
  nature of, 151-52
  challenges of, 160-64
  use in the library and information science field, 152-54
  use in professional fields, 153
  use value of, 158-59, 165
  technology, history of, 157-58
listserv archives controversy. *See* Archives and Archivists listserv controversy.

LISTSERV software, 157
literature
  of information professionals, 9
  on corporate archives, 131, 137
Lytle, Richard
  call for ARMA ethics code revision, 130-31
Manarin, Louis, 65
Mandela, Nelson, 9, 81-84
MARC-based records, 206, 208, 212

Maryland Historical Society, 60
Meissner, Dennis
  on digitizing finding aids, 210
Memoranda of Understanding
  NARA and, 107, 109, 110, 112, 113, 117, 118, 121, 123, 126
memory
  archival, 39, 258
  as archival impulse, 244
  public, 39
mentoring, 21-23
Merewether, Christopher
  on Freud and ruins, 215
Miami University of Ohio, 148, 174, 175, 177
Miller, Harold, 90
Minnesota Historical Society, 51
mission
  archival, vii, x, xii, 38, 81, 97, 104, 130, 187, 188, 194-96, 220, 228, 231, 237, 238, 241, 249, 252, 255, 257, 262-63, 267, 269
  personal, 14
Mississippi State Sovereignty Commission, 89
Montgomery, Bruce
  on "Bush-Cheney" administration, 88, 96-99
Muirhead, Russell
  on vocation, 15
museum
  classification, 217

enterprise, of Charles Wilson Peale, 216
exhibits, 75, 211, 212, 217
exhibitions, and relation to finding aids, 213-14
funding from the public, 214
relating to archives, 213-14, 216, 235
role of, 216
studies, 50, 51, 72, 213-214, 216

N

NARA (National Archives and Records Administration)
history of, 197
leadership of, 185, 186, 189
role in government secrecy, 104, 106
training for classification system, 126, 186
unethical behavior of, 184
NARA reclassification controversy, 103-28
Allen Weinstein reaction to, 108-10, 113
audit report of, 124-25
reactions to, 104
Richard Cox's response to, 104
SAA response to, 104, 106, 118
Nation of Secrets, 91-92
National Archives
funding of, 187
mismanagement of, 186
need for an independent, 185
secret agreements, 103
strengthening of, 102, 108, 118
See also NARA.
National Coalition for History, 104, 115, 117
National Historical Publications and Records Commission, 187
National Security Archive (NSA), 88, 102, 104, 107

Freedom of Information Act, request of, 103
press release of, 105
reclassification program, 69
executive director of, 104
National Union Catalog of Manuscript Collections, criticism of, 211
Native American Archives Protocol, 258, 269
Nazis
destruction of records, 251
stealing artifacts, 253
networking
informal, 23-25
of archival community, 260
professional, 179
technologies, 176
See also social networking.
Nixon records
Bruce Montgomery on, 96-99
Maarja Kursten on, 106
Nixon, Richard, 120
White House materials of, 96-98, 101, 106-07, 127
Norman, Donald
on design and systems, 218
Norriega, Chon A.
on funding museums, 214
Norris, Kathleen
on writing, 66

O

Obama, Barack
administration of, 184, 189
occupation, multiple changes of, 4
Office of Presidential Libraries, xi, 183, 184, 189, 190, 191, 192, 194, 258
organizations, market driven, 17
outreach, archival, 228

INDEX   353

P
Pallitto, Robert M., and William G. Weaver, 88, 91-92
past, unpleasantness of, 250
Patriot Act, 92, 169
Peale, Charles Wilson
    and museums, 216
Pearce-Moses, Richard, SAA President
    and NARA, 105, 112, 189
    on *American Archivist* cover controversy, 142
    on Archives and Archivists listserv controversy, 180
personal archives, 239
Pew Freedom Trust Fund, 43
Philip Morris
    and use of Bill of Rights, 186
Plato
    on property, 33
political posters, 138
Posner, Ernest, on government archives, 40
poster collections, administration of, 138, 202
postmodernist
    approaches to archives, 208, 241, 249-50, 255
practical training vs. theory, 228
preservation
    and reactions to Nicholson Baker's *Double Fold*, 235
presidential doodles, 156-57
presidential libraries, 70-78, 124
    denial of access to, 184
    George W. Bush Presidential Library and Museum, 69, 70, 77, 98, 124, 195-96
    Oval Offices in, 73
    research of history of, 83
    The Truman Library, 71-72, 73, 77, 78
    Washington, George, presidential library of, 71

William J. Clinton Presidential Library, 90
    See also Executive Order 13233.
Presidential Recordings and Materials Preservation Act, 96
presidential records, 69, 71, 74, 79, 92, 96-99, 101, 194
Presidential Records Act of 1978, 69, 96
presidential secrecy
    judiciary role in, 91-92
    research study on, 88
professional schools, 231-34
professor
    role of, 229-30
Prom, Christopher
    on online finding aids, 210
public officials' personal papers
    ownership of, 101
public records, viii-ix, 38-54, 87, 89, 96, 99, 111, 188-89
Public Records Act, 111
Public Records Office (Williamsburg, Virginia). *See* Secretary's Office (Williamsburg, Virginia).
Radoff, Morris, 48
"Raisingate." *See* controversy, American Archivist cover.
reading, 20-21
"Reading Archives," blog of Richard Cox, 183, 185
reading, records, 57
reappraisal, validity of, 246
records professionals
    training of, 28
records retention scheduling, 132
records
    importance of, 12-13
    nature of, 9, 140
Reich, Robert
    on vocation, 17
research vs. practice, 31
Roberts, Alasdair

on government response to 9/11, 88, 94-96
Robinson, Morgan P., 47
Rockefeller, John D. Jr., 39
    Library of, 49

S

SAA. *See* Society of American Archivists (SAA).
SAA listserv archives controversy. *See* Archives and Archivists listserv controversy.
Sarbanes-Oxley Act, 134, 139
Sayers, Dorothy, on Christian doctrine, 14
Schellenberg, T. R., on appraisal, 245, 246
search engines, inadequacies of, 225

secrecy, 87
secrecy, government documents, 92-94, 90
Secretary's Office (Williamsburg, Virginia), viii, 38-54, 56, 65
September 11th, 12-13, 78, 88, 93, 246-47, 248
    commission, 69
    government response to, 88
Sigmund Freud papers, at Library of Congress, 119
Smithsonian
    Enola Gay exhibit at, 221
    First Ladies exhibition at, 71-72
    Showtime agreement, 116
    First Ladies exhibition at, 71-72
social networking, 263, 264, 269
Society for History in the Federal Government, 114
Society of American Archivists (SAA), xi, 22, 26, 29, 61, 88, 90, 130, 139, 140, 141, 147, 170, 182, 245, 251, 260
    and NARA reclassification controversy, 104, 106, 107, 112-14

appraisal decision, 165-70, 171, 172, 173, 174, 180, 181
    response to NARA and reclassification case, 112-14
    student response to, 173
    Ethics Code, 180
    listserv, 150-153
    presidents, 87, 150
Society of American Archivists (SAA), Presidents
    Ericson, Tim, 87-88
    Fleckner, John A., 26-27
    Gottlieb, Peter, 263
    Hirtle, Peter, 116, 117, 118, 119, 121
Southern Methodist University, 195-96
Stasi, East German, 89, 248
State Archivists, 43, 48, 65, 77
    Maryland State Archivist, 48
    New York State Archivist, 77
    Virginia State Archivist, 43, 65
students
    as customers, 230
    graduate, 15-16, 236
Subverting Open Government, 96-99
Sullivan, William, on professionalism, 3
"Sun Mad" poster. *See* controversy, *American Archivist* cover.
Surveillance or Security Age (vs. Information Age), x, 93
surveillance of individuals, 89

T

teaching archival studies, 228
teaching, of archival students, 229, 230, 235, 237
technological entrepreneurialship, 221
technological issues, 250
technology
    effects of, 2

temples, presidential. *See* presidential libraries.
The Collapse of Fortress Bush, 94-96
Theoharis, Athan
  on FBI secrecy, 88
Tibbo, Helen
  on archival description, 206-07
  on historians, 208
Tompkins, Jane
  on teaching, 230
Transportation, Treasury, and Housing and Urban Development, 116
Truman Library,
  Hackman, Larry, Director of, 77
  location, 71-72, 73, 77, 78
truth commissions, 11, 143, 240, 250
truth
  perceptions of, 250
Tschabrun, Susan
  on poster collections, 138
Twitter, 263, 269

U
United States Air Force (USAF), Memoranda of Understanding of, 125-26
US MARC AMC format. *See* MARC-based records.

V
values
  teaching of, 33-35
veteran professionals
  advise of, 17
Vietnam Veterans Memorial, 250
virtual communities
  challenges of, 160-64
  character of, 159
vocational call, 3-16
Vocationalism, 231

W
war on terror, 91

Washington, George
  presidential library of, 71
Web-based archival research, 209
Weblogs. *See* blogs.
Webster, Berenika
  on records management, 27
Weigel, George
  on role of religion in society, 15
Weinstein, Allen, 70, 104, 105
  on NARA reclassification controversy, 108-10, 113
Wertman, John
  on presidential records, 69, 71
whistle-blowing, 143, 144
William J. Clinton Presidential Library, 90
Williamsburg Antiques Forum, 42, 64
Williamsburg, Virginia Secretary's Office. *See* Secretary's Office.
Wilson, Don
  unethical acts of, 186
women's archives, 241
Woodruff, Paul
  on political leaders, 33
writing
  practice of, 66
Wythe House
  criticism of, 52

Y
Yakel, Elizabeth
  on finding aids, 224

Z
Zinn, Howard
  on government secrecy, 87

About the Author

Richard J. Cox is Professor in Library and Information Science at the University of Pittsburgh, School of Information Sciences where he is responsible for the archives concentration in the Master's in Library Science degree and the Ph.D. degree. He was a member of the Society of American Archivists Council from 1986 through 1989. Dr. Cox also served as Editor of the *American Archivist* from 1991 through 1995 and Editor of the *Records & Information Management Report* from 2001 through 2007. He has written extensively on archival and records management topics and has published fifteen books in addition to this one in this area: *American Archival Analysis: The Recent Development of the Archival Profession in the United States* (1990) -- winner of the Waldo Gifford Leland Award given by the Society of American Archivists; *Managing Institutional Archives: Foundational Principles and Practices* (1992); *The First Generation of Electronic Records Archivists in the United States: A Study in Professionalization* (1994); *Documenting Localities* (1996); *Closing an Era: Historical Perspectives on Modern Archives and Records Management* (2000); *Managing Records as Evidence and Information* (2001), winner of the Waldo Gifford Leland Award in 2002; co-editor, *Archives & the Public Good: Records and Accountability in Modern Society* (2002); *Vandals in the Stacks? A Response to Nicholson Baker's Assault on Libraries* (2002); *Flowers After the Funeral: Reflections on the Post-9/11 Digital Age* (2003); *No Innocent Deposits: Forming Archives by Rethinking Appraisal* (2004), winner of the Waldo Gifford Leland Award in 2005; *Lester J. Cappon and Historical Scholarship in the Golden Age of Archival Theory* (2004); *Archives and Archivists in the Information Age* (2005); *Understanding Archives & Manuscripts* (2006) with James M. O'Toole; *Ethics, Accountability, and Recordkeeping in a Dangerous World* (2006); *Personal Archives and a New Archival Calling: Readings, Reflections and Ruminations* (2008); and *The Demise of the Library School: Personal Reflections on Professional Education in the Modern Corporate University* (2010). Dr. Cox was elected a Fellow of the Society of American Archivists in 1989.

www.ingramcontent.com/pod-product-compliance
Lightning Source LLC
Chambersburg PA
CBHW021931290426
44108CB00012B/798